SEXUAL ORIENTATION AND MENTAL HEALTH

Contemporary Perspectives on Lesbian, Gay, and Bisexual Psychology

Gregory M. Herek, Series Editor

Series Titles

HIV+ Sex: The Psychological and Interpersonal Dynamics of HIV-Seropositive Gay and Bisexual Men's Relationships
Edited by Perry N. Halkitis, Cynthia A. Gómez, and Richard J. Wolitski

Sexual Orientation and Mental Health: Examining Identity and Development in Lesbian, Gay, and Bisexual People
Edited by Allen M. Omoto and Howard S. Kurtzman

SEXUAL ORIENTATION AND MENTAL HEALTH

Examining Identity and Development in Lesbian, Gay, and Bisexual People

EDITED BY **ALLEN M. OMOTO**
AND **HOWARD S. KURTZMAN**

American Psychological Association • *Washington, DC*

57579240

Published by
American Psychological Association
750 First Street, NE
Washington, DC 20002
www.apa.org

To order
APA Order Department
P.O. Box 92984
Washington, DC 20090-2984
Tel: (800) 374-2721
Direct: (202) 336-5510
Fax: (202) 336-5502
TDD/TTY: (202) 336-6123
Online: www.apa.org/books/
E-mail: order@apa.org

In the U.K., Europe, Africa, and the Middle
East, copies may be ordered from
American Psychological Association
3 Henrietta Street
Covent Garden, London
WC2E 8LU England

Typeset in Goudy by World Composition Services, Inc., Sterling, VA

Printer: Edwards Brothers, Inc., Ann Arbor, MI
Cover Designer: Berg Design, Albany, NY
Technical/Production Editor: Devon Bourexis

The opinions and statements published are the responsibility of the authors, and such opinions and statements do not necessarily represent the policies of the American Psychological Association.

Library of Congress Cataloging-in-Publication Data

Sexual orientation and mental health : examining identity and development in lesbian, gay, and bisexual people / edited by Allen M. Omoto & Howard S. Kurtzman.
    p. cm.—(Contemporary perspectives on lesbian, gay, and bisexual psychology)
    Includes bibliographical references and index.
    ISBN 1-59147-232-6
    1. Psychoanalysis and homosexuality.   2. Sexual orientation.   3. Gays.
  4. Lesbians.   I. Omoto, Allen Martin.   II. Kurtzman, Howard S. III. Series.

  RC451.4.G39S46 2005
  616.89′17′08664—dc22   2005002995

British Library Cataloguing-in-Publication Data
A CIP record is available from the British Library.

Printed in the United States of America
First Edition

CONTENTS

CONTRIBUTORS

George Ayala, AIDS Project Los Angeles, Los Angeles, CA

Edward Bein, School of Social Welfare, University of California, Berkeley

Henny Bos, Department of Education, University of Amsterdam, the Netherlands

Raymond W. Chan, Isis Research, Columbia, MD

Susan D. Cochran, School of Public Health, University of California, Los Angeles

Steve W. Cole, School of Medicine, University of California, Los Angeles

Anthony R. D'Augelli, Department of Human Development and Family Studies, Pennsylvania State University, University Park

Lisa M. Diamond, Department of Psychology, University of Utah, Salt Lake City

Rafael M. Díaz, Cesar E. Chavez Institute, San Francisco State University, San Francisco, CA

Kirk W. Elifson, Department of Sociology, Georgia State University, Atlanta

Megan Fulcher, Department of Psychology, Washington and Lee University, Lexington, VA

Marya Viorst Gwadz, National Development and Research Institutes, New York, NY

Tonda L. Hughes, College of Nursing and UIC National Center of Excellence in Women's Health, University of Illinois at Chicago

Joyce Hunter, HIV Center for Clinical and Behavioral Studies, New York State Psychiatric Institute and Columbia University, New York

Timothy P. Johnson, Survey Research Laboratory, University of Illinois at Chicago

Howard S. Kurtzman, Washington, DC

Alicia K. Matthews, College of Nursing, University of Illinois at Chicago

Vickie M. Mays, Department of Psychology, University of California, Los Angeles

Allen M. Omoto, School of Behavioral and Organizational Sciences, Claremont Graduate University, Claremont, CA

David W. Pantalone, Department of Psychology, University of Washington, Seattle

Charlotte J. Patterson, Department of Psychology, University of Virginia, Charlottesville

Margaret Rosario, Department of Psychology, City College and Graduate Center of the City University of New York, NY

Stephen T. Russell, John and Doris Norton School of Family and Consumer Sciences, University of Arizona, Tucson

Elizabeth M. Saewyc, School of Nursing, University of Minnesota, Minneapolis; School of Nursing, University of British Columbia, Vancouver, Canada

Steven A. Safren, Department of Psychiatry, Harvard Medical School, Boston, MA; Behavioral Medicine Service, Massachusetts General Hospital, Boston; Research and Evaluation Department, Fenway Community Health, Boston, MA

Theo G. M. Sandfort, HIV Center for Clinical and Behavioral Studies, New York State Psychiatric Institute and Columbia University, New York

Joanna E. Scheib, The Sperm Bank of California, Berkeley; Department of Psychology, University of California, Davis

Claire E. Sterk, Rollins School of Public Health, Emory University, Atlanta, GA

Erin L. Sutfin, Department of Psychology, University of Virginia, Charlottesville

Jessica Tartaro, Department of Psychology, Arizona State University, Tempe

Raymond Vet, Department of Social and Organizational Psychology, Utrecht University, the Netherlands

Sharon C. Wilsnack, Department of Neuroscience, University of North Dakota, Grand Forks

Ann Marie Yali, Department of Psychology, City College and Graduate Center of the City University of New York, NY

ACKNOWLEDGMENTS

We thank Delores L. Parron for the critical support and insights over the years that led to the development of this volume. We are also grateful to the following people for their efforts that helped to make this volume possible and to enhance its quality: Clinton W. Anderson, Timothy P. Condon, Gregory M. Herek, Sherman L. Ragland, Jack B. Stein, and the members of the Committee on Lesbian, Gay, and Bisexual Concerns of the American Psychological Association (APA). We also thank Lansing Hays and Ed Meidenbauer of APA Books for their support and advice throughout the preparation of this volume.

Much of the work described in this volume was supported by the National Institutes of Health (NIH). However, no portion of the volume is an official statement of the views of the NIH, its components, or any other unit of the federal government.

SEXUAL ORIENTATION AND MENTAL HEALTH

INTRODUCTION: CURRENT AND FUTURE RESEARCH ON LESBIAN, GAY, AND BISEXUAL PEOPLE

HOWARD S. KURTZMAN AND ALLEN M. OMOTO

The past decade has witnessed the emergence of an impressive body of rigorous empirical research on mental health and disorders in lesbian, gay, and bisexual (LGB) people. Although homosexuality itself is no longer considered to be a disorder and most LGB people are mentally healthy, a substantial body of evidence indicates that LGB people are at greater risk than the general population for various disorders, including depression, anxiety, and substance abuse. Recently, investigators have aimed not only to characterize this greater risk but also to explain it within frameworks that acknowledge the unique stresses and challenges that LGB people experience, especially in a society in which same-sex orientation remains largely stigmatized. This broad research effort has yielded new knowledge about how LGB people come to understand their sexual orientation, integrate it into their self-concept, make decisions about disclosing it to others, and respond to prejudice and harassment. The work also has produced a better understanding of LGB people's family and social relationships and is beginning to provide insights into their involvements with larger social institutions such as religion and work.

This volume presents some of the most important research in this field from both established and emerging investigators. Some of the chapters describe programs or bodies of research; others focus on individual studies. The chapters also address the implications of the research for clinical practice and service delivery and suggest directions for future investigation. Although not intended to be an exhaustive survey, this collection conveys the wide range of scientific methodologies and thinking currently being directed toward understanding the mental health of LGB people and its social and psychological correlates.

Part I focuses on adolescents and young adults. In the first chapter, Stephen T. Russell reviews evidence from the National Longitudinal Study of Adolescent Health, a comprehensive survey of U.S. adolescents' health and health-related behaviors and social characteristics. LGB youths are shown to have higher levels of mental health and substance use problems than non-LGB youths, with bisexual youths at highest risk for many problems. Other noteworthy findings presented in this chapter include gender differences in the magnitude of particular health problems and changes in self-reported attractions and relationships between the two waves of data collection (18 months apart). These and other findings from this rich data set pose important questions for future analysis and empirical research.

Complementing this population-based research, in chapter 2, Anthony R. D'Augelli's work with participants in LGB youth social groups examines adolescents' awareness and disclosure of their sexual orientations; their family, social, romantic, and sexual interactions; their experiences of harassment and violence; and the relations of all of these to mental health indicators. The findings are discussed in the current sociocultural context, one in which contemporary adolescents are more likely than those from earlier historical periods to acknowledge same-sex attractions and to have access to information and discussion about LGB people.

In chapter 3, Steven A. Safren and David W. Pantalone offer evidence that higher levels of depression and suicidality in LGB adolescents are attributable to such factors as insufficient social support and fewer positive life events, rather than to their sexual orientation per se. Specifically, their research suggests that LGB youths are more likely than non-LGB youths to experience social anxiety, perhaps because of social pressures to be or appear heterosexual, and that it is this social anxiety that interferes with their ability to obtain adequate levels of social support and positive experiences.

Lisa M. Diamond's longitudinal study, in chapter 4, addresses the complexity and continuity of sexual identity. Her data indicate that some nonheterosexual women in their teens and twenties have attractions, behaviors, or identities oriented to both sexes rather than exclusively toward other women, and that these orientations may shift independently over time. Moreover, discordances are seen to arise between physical and emotional attractions. Significantly, those women whose orientations were more complex or variable did not appear to have compromised mental health.

In chapter 5, Elizabeth M. Saewyc's work addresses the surprising finding that LGB adolescents are at least as likely as non-LGB adolescents to become pregnant or to impregnate. Although pregnancy involving adolescents is not itself a disorder, it is often related to social and emotional difficulties and can constrain adolescents' future development. Saewyc reviews a large body of data on the heterosexual behaviors and contraceptive use of LGB youths, as well as their experiences of sexual and other abuse. In light of this evidence, she evaluates the applicability of current explanatory models of adolescent involvement in pregnancies to LGB youths.

The impact of religion on the mental health, substance use, and sexual risk behaviors of LGB adolescents is considered in Part I's final chapter, chapter 6, by Margaret Rosario, Ann Marie Yali, Joyce Hunter, and Marya Viorst Gwadz. Their analyses of questionnaire data completed by LGB youths in New York City indicate protective health effects of religious commitment among males, but little effect among females. The authors draw from earlier literature, including work derived from cognitive dissonance theory,[1] in proposing a model that links religious commitments to positive and negative health outcomes for LGB youths. The model also suggests the processes by which some LGB people (both adolescents and adults) achieve integration of their religious and sexual identities.

Part II, which focuses on adults, begins with a chapter by Susan D. Cochran and Vickie M. Mays. They show how information about the health status of LGB people can be drawn from the data sets of major health surveys of the U.S. population, such as the National Health and Nutrition Examination Survey. On the basis of evidence from these surveys, the authors point to higher rates of mental health and substance abuse problems as well as higher rates of service utilization among LGB than non-LGB adults. In addition, they discuss some of the methodological, interpretive, and sociopolitical issues that arise in conducting such analyses and in attempts to design and gain inclusion of questions about sexual orientation in future national surveys.

The assessment of mental health, alcohol use, and sexual experiences in lesbians is considered in the next two chapters. In chapter 8, Tonda L. Hughes, Sharon C. Wilsnack, and Timothy P. Johnson report a study that examined samples of lesbians and matched heterosexual women in the Chicago area. Their findings are generally consistent with previous research that indicates that lesbians are at higher risk for alcohol abuse and various mental health problems than heterosexual women. However, a comparison of the Chicago lesbian sample with a national sample of urban heterosexual women yielded a pattern of results that differed in a number of significant details. The authors discuss the advantages and disadvantages of their different comparisons and argue that research designs involving comparisons among multiple samples can be useful for tracing the pathways that lead to health problems.

In chapter 9, Alicia K. Matthews, Tonda L. Hughes, and Jessica Tartaro use data from the same Chicago lesbian and heterosexual samples to examine sexual behavior and dysfunction and their relation to mental health, alcohol use, and prior experience of abuse. Overall, their results suggest greater similarities between lesbian and heterosexual women's sexuality than previous investigators have claimed. This study is particularly useful for its consideration of the frequencies and relationship contexts of specific sexual behaviors and experiences.

The study by Rafael M. Díaz, Edward Bein, and George Ayala, in chapter 10, shows independent negative effects of anti-gay discrimination, racial and ethnic discrimination, and poverty on the mental health of Latino gay and bisexual men in three large U.S. cities (New York, Miami, and Los Angeles). The negative effects attributable to these social and structural conditions are shown to be partially mediated by social isolation and low self-esteem. Furthermore, their results indicate that the deleterious effects can be reduced by family and other social supports for the men's gay or bisexual identities. The study is especially noteworthy for its innovative recruitment methods and for its rich data obtained from both focus group discussions and responses to newly developed survey instruments.

Chapter 11, written by Theo G. M. Sandfort, Henny Bos, and Raymond Vet, is the only one in the volume that focuses on data from a sample drawn from outside North America. Investigating the experiences of middle-class Dutch LGB people who work in service fields, the authors find that concealment of sexual orientation and experiences of prejudice and discrimination in the workplace are associated with job burnout, characterized by feelings of emotional exhaustion, depersonalization, and reduced competence. These effects were stronger for men than for women. Burnout was linked, in turn, with reduced levels of job satisfaction and self-reported general health. The authors suggest that a complete understanding of the nature and effects of workplace difficulties related to having an LGB identity will require information about the full range of challenges that LGB people face both within and outside of the workplace.

The linkage between psychosocial processes and physical health is addressed in Steve W. Cole's work. In chapter 12, he provides evidence that concealment of sexual orientation by men who self-identify as gay is associated with faster progression of HIV/AIDS, other infectious diseases, and cancer. Those men with HIV/AIDS who do not conceal their orientation but whose personalities are characterized by high levels of social inhibition also show faster disease progression. Cole presents a detailed integrative model of the psychological and biological mechanisms that may be responsible for these effects and also discusses potential interventions to prevent or reverse them.

In chapter 13, Claire E. Sterk and Kirk W. Elifson present the results of some of their qualitative research with female drug users in the Atlanta area. Their open-ended interviews revealed that women who had sex with other women varied widely in their attractions and in their private and public sexual identities. The women also varied in how they sexually interacted with other women and men, in ways driven both by strategic considerations within the drug-using environment and by their own social and emotional needs. As illustrated by this chapter, careful qualitative research can provide important information about how people understand their sexuality in particular contexts and in relation to their other behaviors and experiences.

The well-being of lesbian couples and their children is addressed in the final chapter by Megan Fulcher, Erin L. Sutfin, Raymond W. Chan, Joanna E. Scheib, and Charlotte J. Patterson. They report a study that examines family functioning and child development in households headed by both lesbian couples and heterosexual couples who conceived through donor insemination. Consistent with earlier research, few differences were found between lesbian- and heterosexual-headed families. The emotional, social, and academic adjustment of children in these families was associated with parents' satisfaction with their couple relationship, no matter their sexual orientation. Such research has implications for the formulation of social policies related to families, as well as raising new research questions about family functioning and child development across diverse household compositions and settings.

Taken together, it is evident that the variety of methodological approaches used in research on LGB mental health is one of the major strengths of the field. Both quantitative and qualitative methods are shown to produce meaningful results, and combinations of these methods may be especially powerful in fleshing out and evaluating models of the processes that lead to particular health outcomes. In addition, provocative and useful findings are shown to emerge from both population-based studies and studies targeted at particular samples of LGB people. Finally, comparisons of LGB with non-LGB people as well as comparisons solely among LGB subgroups prove informative about the range of factors that influence the experiences and health of LGB people.

As several contributors suggest, we can expect to see development of even more sophisticated approaches to defining, sampling, and recruiting from various LGB subgroups in future research efforts. These advances, marked by enhanced rigor and more complete characterization of participant samples, will enable researchers to generalize more confidently from the findings of individual studies as well as to make valuable cross-study comparisons. They will also allow researchers to establish more specific linkages between individual and contextual characteristics of LGB people and their health status. For example, careful attention to sampling concerns is required in any work that seeks to account for the gender differences in health risks or the distinctive health profiles of bisexual people that are reported in a number of the chapters.

At the same time, it will be important in future research to investigate a larger range of LGB subgroups, including considering such dimensions as geography, class, culture, ethnicity, age, and physical and mental capacities. How sexual orientation is manifested and conceived and how it interacts with other characteristics to influence health can vary markedly across groups defined by these dimensions and their combinations. Although a number of the studies reported in this volume examine large and diverse samples or focus on understudied groups, much more work remains to be done. Many subgroups of LGB people, both within and outside the United States, have yet to receive serious and sustained attention from empirical researchers. In relation to this point, it can be suggested that efforts to describe and explain health disparities among other demographic groups (e.g., geographic, ethnic) are likely to be enriched by considering the sexual orientation characteristics of members of those groups.

The chapters hint at other future trends in research methodology. Longitudinal designs are likely to become more widely used. These designs not only provide detailed information about developmental processes but can also be valuable in testing models of causal mechanisms. Further, although researchers will continue to rely heavily on self-report data, we can anticipate greater use of observer-report and biological data. These additional types of data enable a greater variety of research questions to be addressed and can ultimately provide empirical support for integrative theoretical models that link processes at multiple levels of analysis.

As for topics of future research, the work presented in this volume (and elsewhere) points in several directions. First, future research can be expected to consider a broader range of disorders and conditions. Although the chapters in this volume primarily address mood disorders and alcohol abuse, some investigators have begun to turn their attention to eating disorders, body dysmorphic disorders, and conduct disorders, as well as to abuse of tobacco, methamphetamine, and injection drugs. The evidence currently available suggests that particular LGB subgroups may be at higher risk for many of these disorders. As investigators more carefully examine the prevalence and causes of these disorders in LGB people, they may eventually be able to analyze patterns of comorbidity. Such work may in turn shed light on fundamental underlying processes of the disorders in both LGB and non-LGB people.

A second direction for future research focuses not on what causes disorders but rather on protective and resiliency factors. Understanding these factors, from the individual through social and community levels, should help explain why the majority of LGB people are healthy despite the challenges they face, as well as provide a firmer foundation for the development of prevention and treatment interventions. As noted by several contributors to this volume, such interventions can be implemented not only within mental health services but also within other types of social services and school and workplace programs.

Finally, we can expect stronger research interest in the nature and effects of gender-related expression, behaviors, roles, and identity. It has been frequently suggested that gender atypicality, though generally not considered a disorder itself, is associated with greater risk for mental health problems in LGB people. More research is needed to understand the specific forms of gender atypicality, their developmental courses within various social contexts, and how they are related to sexual orientation and to mental health. Moreover, to the extent that transgendered people and LGB people share common experiences and behaviors, or even that there are key differences between them, research with each of these populations should be mutually informative about factors that influence health.

Significant progress in all these directions can be expected in the years ahead. As the contributors to this volume continue to make advances, a growing number of other talented investigators from a variety of disciplines and perspectives are also joining the inquiry into LGB mental health. The findings emerging from all of these researchers' efforts promise to increase scientific understanding of human diversity and, most important, to lead to meaningful improvements in the health and well-being of lesbian, gay, and bisexual people and the families and communities to which they belong.

I

YOUTH

1

SUBSTANCE USE AND ABUSE AND MENTAL HEALTH AMONG SEXUAL-MINORITY YOUTHS: EVIDENCE FROM ADD HEALTH

STEPHEN T. RUSSELL

Dealing with emerging sexuality is a fundamental developmental task of adolescence (Katchadourian, 1990). The normal difficulties associated with this developmental process are likely to be exacerbated for lesbian, gay, and bisexual (LGB) youths; they must simultaneously negotiate the normal challenges of adolescence as they learn to manage the cultural stigma of homosexuality (Rotheram-Borus & Fernandez, 1995). It is believed that

The research described in this chapter was supported by a grant from the Wayne F. Placek Fund of the American Psychological Foundation. This research uses data from Add Health, a program project designed by J. Richard Udry, Peter S. Bearman, and Kathleen Mullan Harris, and funded by Grant P01-HD31921 from the National Institute of Child Health and Human Development, with cooperative funding from 17 other agencies. Special acknowledgment is due Ronald R. Rindfuss and Barbara Entwisle for assistance in the original design. Persons interested in obtaining data files from Add Health should contact Add Health, Carolina Population Center, 123 W. Franklin Street, Chapel Hill, NC 27516–2524 (www.cpc.unc.edu/addhealth/contact.html).

as a result of these developmental challenges, many LGB youths are at risk for substance use and abuse and for compromised mental health. Nearly three decades ago, scientific reports first began to suggest that LGB adolescents were at higher risk than their heterosexual peers for risk behaviors and compromised mental health (Bell & Weinberg, 1978; Hetrick & Martin, 1987, 1988). Through the 1980s and early 1990s, research began to confirm these concerns, showing that LGB adolescents were more likely to report mental health problems (Hammelman, 1993; Hershberger & D'Augelli, 1995; Rotheram-Borus, Hunter, & Rosario, 1994) and to use and abuse drugs and alcohol (Remafedi, 1987, 1994; Rosario, Hunter, & Gwadz, 1997; Rosario, Rotheram-Borus, & Reid, 1996; Rotheram-Borus, Rosario, Van Rossem, & Reid, 1995).

This chapter considers the substance use and abuse and mental health of sexual-minority youths. Attention is first given to barriers in research that have limited our understanding of the lives of sexual-minority youths, including measurement and sampling challenges. Past research on adolescent sexual orientation, substance use and abuse, and mental health is then reviewed, with a focus on recent population-based studies that have included attention to these concerns. Finally, analyses from the National Longitudinal Study of Adolescent Health (the Add Health study) are presented. The Add Health study is the first nationally representative study of U.S. adolescents that incorporates questions relevant to adolescent sexual orientation. Results from analyses of adolescents' reports of same-sex romantic attractions and relationships and their associations with indicators of substance use and abuse and mental health are then presented.

Before considering the barriers to research on adolescent same-sex sexuality, a note on language is important. The term *sexual minority* is used in this chapter for several reasons. First, past research has been largely limited to samples of LGB-identified youths, and thus to indicators of sexual identity alone. This limitation has confined our theoretical and practical understandings of adolescents' (and adults') sexual lives such that the labels of lesbian, gay, and bisexual are often assumed to account for all dimensions of same-sex sexuality. The term sexual minority is used as an umbrella term to include the possibilities of same-sex sexual attractions, behaviors, and identities. Second, the participants in the Add Health study did not report their *sexual identities*. Nevertheless, their same-sex romantic attractions and relationships set them apart from their peers. Finally, this term is an appropriate and convenient general reference to past research; although most past studies have been based on samples of self-identified LGB youths, several are based on reports of same-sex sexual behavior among adolescents. This general term provides summary language when describing past work.

CHALLENGES IN THE STUDY OF
SEXUAL-MINORITY YOUTHS

A fundamental challenge in the study of sexual-minority youths continues to be the development of adequate measures of sexual orientation. More basic to the challenge of measurement is that there remains confusion regarding what it means to be gay, lesbian, or bisexual (or transgender or queer; Doll, 1997; Sandfort, 1997). There is consensus that sexual orientation is composed of the dimensions of (a) physical or emotional *attraction*, (b) sexual *behavior*, and (c) self-*identity* (Sandfort, 1997). These dimensions have been empirically measured in different ways in various studies; it is usually the case that one or perhaps two of these dimensions are included as indicators of "sexual orientation" or "homosexuality" in any given study. Studies of adolescents have relied most heavily on self-identity as gay, lesbian, or bisexual; a handful of studies have considered adolescent same-sex sexual behavior, including the 1993 Massachusetts Youth Risk Behavior Survey (YRBS; see Faulkner & Cranston, 1998) and the 1995 Vermont YRBS (see DuRant, Krowchuk, & Sinal, 1998), and same- and both-sex romantic attractions or relationships (the Add Health study, see Russell, Driscoll, & Truong, 2000; Russell, Franz, & Driscoll, 2001; Russell & Joyner, 2001; Russell, Seif, & Truong, 2001; Russell & Truong, 2001; Udry & Chantala, 2002). In their study of adults in the United States, Laumann, Gagnon, Michael, and Michaels (1994) included each of these three dimensions of sexual orientation. Their results show that these concepts do not neatly overlap, but rather that an individual may report any one or combination of these dimensions as relevant to her or his life.

In addition to the challenges of defining sexual orientation and its possible dimensions is the application of these meanings to the lives of children and adolescents. Past models of the development of sexual orientation during adolescence have often assumed a linear progression that begins in childhood with same-sex attraction, followed by early adolescent same-sex sexual behavior, and culminating in self-labeling as gay or lesbian in late adolescence or young adulthood (Fox, 1996). There was little room in these models for nonfixed identities, or for bisexual identities or behaviors; one's identity was assumed to be gay or lesbian, and the developmental process was one of discovering and labeling that "true" identity. More recent models acknowledge bisexuality as a nontransitory sexual identity (Diamond, 1998; Doll, 1997; Fox, 1996).

It is remarkable, however, that there has been only limited discussion of the fluidity of sexual attractions, behaviors, and identities (e.g., Diamond, 1998), and no known consideration of the degree to which this is developmentally relevant to adolescents. Clearly adolescence is the developmental stage of life when the development of sexuality—the physical, emotional, and psychological aspects—is most distinctive. Indeed, the development of sexuality can be said to be a defining characteristic of adolescence to a much greater extent than is true for any other life stage (Katchadourian, 1990; Konopka, 1973). Thus, although sexuality, and therefore sexual orientation, is fundamentally in the process of development during adolescence (Koch, 1993), current modes for understanding sexual orientation during adolescence remain largely based on a fixed heterosexual–homosexual dichotomy. There is little acknowledgment that contemporary studies of adolescents reveal information that may be only slightly indicative of their later adult sexual behaviors or identities. The fluidity of adolescent sexual desire, behavior, and identity may be a fundamental characteristic of sexuality during the teenage years. Although much has changed during the period of a single generation in the historical context of adolescent sexuality development, the development of adolescent sexuality and sexual orientation can be characterized to a significant degree by a fluidity of attraction, behavior, and identity. Although some have argued that this perspective is, perhaps, uniquely relevant to contemporary youths (Sandfort, 1997), researchers should nevertheless be aware of this possibility in the study of young lives.

There are several notable challenges with regard to sampling sexual-minority individuals of any age (Sandfort, 1997). As a population generally regarded as at risk, it is likely that sexual-minority youths might be underrepresented in regularly sampled populations such as public schools or even households (Russell & Seif, 2002); in fact, past research suggests that LGB youths are overrepresented among homeless youths (Hunter & Schaecher, 1995; Kruks, 1991). Second, there are a number of reasons why the sexual-minority youths who make their way into population-based samples may not disclose their same-sex sexual attractions, behaviors, or identities. Their same-sex sexuality may be unknown to them, they may be unable or unwilling to acknowledge these issues to themselves, or they simply may be unwilling to disclose in the context of a research study. Because of these challenges, most past research on adolescent sexual orientation has relied on samples that include primarily urban youths, usually self-identified gay male participants. It is possible that because of their early self-identification as LGB, adolescents who have participated in past studies (many as self-selected volunteers) make up a unique subgroup within a larger population of sexual-minority youths. If this is the case, it may be that these samples of self-identified LGB youths are at higher initial risk for many of the negative health and behavioral risk outcomes so frequently documented in past studies (Russell & Joyner, 2001; Savin-Williams & Rodriguez, 1993).

A further issue related to these sampling challenges is that gender differences rarely have been included in past studies, and there have been few examinations of differences in experiences between adolescents reporting exclusively homosexual orientations and those reporting bisexual orientations. Ultimately, the fundamental criticism of this past research has been that it is based on nonrepresentative samples of adolescents (Shaffer, Fisher, Hicks, Parides, & Gould, 1995). In recent years, a handful of studies based on state-level random samples have been published about LGB youths and youths who report same-sex sexual behavior; these studies address concerns regarding inadequate samples in past research. They provide more certain evidence regarding the link between sexual orientation and the negative outcomes for youths previously described. The only national-level data from the United States to date have come from the Add Health study (Borowsky, Ireland, & Resnick, 2001; Resnick et al., 1997; Russell & Joyner, 2001; Russell & Truong, 2001; Udry & Chantala, 2002). However, because of the challenges with self-reports of same-sex sexual attraction, behavior, or identity, sexual-minority youths are likely underrepresented in these studies.

SEXUAL-MINORITY YOUTHS, SUBSTANCE USE AND ABUSE, AND MENTAL HEALTH

Substance abuse and compromised mental health are critical problems among youths in the United States (Petersen, Leffert, Graham, Alwin, & Ding, 1997; Weinberg, Rahdert, Colliver, & Glantz, 1998). Past studies of self-identified LGB youths have reported rates of substance use and abuse that are higher than those found in population-based studies of U.S. adolescents (Remafedi, 1987, 1994; Rosario et al., 1997, 1996; Rotheram-Borus et al., 1995; for comparison statistics for U.S. adolescents, see Weinberg et al., 1998). Several recent studies have used population-based data to examine associations between same-sex sexual identity or sexual behaviors and substance use and abuse. Analyses of the Youth Risk Behavior Surveys (YRBS) from two northeastern states indicate that same-sex sexual behavior is linked to substance use (the use of alcohol, marijuana, cocaine, and other illegal drugs) in the 1993 Massachusetts YRBS (Faulkner & Cranston, 1998) and the use of cigarettes, tobacco, alcohol, and marijuana at school by young men in the 1995 Vermont YRBS (DuRant et al., 1998). A study using the 1995 Massachusetts YRBS demonstrated that self-identified LGB youths are more likely to begin using marijuana and alcohol at younger ages, to have higher lifetime rates of crack or cocaine use, and to report more recent use of tobacco than their peers (Garofalo, Wolf, Kessel, Palfrey, & DuRant, 1998).

Data from the Add Health study have shown that youths reporting romantic attraction to the same sex are more likely than their peers to abuse alcohol (Russell & Joyner, 2001). A companion study (Russell et al., 2000) revealed that the substance use and abuse of sexual-minority youths differed between male and female participants and depended on whether the romantic attractions or relationships were to the same sex only, or to both sexes. Specifically, across seven indicators of substance use and abuse, romantic attraction and relationship differences were found more consistently for girls than for boys. Further, teens with both-sex attractions were at somewhat higher risk for substance use and abuse than teens who reported only other-sex attractions. Same-sex attractions appear as risk factors for several substance use and abuse outcomes, but only for girls. It should be noted that a representative community-based study of 106 LGB and 224 unsure youths found that they were not at greater risk for substance abuse than their peers (Lock & Steiner, 1999). However, most past studies indicate that sexual-minority youths are a group at risk for substance use and abuse and that there are important differences in substance use and abuse based on gender and on same-sex versus bisexual orientation.

Comparatively less research has examined the associations between adolescent sexual orientation and indicators of mental health. Although the YRBS includes information on same-sex sexuality and risk outcomes, these studies have not included traditional indicators of mental health status. The main exception in recent population-based studies is attention to suicidality. In fact, suicidality is almost certainly the most researched topic related to adolescent sexual orientation. There is a substantial research literature based on studies of self-identified LGB youths that addresses the high prevalence of suicidal thoughts and attempts among LGB youths (Hammelman, 1993; Rotheram-Borus et al., 1994; for statistics comparing LGB youths with heterosexual U.S. adolescents, see Faulkner & Cranston, 1998; Lewinsohn, Rohde, & Seeley, 1996). More recent population-based studies have affirmed these reports (Garofalo et al., 1998; Remafedi, French, Story, Resnick, & Blum, 1998; Russell & Joyner, 2001).

Several past studies based on samples of LBG-identified youths have reported links between mental health outcomes and stress due to being gay (Meyer, 1995; Rosario et al., 1996), self-esteem (Grossman & Kerner, 1998; Rosario et al., 1996), and victimization (Hershberger & D'Augelli, 1995). However, these past studies do not include comparison groups, and it is therefore unclear whether the mental health of self-identified LGB youths is compromised relative to heterosexual youths. In fact, Rosario, Rotheram-Borus, and Reid (1996) reported that the urban, ethnic-minority gay and bisexual boys in their sample did not have elevated levels of depression or anxiety or low self-esteem when compared with baseline statistics for U.S. adolescents. However, LGB youths from a cohort study in New Zealand reported more depression and anxiety and lower self-esteem than their heterosexual peers (Fergusson, Horwood, & Beautrais, 1999). A recent study based on Add Health reported higher levels of depression among same-sex-attracted youths (Russell & Joyner, 2001). In sum, there is limited and mixed evidence to suggest that sexual-minority youths may experience higher levels of depression and anxiety and lower levels of self-esteem compared with their non–sexual-minority peers.

Finally, substance use and abuse are important correlates of mental health outcomes. Substance abuse is regarded as a major risk factor for adolescent suicide (Brent & Perper, 1995; Felts, Chenier, & Barnes, 1992), and two recent studies have examined the link between substance abuse and the elevated reports of suicidality among sexual-minority youths. A study based on the 1995 Massachusetts YRBS reported that the high rates of substance use among LGB and "not sure" youths are associated with higher rates for reporting suicidality among lesbian and bisexual female youths (Garofalo, Wolf, Wissow, Woods, & Goodman, 1999). In a study using the Add Health data, alcohol abuse was found to be an important mediator of the link between adolescent same-sex romantic attractions and suicidal thoughts and attempts (Russell & Joyner, 2001).

DATA: THE NATIONAL LONGITUDINAL STUDY OF ADOLESCENT HEALTH

The Add Health study is the most recent, comprehensive, national study of adolescents in the United States. Developed in the early 1990s in response to growing concerns about HIV/AIDS among the adolescent population in the United States (Hunt, 1999), the study was designed to provide needed information about factors associated with health risk and promotion. Further, its focus was on the effects of multiple contexts or environments within which adolescents grow and develop—their schools, neighborhoods, families, and friends (Blum & Rinehard, 1997). Since the first major publication, which focused on general indicators of health and well-being (Resnick et al., 1997), widely publicized studies have been published on adolescent heterosexual romantic attraction and emotional health (Halpern, Joyner, Udry, & Schindran, 2000; Joyner & Udry, 2000), virginity pledges and sexual behavior (Bearman & Brückner, 2001), and adolescent suicidality (Borowsky et al., 2001).

Data collection for the study began in 1995 with a school-based sample of over 90,000 youths in grades 7 through 12 (a sample of 80 high schools and one of their feeder schools). From this in-school sample a core sample of over 12,000 were randomly chosen to complete an interview in their homes. Four ethnic groups were oversampled, including Puerto Rican, Cuban, and Chinese adolescents, as well as Black adolescents from well-educated families (families in which one parent had a college degree). Additional oversamples included a saturation sample (all students enrolled in 16 of the schools), a disabled sample, and a genetic sample (pairs of siblings raised in the same household). The core sample and oversamples yielded a total of more than twenty thousand 7th- to 12th-grade students who participated in the Wave 1 in-home interview (Blum & Rinehard, 1997). In addition to the participating youths, one parent (usually the mother) participated in the first wave of the study, answering questions about family background and characteristics of the parent–adolescent relationship. School administrators also provided basic background information about the school. Eighteen months after the first interview, over 70% of eligible students were reinterviewed for the second wave of the study (respondents who were in 12th grade at Wave 1 were not included in the second wave). For the following analyses, the full sample was limited to adolescents who had answered the questions on romantic attractions or relationships and who were between ages 12 and 19 in Wave 1 (sample sizes are reported in the tables that follow).

Sensitive information, including data on same-sex romantic attraction, were collected through the use of audio computer-aided self-interview (Audio-CASI). Using a laptop computer to record their answers, respondents listened to questions through earphones. Past studies reported a high level of self-disclosure bias in interviewer-administered surveys on sensitive behavior (Turner, Miller, & Rogers, 1997). Recent examinations of this method have demonstrated that Audio-CASI reduces the potential for interviewer or parental influence on the responses of adolescents and yields higher reporting levels of sensitive information and behavior (Supple, Aquilino, & Wright, 1999; Turner et al., 1998).

MEASURES

Two dimensions of sexual orientation were included in both waves of the study: romantic attractions and romantic relationships. The Wave 1 in-home survey included two questions on romantic attractions: "Have you ever had a romantic attraction to a female?" and "Have you ever had a romantic attraction to a male?" In the Wave 2 survey, participants were asked if they had had a romantic attraction to a boy or girl since the last survey date. With these measures respondents could be coded as reporting romantic attraction to the other sex only, the same sex only, or to both sexes (and also to neither sex). Measures of romantic relationships were also included in the study. In Wave 1 respondents were asked, "In the last 18 months, have you had a romantic relationship with anyone?" and "What is their sex?" Information was obtained on up to three romantic relationships. At Wave 2 respondents were asked the same question in reference to the period since the last survey (approximately 18 months). The measure for sex of romantic relationship partner(s) was based on the reports of up to three partners. Because one cannot assume that heterosexual, homosexual, or bisexual identities are claimed by the youths on the basis of their romantic attractions or relationships, "other-sex," "same-sex," and "both-sex" are used to describe the attractions and relationships of youths in the Add Health study. The Add Health study does not include measures of sexual identity (self-identification as lesbian, gay, or bisexual); results from this study cannot be directly compared with previous studies of adolescents who identify themselves as lesbian, gay, or bisexual.

Nine measures of substance use and abuse that were included in both Waves 1 and 2 are examined here. *Smoking* (number of cigarettes in last month) is calculated as the product of the number of days the respondents reported smoking in the last 30 days and the number of cigarettes they reported smoking on the days they smoked during that period. *Getting drunk* is a measure of the frequency with which the respondent got drunk in the past 12 months, or since the last survey (0 = *never drank alcohol*; 1 = *drank but never been drunk*; 2 = *once a month or less*; 3 = *2 to 8 days a month*; 4 = *every day or almost every day*). *Problems caused by drinking* is an average of four items measuring whether the respondents' drinking caused them problems with their parents, at school, with their friends, and with someone they were dating in the previous 12 months, or since the last survey (0 = *never drank or no problem*; 1 = *once*, 2 = *twice*; 3 = *3–4 times*; 4 = *5 or more times*). *Sexual regret from drinking* indicates that respondents got into a sexual situation that they later regretted because they had been drinking at some point during the past 12 months, or since the last survey (0 = *never drank or drank but no problem*; 1 = *once*; 2 = *twice*; 3 = *3–4 times*; 4 = *5 or more times*). *Marijuana use* is measured as the number of times respondents reported using marijuana in the last 30 days (0 = *never used*; 1 = *1 or 2 times*; 2 = *3 or more times*). *Drinking alone* is a dichotomous variable measuring whether the respondent reported having drunk alcohol while alone in the past 30 days (1 = *yes*). Finally, *other drug use* includes the reported use of cocaine in any form, inhalants, or other illegal drugs, such as LSD, PCP, or ecstasy in the last 12 months, or since the last survey (dichotomous, 1 = *yes*).

Three measures of mental health are examined in the analyses that follow: self-esteem, anxiety, and depression. The Self-Esteem scale consists of an average of 9 items, including "I like me just the way I am," "I have a lot of energy," and "I have a lot of good qualities" (1 = *strongly disagree*; 5 = *strongly agree*; Cronbach's α: boys = .86; girls = .86). The measure of Anxiety consists of a 7-item scale. Respondents were asked how often they had anxiety-related conditions in the past 12 months, including "trouble falling asleep or staying awake," "moodiness," and "trouble relaxing" (0 = *never*; 4 = *every day*; Cronbach's α: boys = .73; girls = .78). Finally, Depression is measured using an 11-item scale derived from the Center for Epidemiologic Studies Depression Scale (CES–D; Radloff, 1977) based on questions about the previous week (questions include "You were bothered by things that usually don't bother you," "You felt depressed," "You felt lonely," and "You felt sad"; 0 = *never or rarely*; 3 = *most of the time or all of the time*; Cronbach's α: boys = .81; girls = .85).

ANALYSIS PLAN

The prevalence of same-sex and both-sex romantic attractions and relationships are first examined for Waves 1 and 2. The stability of romantic attractions or relationships is then examined across waves. Group differences based on romantic attractions or relationships for substance use and abuse and mental health indicators are then examined for the full sample. Survey regression (and logistic regression) is used to adjust for the stratified sample design and sample weights of the Add Health study (Chantala & Tabor, 1999). In separate models, Wave 1 and Wave 2 measures of romantic attraction and relationships are regressed on Wave 2 indicators of substance use, substance abuse, and mental health outcomes. The presentation of Wave 1 and Wave 2 attractions and relationships models allows for a comparison both of the predictive and contemporaneous effects of same- and both-sex attraction and relationships on these negative outcomes and of the consistencies of the attraction and relationship measures in predicting these outcomes. All multivariate models include dichotomous variables for same-sex, both-sex, and neither-sex attractions or relationships, with other-sex as the reference category. For ease of presentation, only the same- and both-sex coefficients are presented in the tables that follow. In all cases, adolescents who reported attractions or relationships to neither sex reported significantly stronger emotional health, and significantly lower levels of substance use and abuse.

RESULTS

At the time of the first wave, 5.3% of the female adolescents and 7.1% of the male adolescents in the Add Health sample reported some form of same-sex or both-sex romantic attraction (see Table 1.1). In recent population-based samples, adolescents have more often reported bisexual rather than lesbian or gay identities (French, Story, Remafedi, Resnick, & Blum, 1996; Garofalo et al., 1998). Consistent with this past work, more adolescents reported both-sex than same-sex-only attractions. Fewer respondents reported same- or both-sex romantic relationships (2.2% for girls, 1.4% for boys).

TABLE 1.1
Romantic Attractions and Relationships by Sex, Waves 1 and 2 of the Add Health Study

Variable	Wave 1		Wave 2	
	Girls	Boys	Girls	Boys
Romantic attraction[a]				
Neither sex				
%	10.92	12.90	17.33	23.16
n	1,117	1,286	1,284	1,629
Other sex				
%	83.75	79.9	77.84	72.19
n	8,564	7,960	5,768	5,078
Same sex				
%	1.45	0.89	1.15	1.55
n	148	89	85	109
Both sexes				
%	3.88	6.26	3.68	3.10
n	397	624	273	218
Romantic relationships[b]				
Neither sex				
%	33.93	35.64	30.71	35.60
n	3,490	3,581	2,282	2,517
Other sex				
%	63.85	62.99	67.30	62.93
n	6,567	6,330	5,002	4,450
Same sex				
%	1.20	0.72	1.20	0.85
n	123	72	89	60
Both sexes				
%	1.02	0.66	0.79	0.62
n	105	66	59	44

[a]Wave 1: for girls, $n = 10,226$; for boys, $n = 9,959$. Wave 2: for girls, $n = 7,410$; for boys, $n = 7,034$. [b]Wave 1: for girls, $n = 10,285$; for boys, $n = 10,049$. Wave 2: for girls, $n = 7,432$; for boys, $n = 7,071$.

Eighteen months later, reports of same- or both-sex attractions or relationships were generally lower, except for the same-sex attractions or relationships for boys. Recall that at Wave 1 youths could report romantic attractions that had taken place at any time prior to the survey, whereas at Wave 2 they were asked only about the previous 18 months. Thus, they had had less time to experience attractions. This explanation accounts for the larger proportion of the sample that reported no romantic attractions at Wave 2 when compared with Wave 1. A notable contrast between boys and girls in terms of romantic relationships between Waves 1 and 2 is that the proportion of girls involved in other-sex relationships grew and the proportion uninvolved dropped, whereas the distribution for boys remained similar across waves: More girls were initiating dating during the period between Waves 1 and 2.

Consistency in the Report of Romantic Attractions and Relationships

When one links the reports across waves, substantial fluctuation in attractions and relationships is evident (see Table 1.2). This fluctuation reflects the developmental processes inherent in this stage of life. It is also in part a product of the study design: Wave 1 attraction indicators reflect on earlier life experiences; Wave 2 is limited to the past 18 months. Same-sex and both-sex attractions or relationships are combined for ease of presentation and because, when separate, the cell sizes are very small. Other-sex sexuality is the most consistent between waves; it appears that girls are somewhat more likely than boys to be consistent in their reports of other-sex attractions and relationships across waves (by approximately 5%). There is much less consistency in the report of same- or both-sex romantic attractions or relationships. Approximately one quarter of the girls and 16% of boys who reported same- or both-sex attraction at Wave 1 also reported same- or both-sex attraction at Wave 2. Seventeen percent of the boys and 15% of the girls reported same- or both-sex romantic relationships at both waves.

Although these proportions are small in comparison to the consistency in the reports of other-sex romantic attractions and relationships (as well as in those reporting no attractions or relationships), note that the sexual-minority youths of Wave 1 were more likely to be in that category at Wave 2. Boys reporting same- or both-sex attraction at Wave 1 were over 4 times more likely than their peers to report same- or both-sex attraction at Wave 2; girls were over 7 times more likely. For romantic relationship comparisons the factor for both boys and girls is greater than 10 times. Thus, although there is substantial fluidity in the reports of same- and both-sex attractions and relationships, these analyses indicate that at least a small portion of these youths consistently report same- or both-sex attractions and relationships.

Substance Use and Abuse

Survey regression results for ordinal substance use and abuse indicators are presented in Table 1.3; for dichotomous indicators (drinking alone or use of other drugs), survey logistic regression results are presented in Table 1.4. Because of the small number of respondents reporting same- or both-sex relationships who are either drinking alone or using other drugs, it is not possible to calculate logistic equations based on romantic relationship reports with these outcomes. Overall, there are two striking findings: Girls with both-sex attractions or relationships are uniquely and consistently at risk, and same-sex relationships may be protective against alcohol abuse for boys. Results indicate that both-sex attractions or relationships among girls are predictors of all indicators of substance use and abuse, with only one

TABLE 1.2
Consistency in Reports of Romantic Attractions and Relationships Between Waves 1 and 2 of the Add Health Study

| | Wave 2 | | | | | | | |
| | Boys | | | | Girls | | | |
Wave 1	Neither	Other-sex	Same-/Both-sex	Total	Neither	Other-sex	Same-/Both-sex	Total
Romantic attraction								
Neither sex								
Frequency	459	452	41	952	352	459	28	839
Row %	48.21	47.48	4.31	14.15	41.95	54.71	3.34	11.82
Column %	29.35	9.28	13.95		28.97	8.28	3.34	
Other-sex								
Frequency	1,000	4,115	175	5,290	312	4,887	220	5,919
Row %	18.90	77.79	3.31	78.64	13.72	82.56	3.72	83.35
Column %	63.94	84.51	59.52		66.83	88.12	3.72	
Same-/Both-sex								
Frequency	105	302	78	485	51	200	92	343
Row %	21.65	62.27	16.08	7.21	14.87	58.31	26.82	4.83
Column %	6.71	6.21	26.53		4.20	3.61	27.06	
Total								
Frequency	1,564	4,869	294	6,727	1,215	5,546	340	7,101
Row %	23.25	72.38	4.37		17.11	78.10	4.79	
Romantic relationships								
Neither sex								
Frequency	1,617	994	20	2,631	1,628	1,024	25	2,677
Row %	61.46	37.78	0.76	38.62	60.81	38.25	0.93	37.42
Column %	66.08	23.25	22.22		72.91	21.37	19.23	
Other-sex								
Frequency	814	3,223	55	4,092	585	3,661	83	4,329
Row %	19.89	78.76	1.34	60.06	13.51	84.57	1.17	60.51
Column %	33.27	75.37	61.11		26.20	76.41	63.85	
Same-/Both-sex								
Frequency	16	59	15	90	20	106	22	148
Row %	17.78	65.56	16.67	1.32	13.51	71.62	14.86	2.07
Column %	.65	1.38	16.67		.89	2.21	16.92	
Total								
Frequency	2,447	4,276	90	6,813	2,233	4,791	130	7,154
Row %	35.92	62.76	1.32		31.21	66.97	1.82	

TABLE 1.3

Adolescent Sexual Orientation (Waves 1 and 2) Regressed on Substance Use and Abuse Indicators (Wave 2), Survey Regression Beta Coefficients Presented

	Wave 2 substance use or abuse									
	Smoking cigarettes		Getting drunk		Problems caused by drinking		Sexual regret from drinking		Marijuana use	
Variable	Boys	Girls	Boys	Girls	Boys	Girls	Boys	Girls	Boys	Girls
Wave 1										
Same-sex attraction	.09	−.19	.13	.01	−.02	.05	.12	.01	.05	.09
Both-sex attraction	.25***	.35***	.10	.34***	.12*	.32***	.06	.20***	.16*	.32***
Same-sex relationship	−.22	−.11	.04	.05	.18	.09	.01	.14	−.28	−.02
Both-sex relationship	.51	.43*	.59	.23	.16	.15	.12	.23	.61*	.35
Wave 2										
Same-sex attraction	.06	−.04	−.23	−.09	−.24*	.03	−.18	−.08	.16	.16
Both-sex attraction	.18	.56***	.08	.32***	.02	.31***	.10	.20**	.15	.53***
Same-sex relationship	.04	.28	−.69***	.11	−.40*	.04	−.22	−.02	−.28	−.07
Both-sex relationship	.31	.71**	−.12	.20	−.24	.13	−.05	.12	.51	.33

Note. All models control for the following: no reported romantic attractions or relationships, race, age, parental education, welfare status, and intact family status.
*p < .05. **p < .01. ***p < .001.

TABLE 1.4
Adolescent Sexual Orientation (Waves 1 and 2) Regressed on
Substance Use and Abuse Indicators (Wave 2), Survey Logistic
Regression Odds Ratios Presented

	Wave 2 substance abuse			
	Drinking alone		Other drug use	
Variable	Boys	Girls	Boys	Girls
Wave 1				
Same-sex attraction	0.99	0.86	1.53	1.41
Both-sex attraction	1.15	1.89**	1.48	2.44***
Wave 2				
Same-sex attraction	0.56	0.48	1.68	1.99
Both-sex attraction	1.50	2.54***	2.03*	4.29***

Note. All models control for the following: no reported romantic attractions or relationships, race, age, parental education, welfare status, and intact family status. Romantic relationships are not included in these analyses because of small cell sizes for same- and both-sex relationships and for these substance abuse indicators.
*$p < .05$. **$p < .01$. ***$p < .001$.

exception: Wave 2 attraction and cigarette smoking (see Tables 1.3 and 1.4). The results for girls with both-sex attractions and relationships are in stark contrast to the findings for same-sex girls, who are not at risk for higher rates of substance use or abuse on *any* of the indicators.

The pattern of findings for girls is distinct from the results for boys. Among the boys, both-sex attraction at Wave 1 is associated with more frequent smoking, problems caused by drinking, and marijuana use 18 months later, and both-sex attraction at Wave 2 is associated with the contemporaneous use of other drugs. It is surprising that boys reporting same-sex relationships at Wave 2 were less likely to report getting drunk or having problems caused by drinking, and boys who reported same-sex attractions at Wave 2 were less likely to have problems caused by drinking.

Few past studies have been able to make gender comparisons, or comparisons between sexual orientation subgroups. Only one past study that I know of, from a community-based sample of LGB youths (Rosario et al., 1997), compared lesbian and gay youths on substance abuse indicators. That study reported higher substance abuse among lesbian than among gay male youths. The findings outlined in Tables 1.3 and 1.4 suggest that among sexual-minority youths bisexual girls may be at particular risk for substance abuse. Bisexual youths have been routinely excluded from past studies of lesbian and gay youths, or they have been grouped with lesbian-identified youths and labeled "gay or lesbian" (Russell & Seif, 2002). In fact, a significant part of what we know from past research about "lesbian and gay" youths is based on the lives of bisexual adolescents (e.g., French et al., 1996; Garofalo et al., 1998). We have little research or theory to help us understand the development or experiences of adolescent bisexuality; given the risks apparent among the both-sex-attracted and -partnered girls in this study, this is an important area for further research.

Mental Health

For boys, neither attractions nor relationships are associated with self-esteem at Wave 2 (see Table 1.5). Same- and both-sex attractions at Wave 1 predict Wave 2 anxiety for boys. For depression, boys reporting both-sex attractions at Wave 1 reported higher levels of depression than their peers; similarly, same- and both-sex attraction and both-sex relationships from Wave 2 are associated with higher depression for boys. Girls reporting same- or both-sex attraction or both-sex relationships at Wave 1 and both-sex attraction at Wave 2 had lower self-esteem than those who reported only other-sex attraction or relationships. Both-sex-attracted girls appear unique in regard to their elevated levels of anxiety. Finally, although same-sex attraction at Wave 1 is associated with Wave 2 depression, girls with both-sex relationships at Wave 1 and those with both-sex attraction at Wave 2 reported higher depression.

It is difficult to explain the significance of these patterns for mental health outcomes. For girls at Wave 2 both-sex attraction is closely linked to compromised mental health outcomes. This strong effect for all outcomes for girls may overshadow any possible same-sex effect due to the small

TABLE 1.5
Adolescent Sexual Orientation (Waves 1 and 2) Regressed on Mental Health Indicators (Wave 2), Survey Regression
Beta Coefficients Presented

| | Wave 2 mental health indicators | | | | | |
| | Self-esteem | | Anxiety | | Depression | |
Variable	Boys	Girls	Boys	Girls	Boys	Girls
Wave 1						
Same-sex attraction	−.20	−.37***	.20*	.13	.11	.26*
Both-sex attraction	.03	−.17***	.13**	.18**	.12***	.08
Same-sex relationship	−.05	.18	.12	−.05	.13	−.08
Both-sex relationship	−.02	−.23*	.20	.22	.07	.23*
Wave 2						
Same-sex attraction	−.12	−.11	.10	.11	.14*	−.04
Both-sex attraction	.08	−.30***	.10	.27***	.09*	.23***
Same-sex relationship	−.03	.03	−.09	.01	.08	.01
Both-sex relationship	−.11	−.12	.17	.30*	.22*	.23

Note. All models control for the following: no reported romantic attractions or relationships, race, age, parental education, welfare status, and intact family status.
*p < .05. **p < .01. ***p < .001.

number of same-sex-attracted girls at Wave 2. Among boys, however, there is no clear pattern. A possible explanation for the effects of same- and both-sex attraction at Wave 1 on anxiety and at Wave 2 on depression may be that although depression is experienced contemporaneously with emotional stresses, anxiety is reactive and builds over time relative to emotions, feelings, or events.

DISCUSSION

This chapter has considered challenges in the study of adolescent sexual orientation, a topic for which there are multiple definitions and competing measures, and a phenomenon that is fundamentally in development during the period of adolescence. It is important to acknowledge that our understanding of the lives of sexual-minority youths has been limited in fundamental ways not only because of methodological challenges but also because of the considerable political challenges that the social scientific study of sexuality has faced. The study of adolescent same-sex sexuality concerns two issues about which the U.S. public and its policy makers have been ambivalent: adolescent sexuality and homosexuality. Scientific research on either topic, much less the two combined, faces considerable obstacles. Data on same-sex sexual behavior and sexual identities are notably absent from Add Health. The history of the Add Health study is an important example of intervention of politics in sexuality research—specifically with regard to adolescent sexual orientation (Ericksen, 1999; Gardner & Wilcox, 1993; Hunt, 1999; Udry, 1993; for the history of the Add Health study see Ericksen, 1999, and Hunt, 1999). Nevertheless, data from the Add Health study are an important source for understanding the lives of contemporary sexual-minority youths. They illustrate the fluidity of adolescent sexual attractions and relationships. At the same time, the findings on substance use, abuse, and mental health are largely consistent with past research on LGB youths.

No known studies have suggested that same-sex relationships may be protective against problem drinking for young men. This finding is worth more attention and study. The effects were only significant for contemporaneous measures of relationships and problem drinking, indicating that it may be recent or current relationships that make a difference in drinking behavior. Given what is known about gay and youth cultures, this finding makes sense. Both cultures encourage social drinking (for a discussion of drinking and youth culture, see Wooden & Blazak, 2001). In gay culture, single social life often centers on gay bars, and there is anecdotal evidence that many gay male teens view gay bars as a primary destination for finding the gay community (Savin-Williams, 1998). Same-sex romantic relationships may afford young men alternative settings for socializing, and ultimately alternative ways to relate to each other and their communities.

Past research on sexual-minority youths has been characterized by the documentation of risk, a history that has been criticized as overly focused on negative outcomes for sexual-minority youths (Savin-Williams, 1998). This chapter contributes to that history because of the need to replicate the results of studies documenting substance use, abuse, and mental health risks in the lives of sexual-minority adolescents at the national level. Studies like these are important in that they affirm past studies that have documented risk on the basis of nonrandom, self-selected samples. Findings from Add Health and other recent population-based studies provide the needed justification for policies and programs that support sexual-minority youths. It is necessary to replicate the findings of these studies because a great deal of faith has been placed in results based on very small cell sizes, representing the experiences of small numbers of youths (e.g., boys in same-sex relationships). Ultimately, these studies can both inform and be complemented by ethnographic or qualitative studies that explore the daily lives of sexual-minority youths at home, at school, and among peers.

There are, of course, limitations to the data presented here. Although it is the only nationally available study that includes indicators of same-sex sexuality, Add Health does not include self-identification as lesbian, gay, or bisexual; direct comparison to past studies of LGB youths is not possible. However, it is likely that both self-identified and pre-identified LGB youths are included among the participants who responded with same-sex or both-sex answers to questions about romantic attractions and relationships. It is also possible that some youths who are classified as reporting same-sex or both-sex attractions or relationships may never identify as LGB. Future research, both qualitative and quantitative, is needed to better understand the development of sexual behaviors, attractions, and identities during adolescence.

FUTURE DIRECTIONS

It is important for future research to begin to situate adolescent mental health within the broader context of adolescents' lives. Recent studies of gay-related stress offer a promising avenue for the study of adolescent sexual orientation and mental health (Meyer, 1995; Rosario et al., 1996; Rotheram-Borus et al., 1994). The concept of minority stress (internalized homophobia, stigma, and prejudice) has been shown to be an important predictor of psychological distress among gay men (Meyer, 1995). Among urban, gay male youths, gay-related stress (disclosing sexual orientation or being discovered as gay) is related to problem behaviors, emotional distress (Rosario et al.,

1996), and suicide attempts (Rotheram-Borus et al., 1994). Past studies such as these have moved the field beyond simply demonstrating that sexual-minority youths have compromised health outcomes by explicitly examining the characteristics, correlates, and precursors of stress and health for sexual minorities.

Given the need for and limitations of these large-scale, broadly generalizable samples of youths that include attention to sexual orientation, what direction should future research take? First, results like the ones presented here need to be followed up with well-designed community-based studies that can further explore and test some of the population-based patterns that have emerged. Second, further developments in survey language and a consensus on measures are important, so that more studies can include multidimensional measures that give attention to sexual and romantic attractions, behaviors, and identities. Third, it is important for research in this field to move beyond documenting risk (or even health). We should begin to examine the processes that propel some young bisexual women to abuse substances, that may lead to depression among both-sex-attracted boys, or even that enable young male couples to avoid problem drinking. Advances such as these will move the field forward toward understanding the risks—as well as the sources of strength—of sexual-minority youths.

REFERENCES

Bearman, P. S., & Brückner, H. (2001). Promising the future: Virginity pledges as they affect transition to first intercourse. *American Journal of Sociology, 106*(4), 859–912.

Bell, A. P., & Weinberg, M. S. (1978). *Homosexualities: A study of diversity among men and women.* New York: Simon & Schuster.

Blum, R. W., & Rinehard, P. M. (1997). *Reducing the risk: Connections that make a difference in the lives of youth.* Minneapolis: University of Minnesota.

Borowsky, I. W., Ireland, J., & Resnick, M. D. (2001). Adolescent suicide attempts: Risks and protectors. *Pediatrics, 107,* 485–493.

Brent, D. A., & Perper, J. A. (1995). Research on adolescent suicide: Implications for training, service delivery, and public policy. *Suicide and Life-Threatening Behavior, 25,* 222–240.

Chantala, K., & Tabor, J. (1999). *Strategies to perform a design-based analysis using the Add Health data.* Retrieved March 29, 2005, from http://www.cpc.unc.edu/projects/addhealth/files/weight1.pdf

Diamond, L. M. (1998). Development of sexual orientation among adolescent and young women. *Developmental Psychology, 34,* 1085–1095.

Doll, L. S. (1997). Sexual behavior research: Studying bisexual men and women and lesbians. In J. Bancroft (Ed.), *Researching sexual behavior: Methodological issues* (pp. 145–158). Bloomington: Indiana University Press.

DuRant, R. H., Krowchuk, D. P., & Sinal, S. H. (1998). Victimization, use of violence, and drug use at school among male adolescents who engage in same-sex sexual behavior. *The Journal of Pediatrics, 133,* 113–118.

Ericksen, J. A. (with Steffen, S. A.). (Eds.). (1999). *Kiss and tell: Surveying sex in the twentieth century.* Cambridge, MA: Harvard University Press.

Faulkner, A. H., & Cranston, K. (1998). Correlates of same-sex sexual behavior in a random sample of Massachusettes high school students. *American Journal of Public Health, 88*(2), 262–266.

Felts, W. M., Chenier, T., & Barnes R. (1992). Drug use and suicide ideation and behavior among North Carolina public school students. *American Journal of Public Health, 82,* 870–872.

Fergusson, D. M., Horwood, L. J., & Beautrais, A. L. (1999). Is sexual orientation related to mental health problems and suicidality among young people? *Archives of General Psychiatry, 56,* 876–880.

Fox, R. C. (1996). Bisexuality: An examination of theory and research. In R. P. Cabaj & T. S. Stein (Eds.), *Textbook of homosexuality and mental health* (pp. 147–171). Washington, DC: American Psychiatric Press.

French, S. A., Story, M., Remafedi, G., Resnick, M. D., & Blum, R. W. (1996). Sexual orientation and prevalence of body dissatisfaction and eating disordered behaviors: A population-based study of adolescents. *International Journal of Eating Disorders, 19,* 119–126.

Gardner, W., & Wilcox, B. (1993). Political intervention in scientific research. *American Psychologist, 48,* 972–983.

Garofalo, R., Wolf, R. C., Kessel, S., Palfrey, J., & DuRant, R. H. (1998). The association between health risk behaviors and sexual orientation among a school-based sample of adolescents. *Pediatrics, 101,* 895–902.

Garofalo, R., Wolf, R. C., Wissow, L. S., Woods, E. R., & Goodman, E. (1999). Sexual orientation and risk of suicide attempts among a representative sample of youths. *Archives of Pediatric and Adolescent Medicine, 153,* 487–493.

Grossman, A. H., & Kerner, M. S. (1998). Self-esteem and supportiveness as predictors of emotional distress in gay male and lesbian youth. *Journal of Homosexuality, 35,* 25–39.

Halpern, C. T., Joyner, K., Udry, J. R., & Schindran, C. (2000). Smart teens don't have sex (or kiss much either). *Journal of Adolescent Health, 26,* 213–225.

Hammelman, T. L. (1993). Gay and lesbian youth: Contributing factors to serious attempts or considerations of suicide. *Journal of Gay and Lesbian Psychotherapy, 2,* 77–89.

Hershberger, S. L., & D'Augelli, A. R. (1995). The impact of victimization on the mental health and suicidality of lesbian, gay, and bisexual youths. *Developmental Psychology, 31,* 65–74.

Hetrick, E. S., & Martin, A. D. (1987). Developmental issues and their resolution for gay and lesbian adolescents. *Journal of Homosexuality, 14*, 25–43.

Hetrick, E. S., & Martin, A. D. (1988). The stigmatization of the gay and lesbian adolescent. *Journal of Homosexuality, 14*, 163–183.

Hunt, M. (1999). *The new know-nothings: The political foes of the scientific study of human nature*. New Brunswick, NJ: Transaction Publishers.

Hunter, J., & Schaecher, R. (1995). Gay and lesbian adolescents. In L. Beebe (Ed.), *Encyclopedia of social work* (19th ed., pp. 1055–1063). Washington, DC: National Association of Social Workers.

Joyner, K., & Udry, J. R. (2000). You don't bring me anything but down: Adolescent romance and depression. *Journal of Health and Social Behavior, 41*, 369–391.

Katchadourian, H. (1990). Sexuality. In S. S. Feldman & G. R. Elliott (Eds.), *At the threshold: The developing adolescent* (pp. 330–351). Cambridge, MA: Harvard University Press.

Koch, P. B. (1993). Promoting healthy sexual development during early adolescence. In R. M. Lerner (Ed.), *Early adolescence: Perspectives on research, policy, and intervention* (pp. 293–307). Hillsdale, NJ: Erlbaum.

Konopka, G. (1973). Requirements for healthy development of adolescent youth. *Adolescence, 8*, 1–26.

Kruks, G. (1991). Gay and lesbian homeless/street youth: Special issues and concerns. *Journal of Adolescent Health, 12*, 515–518.

Laumann, E. O., Gagnon, J. H., Michael, R. T., & Michaels, S. (1994). *The social organization of sexuality: Sexual practices in the United States*. Chicago: University of Chicago Press.

Lewinsohn, P. M., Rohde, P., & Seeley, J. R. (1996). Adolescent suicidal ideation and attempts: Risk factors and clinical implications. *Clinical Psychology: Science and Practice, 3*, 25–46.

Lock, J., & Steiner, H. (1999). Gay, lesbian, and bisexual youth risks for emotional, physical, and social problems: Results from a community-based survey. *Journal of the American Academy of Child & Adolescent Psychiatry, 38*, 297–304.

Meyer, I. H. (1995). Minority stress and mental health in gay men. *Journal of Health and Social Behavior, 36*, 38–56.

Petersen, A. C., Leffert, N., Graham, B., Alwin, J., & Ding, S. (1997). Promoting mental health during the transition into adolescence. In J. Schulenberg, J. L. Maggs, & K. Hurrelmann (Eds.), *Health risks and developmental challenges during adolescence* (pp. 471–497). Cambridge, England: Cambridge University Press.

Radloff, L. S. (1977). The CES-D scale: A self-report depression scale for research in the general population. *Applied Psychological Measurement, 1*, 385–401.

Remafedi, G. (1987). Male homosexuality: The adolescent's perspective. *Pediatrics, 79*, 326–330.

Remafedi, G. (1994). Cognitive and behavioral adaptations to HIV/AIDS among gay and bisexual adolescents. *Journal of Adolescent Health, 2*, 142–148.

Remafedi, G., French, S., Story, M., Resnick, M. D., & Blum, R. (1998). The relationship between suicide risk and sexual orientation: Results of a population-based study. *American Journal of Public Health, 87,* 1–4.

Resnick, M. D., Bearman, P. S., Blum, R. W., Bauman, K. E., Harris, K. M., Jones, J., et al. (1997). Protecting adolescents from harm: Findings from the National Longitudinal Study of Adolescent Health. *Journal of the American Medical Association, 278,* 823–832.

Rosario, M., Hunter, J., & Gwadz, M. (1997). Exploration of substance use among lesbian, gay, and bisexual youth: Prevalence and correlates. *Journal of Adolescent Research, 4,* 454–476.

Rosario, M., Rotheram-Borus, M. J., & Reid, H. (1996). Gay-related stress and its correlates among gay and bisexual male adolescents of predominantly Black and Hispanic background. *Journal of Counseling Psychology, 24,* 136–159.

Rotheram-Borus, M. J., & Fernandez, M. I. (1995). Sexual orientation and developmental challenges experienced by gay and lesbian adolescents. *Suicide and Life-Threatening Behavior, 25*(Suppl.), 26–34.

Rotheram-Borus, M. J., Hunter, J., & Rosario, M. (1994). Suicidal behavior and gay-related stress among gay and bisexual male adolescents. *Journal of Adolescent Research, 9*(4), 498–508.

Rotheram-Borus, M. J., Rosario, M., Van Rossem, R., & Reid, H. (1995). Prevalence, course, and predictors of multiple problem behaviors among gay and bisexual male adolescents. *Developmental Psychology, 31,* 75–85.

Russell, S. T., Driscoll, A. K., & Truong, N. L. (2000). Adolescent same-sex romantic attractions and relationships: Implications for substance use and abuse. *American Journal of Public Health, 92*(2), 198–202.

Russell, S. T., Franz, B., & Driscoll, A. K. (2001). Same-sex romantic attraction and violence experiences in adolescence. *American Journal of Public Health, 91,* 907–914.

Russell, S. T., & Joyner, K. (2001). Adolescent sexual orientation and suicide risk: Evidence from a national study. *American Journal of Public Health, 91,* 1276–1281.

Russell, S. T., & Seif, H. M. (2002). Bisexual female adolescents: A critical review of past research, and results from a national study. *Journal of Bisexuality, 2,* 73–94.

Russell, S. T., Seif, H., & Truong, N. L. (2001). School outcomes of sexual minority youth in the United States: Evidence from a national study. *Journal of Adolescence, 24,* 111–127.

Russell, S. T., & Truong, N. L. (2001). Adolescent sexual orientation, race and ethnicity, and school environments: A national study of sexual minority youth of color. In K. K. Kumashiro (Ed.), *Troubling intersections of race and sexuality: Queer students of color and anti-oppressive education* (pp. 113–130). New York: Rowman & Littlefield.

Sandfort, T. G. M. (1997). Sampling male homosexuality. In J. Bancroft (Ed.), *Researching sexual behavior: Methodological issues* (pp. 261–275). Bloomington: Indiana University Press.

Savin-Williams, R. C. (1998). ". . . And then I became gay": Young men's stories. New York: Routledge.

Savin-Williams, R. C., & Rodriguez, R. G. (1993). A developmental, clinical perspective on lesbian, gay male, and bisexual youths. In T. P. Gullotta, G. R. Adams, & R. Montemayor (Eds.), Adolescent sexuality (pp. 77–101). Newbury Park, CA: Sage.

Shaffer, D., Fisher, P., Hicks, R. H., Parides, M., & Gould, M. (1995). Sexual orientation in adolescents who commit suicide. Suicide and Life-Threatening Behavior, 25, 64–71.

Supple, A. J., Aquilino, W. S., & Wright, D. L. (1999). Collecting sensitive self-report data with laptop computers: Impact on the response tendencies of adolescents in a home interview. Journal of Research on Adolescence, 9, 467–488.

Turner, C. F., Ku, L., Rogers, S. M., Lindberg, L. D., Pleck, J. H., & Sonenstein, F. L. (1998, May 8). Adolescent sexual behavior, drug use, and violence: Increased reporting with computer survey technology. Science, 280, 867–873.

Turner, C. F., Miller, H. G., & Rogers, S. M. (1997). Survey measurement of sexual behavior: Problems and progress. In J. Bancroft (Ed.), Researching sexual behavior: Methodological issues (pp. 37–60). Bloomington: Indiana University Press.

Udry, J. R. (1993). The politics of sex research. Journal of Sex Research, 30, 103–110.

Udry, J. R., & Chantala, K. (2002). Risk assessment of adolescents with same-sex relationships. Journal of Adolescent Health, 31, 84–92.

Weinberg, N. Z., Rahdert, E., Colliver, J. D., & Glantz, M. D. (1998). Adolescent substance abuse: A review of the past 10 years. Journal of the American Academy of Child & Adolescent Psychiatry, 37, 252–261.

Wooden, W. S., & Blazak, R. (2001). Renegade kids, suburban outlaws: From youth culture to delinquency (2nd ed.). Belmont, CA: Wadsworth.

2

DEVELOPMENTAL AND CONTEXTUAL FACTORS AND MENTAL HEALTH AMONG LESBIAN, GAY, AND BISEXUAL YOUTHS

ANTHONY R. D'AUGELLI

In the past decade, research of increasing sophistication has appeared concerning youths who self-identify as lesbian, gay, or bisexual (LGB; see D'Augelli & Patterson, 2001, for reviews of current research). LGB youths have generally been adolescents ranging in age from 13 through 21, although some studies have also included in their samples of "youth" young adults up to 25 years of age. This chapter focuses predominantly on LGB youths, not young adults. LGB youths made their first appearance in the psychological research literature more than 30 years ago (Roesler & Deisher, 1972), although a non–pathology-oriented analysis of their life challenges did not appear until the early 1980s (Malyon, 1981). The publication of several articles by Remafedi in 1987 (Remafedi, 1987a, 1987b) launched contemporary empirical interest in LGB youths. These articles, based on a small sample of adolescents in Minneapolis, not only focused on their mental health problems but also attended to the circumstances of their lives, including mistreatment by others because of their sexual orientation.

These landmark studies were followed by studies conducted on college students (e.g., D'Augelli, 1991) as well as descriptive survey-based studies that included youths from diverse community settings (e.g., D'Augelli & Hershberger, 1993; Savin-Williams, 1990). Several interview-based studies were conducted in urban social service agencies for LGB youths (e.g., Herdt & Boxer, 1993). Because of the nature of their sampling, early studies had the inevitable problem of generalizability, a problem endemic to research on a highly stigmatized population. Generalizability to the larger population of youths with same-sex attractions is an important contribution of the population-based survey research conducted since the early 1990s (e.g., Remafedi, Resnick, Blum, & Harris, 1992; see Cochran, 2001, for a review of population-based studies). These studies use large representative samples of high school students and sort youths by sexual orientation on the basis of questions about sexual orientation, sexual behavior, or the gender of sexual partners. The population-based surveys share with other survey research on LGB youths limits on the nature of information obtained. For example, only data on sexual behavior were available in some studies and only data on same-sex romantic attractions were collected in others. Unfortunately, conducting an intensive interview study of LGB youths using a large sample of randomly chosen youths who might be representative of the population remains an impossibility.

The available research on LGB youths has endeavored to elucidate the processes of development they undergo as they move through puberty to young adulthood. From the perspective of developmental researchers, these youths provide information about how sexual orientation evolves prior to puberty and crystallizes thereafter, providing critical insights into how these adolescents experience the emergence of sexual identity (Graber & Archibald, 2001). In contrast to earlier generations of LGB people who self-identified as nonheterosexual in early adulthood as they established independence from their families of origin, many LGB youths now self-identify during early adolescence, although we do not know what percentage of all LGB youths do so. The apparent earlier timing of contemporary LGB youths' self-identification highlights the importance of the historical and social context on these youths' development (D'Augelli, 1998). In addition, these youths are, for the most part, still living at home and remain in school, two crucial social contexts for adolescent development. They are adolescents whose cognitive, emotional, and social development is still occurring. They must confront the challenge of a stigmatized identity, as adolescents, in primary social contexts (homes and schools) that are often hostile. Little psychological research on the impact of contextual factors on the development of sexual orientation has occurred to date.

This chapter reviews research on developmental and contextual factors in the lives of LGB youths. A comprehensive review of the research is beyond the scope of the chapter, and the reader is referred to D'Augelli and Patterson (2001). Instead, this chapter highlights findings from studies I have completed on LGB youths, using the results to demonstrate the importance of using developmental-contextual thinking in such research.

ADJUSTMENT PROBLEMS AMONG LESBIAN, GAY, AND BISEXUAL YOUTHS

Much of the interest in LGB youths results from evidence from diverse sources showing that LGB youths are at risk for a range of health and mental health problems, as well as alcohol and drug abuse, and that they engage in sexual behavior that increases their chance of HIV infection. Reviews of these issues can be found in Anhalt and Morris (1999), Rotheram-Borus and Langabeer (2001), and Grossman (2001). Perhaps the most important—and contentious—finding related to LGB youths' adjustment concerns suicidality/suicidal ideation, suicide attempts, and completed suicides. An early synthesis of then-available literature by Gibson (1989) concluded that a disproportionate percentage of completed youth suicides were the result of sexual orientation conflicts and that LGB youths attempted suicide at a considerably higher rate than their heterosexual counterparts. Although no empirical evidence has found LGB youths to be overrepresented among completed suicides, studies based on convenience samples have found high suicide attempt rates among LGB youths (Gould, Greenberg, Velting, & Shaffer, 2003; McDaniels, Purcell, & D'Augelli, 2001; Russell, 2003). Methodological problems in past research, especially problems related to sampling and measurement, make conclusions difficult (Savin-Williams, 2001, 2003). Results from representative samples, however, have generally corroborated findings from the earlier studies showing adjustment difficulties among LGB youths. The rates of suicide attempts for LGB youths found in these studies are considerably higher than estimates of suicide attempts among high school students in general (Lewinsohn, Rohde, & Seeley, 1996).

AN ANALYSIS OF LESBIAN, GAY, AND BISEXUAL YOUTHS' LIVES: RESULTS FROM NONCLINICAL SAMPLES

This chapter presents data on developmental processes and adjustment patterns among LGB youths by using a large sample of youths attending social and recreational groups in community settings. The data are used to answer core questions related to the developmental and contextual factors influencing LGB youths. The questions concern developmental milestones in the development of sexual orientation, social aspects of sexual orientation, family relationships, mental health and adjustment, and victimization based on sexual orientation. Findings are presented about these issues: (a) At what ages do sexual orientation milestones occur for youths who self-identify as LGB? (b) How central is sexual orientation to youths' social lives? (c) How much do parents know of youths' sexual orientation and how do they react? (d) How are LGB youths victimized because of their sexual orientation? and (e) What impact does victimization have on their adjustment? The report includes information on experiences with victimization because of the pervasive stigmatization of same-sex sexual orientation; as a result, the developmental process of sexual orientation integration is conjointly determined by individual biopsychosocial factors and by exogenous cultural and contextual factors heavily influenced by stigma (D'Augelli, 1998). Gender differences are reported, as relatively few empirical studies of lesbian and bisexual female adolescents have been conducted (Schneider, 2001). Evidence suggests young women's sexual orientation development is distinctly different from that of young men (Diamond & Savin-Williams, 2000).

This report is based on two data sets combined for analysis and presented here. The first data were gathered from 1987 through 1989 and the second from 1995 to 1997. Similar data-collection procedures were used both times, with the primary goal the generation of a diverse national sample. Listings of social and recreational groups for LGB youths in the United States and Canada were identified, and personal contact was made with adult group coordinators, requesting that they consult with group members about participation. Details about the procedures can be found in D'Augelli and Hershberger (1993) and D'Augelli, Hershberger, and Pilkington (2001).

A final sample of 542 youths (62% male and 38% female participants) was obtained. Three quarters (74%) self-identified as gay or lesbian; 20% said they were bisexual, but mostly gay or lesbian; and 6% said they were bisexual, but equally gay or lesbian and heterosexual. Significantly more female participants identified as bisexual, $\chi^2(2, N = 542) = 28.57$, $p < .001$. Their ages ranged from 14 to 21, with one third from 14 to 18, and two thirds from 19 to 21. Average age was 19.08 ($SD = 1.5$); male participants were significantly older, $t(540) = 2.53$, $p < .01$. Over three quarters were White; 8% were African American, 4% were of Hispanic origin, 1% were Native American or Canadian, and the rest came from a variety of other backgrounds. Geographical diversity was reasonably represented: 38% lived in major metropolitan areas, 19% in small cities, 28% in medium-sized towns or in the suburbs, 10% in small towns, and 5% in rural areas. Because of small sample sizes, comparisons between youths of different racial and ethnic backgrounds were not attempted.

SEXUAL ORIENTATION MILESTONES

The following information was obtained about ages at which different milestones related to sexual orientation occurred: age of awareness of same-sex attraction; age of self-labeling as LGB; age of disclosure of same-sex sexual orientation; and ages of first sexual experiences with males and with females. Youths were also asked about the number of males and females with whom they had had sexual experiences. Additional descriptors of early sexual orientation experience were calculated. Years of awareness of LGB orientation were computed by subtracting youths' age at first awareness from their current age; years before self-labeling were computed as age of awareness subtracted from age of self-labeling; and years before first disclosure were obtained by subtracting age at self-labeling from age of first disclosure. These scores reflect the duration of the crucial phases of sexual orientation development. The percentage of youths' lives during which they were aware of same-sex feelings was calculated by dividing age of first awareness by chronological age. The percentage of their lives that youths were aware of same-sex feelings but told no one was calculated by subtracting age of awareness from age of first disclosure, and then dividing by age. To calculate the percentage of their lives that youths knew of their sexual orientation but had disclosed to no one, the difference between the age of self-labeling and the age of first disclosure was divided by their ages. Comparisons between male and female youths were conducted; complete results can be found in D'Augelli (2002).

Youths reported being aware of their same-sex feelings at about age 10, with male participants noting the awareness earlier (10 vs. 11). Self-labeling occurred about 5 years after the initial awareness, with male participants once again reaching the milestone sooner (15 vs. 16). First disclosure of sexual orientation for both male and female youths occurred at about 17, though youths reported this occurring as young as 10 and as old as 21. Fourteen percent disclosed between the ages of 10 and 14; 69% between 15 and 18; and 17% disclosed between 19 and 21. On average, youths spent about half of their lives aware of their same-sex feelings, although this ranged from 5% to nearly all of their lives. Youths spent about one third of their lives aware of same-sex feelings but not revealing these feelings to others. There was wide variability in the time youths spent "in the closet," ranging from zero (disclosure occurred in the same year as awareness) to over 80% of their lives. Youths were found to have spent about 7% of their lives self-labeled yet nondisclosed. Clearly self-identification is a crucial step in the development of sexual orientation.

Most (92%) male participants had engaged in sexual behavior with other males. As to the age at which same-sex sexual experience first occurred, 14% said from 4 to 10 years of age; 24% from 11 to 14; 49% from 15 to 18; and 13% from 19 to 21. Most (83%) had their first male sexual experience following their awareness of their sexual orientation; 13% had the sexual experience during the same year as awareness. In only 4% of the male participants did same-sex sexual experience precede awareness. On average, 5 years passed between awareness and first male sexual experiences. Although sexual behavior followed awareness, a different pattern held for self-identification. One third had their first sexual experience with another male before labeling themselves gay or bisexual; 21% had the experience and self-identified in the same year; and almost half (47%) identified as gay first and later had sex with a male. Sexual experience thus ordinarily followed awareness, and self-identification did not predict onset of sexual behavior.

Half of the male participants (57%) also reported heterosexual sexual activity. As to age of first heterosexual experience, 10% said from 4 to 10; 28% from 11 to 14; 55% from 15 to 18; and 7% from 19 to 21. Fewer than half (41%) of the male participants had sex with both males and females. Of these, half (47%) engaged in sex with females first; 44% had sex with males first; and for 9% the ages of initiation did not differ. Many (84%) of the male participants reported awareness of same-sex feelings before having heterosexual sex; 7% said awareness and first heterosexual sex occurred in the same year; and 16% said they had sex with females before awareness. About half of the male participants (53%) had sex with females before self-identifying as gay; 14% had heterosexual sex in the same year they self-identified; and 33% first identified as gay, and later had sexual contact with females.

Most female youths (90%) also reported same-sex sexual behavior. However, females initiated same-sex sexual activities later than males (16 vs. 15). Eight percent said their first sexual experience with a female occurred between ages 4 and 10; 18% said from 11 to 14; 53% from 15 to 18; and 21% from 19 to 21. By age 18, 93% of the males and 79% of the females had had same-sex sexual experience. Most (83%) females were aware of same-sex feelings prior to their first same-sex experience; 12% became aware during the same year that they had their first same-sex experience; and 5% had sex with a female prior to awareness of their feelings. On average, 4 years passed between awareness and first same-sex sexual contact. As to self-labeling and same-sex sexual experience, 20% had their first same-sex sexual experience before labeling themselves as lesbian (or bisexual); 35% had the sexual experience in the same year they self-identified; and 45% self-identified first.

Three quarters (74%) of the female participants had heterosexual experiences, far more than the male participants. Of those having sex with both male and female partners (81% of the females), only 15% had sex

TABLE 2.1
Number of Same-Sex and Opposite-Sex Sexual Partners of Lesbian, Gay, and Bisexual Youths

Number of sexual partners	Same-sex				Opposite-sex			
	Male		Female		Male		Female	
	n^a	%	n^b	%	n^c	%	n^d	%
None	26	8	20	10	131	43	51	26
1	17	5	35	17	72	24	25	13
2–4	84	26	96	47	73	24	62	31
5–7	62	19	29	14	17	6	25	13
8–10	40	12	11	5	5	2	9	5
11–13	27	8	5	2	3	1	11	6
14–19	21	6	3	1	3	1	6	3
20–30	28	9	0	0	1	<1	5	2
31–50	8	2	0	0	0	0	1	<1
51+	15	5	3	1	0	0	1	<1

$^a n = 328.$ $^b n = 202.$ $^c n = 305.$ $^d n = 196.$

with female partners first; three quarters (77%) had heterosexual sexual experiences first; and 8% reported onset of heterosexual and same-sex sexual contact at the same ages. Many (60%) reported having awareness of their same-sex feelings before having heterosexual sex; 10% said these events occurred during the same year; and 29% had sex with male partners and later recognized same-sex sexual feelings. As to self-identification, 68% of the girls had sex with male partners before identifying as lesbian; 11% said the opposite-sex experience occurred during the same year as their identification as lesbian; and 22% said they identified as lesbian first and later initiated heterosexual activity.

In contrast to male participants, for whom the ages of initial heterosexual and same-sex sexual contact did not differ, female participants initiated same-sex sexual activity significantly later than heterosexual contact, $t(135) = 8.37$, $p < .001$.

The number of lifetime sexual partners youths reported appears in Table 2.1. Overall, male youths reported more same-sex sexual partners than did female youths, $\chi^2(9, N = 530) = 83.67$, $p < .001$; female youths reported more opposite-sex sexual partners, $\chi^2(9, N = 501) = 50.41$, $p < .001$. The later ages of female participants' awareness and self-labeling provided more time to engage in heterosexual sexual activity than male participants had. The fewer same-sex partners reported by the female participants might also reflect their relationship status. Nearly half (47%) of the female youths and 38% of the male youths were in same-sex relationships, a significant difference, $\chi^2(1, N = 513) = 4.48$, $p < .05$. Involvement in such relationships would likely decrease the number of sexual partners.

When asked how open they were about their sexual orientation in general, using a 7-point continuum, 23% were *completely out*, and only 3% were *completely hidden from others*, the extreme points on the scale. Three quarters were past the midpoint on outness. There were no sex differences on outness. When asked how likely someone who did not know them would be able to identify them as LGB, 9% said they were very likely to be identified, 44% said it was likely, and 46% said it was not likely, suggesting considerable variability in public presentations. No sex differences in identifiability by strangers were found. When asked to compare themselves with same-sex peers, female participants perceived themselves as more masculine than other girls compared with how masculine the boys felt they were compared with other boys, $t(533) = 12.29$, $p < .01$. It would appear as though these differences in gender presentation were not associated with greater identifiability of one sex over the other. "Masculine" female participants did not cue others' reactions to an attribution of lesbian status, nor were most male participants sufficiently "feminine" to be identified as gay. However, as seen later, male participants were more often targeted for victimization.

Nearly half (45%) of the youths said they often participated in social activities offered by LGB organizations. Most (77%) said they had gone to LGB bars, with 16% going weekly and 30% going several times a month. Attendance at LGB bars was significantly correlated with age, with older youths reporting more frequent attendance, $r(507) = .25$, $p < .001$. When asked how many of their good friends were LGB, 4% said none, 27% said less than half, 22% said half, 40% said more than half, and 7% said all.

More than one third (39%; 36% of the female and 44% of the male participants) reported that they had lost friends as a result of their sexual orientation, $\chi^2(1, N = 504) = 2.96$, $p = .09$. When it came to how best heterosexual friends would react (or have reacted) to disclosure of sexual orientation, most (85%) said their best heterosexual female friend was accepting, and there was no sex difference. However, not only were best heterosexual male friends in general expected to be less accepting (74% were thought to be accepting) but there was a significant sex difference. Male youths expected much more negative reactions from their best male heterosexual friends than from female youths, $\chi^2(3, N = 423) = 17.89$. $p < .001$). About two thirds (67%) of the male participants expected these friends to be accepting compared with 84% of the female participants. Many feared losing additional friends. Although over one third of the youths (36%) feared losing more friends, nearly half of the girls (46%) compared with 30% of the boys had such a fear, a significant difference, $\chi^2(1, N = 512) = 12.88$, $p < .001$.

FAMILY RELATIONSHIPS

Almost three quarters (69%) of the youths' mothers and about half (48%) of their fathers knew of their children's sexual orientation and had discussed the issue. Twice as many fathers as mothers (19% vs. 9%) did not suspect that their children were LGB. Mothers were significantly more aware, $t(421) = 8.47$, $p < .001$, and responded more positively, $t(419) = 5.81$, $p < .001$. Half of the mothers (48%) were accepting, compared with one third (35%) of the fathers; 24% of mothers were intolerant or rejecting, compared with 37% of fathers.

Youths who had told a parent about themselves made their initial disclosure at about age 17, with male and female participants not differing. To determine how long youths kept their sexual orientation from parents, the age of first self-labeling was subtracted from the age of first disclosure to a parent. The average time was approximately 2 years, with male participants having self-identified as LGB and not telling parents for a longer period than female participants, $t(366) = 3.14$, $p < .01$. There is a considerably longer period, however, during which youths were aware of same-sex feelings without informing their parents; a range of up to 17 years was found between age of first awareness of same-sex feelings and telling a parent, with an average of about 7 years. Male participants were aware of their same-sex feelings for longer periods without telling parents than were female participants, $t(369) = 2.96$, $p < .01$.

LIFETIME VICTIMIZATION EXPERIENCES

Information was sought about youths' lifetime experiences of victimization related to their sexual orientation with items commonly used in research on this form of victimization. The results do not include any other forms of victimization youths might have experienced. The six types of victimization were verbal abuse, threats of physical attack, objects being thrown, assaults (being punched, kicked, or beaten), threats with weapons, and sexual assaults. Youths noted how often each type of victimization occurred using these categories: *never, once, twice,* or *three or more times*. A total victimization score was computed by adding the six types of victimization. A log transformation was applied to the total victimization score to decrease the skewness of the distribution.

Most (81%) had experienced verbal abuse related to being LGB; 38% had been threatened with physical attacks, 22% had objects thrown at them, 15% had been physically assaulted, 6% had been assaulted with a weapon, and 16% had been sexually assaulted. More than half (54%) had been subjected to three or more incidents of verbal abuse. Fourteen percent had been threatened with violence three or more times. Only one gender difference was found in specific kinds of victimization: Male participants were more often threatened with violence, $\chi^2(3, N = 496) = 10.36$, $p < .05$. In several other categories (verbal abuse, objects thrown, sexual assault), however, their experiences approached statistically significant differences from those of female participants ($p < .10$). Male participants' lifetime victimization scores were significantly higher than those of female participants, $t(462) = 2.92$, $p < .01$.

The participants were asked if their mothers or fathers had verbally attacked them, threatened to hurt them, or actually hit them because of their sexual orientation. These questions were answered with *yes* or *no*. Youths were also asked if they feared being verbally harassed at home or physically hurt at home. This was answered with *yes* or *no* as well. Of the entire sample of 542, 12% (35 male and 28 female participants) acknowledged that their mothers had verbally abused them, and 7% (31 male and 9 female participants) said their fathers verbally abused them. Being threatened with harm by mothers was reported by 7 male and 5 female participants; threats by fathers were reported by 8 male and 5 female participants. Actual physical attacks by mothers were reported by 8 male and 14 female participants; attacks by fathers were reported by 3 male and 4 female participants. It is interesting to note that male and female participants were verbally abused at similar rates by mothers, yet more fathers verbally abused sons than daughters. However, proportionately more physical attacks by mothers were directed at daughters than at sons. It is important to note that frequencies of parental physical attack were low in this sample.

More fear of victimization at home was reported than actual victimization. Nearly 30% said they were afraid of verbal harassment at home because they were lesbian, gay, or bisexual, with more female (35%) than male (26%) participants fearing verbal attacks, $\chi^2(1, N = 511) = 4.55$, $p < .05$. Thirteen percent reported being afraid of being physically attacked at home. Not only does verbal victimization occur more often but youths are more afraid of future experiences of such victimization. This is not meant to minimize actual physical attacks or fear of physical attacks, as some of these attacks were reported to have been quite severe.

Inspection of data about the nature of the victimizers of these youths revealed that other youths were the most common assailants. Seventy youths (14% of the entire sample) said that they had been hit by another youth because they were LGB. This explains the high fear of verbal harassment at school, with 38% expressing such a fear. Over one quarter (28%) feared physical attack at school, with male and female participants being equally afraid.

MENTAL HEALTH AND ADJUSTMENT

The participants completed the Rosenberg Self-Esteem Inventory (Rosenberg, 1979) and the Brief Symptom Inventory (BSI; Derogatis, 1993). The BSI is a measure of 53 symptoms yielding nine subscales: Somatization, Obsessive–Compulsiveness, Interpersonal Sensitivity, Depression, Anxiety, Hostility, Phobic Anxiety, Paranoid Ideation, and Psychoticism. An overall measure of symptoms called the Global Severity Index (GSI) is calculated by summing item responses. Male and female participants did not differ on self-esteem, $t(538) = 1.51$, ns. However, a multivariate analysis of variance comparing the participants on BSI scores yielded a significant sex difference, Wilks's $\Lambda = .96$, $F(9, 497) = 2.45$, $p < .01$. Follow-up t tests found female participants showing more symptoms than male participants on the three subscales on which there were significant differences, Somatization, Obsessive–Compulsiveness, and Anxiety (all at $p < .05$). GSI scores did not differ between boys and girls, $t(505) = 1.25$, ns. Female participants differed on several types of mental health symptoms, but not on overall symptomatology. The participants' reported symptoms were contrasted to those reported by Derogatis (1993, p. 36) for a nonclinical sample of adolescents. These results can be found in D'Augelli (2002). In general, analyses showed more symptoms reported by the LGB youths on six of the nine BSI scale scores, but not on the overall GSI scores. More research is needed on this issue to determine if the meaning of the symptoms is comparable for LGB youths and their heterosexual counterparts before one would conclude that LGB youths have more mental health symptoms. However, such a conclusion would be consistent with findings from the population-based reports noted earlier in this chapter.

Information was obtained about current suicidal thoughts and past suicide attempts. Youths were asked, "Have you *ever* seriously thought of taking your own life?" which they answered on a 4-point scale (ranging from $1 = never$, through $4 = often$). They were asked whether they had ever tried to kill themselves, answered as *yes* or *no*. Eight percent of male and 15% of the female participants said they often had serious suicidal thoughts; another quarter (27% of male and female participants) sometimes had serious suicidal ideation, with female participants reporting more frequent past suicidal ideation than male participants, $\chi^2(3, N = 537) = 7.87$, $p < .05$. Over one third of the entire sample (37%; 36% of male and 39% of female participants) reported past suicide attempts. More details about suicidality results can be found in D'Augelli, Hershberger, and Pilkington (2001). The reader is referred to Savin-Williams's (2001, 2003) critical analyses of LGB youth suicide data to obtain an important perspective on the meaning of findings such as these.

TABLE 2.2
Correlations of Lifetime Victimization and Parental Reactions With Mental Health Indicators

Victimization	Self-esteem	Suicidal thinking	Overall symptoms[a]
Verbal abuse	−.07	.18***	.22***
Threats of violence	−.02	.14***	.18***
Objects thrown	.01	.08	.15**
Assault	−.05	.12**	.20***
Threatened with weapon	−.02	.03	.10*
Sexual assault	−.05	.12**	.17***
Total victimization	−.04	.18***	.23***
Maternal reaction	−.12**	.08	.19***
Paternal reaction	−.13**	.06	.11*

[a]Brief Symptom Inventory, Global Severity Index.
*p < .05. **p < .01. ***p < .001.

SEXUAL ORIENTATION MILESTONES, FAMILY RELATIONSHIPS, VICTIMIZATION, AND MENTAL HEALTH

Correlations between lifetime victimization and sexual orientation milestones revealed that the earlier milestones were reached the more victimization youths reported. Youths who were aware at earlier ages (r = .13, p < .001), self-identified earlier (r = .27, p < .001), and self-disclosed earlier (r = .23, p < .001) reported more lifetime victimization. Age was unrelated to victimization.

Table 2.2 shows correlations between lifetime sexual orientation victimization and self-esteem, lifetime suicidal ideation, and overall mental health symptoms (BSI total symptoms [GSI scores]). Although parental rejection was more closely related to lower self-esteem than were the other factors considered, no relationship between victimization and self-esteem was found. Past victimization was more closely associated with current mental health problems, including suicidal ideation.

DISCUSSION

These results demonstrate the unique characteristics of adolescents who describe themselves as lesbian, gay, or bisexual. Description of the life experiences of LGB youths not only must include the developmental challenges they face prior to, during, and after puberty as they make the transition to adulthood but also must address the social contexts of these changes because of the cultural stigma such youths face. The interactions between individual developmental processes, family and peer relationships, and integration into community life are at the heart of understanding the challenges faced by all adolescents. Without exception, these interactions are much more complex for LGB youths.

These results show that LGB youths vary considerably in the ages at which they confront developmental milestones in the evolution of their sexual orientations. It is important to avoid the extrapolation of an adult sexual orientation identity model on the experiences of LGB youths. Contemporary LGB youths approach the challenges of self-definition and self-disclosure at chronologically earlier ages than did previous cohorts. For example, in a sample of 400 older LGB adults aged 60 or older, the average age of awareness of same-sex attractions was 13; the age of self-labeling was 21; and the age of first disclosure to anyone was 23 (D'Augelli & Grossman, 2001). It is considerably easier in many (but, of course, not all) cultural contexts for adolescents in this decade to label sexual and emotional arousal by people of the same sex in ways that were unavailable to earlier cohorts. Nor could a youth who self-identified as LGB in earlier years proceed in identity exploration without substantial risk. The risks were so threatening that acknowledgment to others of any same-sex feelings during adolescence was not an option for most. Without the ability to obtain social verification for their identity status, even an uncertain one, LGB youths of earlier generations denied or mislabeled their feelings, often enacting heterosexual expectations, and postponed the integration of their personal identity.

These results show that young lesbians' and bisexual females' experiences are in many ways different from those of young gay and bisexual males. Males are aware of their same-sex feelings at earlier ages and self-identify earlier, yet spend significantly more of their lives "in the closet," being aware of their feelings and not disclosing them. By far the most typical pattern was for youths to engage in same-sex sexual activity following awareness of their feelings; for very few did same-sex sexual behavior precede the feelings. About the same percentage of males and females had initiated same-sex sexual activity (about 90%), but females' ages of onset were significantly later than males'. More males than females (33% compared with 20%) had same-sex sexual activity before self-identifying as gay. There were differences in heterosexual activities as well. About half of the males and three quarters of the females had heterosexual experience; more females had heterosexual sex before same-sex sexual experience. More males than females (84% compared with 60%) were aware of same-sex feelings prior to initiating heterosexual sex. There were more females (68%) who had heterosexual sex before self-identifying as lesbian than there were males who had heterosexual sex before identifying as gay (53%).

The developmental processes of LGB youths must take into account factors other than sexual orientation factors, especially the many forms of stigmatization and victimization youths experience. Parental knowledge of and reactions to youths' emerging sexual orientation are most important in understanding youths' development during adolescence. Few families were completely accepting; in most cases, mothers were more knowledgeable and supportive than fathers. The impact of family rejection is clear in these findings: Parental negative reactions were associated with low self-esteem and with mental health symptoms. Victimization based on sexual orientation also influences mental health and is associated with suicidal ideation and with symptoms. These results suggest that sexual orientation victimization may have a long-lasting impact on youths' adjustment. Only longitudinal research can establish the causal mechanisms for these patterns, but it is difficult to argue the alternative causal model—that LGB youths' mental health symptoms induce victimization based on their sexual orientation or elicit parental rejection.

Many questions remain about the developmental pathways involved in the emergence of sexual orientation during adolescence. Both population-based research and research based on convenience samples have their inherent disadvantages. For instance, there are limitations to generalizing from the findings from youths described in this chapter, despite the relatively large sample and heterogeneous locales sampled. These youths had self-identified as LGB and had attended social and recreational groups in settings in which their sexual orientation was known. Having sought out LGB-identified social settings, such youths might have been those with less family and peer support or with more mental health problems than youths who do not attend such groups. If this is in fact the case, generalizing from these results will overestimate the prevalence of mental health problems among LGB youths. Fortunately, the combination of studies based on convenience-based samples and the increasing number of studies using population-based samples provide a powerful way to develop a more accurate understanding of LGB youths.

Longitudinal studies are also important in this regard, and following youths from the point at which they self-identify through early adulthood would yield important findings. With very few exceptions, the available research is cross-sectional, which makes causal conclusions difficult at best. The problems in making developmental statements about the life course of LGB youths are mirrored in the lack of research on their social contexts. Much remains to be done in researching the families of LGB youths, and the few studies available (e.g., Herdt & Koff, 2000) raise many questions for further study. Research that involves the parents and families of LGB youths, not only youths' perceptions of them, is overdue. Research on LGB youths' experiences in school settings is needed as well, to delineate the circumstances youths face in these social contexts (D'Augelli, Pilkington, & Hershberger, 2001). Perhaps the most important long-term need is for researchers of adolescence to include sexual orientation development in their research. Information about aspects of sexual identity development should be routinely included in studies of youths. By leaving LGB youths and questions about sexual orientation out of their research, researchers perpetuate our ignorance of the development of sexual orientation of all youths. This lack of knowledge allows victimization to continue, as it is often based on misinformation and myths. Given the issues surrounding suicidality among LGB youths, research on adolescent suicide that does not include consideration of sexual identity issues verges on the unethical. Although research on the development of LGB youths has a short history, there is sufficient information about these youths and their needs in the literature to render unjustifiable further exclusion of sexual orientation considerations from research on adolescent development.

REFERENCES

Anhalt, K., & Morris, T. L. (1999). Developmental and adjustment issues of gay, lesbian, and bisexual adolescents: A review of the empirical literature. *Clinical Child and Family Psychology Review, 1,* 215–230.

Cochran, S. D. (2001). Emerging issues in research on lesbians' and gay men's mental health: Does sexual orientation really matter? *American Psychologist, 56,* 931–947.

D'Augelli, A. R. (1991). Gay men in college: Identity processes and adaptations. *Journal of College Student Development, 32,* 140–146.

D'Augelli, A. R. (1998). Developmental implications of victimization of lesbian, gay, and bisexual youth. In G. M. Herek (Ed.), *Stigma and sexual orientation: Understanding prejudice against lesbians, gay men, and bisexuals* (pp. 187–210). Thousand Oaks, CA: Sage.

D'Augelli, A. R. (2002). Mental health problems among lesbian, gay, and bisexual youth ages 14 to 21. *Clinical Child Psychology and Psychiatry, 7,* 433–456.

D'Augelli, A. R., & Grossman, A. H. (2001). Disclosure of sexual orientation, victimization, and mental health among lesbian, gay, and bisexual older adults. *Journal of Interpersonal Violence, 10,* 1008–1027.

D'Augelli, A. R., & Hershberger, S. L. (1993). Lesbian, gay, and bisexual youth in community settings: Personal challenges and mental health problems. *American Journal of Community Psychology, 21,* 421–448.

D'Augelli, A. R., Hershberger, S. L., & Pilkington, N. W. (2001). Suicidality patterns and sexual orientation-related factors among lesbian, gay, and bisexual youth. *Suicide and Life-Threatening Behavior, 31,* 250–265.

D'Augelli, A. R., & Patterson, C. J. (Eds.). (2001). *Lesbian, gay, and bisexual identities and youth: Psychological perspectives.* New York: Oxford University Press.

D'Augelli, A. R., Pilkington, N. W., & Hershberger, S. L. (2001). The mental health impact of sexual orientation victimization of lesbian, gay, and bisexual youths in high school. *School Psychology Quarterly, 17,* 148–167.

Derogatis, L. R. (1993). *The Brief Symptom Inventory: Administration, scoring, and procedures manual.* Minneapolis, MN: National Computer Systems.

Diamond, L. M., & Savin-Williams, R. C. (2000). Exploring diversity in the development of same-sex sexuality among young women. *Journal of Social Issues, 56,* 297–313.

Gibson, P. (1989). Gay male and lesbian youth suicide. In Alcohol, Drug Abuse, and Mental Health Administration (Ed.), *Report of the Secretary's Task Force on Youth Suicide* (Vol. 3, pp. 110–142; DHHS Publication No. ADM 89-1623). Washington, DC: U.S. Government Printing Office.

Gould, M. S., Greenberg, T., Velting, D. M., & Shaffer, D. (2003). Youth suicide risk and preventive interventions: A review of the past 10 years. *Journal of the American Academy of Child & Adolescent Psychiatry, 42,* 386–405.

Graber, J. A., & Archibald, A. B. (2001). Psychosocial change at puberty and beyond: Understanding adolescent sexuality and sexual orientation. In A. R. D'Augelli & C. J. Patterson (Eds.), *Lesbian, gay, and bisexual identities and youth: Psychological perspectives* (pp. 3–26). New York: Oxford University Press.

Grossman, A. H. (2001). Avoiding HIV/AIDS and the challenge of growing up gay, lesbian, and bisexual. In A. R. D'Augelli & C. J. Patterson (Eds.), *Lesbian, gay, and bisexual identities and youth: Psychological perspectives* (pp. 155–180). New York: Oxford University Press.

Herdt, G. H., & Boxer, A. M. (1993). *Children of horizons: How gay and lesbian teens are leading a new way out of the closet.* Boston: Beacon Press.

Herdt, G. H., & Koff, B. (2000). *Something to tell you: The road families travel when a child is gay.* New York: Columbia University Press.

Lewinsohn, P. M., Rohde, P., & Seeley, J. R. (1996). Adolescent suicide ideation and attempts: Prevalence, risk factors, and clinical implications. *Clinical Psychology: Science and Practice, 3*(1), 25–46.

Malyon, A. K. (1981). The homosexual adolescent: Development issues and social bias. *Child Welfare, 60,* 321–330.

McDaniels, J. S., Purcell, D. W., & D'Augelli, A. R. (2001). The relationship between sexual orientation and risk for suicide: Research findings and future directions for research and prevention. *Suicide and Life-Threatening Behavior, 31*(Suppl.), 60–83.

Remafedi, G. (1987a). Adolescent homosexuality: Psychosocial and medical implications. *Pediatrics, 79,* 331–337.

Remafedi, G. (1987b). Male homosexuality: The adolescent's perspective. *Pediatrics, 79,* 326–330.

Remafedi, G., Resnick, M., Blum, R., & Harris, L. (1992). Demography of sexual orientation in adolescents. *Pediatrics, 89,* 714–721.

Roesler, T., & Deisher, R. W. (1972). Youthful male homosexuality: Homosexual experience and the process of developing homosexual identity in males aged 16 to 22 years. *Journal of the American Medical Association, 219,* 1018–1023.

Rosenberg, M. (1979). *Conceiving the self.* New York: Basic Books.

Rotheram-Borus, M. J., & Langabeer, K. A. (2001). Developmental trajectories of gay, lesbian, and bisexual youths. In A. R. D'Augelli & C. J. Patterson (Eds.), *Lesbian, gay, and bisexual identities and youth: Psychological perspectives* (pp. 97–128). New York: Oxford University Press.

Russell, S. T. (2003). Sexual minority youth and suicide risk. *American Behavioral Scientist, 46,* 1241–1257.

Savin-Williams, R. C. (1990). *Gay and lesbian youth: Expressions of identity.* New York: Hemisphere Publication Services.

Savin-Williams, R. C. (2001). A critique of research on sexual-minority youths. *Journal of Adolescence, 24*(1), 5–13.

Savin-Williams, R. C. (2003). Suicide attempts among sexual minority youth: Population and measurement issues. *Journal of Consulting and Clinical Psychology, 69,* 983–991.

Schneider, M. S. (2001). Toward a reconceptualization of the coming-out process for adolescent females. In A. R. D'Augelli & C. J. Patterson (Eds.), *Lesbian, gay, and bisexual identities and youth: Psychological perspectives* (pp. 71–96). New York: Oxford University Press.

3

SOCIAL ANXIETY AND BARRIERS TO RESILIENCE AMONG LESBIAN, GAY, AND BISEXUAL ADOLESCENTS

STEVEN A. SAFREN AND DAVID W. PANTALONE

Lesbian, gay, and bisexual (LGB) adolescents represent a subset of youths that is at increased risk of experiencing a variety of clinically significant difficulties. These difficulties include chronic stress from such factors as verbal and physical abuse as a result of one's sexual orientation (see Savin-Williams, 1994) and the absence of role models or easily available social supports to aid in negotiating the development of one's identity as a sexual-minority person (see Patterson, 1995; Rotheram-Borus & Fernandez, 1995). As a result, there is growing evidence that disproportionate numbers of LGB youths experience problems such as depression, hopelessness, and suicidality (Davidson, Potter, & Ross, 1999; Faulkner & Cranston, 1998; Garofalo, Wolf, Kessel, Palfrey, & DuRant, 1998; Garafolo, Wolf, Wissow, Woods, & Goodman, 1999; Remafedi, French, Story, Resnick, & Blum, 1998; Safren & Heimberg, 1999).

We thank Richard G. Heimberg for his assistance and mentorship on this project and Anthony D'Augelli and Richard C. Savin-Williams for their assistance in the early conceptualization of this research.

This chapter describes analyses that examine a potential pathway toward depression and suicidality in LGB youths. First, we review a previous study by our team (Safren & Heimberg, 1999) providing evidence that differences between LGB adolescents and their heterosexual peers in depression and suicidality could be accounted for by risk and protective factors: stress, engagement in positive events, social support, and coping. Second, to examine a potential barrier to some of the protective factors (positive events and social support), we present additional, previously unpublished analyses of social anxiety in this sample. We reasoned that social anxiety may be a barrier to obtaining social support as well as to engaging in positive events for the following reasons. Sexual-minority youths typically experience adolescent development with various social pressures, including pressures to conform to heterosexual social and dating behaviors and experiences and thus to hide their sexual orientation from others. Fear and avoidance of social interactions (social anxiety) can inhibit the ability to attain satisfactory social support from peers and engage in positive, competence-building activities.

DEPRESSION, HOPELESSNESS, AND SUICIDALITY AMONG LGB YOUTHS

We (Safren & Heimberg, 1999) sampled 56 lesbian, gay, or bisexual and 48 heterosexual adolescents between the ages of 16 and 21. The LGB youths came from after-school recreational and educational programs specifically for sexual-minority youths. To obtain a similar sample in terms of age, gender, ethnicity, and education, we recruited heterosexual participants from after-school programs (e.g., a job training program, the YMCA) for youths in general. Because the programs for LGB youths were aimed at youths considered at risk because of their sexual orientation, the sampling strategy for heterosexual youths mainly focused on programs that provide services for teens considered at risk because of economic or other factors related to urban living. Over 60% of the participants were from communities of color, and the two subsamples (LGB vs. heterosexual) did not statistically differ on any of the demographic variables.

All participants completed a self-report battery of psychometrically valid instruments that assess both variables related to suicidality and variables related to risk or resilience. Suicidality and related variables included depression as assessed by the Beck Depression Inventory (BDI; Beck, Ward, Mendelson, Mock, & Erbaugh, 1961); hopelessness as assessed by the Beck Hopelessness Scale (Beck, Weissman, Lester, & Trexler, 1974); and suicidality as assessed by a subset of factor-analyzed items (Cole, 1988; Range & Antonelli, 1990) from the Suicidal Behaviors Questionnaire (Linehan &

Nielsen, 1981), which included an assessment of past suicidal behaviors as well as present and future suicidality.

Variables hypothesized to be protective of suicidality and depression included perceived satisfaction with social support as assessed by the Social Support Questionnaire (Sarason, Levine, Basham, & Sarason, 1983); coping through acceptance as assessed by the COPE (Carver, Scheier, & Weintraub, 1989); and frequency of self-reported positive events on the Adolescent Perceived Events Scale (Compas, Davies, Forsythe, & Wagner, 1987). Negative life events were also assessed with this scale as a measure of stress.

In univariate analyses, LGB youths had higher overall scores[1] for past suicidality compared with the heterosexual comparison group, with sexual orientation accounting for 19% of the variance in mean standardized past suicidality scores, $F(1, 100) = 23.78$, partial $\eta^2 = .19$, $p < .0001$. It is important to note that the item that assessed present suicidality ("How likely is it that you will attempt suicide someday?") was analyzed separately, and the LGB youths also had higher scores on this item, with sexual orientation accounting for 10% of the variance, $F(1, 94) = 10.04$, partial $\eta^2 = .10$, $p < .01$. The LGB group also had significantly higher self-reported depression, $F(1, 100) = 5.82$, partial $\eta^2 = .06$, $p < .05$, and feelings of hopelessness, $F(1, 100) = 8.88$, partial $\eta^2 = .08$, $p < .01$, than the heterosexual youths. These results would suggest that LGB youths have higher rates of distress and suicidality than similar heterosexual youths.

Furthermore, with statistical control for environmental risk and protective factors (stress, satisfaction with social support, coping, positive events), a dramatically different pattern emerged. For depression and hopelessness, the initial difference between groups disappeared such that sexual orientation was no longer a significant unique predictor (semipartial $r^2 = .02$ for both, ns). For present suicidality ratings, significant differences between the two groups also disappeared (semipartial $r^2 = .01$, ns) when these risk and protective factors, as well as depression and hopelessness, were accounted for. The only analysis that retained sexual orientation as a unique predictor of distress was the regression analysis predicting past suicidality scores (semipartial $r^2 = .05$, $p < .05$), and the variance predicted was reduced from 19% to only 5%. Recall that in this equation, all risk and protective variables (e.g., social support, positive and negative events, and coping) were geared toward the present day, whereas the dependent variable (past suicidality scores) was geared toward the past. The sexual-minority sample also reported fewer social supports, $F(1, 100) = 13.47$, $p < .0001$, partial $\eta^2 = .12$, less

---

[1] Mean standardized scores for items assessing (a) number and seriousness of past attempts, (b) frequency of suicidal thoughts in the past year, and (c) frequency of expressing suicidal thoughts to others.

satisfaction with social support, $F(1, 100) = 6.24$, $p < .05$, partial $\eta^2 = .06$, and fewer positive events, $F(1, 94) = 10.04$, $p < .01$, partial $\eta^2 = .10$, than the heterosexual youths.

The main conclusion from this study is that sexual orientation per se did not predict present distress (depression, hopelessness, or present suicidality) among LGB youths. Instead, it suggested that other environmental variables are critical risk and protective factors. Previous studies have found high rates of suicidality among samples of LGB youths and have suggested that this population is one at high risk for suicidality. Our study suggested that many of the variables that put LGB youths at risk for suicide are environmental and amenable to change—that it is not simply their identity as a lesbian, gay, or bisexual person that predicts suicidality—and these young people can be helped by providing the appropriate forms of support.

Developmentally, adolescents face a number of milestones (see Buhrmester, 1996; Cichetti & Cohen, 1995; Zani, 1994) including beginning to date, learning about friendships and intimacy, and developing their sexuality. As previously detailed, LGB youths face these challenges in addition to the challenge of "being different" in a way that is rejected by peers and society at large (Anhalt & Morris, 1998; Patterson, 1995; Rotheram-Borus & Fernandez, 1995). The LGB youths in the study were sampled from an existing after-school intervention program that already provided them with social support and positive events. This program provided a safe meeting place, access to peers, and referrals to therapy or other services as needed. Despite this potential outlet to find social support and experience positive events, there was considerable variance within the sample of LGB youths in terms of these variables, and in terms of suicidality and related factors. The question remains, therefore, as to why, even among those who attend a support program, some LGB youths were able to obtain satisfactory social support and experience enjoyable activities and others with the same opportunities were not. Hence, we hypothesized that social anxiety may be one important barrier. Arguably, if an adolescent already had some of the genetic, biological, or environmental variables that cause social anxiety (see Kagan, 2001; McNeil, Lejuez, & Sorrell, 2001; Saudino, 2001), feeling different as a result of experiencing same-sex sexual attractions would likely increase the chances of his or her developing social phobia and experiencing the negative consequences that generally follow.

SOCIAL ANXIETY AS A BARRIER

Social anxiety is defined as fear and avoidance of situations that may involve evaluation by others. Social phobia, according to Kessler et al. (1994) the third most prevalent psychiatric disorder found in the *Diagnostic* and *Statistical Manual of Mental Disorders* (4th ed., text revision; American Psychiatric Association, 2000), reflects a more severe set of symptoms of social anxiety and is associated with significant impairments in overall quality of life (Safren, Heimberg, Brown, & Holle, 1997). Particularly in adolescence, social phobia is associated with other maladaptive behaviors including depression, school refusal, a lack of social competence and skills, and fewer friendships (e.g., Beidel & Turner, 1998). One main component of social anxiety is social interaction anxiety, which is characterized by a fear of interacting with others in such ways as initiating or maintaining conversations or attending social events. The other main component is social performance anxiety. For the purpose of this research, we have elected to focus on social interaction anxiety. We view social interaction anxiety as the most relevant indicator of an individual's ability to acquire and maintain social supports, as it can, for example, be a barrier to seeking out friendships even in situations or venues where like peers are present. In addition, because social interactions can be a major component of positive events, especially among adolescents, it is also likely that higher levels of social interaction anxiety will be a barrier to both receiving satisfactory social support and experiencing positive events.

The present set of analyses was designed to investigate two hypotheses as a follow-up to the findings of Safren and Heimberg (1999). First, we sought to examine whether LGB youths would report greater social interaction anxiety than heterosexual youths. Second, we sought to test the impact of social interaction anxiety on attaining perceived social support among LGB adolescents. We reasoned that LGB adolescents require social support, coping resources, and positive events to help them with the chronic stress associated with living as a sexual-minority person. Having elevated social interaction anxiety could inhibit the ability to attain these resources. For example, social interaction anxiety could inhibit an individual's ability to seek out social supports and enjoyable peer-oriented activities that typically occur at this time in one's development. In addition, being lesbian, gay, or bisexual may increase the chances of experiencing peer-related social anxiety because these youths may perceive that they are different in a way that is generally rejected by peers.

METHOD

To investigate the hypothesis that social anxiety may serve as a barrier to obtaining social support and engaging in positive events for LGB youths, we investigated this question in the sample previously mentioned (Safren & Heimberg, 1999). Recall that LGB and heterosexual youths were recruited from after-school programs, and that the groups were similar in terms of age, gender, ethnicity, and education. Procedures were identical but different measures were administered and, thus, different analyses conducted.

Informed Consent

Informed consent issues are detailed here, given their high level of importance, the complexities of research ethics in studying at-risk youths, and the fact that at-risk youths are necessarily highly important to study. As previously stated, the age of participants ranged from 16 to 21. It is argued here and elsewhere (e.g., Brooks-Gunn & Rotheram-Borus, 1994; Rotheram-Borus & Koopman, 1992) that for certain populations of adolescents, parental consent may potentially harm the participant rather than protect his or her welfare. As outlined by Fisher (1993), examples of populations in which waiving parental consent for adolescent participation in research is justified on the basis of potential harm specifically include studies of adolescent substance abuse and sexual activity. Waiving of parental consent for adolescents below the age of 18 is a common practice in studies that have targeted LGB individuals (Pilkington & D'Augelli, 1995). Further, it is consistent with clinical reports that stress the importance of waiving parental consent for counseling or medical procedures in areas of sexuality (Sobocinski, 1990) and for certain types of interventions (e.g., treatment of sexually transmitted infections, drug abuse treatment, pregnancy testing) when the adolescent is judged to be competent to consent to treatment (Fisher, 1993).

Waiving parental consent is of particular importance to the sexual-minority adolescents in the study, as they may not have disclosed their sexual orientation to their parents. Disclosing this information could cause considerable stress and harm to the adolescent (e.g., Cramer & Roach, 1988; Gonsiorek, 1993; Savin-Williams, 1994). This particular stress and variables related to support from parents are of primary interest to the present study. As previously discussed, it was expected that a sizable proportion of adolescents would experience various forms of maladjustment, partially as a result of their perceived lack of social support from family members. Thus, in the present study, parental consent was waived.

Procedure

After conducting the informed-consent process, participants responded to the questionnaire battery. Upon completion of the surveys, participants were given a separate information sheet that included free or low-cost referrals for counseling, shelter, health care, and other services in the area for adolescents in need, with additional LGB-specific referral resources pro-

TABLE 3.1
Demographic Characteristics of the Study Sample

Demographic	Total sample (N = 104)	Lesbian, gay, and bisexual youths (n = 56)	Heterosexual youths (n = 48)
Age			
M	18.2	18.4	17.9
SD	1.6	1.6	1.6
Gender			
Male			
n	50	29	21
%	48	52	44
Female			
n	54	27	27
%	52	48	56
Ethnicity			
African American			
n	55	27	28
%	53	48	58
Asian			
n	1	1	0
%	1	2	0
White			
n	37	18	19
%	36	32	40
Hispanic/Latino			
n	4	4	0
%	4	7	0
Biracial			
n	6	5	1
%	6	9	2
Arabic			
n	1	1	0
%	1	2	0

(continued)

vided for the sexual-minority sample. Participants were paid $10 each for their participation. Demographic information about the two samples is presented in Table 3.1.

MEASURES

Participants completed self-report survey instruments in a pencil-and-paper format. Whenever possible, the field's standard, psychometrically valid instruments were utilized to assess the key variables related to risk or resilience.

TABLE 3.1 *(Continued)*
Demographic Characteristics of the Study Sample

Demographic	Total sample (*N* = 104)	Lesbian, gay, and bisexual youths (*n* = 56)	Heterosexual youths (*n* = 48)
Education (years)			
M	12.3	12.1	12.4
SD	1.7	1.5	1.9
Living situation			
Sibling(s) only			
n	6	3	3
%	6	5	6
Parent(s)			
n	56	32	24
%	54	57	50
Grandparent(s)			
n	4	3	1
%	4	5	2
Foster care			
n	1	0	1
%	1	0	2
Group or residential			
n	1	1	0
%	1	2	0
Roommates			
n	21	9	12
%	20	16	10
Self			
n	2	2	0
%	2	4	0
Other adult relative			
n	13	6	7
%	13	11	11

Note. Percentages may not sum to 100% because of rounding.

Demographics and Sexual Orientation

Participants completed a demographics questionnaire, which included questions addressing age, gender, educational attainment, ethnicity, sexual orientation, and living situation. Participants separately rated their sexual orientation on a 1-to-5 scale (1 = *exclusively heterosexual*; 2 = *heterosexual with some homosexual experience*; 3 = *bisexual*; 4 = *homosexual with some heterosexual experience*; 5 = *exclusively homosexual*). The 48 heterosexual participants all gave a rating of 1 on this scale. The sexual-minority sample consisted of 11 persons who rated themselves as 3, 23 who rated themselves as 4, and 22 who rated themselves as 5. No participants' rating conflicted with their self-identification.

Social Anxiety

The Social Interaction Anxiety Scale (SIAS; Mattick & Clarke, 1998) is a widely used, validated (Brown et al., 1997), and reliable (Cronbach's α in present sample = .83) self-report measure of social interaction anxiety (with items including "I find myself worrying that I won't know what to say in social situations" and "I am nervous mixing with people I don't know very well"), and its items measure aspects of social anxiety that do not overlap with social performance anxiety (Safren, Turk, & Heimberg, 1998). Despite the psychometric history of the SIAS, one of the items reads, "I find it difficult talking to attractive people of the opposite sex." Because of the potential for heterosexual bias, as well as the potential of having a Type II error (i.e., LGB youths may not endorse this item as strongly though they may indeed experience social anxiety), this item was eliminated. For scores to be comparable to the mean for the measure, an average item score for each participant was calculated and substituted for this item to achieve the total score.

Additional Measures

Other measures administered included the Social Support Questionnaire (Sarason et al., 1983); the Adolescent Perceived Events Scale (Compas et al., 1987); and the Marlow-Crowne Social Desirability Scale—Short Form (Reynolds, 1992).

RESULTS

Measures were administered in two different counterbalanced orders, and there were no significant interactions between group assignment and order. The measure of social desirability did not correlate with any of the assessment measures and therefore was dropped from further analyses.

Preliminary Analyses

White participants reported a mean of 4.16 social supports (SD = 2.2) and ethnic-minority participants reported a mean of 2.7 (SD = 1.2), $t(48.5)$ = 3.63, $p < .01$, and therefore minority status was included in the analysis of number of social supports.

Social Anxiety in LGB and Heterosexual Adolescents

A 2 (male vs. female) × 2 (LGB vs. heterosexual) between-groups analysis of variance revealed that the LGB youths reported greater social

TABLE 3.2

Associations Among Social Interaction Anxiety and Protective Factors

Variable	1	2	3	4
1. Social interaction anxiety	—	ns	−.30*	−.28*
2. No. of social supports		—	.40***	ns
3. Satisfaction with social support			—	.21*
4. No. of positive events				—

*p < .05. **p < .01. ***p < .001.

anxiety than did the heterosexual youths, $F(1, 100) = 5.62$, $p < .03$, $\eta^2 = .053$. There were no main effects for gender, and no interaction effects. For the heterosexual youths, the mean was 23.75 ($SD = 9.92$), whereas for the LGB youths it was 29.02 ($SD = 12.09$). These figures are lower than the mean for individuals diagnosed with social phobia (49.0), but higher than the mean of 19.9 for the general population (Heimberg, Mueller, Holt, & Hope, 1992).

Associations of Social Interaction Anxiety With Protective Factors

First, we examined a correlation matrix with social interaction anxiety, number of social supports, satisfaction with social support, and number of positive events (see Table 3.2). All variables were significantly associated with each other except that number of social supports was not associated with number of positive events or with social interaction anxiety.

The Effects of Social Interaction Anxiety and Sexual Orientation on Protective Factors

The next set of analyses used multiple regression to examine the effect of social interaction anxiety on satisfaction with social support, number of social supports, and number of positive events, over and above the effects of sexual orientation on these variables. Sexual orientation was dummy-coded (Pedhazur, 1982), and interaction effects were tested by multiplying sexual orientation by the social interaction anxiety score. Accordingly, social interaction anxiety and sexual orientation were entered on the first step and the interaction term on the second step. The details of each regression analysis are reported in Table 3.3.

Satisfaction With Social Support

Together, social anxiety and sexual orientation accounted for 13% of the variance in satisfaction with social support. Higher social anxiety was

TABLE 3.3
Effects of Social Interaction Anxiety and Sexual Orientation on Protective Factors

Regression variable	R^2	ΔR^2	F	dfs	sr	sr^2
Satisfaction with social support						
Step 1	.13**	.13**	7.2	2, 101		
Sexual orientation					−.18†	.03
Social interaction anxiety					−.25**	.06
Step 2: Interaction term		.00	5.0	3, 100		
No. of social supports						
Step 1	.26***	.26***	11.8	3, 100		
Sexual orientation					−.30**	.09
Social interaction anxiety					−.08	.01
Ethnic-minority status					−.37***	.14
Step 2: Interaction term		.03	8.2	5, 98		
No. of positive events						
Step 1	.15**	.15**	8.2	2, 95		
Sexual orientation					−.27**	.07
Social interaction anxiety					−.21*	.04
Step 2: Interaction term		.02	6.0	3, 94		

†$p < .10.$ *$p < .05.$ **$p < .01.$ ***$p < .001.$

a significant predictor of less satisfaction with social support over and above the effects of sexual orientation. There was a trend ($p = .05$) for LGB youths to have less overall satisfaction with social support than heterosexual youths when factoring out the effects of social anxiety. The interaction term entered on the second step of the regression analysis was not significant, revealing that the deleterious effects of social anxiety were not differentially associated with satisfaction with social support for heterosexual versus sexual-minority youths.

Number of Social Supports

Because ethnic-minority status was associated with number of social supports on the univariate level, it was also included in this analysis as a predictor. Together, social anxiety, sexual orientation, and ethnic-minority status accounted for 26% of the variance in number of social supports. Sexual orientation and ethnic-minority status had unique effects such that both sexual minorities and ethnic minorities reported fewer social supports. Social interaction anxiety was not associated with number of social supports, and neither were the interaction terms entered on Step 2 of the regression analysis.

Number of Positive Events

Together, sexual orientation and social interaction anxiety accounted for 15% of the variance in number of positive events reported by the youths in this sample. Both predictors accounted for significant unique variance, with LGB youths and those with higher social anxiety experiencing fewer positive events. Their interaction was not significant on the second step.

DISCUSSION

The higher levels of social interaction anxiety among the LGB youths may be a result of the unique developmental challenges faced by LGB youths during adolescence. Rotheram-Borus and Fernandez (1995) contrasted some of the different developmental issues faced by LGB and heterosexual adolescents. Adolescence is typically a time when youths more fully develop their sense of self through a process of challenges and struggles, which is an integral part of the transition toward adulthood. During this time, exploring one's sexual orientation may become more salient to LGB youths than it might be to heterosexual youths, especially because of the increasing social pressures toward heterosexual dating. Rotheram-Borus and Fernandez argued that, to cope with these challenges, LGB youths require "strong personal resources and multiple strategies for developing and maintaining a positive sense of self in the face of negative feedback from others" (p. 30). Few adolescents have developed these types of resources, and therefore LGB youths may be put at heightened risk for a variety of difficulties. These skill and resource deficits may lead to increased levels of social anxiety among LGB youths, which may, in turn, result in more deficits such as having few friends, supports, or competence-building positive activities.

The fact that sexual orientation remained a significant predictor of number of social supports and number of positive events (and had a trend for satisfaction with social support) over and above the significant effects of social anxiety suggests that there may be other variables besides social anxiety that may make it difficult for LGB youths to attain satisfactory social support and experience positive events. For example, an LGB adolescent who does not have clinically significant social interaction anxiety may still realistically have less access to social support or positive events because of his or her living situation, family dynamics, or other internal or external limitations to what would otherwise be adaptive problem-solving behaviors or strategies.

There may be differences between one's sexual-minority status as an adolescent and one's ethnic-minority status with regard to attaining social support and positive events. Although both ethnic- and sexual-minority youths reported fewer social supports than their peers, ethnic-minority youths did not report less satisfaction with social support or fewer positive events than White youths (regardless of sexual orientation), but sexual-minority youths did. One reason may be that heterosexual ethnic minorities, in general, have extended family members whose relationship to society at large is similar to theirs. This situation would likely allow for mutual and satisfactory support and shared experiences. For sexual-minority youths, however, being a sexual minority can set one apart from one's family. Being lesbian, gay, or bisexual can lead to family discord if young persons perceive that their families will not accept their sexual orientation. In this case, for example, access to satisfactory social support would be limited.

FUTURE CLINICAL AND RESEARCH DIRECTIONS

Although many studies have suggested that LGB youths are at increased risk for problems associated with depression and suicidality, few have examined the particular factors that explain this relationship. The two series of analyses presented found evidence supporting the existence of one pathway toward problems associated with depression and suicidality among this population. Accordingly, LGB youths may be at increased risk for developing increased social interaction anxiety because they are different in a way that is typically rejected by their predominantly heterosexual peers and family members. This finding is important because social interaction anxiety may be a barrier to attaining protective factors that are typically associated with resilience among youths at risk.

The data presented are limited to LGB youths who participated in a support program for sexual-minority youths. Despite this participation, we found considerable variance in the level of social support and positive events reported by LGB youths. Both social support and positive events are variables considered to be protective of a variety of maladaptive behaviors in youth, including depression, hopelessness, and suicidality. Although the study is limited in that the findings cannot be generalized to all LGB youths, the fact that the rates of depression and suicidal behaviors are high in this subpopulation of LGB youths (even among those who already attend support programs) makes the study consistent with the need to target research and clinical efforts at the youths who need it the most.

An important clinical and practical implication of these findings involves the potential to increase the availability of protective factors among LGB youths. A variety of psychosocial (cognitive–behavioral therapy) and pharmacological interventions have been empirically supported for adolescents and adults with social phobia (see Heimberg, Liebowitz, Hope, & Schneier, 1995; Hofmann & DiBartolo, 2001), and these treatments lead to reductions in comorbid depression as well (see meta-analysis by Gould, Buckminster, Pollack, Otto, & Yap, 1997). Such treatments can be applied to, or adapted for, LGB youths who experience clinically significant social anxiety (Safren, Hollander, Hart, & Heimberg, 2001) and should be evaluated empirically. Because of sample size limitations, case study and multiple baseline approaches (see Hersen & Barlow, 1992) may be most useful for starting research in this area.

At present, when working with LGB youths or any group of at-risk young people, counselors can familiarize themselves with local service providers who offer validated treatments for social phobia in their area and have referral or internal resources available to help youths with social phobia. With the alarming rates of suicidality documented in adolescents in general (e.g., Davidson et al., 1999), and in LGB youths in particular, the development and use of prevention and intervention efforts has the potential to help mitigate a major public health problem.

REFERENCES

American Psychiatric Association. (2000). *Diagnostic and statistical manual of mental disorders* (4th ed., text rev.). Washington, DC: Author.

Anhalt, K. A., & Morris, T. L. (1998). Developmental and adjustment issues in gay, lesbian, and bisexual adolescents. *Clinical Child and Family Psychology Review, 1*, 215–230.

Beck, A. T., Ward, C. H., Mendelson, M., Mock, J., & Erbaugh, J. (1961). An inventory for measuring depression. *Archives of General Psychiatry, 4*, 561–571.

Beck, A. T., Weissman, A., Lester, D., & Trexler, L. (1974). The measurement of pessimism: The Hopelessness Scale. *Journal of Consulting and Clinical Psychology, 42*, 861–865.

Beidel, D. C., & Turner, S. M. (1998). *Shy children, phobic adults*. Washington, DC: American Psychological Association.

Brooks-Gunn, J., & Rotheram-Borus, M. J. (1994). Rights to privacy in research: Adolescents versus parents. *Ethics and Behavior, 4*, 102–121.

Brown, E. J., Turovsky, J., Heimberg, R. G., Juster, H. R., Brown, T., & Barlow, D. H. (1997). Validation of the Social Interaction Anxiety Scale and the Social Phobia Scale across the anxiety disorders. *Psychological Assessment, 9*, 21–27.

Buhrmester, D. (1996). Need fulfillment, interpersonal competence, and the developmental contexts of early adolescent friendship. In W. M. Bukowski, A. F. Newcomb, & W. W. Hartup (Eds.), *The company they keep: Friendship in childhood and adolescence* (pp. 158–185). New York: Cambridge University Press.

Carver, C. S., Scheier, M. F., & Weintraub, J. K. (1989). Assessing coping strategies: A theoretically based approach. *Journal of Personality and Social Psychology, 56*, 267–283.

Cicchetti, D., & Cohen, D. J. (1995). *Developmental psychopathology: Vol 2. Risk, disorder, and adaptation*. New York: Wiley.

Cole, D. A. (1988). Hopelessness, social desirability, depression, and parasuicide in two college student samples. *Journal of Consulting and Clinical Psychology, 56*, 131–136.

Compas, B. E., Davies, G. E., Forsythe, C. J., & Wagner, B. M. (1987). Assessment of major and daily stressful events during adolescence: The Adolescent Perceived Events Scale. *Journal of Consulting and Clinical Psychology, 55*, 534–541.

Cramer, D. W., & Roach, A. J. (1988). Coming out to mom and dad: A study of gay males and their relationships with their parents. *Journal of Homosexuality, 15*, 79–91.

Davidson, L., Potter, L., & Ross, V. (1999). *The surgeon general's call to action to prevent suicide*. Washington, DC: U.S. Public Health Service.

Faulkner, A. H., & Cranston, K. (1998). Correlates of same-sex sexual behavior in a random sample of Massachusetts high school students. *American Journal of Public Health, 88*, 262–266.

Fisher, C. B. (1993). Integrating science and ethics in research with high-risk children and youth. *Social Policy Report: Society for Research in Child Development, 7*, 1–26.

Garofalo, R., Wolf, R. C., Kessel, S., Palfrey, J., & DuRant, R. H. (1998). The association between health risk behaviors and sexual orientation among a school-based sample of adolescents. *Pediatrics, 101*, 895–902.

Garofalo, R., Wolf, R. C., Wissow, L. S., Woods, E. R., & Goodman, E. (1999). Sexual orientation and risk of suicide attempts among a representative sample of youth. *Archives of Pediatric Adolescent Medicine, 153*, 487–493.

Gonsiorek, J. C. (1993). Mental health issues of gay and lesbian adolescents. In L. D. Garnets & D. C. Kimmel (Eds.), *Psychological perspectives on lesbian and gay male experiences* (pp. 469–485). New York: Columbia University Press.

Gould, R. A., Buckminster, S., Pollack, M. H., Otto, M. W., & Yap, L. (1997). Cognitive–behavioral and pharmacological treatment for social phobia: A meta-analysis. *Clinical Psychology: Science and Practice, 4*, 291–306.

Heimberg, R. G., Liebowitz, M. L., Hope, D. A., & Schneier, F. R. (1995). *Social phobia: Diagnosis, assessment, and treatment*. New York: Guilford Press.

Heimberg, R. G., Mueller, G. P., Holt, C. S., & Hope, D. A. (1992). Assessment of anxiety in social interaction and being observed by others: The Social Interaction Anxiety Scale and the Social Phobia Scale. *Behavior Therapy, 23*, 53–73.

Hersen, M., & Barlow, D. H. (1992). *Single case experimental designs: Strategies for studying behavior change*. New York: Pergamon Press.

Hofmann, S., & DiBartolo, P. M. (2001). *From social anxiety to social phobia: Multiple perspectives* (pp. 216–234). Boston: Allyn & Bacon.

Kagan, J. (2001). Temperamental contributions to affective and behavioral profiles in childhood. In S. G. Hofmann & P. M. DiBartolo (Eds.), *From social anxiety to social phobia: Multiple perspectives* (pp. 216–234). Boston: Allyn & Bacon.

Kessler, R. C., McGonagle, K. A., Zhao, S., Nelson, C. B., Hughes, M., Eshleman, S., et al. (1994). Lifetime and 12-month prevalence of *DSM–III–R* psychiatric disorders in the United States: Results from the National Comorbidity Survey. *Archives of General Psychiatry, 51*, 8–19.

Linehan, M. M., & Nielsen, S. L. (1981). Assessment of suicide ideation and parasuicide: Hopelessness and social desirability. *Journal of Consulting and Clinical Psychology, 49*, 773–775.

Mattick, R. P., & Clarke, J. C. (1998). Development and validation of measures of social phobia scrutiny fear and social interaction anxiety. *Behaviour Research and Therapy, 36*, 455–470.

McNeil, D. W., Lejuez, C. W., & Sorrell, J. T. (2001). Behavioral theories of social phobia: Contributions of basic behavioral principles. In S. G. Hofmann & P. M. DiBartolo (Eds.), *From social anxiety to social phobia: Multiple perspectives* (pp. 235–253). Boston: Allyn & Bacon.

Patterson, C. (1995). Sexual orientation and human development: An overview. *Developmental Psychology, 31*, 3–11.

Pedhazur, E. J. (1982). *Multiple regression in behavioral research: Explanation and prediction*. New York: Harcourt Brace.

Pilkington, N. W., & D'Augelli, A. R. (1995). Victimization of lesbian, gay, and bisexual youth in community settings. *Journal of Community Psychology, 23*, 34–56.

Range, L. M., & Antonelli, K. B. (1990). A factor analysis of six commonly used instruments associated with suicide using college students. *Journal of Personality Assessment, 55*, 804–811.

Remafedi, G., French, S., Story, M., Resnick, M. D., & Blum, R. (1998). The relationship between suicide risk and sexual orientation: Results of a population based study. *American Journal of Public Health, 88*, 57–60.

Reynolds, W. M. (1992). Development of reliable and valid short forms of the Marlowe-Crowne Social Desirability Scale. *Journal of Clinical Psychology, 38*, 119–125.

Rotheram-Borus, M. J., & Fernandez, M. I. (1995). Sexual orientation and developmental challenges experienced by gay and lesbian youths. *Suicide and Life Threatening Behavior, 25*(Suppl.), 26–34.

Rotheram-Borus, M. J., & Koopman, C. (1992). Protecting children's rights in AIDS research. In B. Stanley & J. E. Sieber (Eds.), *Social research on children and adolescents: Ethical issues* (pp. 143–161). Newbury Park, CA: Sage.

Safren, S. A., & Heimberg, R. G. (1999). Depression, hopelessness, suicidality and related factors in sexual minority and heterosexual adolescents. *Journal of Consulting and Clinical Psychology, 67*, 859–886.

Safren, S. A., Heimberg, R. G., Brown, E. J., & Holle, C. (1997). Quality of life in persons with social phobia. *Depression and Anxiety, 4*, 126–133.

Safren, S. A., Hollander, G., Hart, T. A., & Heimberg, R. G. (2001). Cognitive–behavioral therapy with gay, lesbian, and bisexual youth. *Cognitive and Behavioral Practice, 8*, 215–223.

Safren, S. A., Turk, C., & Heimberg, R. G. (1998). Factor structure of the Social Phobia Scale and the Social Interaction Anxiety Scale. *Behaviour Research and Therapy, 36*, 443–453.

Sarason, I. G., Levine, H. M., Basham, R. B., & Sarason, B. R. (1983). Assessing social support: The social support questionnaire. *Journal of Personality and Social Psychology, 44*, 127–139.

Saudino, K. J. (2001). Behavioral genetics, social phobia, social fears, and related temperaments. In S. G. Hofmann & P. M. DiBartolo (Eds.), *From social anxiety to social phobia: Multiple perspectives* (pp. 200–215). Boston: Allyn & Bacon.

Savin-Williams, R. C. (1994). Verbal and physical abuse as stressors in the lives of lesbian, gay male, and bisexual youths: Associations with school problems, running away, substance use, prostitution, and suicide. *Journal of Consulting and Clinical Psychology, 62*, 261–269.

Sobocinski, M. R. (1990). Ethical principles in the counseling of gay and lesbian adolescents: Issues of autonomy, competence, and confidentiality. *Professional Psychology: Research and Practice 21*, 240–247.

Zani, B. (1994). Dating and interpersonal relationships in adolescence. In S. Jackson & H. Rodriguez-Tome (Eds.), *Adolescence and its social worlds* (pp. 95–116). Hove, England: Erlbaum.

4

WHAT WE GOT WRONG ABOUT SEXUAL IDENTITY DEVELOPMENT: UNEXPECTED FINDINGS FROM A LONGITUDINAL STUDY OF YOUNG WOMEN

LISA M. DIAMOND

The process by which individuals with same-sex attractions (here denoted *sexual minorities*) come to conceive and present themselves as lesbian, gay, or bisexual has received extensive attention by social scientists over the past 30 years. This process, commonly called *sexual identity development*, has been a topic of particular interest with respect to sexual-minority youths. This body of research has given rise to a generalized portrait of sexual-minority development that is widely disseminated not only in social scientific journals but in publications geared toward psychotherapists, social workers, physicians, educators, and parents (e.g., Barber & Mobley, 1999; Fairchild & Hayward, 1979; Hollander, 2000; Meyer & Schwitzer, 1999; Ryan & Futterman, 1998). The stated aim of many of these publications is to raise awareness of the basic developmental process of sexual identity formation so that supportive adults can better facilitate this process among youths wrestling with nascent same-sex attractions.

There is only one problem: Much of this information is incomplete or inaccurate. The generalized models of sexual identity development that are most familiar to social scientists and laypeople alike (reviewed in Cohen & Savin-Williams, 1996; Sophie, 1986) are based on retrospective data from a highly selected subset of the sexual-minority population: typically, openly identified gay men who are exclusively attracted to the same sex. Correspondingly, the information on identity development that eventually trickles down to youths, parents, educators, and media outlets paints a fairly uniform, overly simplistic portrait of this process that does not apply to all youths. To effectively promote the health and well-being of sexual-minority youths and adults, social scientists must collect and disseminate information that more accurately represents how sexual identity development is actually experienced rather than recollected.

Toward this end, I present data from an ongoing longitudinal study of sexual identity development among 89 young sexual-minority women. These women's experiences, tracked in four waves of data collection spanning an 8-year period, highlight several salient "mistakes" we have made in previous conceptualizations of sexual identity development. The first mistake has to do with *characteristics* of sexual minorities themselves; specifically, it concerns the supposition that most sexual minorities are exclusively attracted to the same sex and that individuals with nonexclusive attractions are "special cases." The second mistake has to do with the *process* of identity development; specifically, it involves the supposition that sexual questioning (the private reckoning with same-sex attractions that sets the whole process of sexual identity development in motion) is a one-time-only event that is never revisited once an individual settles on a sexual-minority identity. The third mistake has to do with the *outcome* of identity development; specifically, it concerns the supposition that adopting a lesbian, gay, or bisexual label is the uniform and uniformly healthful outcome of the sexual questioning process.

This is not to say that these suppositions are uniformly wrong—certainly, they provide apt descriptions of some sexual minorities, some of the time. The problem is that they have been vastly overgeneralized, precluding investigation of alternative developmental trajectories. I am certainly not the first to argue for more complex and differentiated conceptualizations of sexual identity development (e.g., see Cass, 1990; Golden, 1987), but in this chapter I bring more data to bear on this argument than has previously been possible. Although these data provide a valuable starting point for revising and expanding current conceptualizations of sexual identity development, they have important limitations that must be noted. Most important, this study focuses only on women, leaving open the possibility that traditional sexual identity models are not fundamentally flawed, but rather gender-specific. Although there is some data in support of this possibility

(Diamond, 1998; Savin-Williams & Diamond, 2000), there is also growing evidence that conventional sexual identity models oversimplify this process for both genders (Savin-Williams, 1998; Weinberg, Williams, & Pryor, 1994; Whisman, 1996). Future longitudinal research on male sexual-minority youths is needed to resolve this issue. Another limitation of the current study is that the respondents are predominantly White and middle class; longitudinal investigation of a more ethnically and socioeconomically diverse sample of sexual minorities is clearly needed to discern how their unique sociocultural contexts shape their long-term identity development.

PREVIOUS RESEARCH

Historically, efforts to study sexual identity development have been hampered by a number of methodological shortcomings: the underrepresentation of women, the underrepresentation of bisexual people, the underrepresentation of ethnic minorities, and the complete nonrepresentation of sexual-minority youths who decline to identify as lesbian, gay, or bisexual. An even more important methodological problem is the long-standing reliance on retrospective data, which (by default) defines the outcome of sexual identity development to be whatever identity an individual claims when he or she happens to be surveyed. Thus, the small number of studies that have examined changes in sexual attractions or identity longitudinally have made critical contributions to our understanding of sexual identity development (Blumstein & Schwartz, 1977; Pattatucci & Hamer, 1995; Stokes, Damon, & McKirnan, 1997; Stokes, McKirnan, & Burzette, 1993; Weinberg et al., 1994). For example, Weinberg and colleagues (1994) collected 5-year follow-up data on a small sample of women ($n = 27$) and men ($n = 28$) recruited through a San Francisco bisexual organization in the early 1980s, nearly all of whom were over 30 years old. They found that approximately two thirds of their respondents reported changes in their self-reported ratio of same-sex to other-sex attractions over the 5-year assessment period, and 85% reported changes in their ratio of same-sex to other-sex sexual behavior. However, because longitudinal assessments were collected from only bisexual men and women, comparisons cannot be drawn between changes experienced by lesbian and bisexual women.

Pattatucci and Hamer (1995) collected 18-month follow-up data from 175 lesbian, bisexual, and heterosexual women recruited from lesbian, gay, and bisexual (LGB) organizations. This study had a shorter time frame than that of Weinberg and colleagues (1994) but is distinguished by its larger and more diverse sample. The authors averaged respondents' ratings of sexual attraction, fantasy, behavior, and self-identification at each assessment, thereby precluding investigation into whether changes in different domains corresponded with one another. Using these averaged ratings, they found fairly little change over the 18-month assessment period, in contrast to the findings of Weinberg and colleagues: Approximately 80% of their sample maintained the same rating, and those that changed ratings did not change them drastically. Stokes and his colleagues (Stokes et al., 1993, 1997) collected 1-year follow-up data from a sample of 216 sexual-minority men recruited through LGB community activities, print advertising, and snowball sampling. This study included significantly more ethnic-minority participants than the other studies—specifically, 50% of their respondents were African American—but like Weinberg and colleagues' study, it included only bisexuals (and only bisexual men, at that). Overall, they found that approximately 50% of their respondents reported some change in their sexual attractions over the 1-year assessment period, with two thirds of these individuals reporting having become more attracted to the same sex.

Clearly, these studies provide important empirical counterpoints to traditional sexual identity models by demonstrating that sexuality continues to evolve even after "coming out." Yet each was conducted with adults who self-identified as sexual minorities in the 1970s and 1980s and who had traversed the critical processes of sexual identity development years or even decades earlier. Thus, they provide little information about how sexual identity development unfolds among contemporary youths who are still in the throes of this process. The data presented here provide some of this missing information. I begin with a brief overview of the methods and procedures of the current study and then combine abbreviated reviews of each "mistake" with corresponding analyses.

OVERVIEW OF THE STUDY

For the first wave of data collection in this study, I interviewed 89 nonheterosexual women between the ages of 16 and 23 (Diamond, 1998). Of these 89 women, 42% identified as lesbian and 30% as bisexual, and 28% declined to adopt a sexual identity label. The mean and median age of the participants was 19, and there were no significant age differences across sexual identity categories. I reinterviewed respondents over the phone three times, approximately every 2 to 3 years. Thus, the T2, T3, and T4 interviews represent 2-year, 5-year, and 8-year follow-ups, respectively. Four lesbians, one bisexual woman, and four *unlabeled* participants could not be relocated at T2. At T3, an additional three lesbians and one bisexual woman could not be located, but the four unlabeled women who had been missing at T2 were successfully recontacted. Two respondents could not be recontacted between T3 and T4 (one had identified as unlabeled and the other as bisexual at T1). One T1 lesbian who had been lost between T2 and T3 was successfully recontacted for T4. Thus, the final T4 sample size was 79, comprising 89% of the original respondents. None of the women who were recontacted declined to be reinterviewed.

Initial sampling took place in two moderately sized cities and a number of smaller urban and rural communities in central New York State. The settings that were sampled included (a) LGB community events (e.g., picnics, parades, social events) and youth groups, (b) classes on gender and sexuality issues taught at a large university with a moderately ethnically diverse— but largely middle-class—student population, and (c) LGB student groups at a large public university with a predominantly White but more socioeconomically diverse population and a small private women's college with a predominantly White and middle-class student population. This recruitment strategy succeeded in sampling sizable numbers of bisexual women as well as nonheterosexual women who declined to label their sexual identity, both groups that are underrepresented in most research on sexual minorities. However, the sample shares a chronic drawback with other samples of sexual minorities in that it comprises predominantly White, highly educated, middle- to upper-class individuals. Nearly all of the college-age participants had enrolled in college at one point, and 75% came from families in which at least one parent had completed college. Sixty-three percent of women came from families in which at least one parent had a professional or technical occupation, and 84% were White.

Detailed information regarding interview procedures and questions can be found in previously published reports on this sample (Diamond, 1998, 2000b, 2003a, 2003b, 2005). Briefly, at each of the three interviews women were asked to describe their current sexual identity, to recall the process by which they first questioned their sexuality, and to recount any changes they had recently undergone regarding their experience or conceptualization of their sexuality. To assess their same-sex attractions, women were asked to report the percentage of their current attractions that were directed toward the same sex on a day-to-day basis; separate estimates were provided for sexual versus romantic–affectional attractions. This yields an estimate of the relative frequency of same-sex versus other-sex attractions, regardless of the intensity of these attractions or the total number of sexual attractions experienced on a day-to-day basis. At T2, T3, and T4, participants also indicated the number of men and women with whom they had engaged in sexual contact (defined as any sexually motivated intimate contact) since the preceding interview, as well as the number of men and women with whom they had had romantic relationships. At T3, women completed questionnaires measuring neuroticism (Costa & McCrae, 1985), trait levels of positive and negative affect (Watson, Clark, & Tellegen, 1988), and endorsement of positive versus negative schemas about sexuality (Andersen & Cyranowski, 1994).

Mistake 1: Most Sexual-Minority Women Are Exclusively Attracted to Women

Perhaps the most significant failing of existing models of sexual identity development is that they focus exclusively on lesbian and gay male development, ignoring bisexuality altogether. In fact, most publications on sexual identity development do not even mention the word *bisexual* in the title (Boxer & Cohler, 1989; Gramick, 1984; Herdt & Boxer, 1993; Joseph, Adib, Joseph, & Tal, 1991; Rotheram-Borus & Fernandez, 1995; Schneider, 1991; Troiden, 1979, 1988; Wooden, Kawasaki, & Mayeda, 1983; Zera, 1992). To some extent, this is a historical problem. With a few notable exceptions (Blumstein & Schwartz, 1977; Dixon, 1984), it was not until the late 1980s and early 1990s that bisexuality began to receive significant research attention by social scientists studying sexual orientation (Fox, 1993, 1995; George, 1993; Klein, 1993; Nichols, 1988; Paul, 1985; Rust, 1993; Shuster, 1987; Weinberg et al., 1994).

Yet even now, many studies of sexual minorities continue to exclude bisexual individuals. Sometimes this is done for practical reasons. In many samples, there are too few openly identified bisexual men and women to permit substantive comparisons with openly identified lesbians or gay men, and therefore they are excluded to simplify data analysis and interpretation. In other cases, bisexual men and women are excluded to preserve conceptual clarity (reviewed in Rust, 1993, 2000). After all, some bisexual men and women might be closeted lesbians or gay men who have not yet accepted their sexual orientation, or perhaps confused heterosexual men and women. Either way, the inclusion of such individuals might distort otherwise straightforward comparisons between lesbian or gay and heterosexual men and women. Of course, the possibility that openly identified lesbians and gay men might actually be closeted or confused bisexual individuals is rarely considered, reflecting the widespread assumption that in matters of sexual orientation, exclusive same-sex attractions are the norm and nonexclusive attractions the exception.

We now know that this is not the case: Recent representative studies of American adults (Laumann, Gagnon, Michael, & Michaels, 1994) and adolescents (French, Story, Remafedi, Resnick, & Blum, 1996; Garofalo, Wolf, Wissow, Woods, & Goodman, 1999) have found that individuals with nonexclusive attractions outnumber those with exclusive same-sex attractions, especially among women. This does not mean that most sexual-minority individuals experience same-sex and other-sex attractions with equal frequency or intensity; rather, most appear to gravitate toward one sex or the other (Diamond, 1998; Rust, 1992, 1993; Weinberg et al., 1994). The critical point is that the coexistence of same-sex and other-sex attractions is a normative rather than exceptional feature of the sexual-minority life course, and sexual identity models that ignore the push and pull between these attractions provide only a partial perspective on this process.

The results of the current study further illustrate this fact. Among the women who identified as lesbian at T1, 70% acknowledged attractions to both sexes at that time, despite their predominant interest in women. By the fourth interview, all of the T1 lesbians acknowledged occasional attractions to men. Thus, consistent with studies cited earlier, nonexclusive attractions were the norm rather than the exception among these young women. A similar pattern emerged for sexual behavior: Nearly two thirds of the T1 lesbians ended up having sexual contact with at least one man in the ensuing 8 years.

Thus, whereas researchers and laypeople have long wondered whether bisexually identified individuals were "really" lesbian or gay, one might rather argue that many lesbian-identified individuals are "really" bisexual. In fact, a number of lesbians in the current study explicitly acknowledged this fact, noting that although they were "technically" bisexual, they maintained a flexible definition of lesbianism that accommodated periodic other-sex attractions and behaviors, especially if they were "just sex." As one woman said, "I've had physical relations with men, but no other types of relationships. Just random, stupid things, no emotional ties. . . . men are just a lot easier to obtain than women are." Another noted that having sexual contact with men "didn't make me think that I wasn't a normal lesbian or anything. . . . At this point in my life, it's not about sexual intimacy as much as it is about being in a committed relationship, and I just don't think that I would want one with a man. And that's a more important criteria for me in terms of identifying as a lesbian, than just having a sexual thing."

Thus, whereas traditional sexual identity models presume that the main "work" of sexual identity development involves acknowledging and accepting same-sex attractions, these findings show that reconciling, reconsidering, or rediscovering other-sex attractions is a common and important part of long-term identity maintenance that may have important developmental implications. For example, Weinberg and colleagues' (1994) longitudinal study of bisexual adults found that nonexclusive attractions prompted many individuals to periodically reconsider the fit between their identity label and their subjective sexual experience as they moved through different environments and relationships over time. This was certainly true of the present sample: Among respondents who experienced at least 95% of their day-to-day attractions to women (averaged across the four assessments), approximately one sixth changed their identity label over the 8 years of the study. In contrast, three fourths of respondents reporting that 50% or fewer of their day-to-day attractions were to women ended up changing their identity labels over time. Clearly, to effectively model the developmental significance of nonexclusive attractions, we must actively recruit women with such attractions into our research samples and systematically explore what their experiences have to teach us about long-term processes of identity development.

Mistake 2: Sexual Questioning Ends Once You Identify as Lesbian, Gay, or Bisexual

Classic stage models of sexual identity development typically posit a clear-cut beginning, middle, and definitive end to this process (Sophie, 1986). It is generally presumed that although delays and perturbations might pockmark the journey, individuals move inexorably from initial confusion about their sexuality toward eventual certainty and consolidation, especially those with supportive friends and family members, frequent contact with other sexual-minority individuals, and successful same-sex intimate relationships (Cohen & Savin-Williams, 1996). Yet this is not always the case. Rather, some individuals (particularly women) revisit the process of sexual questioning many years after first adopting their sexual-minority identity, typically because they find that the identity they initially adopted does not accord with their current attractions or relationships (Blumstein & Schwartz, 1977; Golden, 1996; Rust, 1992; Weinberg et al., 1994).

Overall, this phenomenon has received little substantive attention because it has been viewed the same way that bisexuality has been viewed: as exceptional rather than normative. Furthermore, because individuals are highly motivated to construct coherent and consistent life histories (Boxer & Cohler, 1989; Cass, 1990), those who periodically requestion their sexual identities are likely to edit out these experiences from the retrospective identity narratives they tell to researchers, or to dismiss them as artifacts of protracted denial of their true sexual orientation (Blumstein & Schwartz, 1977). The longitudinal data presented here therefore provide an indispensable perspective on how frequently individuals requestion their sexual identities and how they experience this process at the time it occurs.

Directly contrary to the notion that sexual questioning wraps up after an individual adopts a sexual-minority identity, 70% of the women in the current sample ended up changing their identity label at least one more time after first coming out (as a basis for comparison, Rust's 1993 retrospective study found that 75% of the bisexual respondents reported having once identified as lesbian, and over 40% of the lesbian respondents reported having once identified as bisexual). Approximately one sixth of these changes took place prior to the first interview, and these pre-T1 transitions typically involved women switching from bisexual to lesbian labels as they achieved greater comfort and awareness regarding the strength and predominance of their same-sex attractions, just as traditional sexual identity models would predict.

Yet the vast majority of identity changes took place after the T1 interview, and these transitions appeared to be a different type of phenomenon altogether. For example, whereas transitions to lesbian labels were the most common type of identity change undertaken prior to the T1 interview, they were the least common after this point. Of the 73 transitions that occurred (note that some women underwent more than one), 19% involved switching to a lesbian label, 23% involved switching to bisexual, 21% involved switching to heterosexual, and 37% involved switching to unlabeled, an altogether unexpected phenomenon discussed in more detail later in this chapter (as well as in Diamond, 2003a).

As noted earlier, women with more nonexclusive attractions were more likely to undergo post-T1 identity transitions. This makes sense when one considers that women with nonexclusive attractions must resolve a broader and more complex set of questions in selecting an appropriate identity label than do women with more exclusive attractions. Specifically, acknowledging same-sex attractions is only the first step. To settle on a lesbian or bisexual label they must consider exactly how strongly they lean toward women versus men; whether sexual and emotional feelings are equally important; whether behavior trumps fantasy or vice versa. Many women described having become increasingly aware of how arbitrary and subjective such decisions are, and the extent to which any label they chose could provide only a partial representation of their overall sexuality. As one woman noted, "My full life experience and even my daily experience isn't encompassed by any one label anymore."

For some women, reconsideration of the relative strength of their attractions to women versus men prompted them to reevaluate the overall role of sexual attractions in their sexual identity to begin with, in comparison with other factors such as emotional bonds, specific relationships, social networks, and ideological beliefs. As one woman noted regarding her sexual identity,

> In the past couple of years I've become very comfortable with the fact that there are some men that I will be attracted to, but that any long-term emotional, sexual commitment will be to a woman. I felt comfortable saying to myself "I feel like I'm a lesbian intellectually, but it's okay that I'm still attracted to men physically."

Similarly, another respondent reported that although her attractions to women had substantially dissipated over the years, she maintained a bisexual identity partly out of disdain for mainstream heterosexual culture: "I've kind of straightened out! I still call myself bisexual but I'm on the edge of heterosexual, which I'm not pleased about. I mean, straight culture—yuck, bad!"

For many women, the process of requestioning their identities had led them to conclude that their emotional feelings were more important criteria for sexual identification than their sexual attractions. Perhaps for this reason, the small number of T1 lesbians who had full-fledged love affairs with men ($n = 10$) had greater difficulty reconciling these relationships with their lesbian identities than those who had only casual sexual affairs with men. This was the case for one woman who unexpectedly fell in love with a close male friend.

> Overall, people have been supportive, but I've definitely seen some nastiness because of it. One lesbian I know, she said that it was just a phase, that I was misguided, that she didn't want him in her house. It made me angry, it made me cry, it made me question—I mean, these were the same types of things I heard from straight people when I first came out about having relationships with *women*.

Given such difficulties, it is perhaps not surprising that none of the T1 lesbians who became romantically involved with a man maintained her lesbian identity; six stopped labeling altogether, and four started identifying as bisexual. In contrast, 40% of the lesbians who had engaged in "just sexual" contact with men continued to identify as lesbians.

Thus, whereas researchers have historically described sexual identity development as concluding when individuals come out and claim a sexual-minority identity, these data indicate that for many women—especially those with nonexclusive attractions—coming out may be just the beginning of a longer series of ongoing reevaluations and realignments. Future research is necessary to further investigate the multiple psychological, interpersonal, and sociocultural factors that trigger requestioning and shape its resolution in different contexts and at different stages of life.

Mistake 3: It's Better to Have a Sexual Identity Label Than Not To

Whereas the second mistake concerns the process of resolving one's sexual identity, the third mistake concerns the content of that resolution: a clear-cut lesbian, gay, or bisexual identity. All existing sexual identity models posit a final stage involving the synthesis, resolution, integration, or consolidation of a clearly defined lesbian, gay, or bisexual identity (Cass, 1979; Coleman, 1981/1982; Lee, 1977; Minton & McDonald, 1983; Mohr & Fassinger, 2000; Troiden, 1979), and this final stage is presumed to be critical for future healthy development. Ambivalence or uncertainty about claiming a lesbian, gay, or bisexual label is typically taken as a sign that the individual continues to experience internalized homophobia and self-stigmatization.

The mental health benefits of adopting a lesbian, gay, or bisexual identity have been demonstrated in research showing that stable and well-integrated LGB identities are associated with greater ego strength, self-esteem, general adjustment, and overall well-being (Brady & Busse, 1994; Levine, 1997; Miranda & Storms, 1989; Walters & Simoni, 1983; Wells & Kline, 1987). Yet much of this research has failed to tease out whether such benefits are attributable to the acceptance and integration of a lesbian, gay, or bisexual identity or to the acceptance and integration of one's same-sex sexuality, labeled or not. For example, one of the items that Mohr and Fassinger (2000) used to measure identity synthesis among lesbians was "I am at the point where I feel a deep contentment about my love for other women." Mohr and Fassinger implicitly suggested that any woman agreeing with this statement would identify as lesbian or bisexual, yet the present research shows that this is not necessarily the case.

Contrary to the notion that increasing certainty and self-acceptance of same-sex attractions lead inexorably to stable and clearly articulated sexual-minority identities, many of the women in the current sample reported that the more comfortable they became with their attractions over the years, the more they doubted the value and appropriateness of adopting a fixed lesbian or bisexual label. Of the women who were unlabeled at T1, over one third continued to resist labeling their identities 8 years later. Furthermore, as noted earlier, 37% of the identity transitions that were observed over the 8 years of the study involved giving up sexual-minority identities in favor of unlabeled identities. Traditional identity models would characterize these transitions as representing stunted, stalled, or retrograde development, perhaps attributable to shame, social pressure, or denial. Yet rather than displaying stunted development, the explanations these women provided for their reluctance to adopt sexual-minority identity labels typically displayed a sophisticated understanding of the inherent limitations of sexual categorization.

> The reason why I haven't labeled myself is because I feel like I'm putting myself in a box. I don't want to close off any possibilities. I'm with a woman now but I'm not sure about what will happen in the future and that's okay. I feel that whatever decisions I make will be fine.
>
> I think these days I'm much more comfortable just allowing myself to feel whatever I feel. Growing up, there was society around me telling me to date boys, or whatever, and then I came out as a lesbian and there was an equal pressure to date women. Now I am mainly going through life and seeing who I meet, and I'm much less panicked about the whole thing. Whatever I feel is all right, you know?

Further evidence for the fact that such women are just as psychologically healthy as openly identified lesbians and bisexual women comes from the fact that T4 unlabeled women were no different from T4 lesbians or bisexuals with regard to neuroticism, trait levels of positive and negative affect, and endorsement of positive versus negative schemas about sexuality (all of which were measured at T3). Clearly, traditional sexual identity models may have erred in placing so much emphasis on the adoption of a lesbian, gay, or bisexual identity rather than focusing on the multiple ways in which individuals might manifest a deep acceptance and integration of their same-sex sexuality.

One might go even further to suggest that given the prevalence of fluid and nonexclusive attractions among women, rejection or skepticism of categorical identity labels is a sign of psychological health and self-confidence rather than maladjustment and denial. In a recent (and rare) discussion of the increasing numbers of sexual-minority youths who describe themselves as "questioning" rather than lesbian, gay, or bisexual, Hollander (2000) noted that many of these youths are not, in fact, engaged in a protracted process of sexual questioning at all. Rather, they openly reject the classification of sexuality into heterosexual, bisexual, and homosexual categories, and call themselves "questioning" to acknowledge the vast possibilities they perceive for their sexual attractions and behaviors.

The same phenomenon was detected in the current sample. Numerous respondents—even those who maintained a lesbian or bisexual identity—denounced the implicit restrictions entailed by identity labels. As one woman noted, "I hate boxes. Hate them, hate them. And I hate this whole dichotomy paradigm that our society tends to revolve around. It's black, it's white, it's male, it's female, it's straight, it's gay, whatever. None of those fits." Another woman remarked as follows:

> I don't know, I personally don't like the whole label thing. I guess because I feel that you just never know how someone will affect you, and I just never know who my soul mate is going to be. I feel like for a great majority of people, sexuality is very fluid. There are definitely people who are just one way, like either lesbian or straight, but most people flow in the middle.

Many respondents indicated that they had trouble labeling their sexuality because their sexual desires did not consistently revolve around one gender versus the other but, rather, depended on the specific personalities and attributes of specific individuals. As one woman noted, "Labels don't really matter because when I'm falling in love or whatever, I'm falling in love with the person's soul, and packaging is incidental." Another woman claimed, "I don't label because I'm not attracted to either sex until I get to know the person, and there's no label that reflects that." Similar claims were made by many respondents in Weinberg and colleagues' (1994) study, and they described these respondents as possessing "open gender schemas" when it came to sexuality. In other words, these individuals (most of whom, notably, were women) appeared to have cognitively disconnected *gender* from *sexual desire*. The cues to which they responded sexually were fairly broad, and highly responsive to environmental and interpersonal contexts.

Along the same lines, one pattern that proved distinctive among women who relinquished their identity labels between T1 and T4, or who had never adopted a label to begin with, concerned gaps between their emotional and physical attractions. Of course, most traditional conceptualizations of sexual orientation presume that emotional and physical attractions are always concordant, such that individuals always fall in love with whatever gender they find sexually attractive. Yet not only is there little scientific data to suggest whether and why this might be so (Diamond, 2003b) but this notion directly contradicts the experiences of many women in this sample. One woman who was unlabeled at all three interviews indicated that the gap between her emotional and physical feelings left her questioning all of her attractions.

> I guess the reason that I don't want to label is that I don't necessarily know why I'm sexually attracted to *anyone* anymore. I no longer believe what I used to think. I used to think that you fell in love with the person, and then you would be sexually attracted. I kind of always thought that I could be with women because I did find women attractive, and it seems like I love some of my female friends so much, but now I realize there's something there that I don't understand that makes it so that the friends I become sexually attracted to happen to be men, and I don't know why that is, and why it's not true with my best female friends.

Exploratory analyses were conducted to test whether women who gave up their identity labels between T1 and T4, or who had been unlabeled at all four interviews, experienced disproportionately large discrepancies between their day-to-day physical and emotional same-sex attractions (recall that these attractions were assessed as ratios of same-sex to other-sex attractions). Absolute differences between each woman's 8-year average for each type of attraction were calculated, and these difference scores served as an index of whether women found themselves falling in love with women to the same degree that they found themselves sexually attracted to women. Compared with respondents who identified as lesbian or bisexual at T4, the unlabeled women reported significantly greater absolute gaps between their percentage of physical versus emotional same-sex attractions ($M_{labeled}$ = 11.5, SD = 9.7 vs. $M_{unlabeled}$ = 18.0, SD = 7.5), $t(78)$ = 3.4, p = .001.

This finding demonstrates that the overall fit between a woman's physical and emotional feelings for women and men is a key piece of evidence she might use to assess her sexual identity. As one woman said, quite straightforwardly, during her second interview,

> Sometimes I worry that I will never settle down with anyone, because the way I feel about guys is mainly sexual, and the way I feel about women is mainly emotional. So I'm always going between the two, and I don't know *what* to call that, you know?

Yet traditional sexual identity models make no accommodation for this sort of quandary. According to the traditional paradigm, women claiming discrepancies between their emotional and physical attractions are either confused heterosexuals or repressed lesbians.

This interpretation does not do justice to the complexity of such experiences. In fact, what is particularly compelling about the current sample's descriptions of change in attractions and identities is how infrequently they disavow previous feelings, relationships, or identities as false or misguided. Rather, women who underwent major shifts in how they conceptualized their sexuality generally acknowledged that feelings and experiences that were authentic, compelling, and transformative in one context might not be so in another. As one woman noted, "Your core sexuality probably stays the same, but if the moment that you're living in is strong enough for you, then that's your sexuality at that moment." An important implication of this perspective is that although early coming-out experiences can be ably documented with single-shot retrospective assessments, longitudinal observation is indispensable for investigating how individuals' sexual identities undergo ongoing development and elaboration as they move through different moments, contexts, and relationships at different stages of life. In other words, perhaps it is not so much that we have been wrong about sexual identity development for the past 20 years, but that we were never really observing it to begin with.

FUTURE DIRECTIONS

Now that we have identified our previous missteps, the task of fixing them remains. Toward this end, some of the most straightforward goals for future research involve (a) paying greater attention to nonexclusive attractions, (b) assessing sexual identity development over longer periods of time, and (c) acknowledging the legitimacy of unlabeled identities. Yet although such changes will surely foster a more thorough and nuanced understanding of sexual identity development, they may not be enough.

Rather, a more substantive overhaul of theory and research on sexual identity and same-sex sexuality is in order, one that supplants the traditional emphasis on sexual categories with an emphasis on investigating how specific person–context interactions shape diverse manifestations of same-sex sexuality over the life course.

This is by no means a novel proposal (see Blumstein & Schwartz, 1990; Cass, 1990; DeCecco & Shively, 1984; Gagnon, 1990; Golden, 1987; Kinsey, Pomeroy, & Martin, 1948; Kinsey, Pomeroy, Martin, & Gebhard, 1953; Kitzinger, 1987; Kitzinger & Wilkinson, 1995; Klein, Sepekoff, & Wolf, 1985; Laumann et al., 1994; Rich, 1980; Weinberg et al., 1994), but so far, such recommendations have not generally trickled down to influence mainstream research practice. Consequently, although powerful critiques of rigid sexual classifications regularly appear in the social scientific literature (most recently in Blackwood, 2000; Peplau & Garnets, 2000; Rothblum, 2000; Rust, 2000), it is still the case that the first piece of information reported in most empirical studies of same-sex sexuality is how many "gays" and "straights" there were in the sample. Furthermore, as Rothblum (2000) noted, although Kinsey's famous 0 to 6 scale (Kinsey et al., 1948; Kirby et al., 1994) provides for continuous rather than categorical representations of sexual desire, identity, and behavior, many researchers turn these continua right back into categories by designating certain scale ranges (0–1 = *heterosexual*; 2–4 = *bisexual*; 5–6 = *lesbian/gay*).

I therefore conclude with several specific recommendations for how researchers might change the way we investigate sexual identity and same-sex sexuality. First (and most obvious), we must make concerted efforts to sample individuals with nonexclusive attractions and behaviors—especially those who decline to identify as lesbian, gay, or bisexual—and all research materials should be carefully edited to avoid presumptions of sexual-minority identification. Second, when describing sexual minorities, we should only use the terms *gay*, *lesbian*, and *bisexual* to denote individuals' self-ascribed sexual identities, and not to denote categories of sexual orientation.

Third, sexual identity researchers should consider setting aside discussions of sexual orientation altogether in favor of describing *same-sex sexuality*, a broader phenomenon including everything from fleeting sexual fantasies, enduring sexual attractions, temporary sexual experimentation, and "romantic" friendships to full-fledged sexual and romantic affairs. When we wish to distinguish between individuals with exclusive versus nonexclusive same-sex attractions, or those who have had same-sex sexual contact once versus many times, or those with strong versus weak other-sex attractions, or those whose sexual feelings are concordant or discordant with their romantic feelings, then these are precisely the types of specific and circumscribed descriptions we should use. In this manner, researchers can avoid erroneously suggesting that same-sex sexual attractions, romantic feelings, fantasies, sexual behavior, and romantic relationships always cluster together in convenient homosexual and heterosexual packages.

Furthermore, focusing on specific aspects and instances of same-sex sexuality frees us from the futile (and perhaps impossible) task of differentiating between individuals who are "really" gay and those who are supposedly "confused," "experimenting," and so forth. Although some would argue that investigations of same-sex sexuality should focus on only the former group, I maintain that we cannot fully understand the nature and development of same-sex sexuality unless we understand all of its origins and manifestations. It is important to note that this does not imply that there is no such thing as sexual orientation or that it is not a worthy topic of study in its own right. To the contrary, extant research (ranging from the seminal work of Kinsey and his colleagues to more recent and methodologically sophisticated studies, such as Gangestad, Bailey, & Martin, 2000; Laumann et al., 1994) suggests that it is meaningful to distinguish between individuals who are generally more sexually attracted to the same sex, the other sex, or both sexes. Yet until we know more about the nature, origins, and stability of these distinctions, we should avoid implicitly reifying them with our terminology. After all, these distinctions might not be the most important ones: Weinberg and colleagues (1994) suggested, for example, that "homosexuals" and "heterosexuals" may actually have far more in common with each other than either group shares with individuals whose sexuality revolves around the person and not the gender. Until we have substantively investigated such possibilities, we should reserve sexual identity labels for just that: sexual identities.

Finally, we must revise our conceptualization and operationalization of sexual identity itself. Traditionally, sexual identity has been defined as a personal understanding and social presentation of the "truth" of one's sexual orientation. According to this framework, sexual identity development amounts to simply matching one's identity to one's orientation, and subsequent changes in identification are interpretable only as movements toward or away from this idealized, one-to-one match. Clearly, many of the identity changes observed in the current study do not fit this conceptualization. Rather, women's reidentifications typically reflected careful consideration of the personal meaning of specific identities in specific interpersonal and social contexts (for other excellent discussions and examples of such processes, see Kitzinger & Wilkinson, 1995; Rust, 1992, 1993, 2000).

Thus, a more appropriate operational definition of sexual identity is that proposed by Weinberg and colleagues (1994): "the choice of a particular perspective from which to make sense of one's sexual feelings and behaviors" (p. 292). This definition makes no presumption about "authentic" identities or "true" orientations but allows for multiple, culture-bound, context-specific solutions to the ever-present "problem" posed by nonnormative attractions and behaviors. One of the strengths of this notion of sexual identity is its implicit acknowledgment that the same solution might not be equally healthful or adaptive for all individuals. Thus, one person might avoid labeling his or her sexual identity solely to avoid social rejection; another might do so as an affirmation of sexual fluidity; yet another might do so because Western sexual identity labels have little meaning in his or her own cultural tradition.

This operationalization of sexual identity necessitates a far different approach to studying sexual identity development than has characterized most prior research. Instead of snapshot assessments of the degree to which sexual minorities acknowledge, accept, and disclose their same-sex attractions, we require in-depth, longitudinal, qualitative analyses of how different individuals experience and interpret different manifestations of same-sex sexuality over the life course. Even the most elemental, taken-for-granted aspect of sexual-minority experience—same-sex attractions—is due for substantive reexamination, as qualitative research suggests that individuals use vastly different criteria in classifying various thoughts, urges, desires, fantasies, and affections as attractions (Diamond & Savin-Williams, 2000). The complicated role of sexually and emotionally intimate relationships in long-term identity development also requires more intensive investigation. For many women, changes in their participation in same-sex or other-sex romantic and sexual relationships played a notable role in their emerging sexual self-concepts. This is perhaps most evident among the lesbians who pursued casual sexual contact with men, yet who did not think these experiences contradicted their lesbian identities as long as they remained devoid of emotional intensity. Clearly, such issues require rigorous study if we are to develop more accurate and flexible models of sexual identity development over the life course.

CONCLUSION

For those of us who question, your whole life becomes a question. Do you then reach some level of understanding, and then it's static? I don't think so. When I'm with a woman, I'm not really a lesbian, and when I'm with a man I'm not really straight. Maybe if I spent ten years with a woman it would change the way I thought, and I would call myself a lesbian. I think your definition changes based on your experiences. I can't really say. I still feel young, I still feel that I have a lot left to learn.

So do we. Although research on sexual identity development has proliferated dramatically over the past 20 years, there is much that we still do not understand about this process. The results of this study demonstrate that, contrary to conventional wisdom, the years after coming out involve far more than simple identity consolidation. Rather, they may involve full-fledged replays of the sexual questioning process as different experiences and environments render different attractions, behaviors, affections, and self-concepts more or less salient. To fully understand these processes, researchers must systematically assess the long-term developmental trajectories of as broad and diverse a range of sexual minorities as possible.

One of the most important reasons to undertake such investigations is to provide sexual minorities themselves with more accurate information about these issues. Notably, many of the women in this study expressed embarrassment when explaining changes in their sexual feelings, relationships, or identities, having internalized the prevailing cultural message that such experiences were highly atypical. At this point, it is impossible to say just how typical or atypical they are, but the findings of the present study demonstrate the critical importance of investigating this question. Psychologists, clinicians, and policymakers are increasingly designing educational programming for schools and social service agencies aimed at dispelling myths about sexual orientation and providing support to sexual-minority youths as they embark on the identity development process. For youths to benefit from these efforts, the scientific knowledge behind them should speak to the full range of diverse experiences that characterize the sexual-minority life course.

REFERENCES

Andersen, B. L., & Cyranowski, J. M. (1994). Women's sexual self-schema. *Journal of Personality and Social Psychology, 67,* 1079–1100.

Barber, J. S., & Mobley, M. (1999). Counseling gay adolescents. In A. M. Horne & M. S. Kiselica (Eds.), *Handbook of counseling boys and adolescent males: A practitioner's guide* (pp. 161–178). Thousand Oaks, CA: Sage.

Blackwood, E. (2000). Culture and women's sexualities. *Journal of Social Issues, 56,* 223–238.

Blumstein, P., & Schwartz, P. (1977). Bisexuality: Some social psychological issues. *Journal of Social Issues, 33,* 30–45.

Blumstein, P., & Schwartz, P. (1990). Intimate relationships and the creation of sexuality. In D. P. McWhirter, S. A. Sanders, & J. M. Reinisch (Eds.), *Homosexuality/heterosexuality: Concepts of sexual orientation* (pp. 307–320). New York: Oxford University Press.

Boxer, A., & Cohler, B. (1989). The life course of gay and lesbian youth: An immodest proposal for the study of lives. *Journal of Homosexuality, 17,* 315–355.

Brady, S., & Busse, W. J. (1994). The gay identity questionnaire: A brief measure of homosexual identity formation. *Journal of Homosexuality, 26,* 1–22.

Cass, V. (1979). Homosexual identity formation: A theoretical model. *Journal of Homosexuality*, *4*, 219–235.

Cass, V. (1990). The implications of homosexual identity formation for the Kinsey model and scale of sexual preference. In D. P. McWhirter, S. A. Sanders, J. M. Reinisch (Eds.), *Homosexuality/heterosexuality: Concepts of sexual orientation* (pp. 239–266). New York: Oxford University Press.

Cohen, K. M., & Savin-Williams, R. C. (1996). Developmental perspectives on coming out to self and others. In R. C. Savin-Williams & K. M. Cohen (Eds.), *The lives of lesbians, gays, and bisexuals: Children to adults* (pp. 113–151). Fort Worth, TX: Harcourt Brace.

Coleman, E. (1981/1982). Developmental stages of the coming out process. *Journal of Homosexuality*, *7*, 31–43.

Costa, P. T., & McCrae, R. R. (1985). *The NEO Personality Inventory*. Odessa, FL: Psychological Assessment Resources.

DeCecco, J., & Shively, M. (1984). From sexual identity to sexual relationships: A contractual shift. *Journal of Homosexuality*, *9*, 1–26.

Diamond, L. M. (1998). Development of sexual orientation among adolescent and young adult women. *Developmental Psychology*, *34*, 1085–1095.

Diamond, L. M. (2000a). Passionate friendships among adolescent sexual-minority women. *Journal of Research on Adolescence*, *10*, 191–209.

Diamond, L. M. (2000b). Sexual identity, attractions, and behavior among young sexual-minority women over a two-year period. *Developmental Psychology*, *36*, 241–250.

Diamond, L. M. (2003a). Was it a phase? Young women's relinquishment of lesbian/ bisexual identities over a 5-year period. *Journal of Personality and Social Psychology*, *84*, 352–364.

Diamond, L. M. (2003b). What does sexual orientation orient? A biobehavioral model distinguishing romantic love and sexual desire. *Psychological Review*, *110*, 173–192.

Diamond, L. M. (2005). A new view of lesbian subtypes: Stable vs. fluid identity trajectories over an 8-year period. *Psychology of Women Quarterly*, *29*, 119–128.

Diamond, L. M., & Savin-Williams, R. C. (2000). Explaining diversity in the development of same-sex sexuality among young women. *Journal of Social Issues*, *56*, 297–313.

Dixon, J. K. (1984). The commencement of bisexual activity in swinging married women over age thirty. *Journal of Sex Research*, *20*, 71–90.

Fairchild, B., & Hayward, N. (1979). *Now that you know*. New York: Harper & Row.

Fox, R. C. (1993). *Coming out bisexual: Identity, behavior, sexual orientation self-disclosure*. Unpublished doctoral dissertation, California Institute of Integral Studies, San Francisco.

Fox, R. C. (1995). Bisexual identities. In A. R. D'Augelli & C. Patterson (Eds.), *Lesbian, gay, and bisexual identities over the lifespan* (pp. 48–86). New York: Oxford University Press.

French, S. A., Story, M., Remafedi, G., Resnick, M. D., & Blum, R. W. (1996). Sexual orientation and prevalence of body dissatisfaction and eating disordered behaviors: A population-based study of adolescents. *International Journal of Eating Disorders, 19*, 119–126.

Gagnon, J. (1990). Gender preference in erotic relations: The Kinsey scale and sexual scripts. In D. P. McWhirter, S. A. Sanders, & J. M. Reinisch (Eds.), *Homosexuality/heterosexuality: Concepts of sexual orientation* (pp. 177–207). New York: Oxford University Press.

Gangestad, S. W., Bailey, J. M., & Martin, N. G. (2000). Taxometric analyses of sexual orientation and gender identity. *Journal of Personality and Social Psychology, 78*, 1109–1121.

Garofalo, R., Wolf, R. C., Wissow, L. S., Woods, E. R., & Goodman, E. (1999). Sexual orientation and risk of suicide attempts among a representative sample of youth. *Archives of Pediatrics and Adolescent Medicine, 153*, 487–493.

George, S. (1993). *Women and bisexuality*. London: Scarlet Press.

Golden, C. (1987). Diversity and variability in women's sexual identities. In Boston Lesbian Psychologies Collective (Ed.), *Lesbian psychologies: Explorations and challenges* (pp. 19–34). Urbana: University of Illinois Press.

Golden, C. (1996). What's in a name? Sexual self-identification among women. In R. C. Savin-Williams & K. M. Cohen (Eds.), *The lives of lesbians, gays, and bisexuals: Children to adults* (pp. 229–249). Fort Worth, TX: Harcourt Brace.

Gramick, J. (1984). Developing a lesbian identity. In T. Darty & S. Potter (Eds.), *Women-identified women* (pp. 31–44). Palo Alto, CA: Mayfield Publishing.

Herdt, G., & Boxer, A. M. (1993). *Children of Horizons: How gay and lesbian teens are leading a new way out of the closet*. Boston: Beacon Press.

Hollander, G. (2000). Questioning youths: Challenges to working with youths forming identities. *School Psychology Review, 29*, 173–179.

Joseph, K. M., Adib, S. M., Joseph, J. G., & Tal, M. (1991). Gay identity and risky sexual behavior related to the AIDS threat. *Journal of Community Health, 16*, 287–296.

Kinsey, A. C., Pomeroy, W. B., & Martin, C. E. (1948). *Sexual behavior in the human male*. Philadelphia: W. B. Saunders.

Kinsey, A. C., Pomeroy, W. B., Martin, C. E., & Gebhard, P. H. (1953). *Sexual behavior in the human female*. Philadelphia: W. B. Saunders.

Kirby, D., Short, L., Collins, J., Rugg, D., Kolbe, L., Howard, M., et al. (1994). School-based programs to reduce sexual risk behaviors: A review of effectiveness. *Public Health Reports, 109*, 339–360.

Kitzinger, C. (1987). *The social construction of lesbianism*. London: Sage.

Kitzinger, C., & Wilkinson, S. (1995). Transitions from heterosexuality to lesbianism: The discursive production of lesbian identities. *Developmental Psychology, 31*, 95–104.

Klein, F. (1993). *The bisexual option* (2nd ed.). New York: Harrington Park Press.

Klein, F., Sepekoff, B., & Wolf, T. J. (1985). Sexual orientation: A multi-variable dynamic process. In F. Klein & T. Wolf (Eds.), *Two lives to lead: Bisexuality in men and women* (pp. 35–49). New York: Harrington Park Press.

Laumann, E. O., Gagnon, J. H., Michael, R. T., & Michaels, S. (1994). *The social organization of sexuality: Sexual practices in the United States.* Chicago: University of Chicago Press.

Lee, J. A. (1977). Going public: A study in the sociology of homosexual liberation. *Journal of Homosexuality, 3,* 47–78.

Levine, H. (1997). A further exploration of the lesbian identity development process and its measurement. *Journal of Homosexuality, 34,* 67–78.

Meyer, S., & Schwitzer, A. M. (1999). Stages of identity development among college students with minority sexual orientations. *Journal of College Student Psychotherapy, 13,* 41–65.

Minton, H. L., & McDonald, G. J. (1983). Homosexual identity formation as a developmental process. *Journal of Homosexuality, 9,* 91–104.

Miranda, J., & Storms, M. (1989). Psychological adjustment of lesbians and gay men. *Journal of Counseling and Development, 68,* 41–45.

Mohr, J., & Fassinger, R. (2000). Measuring dimensions of lesbian and gay male experience. *Measurement and Evaluation in Counseling and Development, 33,* 66–90.

Nichols, M. (1988). Bisexuality in women: Myths, realities, and implications for therapy. *Women and Therapy, 7,* 235–252.

Pattatucci, A. M. L., & Hamer, D. H. (1995). Development and familiality of sexual orientation in females. *Behavior Genetics, 25,* 407–420.

Paul, J. P. (1985). Bisexuality: Reassessing our paradigms of sexuality. In F. Klein & T. Wolf (Eds.), *Two lives to lead: Bisexuality in men and women* (pp. 21–34). New York: Harrington Park Press.

Peplau, L. A., & Garnets, L. D. (2000). A new paradigm for understanding women's sexuality and sexual orientation. *Journal of Social Issues, 56,* 329–350.

Rich, A. (1980). Compulsory heterosexuality and lesbian existence. *Signs, 5,* 631–660.

Rothblum, E. D. (2000). Sexual orientation and sex in women's lives: Conceptual and methodological issues. *Journal of Social Issues, 56,* 193–204.

Rotheram-Borus, M. J., & Fernandez, M. I. (1995). Sexual orientation and developmental challenges experienced by gay and lesbian youths. *Suicide and Life-Threatening Behavior, 25*(Suppl.), 26–34.

Rust, P. (1992). The politics of sexual identity: Sexual attraction and behavior among lesbian and bisexual women. *Social Problems, 39,* 366–386.

Rust, P. (1993). Coming out in the age of social constructionism: Sexual identity formation among lesbians and bisexual women. *Gender and Society, 7,* 50–77.

Rust, P. (2000). Bisexuality: A contemporary paradox for women. *Journal of Social Issues, 56,* 205–221.

Ryan, C., & Futterman, D. (1998). *Lesbian and gay youth: Care and counseling*. New York: Columbia University Press.

Savin-Williams, R. C. (1998). *". . . And then I became gay": Young men's stories*. New York: Routledge.

Savin-Williams, R. C., & Diamond, L. M. (2000). Sexual identity trajectories among sexual-minority youths: Gender comparisons. *Archives of Sexual Behavior, 29,* 419–440.

Schneider, M. (1991). Developing services for lesbian and gay adolescents. *Canadian Journal of Mental Health, 10,* 133–151.

Shuster, R. (1987). Sexuality as a continuum: The bisexual identity. In Boston Lesbian Psychologies Collective (Ed.), *Lesbian psychologies* (pp. 56–71). Urbana: University of Illinois Press.

Sophie, J. (1986). A critical examination of stage theories of lesbian identity development. *Journal of Homosexuality, 12,* 39–51.

Stokes, J. P., Damon, W., & McKirnan, D. J. (1997). Predictors of movement toward homosexuality: A longitudinal study of bisexual men. *Journal of Sex Research, 34,* 304–312.

Stokes, J. P., McKirnan, D., & Burzette, R. (1993). Sexual behavior, condom use, disclosure of sexuality, and stability of sexual orientation in bisexual men. *Journal of Sex Research, 30,* 203–213.

Troiden, R. R. (1979). Becoming homosexual: A model of gay identity acquisition. *Psychiatry, 42,* 362–373.

Troiden, R. R. (1988). *Gay and lesbian identity: A sociological analysis*. Six Hills, NY: General Hall.

Walters, K. L., & Simoni, J. M. (1983). Lesbian and gay male group identity, attitudes, and self-esteem: Implications for counseling. *Journal of Counseling Psychology, 40,* 94–99.

Watson, D., Clark, L. A., & Tellegen, A. (1988). Development and validation of brief measures of positive and negative affect: The PANAS scales. *Journal of Personality and Social Psychology, 54,* 1063–1070.

Weinberg, M. S., Williams, C. J., & Pryor, D. W. (1994). *Dual attraction: Understanding bisexuality*. New York: Oxford University Press.

Wells, J. W., & Kline, W. B. (1987). Self-disclosure of homosexual orientation. *Journal of Social Psychology, 127,* 191–197.

Whisman, V. (1996). *Queer by choice: Lesbians, gay men, and the politics of identity*. New York: Routledge.

Wooden, W. S., Kawasaki, H., & Mayeda, R. (1983). Lifestyles and identity maintenance among gay Japanese-American males. *Alternative Lifestyles, 5,* 236–243.

Zera, D. (1992). Coming of age in a heterosexist world: The development of gay and lesbian adolescents. *Adolescence, 27,* 849–854.

5

PREGNANCY AMONG LESBIAN, GAY, AND BISEXUAL ADOLESCENTS: INFLUENCES OF STIGMA, SEXUAL ABUSE, AND SEXUAL ORIENTATION

ELIZABETH M. SAEWYC

A young homeless teen sits in the waiting room of a teen pregnancy clinic. She is accompanied to her appointment by another homeless young woman, who sits close by, and occasionally rubs her growing belly affectionately. When the nurse shows her to the exam room to begin the health assessment, both women rise to follow. The pregnant teen warily introduces her "street sister," and the nurse smiles and welcomes her to the clinic too.

Preliminary data from the author's various studies reported in this chapter were presented at the Society for Adolescent Medicine meetings in Vancouver, British Columbia, Canada, 1995; Washington, DC, 1996; San Francisco, 1997; Washington, DC, 2000; San Diego, 2001; and Seattle, 2004. Other preliminary data related to sexual abuse and teen pregnancy or sexual orientation and pregnancy were presented in papers at the 7th International Congress of Health in Adolescence, 2001, in Salvador, Bahia, Brazil; at the 13th International Congress on Women's Health Issues, 2002, Seoul, Korea; and at the 14th International Congress on Women's Health Issues, 2003, Victoria, British Columbia, Canada.

These studies have been supported in full or in part by grants from several institutions, including the National Institute of Mental Health (R01 MH6258601, Elizabeth M. Saewyc, principal investigator); the National Institute of Nursing Research (F31 NR07352, Elizabeth M. Saewyc, principal investigator); the National Institute on Drug Abuse (R01 DA1797901, Elizabeth M.

In the exam room, the young women notice a small poster with a Gay Pride symbol on the back of the door, but say nothing. It is not until the third prenatal clinic visit that the teen decides to confide to the nurse, "She's not just my street sister, she's my girlfriend. I'm bi."

This scenario (drawn from actual clinical experience) is relatively uncommon, but not necessarily because so few lesbian and bisexual adolescents become pregnant. The common assumption among many clinicians is that a pregnant teen must be heterosexual by definition, and this assumption is conveyed to clients in myriad ways within the clinical encounter. Because this assumption is so pervasive, it is unlikely a lesbian or bisexual pregnant teen will feel comfortable disclosing her orientation to her health care providers, and equally unlikely an expectant teen father will identify as gay or bisexual.

But is this assumption warranted? In the past two decades, large-scale school-based adolescent health surveys (AHSs) that include questions about sexual orientation, sexual behaviors, and pregnancy have brought to light unexpected evidence: Lesbian, gay, and bisexual (LGB) teens may be more likely than their heterosexual peers to become pregnant or to father a pregnancy during their adolescence (Reis & Saewyc, 1999; Saewyc, Bearinger, Blum, & Resnick, 1999; Saewyc, Pettingell, & Skay, 2004; Saewyc, Skay, Bearinger, Blum, & Resnick, 1998c). In some studies, sexual-minority adolescents have been twice as likely to report a previous pregnancy as heterosexual teens. Although rates of teen pregnancy in the general population have declined every year since 1990 (Feldmann & Middleman, 2002), preliminary evidence suggests pregnancy rates among sexual-minority teens have not (Saewyc, Pettingell, & Skay, 2004). The reasons LGB teens become involved in pregnancy may be quite different from those of heterosexual teens, so pregnancy prevention strategies targeted to the general population may not be equally effective for this population.

Why might a lesbian, gay, or bisexual teen become pregnant or father a pregnancy? In this chapter, both the theoretical explanations and the empirical evidence for the phenomenon of teen pregnancy among sexual-minority young people are explored. Drawing on theories of adolescent risk behavior, stigma management, and the traumatic effects of victimization, I examine the health sciences research linking sexual behaviors, sexual orientation, and teen pregnancy. I evaluate its support for the theoretical

Saewyc, principal investigator); and the Office of the Vice President of Research of the Graduate School, University of Minnesota. Support was also provided by the Center for Adolescent Nursing at the University of Minnesota, which is funded by the Maternal and Child Health Bureau of the U.S. Department of Health and Human Services, and both the School of Nursing and the Division of Adolescent Medicine, University of Washington, Seattle. The preparation of this chapter has also been supported in part by a recent career scholar award from the Michael Smith Foundation for Health Research, Vancouver, British Columbia, Canada.

explanations offered, and I provide recommendations for future directions in theory development, research, and practice.

THEORETICAL PERSPECTIVES TO EXPLAIN PREGNANCY AMONG SEXUAL-MINORITY TEENS

Several theories have been advanced to help explain teen pregnancy in the general population. Developmental stages of adolescence, earlier ages of sexual debut (i.e., age at first heterosexual intercourse), fertility patterns, access to contraception or abortion services, even the status of women in society have been thought to play a role in early childbearing in the United States (Burke, 1987; Luker, 1996; Ward, 1995; Zabin, Astone, & Emerson, 1993). Some theories focus on the reasons for heterosexual intercourse during the teen years. Others focus on contraceptive behaviors (or lack of such behaviors). Still others focus on the reasons teens might choose to conceive a pregnancy, continue a pregnancy, or decide to parent. For specific groups (homeless adolescents, teen prostitutes, sexually abused adolescents, or incarcerated teens) other factors have been suggested, such as exposure to "deviant" norms, sexual victimization, or pregnancy as an adaptive response to damaging environments (N. L. Anderson, 1990; Barker & Musick, 1994; Boyer & Fine, 1992; Saewyc, 1999). Because teens do not have ready access to fertility clinics and artificial insemination, a reasonable premise is that heterosexual intercourse is taking place, and pregnancy is the consequence, intended or otherwise, of this heterosexual behavior.

But what about LGB adolescents? It is not hard to believe heterosexual sex happens among LGB teens, because this group does include bisexual adolescents, who could have opposite-gender partners. Sexual orientation development unfolds during the teen years, with a lot of tentative questioning and experimentation during the process (see Diamond, chap. 4, this volume). But pregnancy? Especially higher rates of pregnancy? This becomes a counterintuitive leap. There are several theories that help explain why LGB adolescents might be more likely to become involved in a pregnancy during their teen years.

Deviance Theory: Jessor's Theory of Problem Behavior

One of the most commonly observed associations in adolescent health behavior research is the clustering of problem behaviors. Teens who smoke are more likely to drink, those who use drugs are more likely to skip school, and gang-involved youths and runaways report substance use, violence, and risky sexual behaviors far more often than other teens (Rotheram-Borus, Mahler, Koopman, & Langabeer, 1996). Teen pregnancy is no exception:

Adolescents involved in a pregnancy are more likely to engage in other risky behaviors (Felice et al., 1999; Resnick, Chambliss, & Blum, 1993).

One explanation for this clustering of risk behaviors comes from deviance theory, articulated for adolescent health behavior in Jessor's theory of problem behavior (Jessor, 1992; Jessor, Donovan, & Costa, 1991). Deviance theory suggests people who do not fit the social norms of a group are treated differently by, and set themselves apart from, the group. In Jessor's theory, adolescents who depart from social norms in one area of behavior are less likely to adhere to norms governing other areas. It could be they are less connected to the community, and so less influenced by the group's norms. Or they may find a smaller group of nonnormative peers, and together they reinforce each other's risky behaviors. This part of Jessor's theory can be likened to society's explanation of adolescents who "get into a bad crowd."

LGB teens who recognize their orientation during adolescence clearly do not fit the normative social messages of heterosexual erotic attractions, leading to heterosexual romantic involvement, leading to heterosexual marriage, then heterosexual intercourse, and ultimately, heterosexual procreation. Jessor's theory would suggest their deviance from heterosexual norms in sexual attractions and romantic involvement disengages them from the influence of norms in other areas. Early sexual debut and pregnancy are still not considered normative for teens in general, so sexual-minority teens could feel less constraint about engaging in these behaviors—they might even feel a gay, lesbian, or bisexual identity is compatible with any sort of nonnormative sexual behavior. This disengagement could also foster other nonnormative behaviors such as smoking, drinking, illegal drug use, and violence. LGB teens may seek friendships with their peers in community support groups, in gay–straight alliance groups at school, and through the Internet (Rosario et al., 1996). If those LGB friends are adults in the urban gay bar scene, they might reinforce behaviors such as underage drinking or drug use.

Managing a Stigmatized Identity: Goffman's Theory and Troiden's Model

A different approach, although still derived from deviance theory, is Goffman's theory of stigma and its effects on identity (Goffman, 1963, 1968). In Goffman's theory, the focus is on identity rather than just behavior (i.e., a self-identity as gay, lesbian, or bisexual rather than a focus on same-gender sexual attractions or sexual behaviors). For Goffman, deviant characteristics carry stigma in the community, and identities associated with those characteristics are stigmatized. Depending on how visible the stigmatizing characteristics are, such identities can be already discredited (clearly stigmatized) or discreditable (only stigmatized if people know about it), so people engage in a variety of strategies to hide, reduce, or manage the stigma. Some people may adopt the normative group's behaviors to try to hide the stigma (i.e., as camouflage). Some may do so to completely deny their stigmatized identity or to try to "cure" themselves of their stigma. Troiden (1988) identified coping responses in early stages of LGB development from Goffman's idea of stigma management. He described denial and avoidance strategies, such as "heterosexual immersion," or frequent heterosexual intercourse, to cure oneself of same-gender attractions or to hide one's identity. Troiden noted, "an adolescent girl may purposely become pregnant to 'prove' that she isn't lesbian" (p. 108). Thus sexual-minority teens may choose heterosexual intercourse or pregnancy to avoid or hide the stigma linked to same-gender attractions, behaviors, or identity.

Response to Trauma and Violence: Finkelhor's Traumagenic Dynamics Model

Another explanation involves coping with stigma, but a different type of stigma. Several studies in the past two decades have noted a higher prevalence of sexual abuse history among LGB adolescents and adults than among heterosexual peers (Murphy, Sidhu, & Tonkin, 1999; Peters & Cantrell, 1991; Saewyc, Skay, Bearinger, Blum, & Resnick, 1998a; Saewyc, Skay, & Pettingell, 2004; Simari & Baskin, 1982). The reasons suggested for this higher risk vary. Early theories posited sexual abuse and negative sexual experiences were actually a cause of homosexuality, especially for women (Simari & Baskin, 1982). It has also been linked to higher risk of sexual assault among homeless or runaway teens because LGB adolescents are disproportionately represented among homeless teens (Farrow, Deisher, Brown, Kulig, & Kipke, 1992; Murphy, Peters, & Tonkin, 1994; Murphy et al., 1999). Homeless teens often use survival sex or prostitution to support themselves (Rotheram-Borus, Marelich, & Srinivasan, 1999). Another theory, derived from studies of sexual abuse of young boys (Holmes & Slap, 1998), suggests that gender-atypical behaviors in childhood, or same-gender attractions in adolescence, may marginalize sexual-minority teens, so they are more vulnerable to abuse. Disclosing a gay or bisexual orientation can lead a youth to be targeted by family or others for violence, including sexual violence (D'Augelli, Hershberger, & Pilkington, 1998); in a study of Vancouver LGB and transgender adolescents (Murphy et al., 1999), nearly 10% reported at least one sexual abuse experience was directly due to perceived sexual orientation.

Sexual abuse has also been associated with teen pregnancy in the general population (Boyer & Fine, 1992; Saewyc, Magee, & Pettingell, 2004; Stevens & Reichert, 1994). Whatever the reasons for a higher prevalence, the traumatic effects of sexual abuse may play the same role in teen pregnancy for LGB teens as for heterosexual teens. Finkelhor and Browne (1985) described these effects in their traumagenic dynamics model of sexual abuse. According to this theory, four trauma-causing factors, or traumagenic dynamics, alter abused children's cognitive and emotional interactions and distort their sense of self and worldviews. Their attempts to cope with their environments within these distorted perceptions may include risky behaviors and ongoing mental health problems. The four traumagenic dynamics are (a) *traumatic sexualization*, in which a child's sexuality is profoundly shaped by abuse, resulting in dysfunctional or developmentally inappropriate sexual behaviors; (b) *betrayal*, by the abuser, who may hold a position of love, trust, or authority, and by family members who do not protect or believe the victim; (c) *powerlessness* or *disempowerment*, as the child's self-efficacy and will are constantly denied during abuse, or by an inability to get adults to intervene; and (d) *stigmatization*, guilt and shame for being forced into activity that is considered wrong and needing to keep the abuse secret, even after it may have stopped.

As a result of these dynamics, sexually abused teens are more likely to engage in compulsive sexual behaviors, risky sex work or prostitution, and unprotected intercourse with multiple partners, which in turn can lead to pregnancy (Boyer & Fine, 1992; Fiscella, Kitzman, Cole, Sidora, & Olds, 1998; Widom & Kuhns, 1996). According to Finkelhor and Brown (1985), teens with a history of sexual abuse may be less able to negotiate sexual practices and contraception and are at increased risk for further sexual victimization. Several studies suggest they may use illicit drugs as a coping method (C. M. Anderson, Teicher, Polcari, & Renshaw, 2002) and are more prone to depression and suicidal behavior (Holmes & Slap, 1998).

Coping With Toxic Environments: Barker and Musick's International View of Teen Pregnancy

A related approach to teen pregnancy that may be salient for LGB teens is the suggestion that teen pregnancy is a method of coping with developmentally toxic environments for vulnerable young people around the world, including street-involved teens, prostitutes, and sexually abused teens (Barker & Musick, 1994). In their exploration of "survival nests," the cluster of behaviors that vulnerable adolescents use to lessen effects of damaging life circumstances (drug use, risky sex, pregnancy, and violence), Barker and Musick concluded pregnancy may be one of the most positive coping methods. Recent studies have tended to support that assertion for incarcerated adolescents (N. L. Anderson, 1990) and homeless pregnant teens (Saewyc, 2003). Given that LGB teens are disproportionately represented among runaways and homeless adolescents in the United States and

Canada (Farrow et al., 1992; Murphy et al., 1994), such teens may cope with toxic environments by becoming involved in a pregnancy.

Clearly, adolescent pregnancy has no simple cause, or single causal factor, in the general population, and this is likely to be the same among sexual-minority teens. These main theoretical perspectives, although developed among primarily heterosexual populations, may be useful in explaining the higher prevalence of teen pregnancy among LGB adolescents. However, is there empirical evidence that supports any or all of these theoretical approaches?

EMPIRICAL EVIDENCE ON THE CAUSES AND CORRELATES OF TEEN PREGNANCY

Teen pregnancy, like all pregnancy, requires a particular event: heterosexual intercourse without effective contraception at a time when conception is possible. In human fertility, it is generally a numbers game: The earlier intercourse begins after puberty, and the more often unprotected intercourse occurs, the more likely a pregnancy will be conceived. For adolescents in the general population, certain risk behaviors have been associated with teen pregnancy: (a) early age of sexual debut (age 14 or younger); (b) multiple opposite-sex partners; (c) frequent intercourse; (d) lack of effective contraception (or infrequent use of contraceptives); and (e) using alcohol or drugs before sex, which usually contributes to lack of contraception (Felice et al., 1999). These same risk behaviors have been linked to sexual abuse history, itself a risk factor for teen pregnancy (Boyer & Fine, 1992; Pierre, Shrier, Emans, & DuRant, 1998; Saewyc, Magee, & Pettingell, 2004). Although LGB adolescents are seldom identified in large-scale studies of the general population, there is growing evidence they engage in these identified risk behaviors. This evidence is found both in subsamples of population-based studies and in smaller studies with convenience samples of sexual-minority teens. However, we have just begun to explore whether these same risks are actually linked to teen pregnancy among LGB adolescents.

What Do We Know About the Heterosexual Behaviors of Lesbian, Gay, and Bisexual Teens?

There is extensive evidence that sexual-minority adolescents are as likely to engage in heterosexual intercourse as their heterosexual peers, both before and after coming out, and they may have more lifetime sexual partners. Five recent studies with nonprobability samples of sexual-minority teens show a high proportion are sexually experienced. In a study of 76 lesbian or bisexual girls and 80 gay or bisexual boys in New York City, for example, Rosario and colleagues (1996) found 61% of girls and 46% of boys had a history of penile–vaginal sex, and the majority of both girls (80%) and boys (56%) had some history of sexual activity with other-sex partners. Nearly half of 77 self-identified LGB teens interviewed in Vancouver in 1997 reported opposite-gender sexual intercourse, similar to heterosexual students in an earlier school-based survey in British Columbia, where 54% of 12th-grade students reported intercourse (Murphy et al., 1999). However, the LGB teens reported a greater number of opposite-gender partners, both lifetime and in the past 3 months. In a study of 544 adolescents from the United States and Canada, D'Augelli (2000) found 73% of girls and 52% of boys reported heterosexual experience. In an earlier study of 239 gay and bisexual young men, Remafedi (1994) found 42% reported recent vaginal sex with female partners. Likewise, in a study of 89 lesbian and bisexual young women in New York state, Diamond (1998) noted 80% of respondents reported at least one other-sex romantic-sexual relationship. Since fewer than half of school-based adolescents in general have reported heterosexual intercourse in recent years of the national Youth Risk Behavior Surveys (YRBS; Kann et al., 1998) the evidence above suggests at least self-identified LGB teens are as likely to have experienced heterosexual sex as their peers.

There is also evidence for this in the population-based or large-scale school-based surveys. In 1986, the school-based statewide Minnesota AHS, a stratified random sample of more than 34,000 teens (French, Story, Remafedi, Resnick, & Blum, 1996), found students with same-gender sexual experiences were more likely to also report opposite-gender sexual experiences than those without same-gender experience (73% vs. 61%), and students who identified as homosexual were just as likely as those who identified as heterosexual to have heterosexual sexual experiences (65%). Using a matched sample of 3,816 female students from that study, Saewyc et al. (1999) explored sexual behaviors among self-identified lesbian and bisexual girls, "unsure" girls, and self-identified heterosexual girls. We found lesbian and bisexual students were as likely as heterosexual students to report intercourse (33% vs. 29%) but were significantly more likely to have frequent intercourse (daily or more than twice a week, 22% vs. 14.5%, $p < .001$). They were also more likely to report a sexual debut before age 14 (62% vs. 45%, $p < .05$). However, because lesbian and bisexual girls reported a higher prevalence of sexual abuse history than the heterosexual girls (22.1% vs. 15.3%, $p < .01$), we conducted further analyses to control for abuse history. When we did so, the significant difference in early sexual debut between lesbian or bisexual girls and heterosexual girls disappeared, whereas likelihood of intercourse remained the same between the two groups, and frequency of intercourse remained significantly higher.

In a 1991 national survey of 13,454 reservation-based American Indian adolescents, Saewyc et al. (1998a) found that self-identified bisexual girls reported the highest prevalence of intercourse (43%), compared with 38% of heterosexual and 25% of lesbian girls, whereas heterosexual, bisexual, and gay boys were all as likely to report having heterosexual intercourse (46%–48%). Among sexually experienced American Indian adolescents in the same survey, lesbian and bisexual girls were more likely to report early sexual debut (before age 14) and more frequent intercourse; gay and bisexual boys were more likely than heterosexual peers to report early sexual debut (Saewyc et al., 1998a). The 1995 Massachusetts YRBS, which included an item on self-identified orientation, found gay, lesbian, or bisexual orientation was linked to intercourse before 13 years old and with four or more sexual partners, both over the lifetime and in the past 3 months (Garofalo et al., 1998).

A word of caution is needed here. Most surveys use the term *sexual intercourse*, and the context of the question usually implies heterosexual intercourse; there is recent evidence gay, lesbian, or bisexual teens interpret it this way (Austin, Conron, & Patel, 2004). However, because these are cross-sectional surveys, they cannot reveal whether the heterosexual behavior occurred before or after self-identity for most teens. Further, surveys that ask about gender of recent sexual partners usually do not ask about identity also, and there is often some discordance between identity, attractions, and behavior during adolescence, when orientation unfolds (Saewyc, Bauer, et al., 2004). Thus, the way orientation is measured may slightly change the samples under consideration. Equally important, studies often combine gay and bisexual teens in a single category. Depending on which group is larger, this may mask findings that differ for the other group (i.e., bisexual teens may be responsible for all the teen pregnancy involvement). However, studies of sexual orientation development have demonstrated teens may switch labels between gay and bisexual and back over adolescence (Diamond, 1998; Rosario et al., 1996), so it may not be important to differentiate between groups.

What Do We Know About Contraceptive Practices of Lesbian, Gay, and Bisexual Teens?

Research examining the contraceptive practices among sexual-minority teens is less common than research on their sexual behaviors, but provides some evidence that LGB adolescents may not use contraceptives as frequently as their sexually active heterosexual peers. In the Vancouver study, Murphy et al. (1999) found that LGB teens reported rates of condom use at last heterosexual intercourse (54%) similar to that of 12th graders in British Columbia (51%), but only 17% reported they or their partner used birth control pills at last intercourse, compared with 39% of 12th graders surveyed. In Remafedi's study of HIV risk among gay and bisexual boys (1994), 41% of respondents said they never used condoms during vaginal sex in the past year, and only 25% said they always used condoms during vaginal sex.

In contrast, a study of 512 high-risk gay, lesbian, bisexual, and heterosexual adolescents from New York, San Francisco, and Los Angeles (Rotheram-Borus et al., 1999) found that although heterosexual and bisexual boys and girls were more likely to engage in vaginal intercourse than gay or lesbian youths, the LGB adolescents were more likely to use condoms during vaginal intercourse than their heterosexual counterparts. Because the study was focused on risk for HIV and other sexually transmitted infections rather than pregnancy, it did not ask about other forms of contraception. These studies by Murphy et al., Remafedi, and Rotheram-Borus and colleagues drew their samples from among exclusively urban, "out" sexual-minority adolescents from different regions; thus, regional influences may account for reported differences in contraceptive practices, and these findings may not be representative of all LGB teens.

Among the large-scale school-based surveys, at present only two published studies my colleagues and I conducted (Saewyc et al., 1998a, 1999) and a further study's preliminary findings recently presented in Gallart and Saewyc (2004) have explored contraceptive behaviors among sexual-minority adolescents. The first study (Saewyc et al., 1998a) focused on the National American Indian AHS of 1991. Among sexually experienced American Indian adolescents, lesbian and bisexual girls were far more likely to report they rarely or never used contraceptives than were heterosexual girls (38.9% vs. 18.4%, $p < .001$); however, they were no more likely than their heterosexual peers to use ineffective methods, such as withdrawal, the rhythm method, or "no method." For American Indian boys, findings were the same: Gay and bisexual boys were significantly more likely to report they rarely used contraceptives compared with heterosexual boys (35.5% vs. 28%, $p < .05$), but they were just as likely to use effective methods when they did use contraception.

In the second study (Saewyc et al., 1999), we explored contraceptive behaviors in the matched sample of lesbian, bisexual, unsure, and heterosexual teens from the 1986 Minnesota AHS (matched by age and ethnicity). In this mostly European American sample, sexually experienced lesbian and bisexual girls were less likely to use contraception than were heterosexual girls (30% vs. 23% no contraception, respectively, $p < .001$); but among those who used any method, they were no more likely than peers to use ineffective methods (12% vs. 15%, ns).

Finally, Gallart and Saewyc (2004) recently presented a preliminary study of sexually experienced students from the 1998 Minnesota Student

Survey (MSS) who indicated gender of sexual partners in the past year (opposite-gender only, both-genders, and same-gender only, $N = 22,241$). The MSS is a statewide census of 9th and 12th graders conducted every 3 years. In this study, boys with exclusively opposite-gender partners were more likely to use a condom at last intercourse than either both-gender or same-gender groups (61.6% vs. 46.2% vs. 38.6%, $p < .001$); we identified similar patterns for girls (53.9% opposite-gender only, 47.5% both-gender, and 42.9% same-gender, $p < .05$). Both male and female students with only opposite-gender partners reported a higher frequency of birth control and of condom use than did their peers with both-gender or same-gender-only partners (Gallart & Saewyc, 2004).

Thus, the majority of studies to date report sexual-minority teens are less likely to use contraceptive methods than are their heterosexual peers, but when they do use contraceptives, they are just as likely to choose effective methods. Because the wording of such items on cross-sectional health surveys often refers to "last intercourse" without specifying time, it is unclear if responses refer to opposite-gender sexual experiences that are recent or long past.

Studies of Sexual Abuse and Sexual Orientation

As already mentioned, research has documented a higher prevalence of sexual abuse history among LGB adolescents. Although estimates of the prevalence of sexual abuse in the general population of adolescents varies widely depending on study sample, item wording, geographic region, or cohort in time, one of the largest recent studies of two populations of adolescents in the Midwest (73,000-plus and 77,000-plus youths in 1992 and 1998) found 10% to 15% of girls and 3% to 5% of boys reported a history of either incest, sexual abuse by a nonfamily adult, or both (Saewyc, Pettingell, & Magee, 2003). Similarly, the population-based 1995 Massachusetts YRBS found 8.1% of male students reported a history of forced sexual contact (Pierre et al., 1998). The prevalence of sexual abuse among LGB teens stands in stark contrast. In Remafedi's study (1994) of gay or bisexual boys, 42% reported a history of sexual abuse or sexual assault. In the Vancouver study (Murphy et al., 1999), 40% of those interviewed reported a history of sexual abuse.

How do these findings compare with population-based studies? In the Minnesota AHS, 22.1% of lesbian and bisexual girls reported a history of sexual abuse, compared with 15.3% of heterosexual peers (Saewyc et al., 1999). For American Indian girls, regardless of orientation, sexual abuse appears much higher than the general population: 42.4% of lesbian and bisexual girls from the 1991 survey indicated sexual abuse, as did 31.1% of heterosexual girls (Saewyc et al., 1998a). Among American Indian boys,

17.8% of gay and bisexual boys reported a history of abuse, compared with only 3.4% of heterosexual boys (Saewyc et al., 1998a). In the 1995 Massachusetts YRBS, Garofalo and colleagues (1998) reported gay, lesbian, and bisexual adolescents were more than three times as likely to report sexual abuse histories as their heterosexual peers. Saewyc, Pettingell, and Skay (2004) conducted a recent study of teen pregnancy and orientation in six different school-based surveys: the 1992 and 1998 British Columbia AHS (weighted; 1992, N = 237,748; 1998, N = 278,102); the 1992 and 1998 MSS (1992, N = 24,880; 1998, N = 22,007), and the 1995 and 1999 Seattle AHS (1995, N = 7,448; 1999, N = 7,610). We found bisexual boys had significantly higher odds of sexual abuse history than heterosexual boys (age-adjusted odds ratios, 5.67 to 16.67, all p < .01) and bisexual girls had higher odds of abuse than heterosexual girls, although differences were not as striking as for boys (age-adjusted odds ratios, 1.13 to 5.14, all p < .05). Odds of abuse for gay and lesbian teens in most surveys were similar to those for bisexual teens; nearly two in five lesbian or bisexual girls, and up to one in three gay and bisexual boys, reported sexual abuse.

Thus, regardless of region, year, and sample, 2 to 16 times as many LGB teens reported a history of sexual abuse as same-age heterosexual teens.

Studies of Homelessness and Prostitution Among Lesbian, Gay, and Bisexual Teens

Homeless adolescents and adolescents involved in prostitution or survival sex are far more likely to report pregnancy involvement than those who live with their families. Whereas an estimated 5% to 10% of teens throughout the United States report pregnancy involvement (Felice et al., 1999), nearly 10 times as many homeless adolescents are involved in pregnancy. A national study of homeless adolescents and runaways (Greene & Ringwalt, 1998) found 48% of street-involved teens and 33% of those living in shelters involved in pregnancy, as were 55% of girls and 42% of boys among homeless adolescents in Vancouver (Murphy et al., 1994).

LGB adolescents are disproportionately found among homeless teens and runaways (Cwayna, 1993; Farrow et al., 1992). In Murphy and colleagues' study of street-involved teens (1994), 23% of girls and 11% of boys identified as bisexual, and 4% of girls and 6% of boys identified as gay or lesbian. In contrast, in the province-wide, 1992 British Columbia school-based survey, only 1.6% identified as bisexual and fewer than 1% identified as gay or lesbian.

Similarly, prostitution or survival sex may be more prevalent among LGB adolescents, perhaps because of this increased risk for homelessness. In a study of HIV risk behaviors among LGB teens in New York, Rosario and colleagues (1999) reported 33% of sexual-minority girls and 17% of boys had exchanged sex for goods. In the Minnesota AHS, Saewyc et al. (1999) found sexually experienced lesbian and bisexual girls were five times as likely to report prostitution involvement in the past year as their heterosexual peers (9.7% vs. 1.9%, $p < .05$). Among those who had ever been pregnant, the association was even more profound: 44.4% of lesbian and bisexual teens had engaged in prostitution in the past year, as had only 5.5% of heterosexual peers ($p < .001$).

Studies Linking Sexual Abuse and Pregnancy

In the general population, there have been several studies linking adolescent pregnancy and a history of sexual abuse, mostly for girls, but increasingly for boys as well (Boyer & Fine, 1992; Fiscella et al., 1998; Pierre et al., 1998; Saewyc, Magee, & Pettingell, 2004; Stevens & Reichert, 1994; Widom & Kuhns, 1996). However, only one published study to date has examined the link between sexual abuse and pregnancy among sexual-minority adolescents, with mixed results. Among the 3,749 sexually experienced students who completed the National American Indian AHS, Saewyc et al. (1998a) found no difference in sexual abuse history among lesbian and bisexual versus heterosexual girls, and no significant difference in prevalence of pregnancy between sexual-minority and heterosexual girls either. In the same study, however, we found gay and bisexual boys were more likely to report sexual abuse than heterosexual boys, but no more likely to report a history of pregnancy involvement.

Beyond this indirect examination, however, as part of the same study we explored the risk factors significantly associated with adolescent pregnancy for each group of adolescents separately (heterosexual, gay, lesbian, bisexual, and unsure) to see if the patterns of risks associated with pregnancy were the same for each group, given the prevalence of pregnancy was the same. Among lesbian or bisexual girls and gay or bisexual boys, sexual abuse was *not* significantly associated with pregnancy. Indeed, for all American Indian girls in this sample, regardless of orientation, sexual abuse was not related to pregnancy, whereas for heterosexual and unsure boys, sexual abuse was significantly associated with pregnancy involvement.

These findings should also be considered with caution. In a demographic comparison between the American Indian national sample and rural Anglo-American adolescents from the Minnesota AHS using identically worded items, we found both a much higher prevalence of sexual-minority teens among American Indian adolescents and a much larger nonresponse rate to the orientation question (Saewyc et al., 1998a). Fewer than half of American Indian adolescents selected "100% heterosexual" as their response, compared with over 97% of Anglo-American teens from Minnesota, although the most frequent other response among American Indians was "unsure" rather than "bisexual," "mostly homosexual," or "100% homosexual (gay or lesbian)." Likewise, 17.4% to 26.7% of American Indian adolescents did not respond to the orientation questions, whereas only 4% to 11% of Minnesota students did not answer the same items. This raises questions about the cultural relevance of the survey for reservation-based adolescents. It could mean American Indian adolescents do not perceive the same levels of stigma around sexual-minority status; a wide array of historical evidence documents positive nonheterosexual identities within tribes across the United States (Saewyc et al., 1998a). The nonresponse rate, however, suggests American Indian adolescents may not conceptualize sexual orientation the same way Anglo-American adolescents do. The orientation questions with the largest nonresponse rate were those with wording that focused on same-gender and opposite-gender orientation, rather than labels like gay, lesbian, or bisexual; a startling 5% of the American Indian sample did not identify their gender, and these respondents were most likely not to answer the orientation questions (Saewyc, Skay, Bearinger, Blum, & Resnick, 1998b).

In our study of pregnancy among American Indian teens, the common correlates of teen pregnancy among heterosexual teens were different or absent for sexual-minority teens, especially for girls (Saewyc et al., 1998c). Because age was significantly associated with pregnancy for heterosexual girls and unsure and heterosexual boys, we controlled for age in our analyses. Among lesbian and bisexual American Indian girls, none of the common risk factors (such as abuse, early sexual debut, frequent intercourse, lack of contraception, or multiple partners) were significantly associated with a history of pregnancy, whereas for gay and bisexual boys, only frequency of intercourse, ineffective contraception, and a history of physical abuse were associated with pregnancy involvement.

Another approach to disentangling the influences of sexual abuse and sexual orientation on teen pregnancy involvement is to control for sexual abuse within the sample. In such a study my colleagues and I (Saewyc, Pettingell, & Magee, 2002) explored risk and protective factors for teen pregnancy involvement within two cohorts of sexually abused adolescents from the MSS in the 1990s (1992, $N = 4,674$; 1998, $N = 3,747$). In the MSS, two items assess incest and nonfamily sexual abuse. We used logistic regression and probability profiling to explore the likelihood of pregnancy involvement based on combinations of risk and protective factors, and we conducted separate analyses for girls and boys by type of abuse: incest only, nonfamily abuse only, or both. Sexual orientation was not directly measured in this survey, but two items asked about the number of male and female sexual partners in the past 12 months. (To reduce the chance that students reporting same-gender sexual partners were reporting a sexual abuse perpetrator as their only same-gender sexual partner, we defined same-gender sexual experience as two or more same-gender sexual partners in the past year. This inevitably undercounted sexual-minority teens with only one sexual partner, but because there was no way to determine consensual sexual behavior in this survey, we felt a more conservative approach was needed). With the exception of girls in 1998 who reported only nonfamily sexual abuse, among girls and boys in both years, regardless of type of abuse, same-gender sexual experience was one of the strongest risk factors for teen pregnancy involvement (adjusted odds ratios, 1.93–8.03, $p < .001$) and even when protective factors were present, same-gender sexual experience in the past year increased the probability of pregnancy involvement by 30% to 50%. This would suggest that not only are LGB teens more likely to experience sexual abuse and thus an increased risk for teen pregnancy but sexual-minority orientation exerts an additional, separate influence on teen pregnancy involvement.

Teen Pregnancy Among Sexual-Minority Adolescents

Although several studies report risk behaviors for pregnancy among LGB teens, there are fewer studies that actually report the prevalence of pregnancy among such teens, compare their pregnancy rates with those of heterosexual teens, or explore associated risk and protective factors. Among those already reported, Saewyc et al. (1999), a study of girls from the Minnesota AHS of 1986, found lesbian and bisexual girls were more than twice as likely to have been pregnant than heterosexual girls, 12.3% versus 5.3% ($p < .01$). In contrast, among sexually experienced adolescents in the National American Indian AHS of 1991, Saewyc et al. (1998a) found no significant differences in prevalence of pregnancy by orientation for either boys or girls.

Other population-based surveys report increased prevalence of pregnancy among sexual-minority teens. In the 1997 Massachusetts YRBS, twice as many gay, lesbian, or bisexual adolescents reported pregnancy involvement as other respondents, 24% versus 12% (reported in Reis & Saewyc, 1999). Similarly, in the 1997 Vermont YRBS, sexually experienced adolescents who reported same-gender sexual experience were seven times as likely to report having been pregnant or gotten someone pregnant twice or more, 15% as compared with 2% (reported in Reis & Saewyc, 1999).

Most of these studies have combined gay or lesbian with bisexual teens. In Saewyc, Pettingell, and Skay (2004), a recent examination of teen pregnancy in the six school-based surveys from three regions in the 1990s, my colleagues and I disaggregated bisexual adolescents and gay or lesbian teens—or, in the MSS, teens with recent both-gender sexual partners—from those with exclusively same-gender partners. We found bisexual teens in all surveys significantly more likely than heterosexual teens to report pregnancy involvement (odds ratios ranged from 2.08–9.03 for bisexual vs. heterosexual, all $p < .001$). In most surveys gay and lesbian teens were just as likely to report prior pregnancy as the bisexual teens. We found the prevalence of pregnancy involvement declined among heterosexual teens in each pair of surveys from the earlier to later 1990s, as expected, but it increased among bisexual teens and was mixed for the gay and lesbian teens. When we controlled for sexual abuse history, it reduced the difference in pregnancy risk between bisexual and heterosexual teens and the bisexual and gay or lesbian teens, but most differences remained significant. Thus, sexual-minority teens are significantly more likely to be involved in pregnancy, a finding not solely driven by bisexual teens' behaviors, and during the 1990s pregnancy rates increased for sexual-minority teens while decreasing for heterosexual teens.

EVALUATING THEORIES OF TEEN PREGNANCY AND SEXUAL ORIENTATION

There is evidence to support each theory offered as an explanation for higher teen pregnancy rates among LGB adolescents. Several studies link sexual-minority status with sexual risk behaviors that lead to pregnancy; thus, Jessor's Theory of Problem Behavior seems to be supported by these studies. However, the competing explanations of Goffman and Finkelhor, of adolescents coping with stigma (either of non-normative sexual orientation or of sexual abuse), can also explain these increased risk behaviors. Likewise, Barker and Musick's theory that pregnancy may be a method of surviving the toxic environments of homeless youths, prostitutes, and sexually abused adolescents, is supported by evidence that sexual-minority teens are more likely to be homeless, to engage in prostitution, or to be sexually abused.

With four different theories supported by roughly the same findings, how do we decide which theory best explains the phenomenon? Unfortunately, current studies do not provide enough evidence to disentangle competing explanations. Many studies do not assess sexual abuse; even those with sexual abuse items do not necessarily control for that abuse in examining behaviors among groups who differ by orientation. Likewise, the studies are primarily cross-sectional, which creates the possibility that sexual abuse came after sexual debut, or after pregnancy, with no way to determine the actual order either way. Similarly, most of the studies cannot reveal whether the heterosexual behavior or pregnancy came before or after teens identified as gay, lesbian, or bisexual. Of the few studies that consider homelessness or prostitution, only Saewyc et al. (1999) directly connects prostitution and pregnancy among sexual-minority teens. And population-based studies do not usually include items to measure perceived stigma. For that matter, studies that explore some risks for teen pregnancy, such as unprotected sexual behaviors or multiple partners, often focus on sexually transmitted infections like HIV and do not ask about pregnancy. Many large-scale, school-based studies report prevalence of pregnancy but do not explore the patterns of risk behaviors associated with pregnancy for sexual-minority teens. This last issue may be particularly critical, in that the only study that compares pregnancy risk factors among gay, lesbian, bisexual, and heterosexual teens found patterns were quite different, even with a similar prevalence of pregnancy; but the study was among reservation-based American Indian adolescents only (Saewyc et al., 1998c).

Although all four theories have potential salience for explaining increased prevalence of pregnancy among LGB adolescents, I tend to support a synthesis of theories focused around stigma and coping with trauma, but with a different, potentially positive spin. Both Goffman's stigma management theory and the traumagenic dynamics theory identify stigma as a potent motivator for behaviors that can lead to pregnancy, whether that stigma is from sexual-minority status or from sexual abuse. Likewise, the traumagenic dynamics theory and Barker and Musick's "survival nests" identify similar behaviors used for coping with trauma and violence. The evidence from the research is clear: Many LGB teens are exposed to the toxic environments of harassment, homelessness, sexual abuse, and constant negative messages that reinforce their stigma. Confronted with the damaging mirror of society's attitudes toward gay, lesbian, or bisexual orientation, who would not want to change the face in the mirror? What alternate status can be a site of resistance to that stigma, a cry of hope for the future, a reclaiming of sexuality and worth? In our society, there is one status readily accessible to adolescents, imbued with positive virtues and value of mythic proportions: parenthood.

In 1999, I conducted an ethnographic study of homeless pregnant teens in Seattle to explore meanings of pregnancy and motherhood (Saewyc, 1999, 2003). I heard stories of sexual abuse, family abandonment, violence, substance use, survival sex, prior suicide attempts, and stigma. Most participants (one of whom identified as bisexual) told about escaping damaging family situations to find equally dangerous situations on the streets, of being the "bad girl," negotiating a life with few choices and less power. For these young women, pregnancy was a strong, positive event, which worked in several ways to change their life trajectories. The bisexual young woman in particular spoke of profound changes in her status with motherhood, of how her family, friends, even strangers treated her differently, and in turn, how pregnancy let her step away from harmful behaviors and forge a new life for herself and her child. I commonly heard from participants in the study and from homeless pregnant teens in my clinical practice a chilling assessment: If they had not gotten pregnant, they were not sure where they would be now, but they most likely would be dead. Given their life experiences, the prediction was a realistic and sobering one. The challenge is to find other ways to address the needs that pregnancy fulfills for these young women. A similar challenge confronts us among sexual-minority teens.

What does pregnancy mean for LGB adolescents? Is it an accidental and unwelcome side effect of behaviors that are used to cope with stigma? Is it a deliberate step toward a future with more hopeful outcomes, a greater sense of self-worth, or a more positive status? Until we actually offer LGB adolescents a chance to tell their stories and share their perspectives, we are left with a tantalizing finding, some potential theoretical explanations, and ambiguous evidence from which to suggest interventions.

WHERE DO WE GO NEXT? RECOMMENDATIONS FOR FURTHER RESEARCH

The evidence presented here, although it forms a compelling picture, really consists of indirect observations from studies designed for very different purposes, or preliminary investigations into a phenomenon that has gone unnoticed until quite recently. One of the most important next steps is to further document the prevalence of teen pregnancy among different populations of sexual-minority teens across the world, to substantiate the trend we observed in specific locations in the United States and Canada from two decades of school-based research. A related question not yet examined is pregnancy outcome: How many pregnant lesbian or bisexual teens terminate their pregnancies? How many suffer miscarriage or prenatal complications? How many choose to parent—or relinquish for adoption?

At the same time, it is equally important to explore LGB teens' own views of their heterosexual behavior and pregnancy involvement. Qualitative studies can develop rich knowledge of the contexts in which teens negotiate sexual and reproductive health. They help us create interventions that are teen-centered and more likely to be effective. If gay, lesbian, or bisexual teens have different reasons than their heterosexual peers for being involved in pregnancy, current pregnancy prevention efforts in mainstream society may be ineffective, and may need to be adapted to address their unique needs.

In surveys that explore sexual behaviors, pregnancy, and sexual orientation among adolescents, it is important to include items assessing sexual abuse, to help disentangle the influences of orientation and abuse. Large-scale, cross-sectional studies of diverse populations of teens in schools or community settings can help track the prevalence of health behaviors.

Longitudinal studies can track their sequence among LGB adolescents, can help determine environmental and developmental contexts in which teen pregnancy is likely, and can further refine theories. An understanding of geographic, cultural, and age-related variations in teen pregnancy among sexual-minority adolescents is also needed and, where possible, the opportunity to compare gay and lesbian teens separately from bisexual teens, and from their heterosexual and unsure peers. Further, do pregnant lesbian and bisexual teens and their partners access prenatal care early enough (or at all?), and do they receive enough supportive care to ensure healthy outcomes? What about parenting? What are the environments and contexts for LGB teen parents?

The pregnant young women, their supportive girlfriends, the young expectant fathers and their male buddies, all nervously seated in the waiting room of a maternity clinic, might be heterosexual. Then again, they might not.

REFERENCES

Anderson, C. M., Teicher, M. H., Polcari, A., & Renshaw, P. F. (2002). Abnormal T2 relaxation time in the cerebellar vermis of adults sexually abused in childhood: Potential role of the vermis in stress-enhanced risk for drug abuse. *Psychoneuroendocrinology, 27,* 231–244.

Anderson, N. L. (1990). Pregnancy resolution decisions in juvenile detention. *Archives of Psychiatric Nursing, 4,* 325–31.

Austin, S. B., Conron, K. J., & Patel, A. (2004). Measures of sexual orientation in epidemiologic surveys: Findings from a cognitive processing study with adolescents [Abstract]. *Journal of Adolescent Health, 34,* 113–114.

Barker, G., & Musick, J. (1994). Rebuilding nests of survival: A comparative analysis of the needs of at-risk adolescent women and adolescent mothers in the U.S., Latin America, Asia and Africa. *Childhood, 2,* 152–163.

Boyer, D., & Fine, D. (1992). Sexual abuse as a factor in adolescent pregnancy and child maltreatment. *Family Planning Perspectives, 24,* 4–11.

Burke, P. J. (1987). Adolescents' motivation for sexual activity and pregnancy prevention. *Issues in Comprehensive Pediatric Nursing, 10,* 161–171.

Cwayna, K. (1993). *Knowing where the fountains are: Stories and stark realities of homeless youth.* Minneapolis, MN: Deacon Press.

D'Augelli, A. R. (2000, June). *Sexual orientation milestones and adjustment among lesbian, gay, and bisexual youths from 14 to 21 years of age.* Paper presented at the 7th Biennial Conference of the European Association for Research on Adolescence, Jena, Germany.

D'Augelli, A. R., Hershberger, S. L., & Pilkington, N. W. (1998). Lesbian, gay, and bisexual youth and their families: Disclosure of sexual orientation and its consequences. *American Journal of Orthopsychiatry, 68,* 361–375.

Diamond, L. M. (1998). Development of sexual orientation among adolescent and young adult women. *Developmental Psychology, 34,* 1085–1095.

Farrow, J. A., Deisher, R. W., Brown, R., Kulig, J. K., & Kipke, M. (1992). Health and health needs of homeless and runaway youth: A position paper of the Society for Adolescent Medicine. *Journal of Adolescent Health, 13,* 717–726.

Feldmann, J., & Middleman, A. B. (2002). Adolescent sexuality and sexual behavior. *Current Opinion in Obstetrics and Gynecology, 14,* 489–493.

Felice, M. E., Feinstein, R. A., Fisher, M. M., Kaplan, D. W., Olmedo, L. F., Rome, E. S., & Staggers, B. C. (1999). Adolescent pregnancy—Current trends and issues: 1998 American Academy of Pediatrics Committee on Adolescence. *Pediatrics, 103,* 516–519.

Finkelhor, D., & Browne, A. (1985). The traumatic impact of child sexual abuse: A conceptualization. *American Journal of Orthopsychiatry, 55,* 530–540.

Fiscella, K., Kitzman, H. J., Cole, R. E., Sidora, K. J., & Olds, D. (1998). Does child abuse predict adolescent pregnancy? *Pediatrics, 101,* 620–624.

French, S. A., Story, M., Remafedi, G., Resnick, M. D., & Blum, R. W. (1996). Sexual orientation and prevalence of body dissatisfaction and eating disordered behaviors: A population-based study of adolescents. *International Journal of Eating Disorders, 19,* 119–126.

Gallart, H., & Saewyc, E. (2004). Sexual orientation and contraceptive behaviors among Minnesota adolescents [Abstract]. *Journal of Adolescent Health, 34,* 141.

Garofalo, R., Wolf, R. C., Kessel, S., Palfrey, J., & DuRant, R. H. (1998). The association between health risk behaviors and sexual orientation among a school-based sample of adolescents. *Pediatrics, 101,* 895–902.

Goffman, E. (1963). *Stigma: Notes on the management of spoiled identity.* Englewood Cliffs, NJ: Prentice-Hall.

Goffman, E. (1968). Management of spoiled identity. In E. Rubington & M. S. Weinberg (Eds.), *Deviance, the interactionist perspective: Text and readings in the sociology of deviance* (pp. 344–348). New York: MacMillan.

Greene, J. M., & Ringwalt, C. L. (1998). Pregnancy among three national samples of runaway and homeless youth. *Journal of Adolescent Health, 23,* 370–377.

Holmes, W. C., & Slap, G. B. (1998). Sexual abuse of boys: Definition, prevalence, correlates, sequelae, and management. *Journal of the American Medical Association, 280,* 1855–1862.

Jessor, R. (1992). Risk behavior in adolescence: A psychosocial framework for understanding and action. In D. E. Rogers & E. Ginzberg (Eds.), *Adolescents at risk: Medical and social perspectives* (pp. 19–34). Boulder, CO: Westview Press.

Jessor, R., Donovan, J. E., & Costa, F. M. (1991). *Beyond adolescence: Problem behavior and young adult development.* Cambridge, England: Cambridge University Press.

Kann, L., Kinchen, S. A., Williams, B. I., Ross, J. G., Lowry, R., Hill, C. V., et al. (1998). Youth Risk Behavior Surveillance—United States, 1997. *Morbidity and Mortality Weekly Report, 47.*

Luker, K. (1996). Bastardy, fitness, and the invention of adolescence. In K. Luker (Ed.), *Dubious conceptions: The politics of teenage pregnancy* (pp. 15–42). Cambridge, MA: Harvard University Press.

Murphy, A., Peters, L., & Tonkin, R. (1994). *Adolescent health survey: Street youth in Vancouver.* Burnaby, British Columbia, Canada: McCreary Centre Society.

Murphy, A., Sidhu, A., & Tonkin, R. (1999). *Being out: Lesbian, gay, bisexual, and transgender youth in BC, an adolescent health survey.* Burnaby, British Columbia, Canada: McCreary Centre Society.

Peters, D. K., & Cantrell, P. J. (1991). Factors distinguishing samples of lesbian and heterosexual women. *Journal of Homosexuality, 21,* 1–15.

Pierre, N., Shrier, L. A., Emans, S. J., & DuRant, R. H. (1998). Adolescent males involved in pregnancy: Associations of forced sexual contact and risk behaviors. *Journal of Adolescent Health, 23,* 362–369.

Reis, E., & Saewyc, E. (1999). *83,000 youth: Selected findings of eight population-based studies as they pertain to anti-gay harassment and the safety and well-being of sexual minority students.* Seattle: Safe Schools Coalition of Washington.

Remafedi, G. (1994). Predictors of unprotected intercourse among gay and bisexual youth: Knowledge, beliefs, and behavior. *Pediatrics, 94,* 163–168.

Resnick, M. D., Chambliss, S., & Blum, R. W. (1993). Health and risk behaviors of urban adolescent males involved in pregnancy. *Families in Society, 74,* 366–374.

Rosario, M., Meyer-Bahlburg, H. F., Hunter, J., Exner, T. M., Gwadz, M., & Arden, K. M. (1996). The psychosexual development of urban lesbian, gay, and bisexual youths. *Journal of Sex Research, 33,* 113–126.

Rosario, M., Meyer-Bahlburg, H. F., Hunter, J., & Gwadz, M. (1999). Sexual risk behaviors of gay, lesbian and bisexual youths in New York City: Prevalence and correlates. *AIDS Education and Prevention, 11,* 476–496.

Rotheram-Borus, M. J., Mahler, K. A., Koopman, C., & Langabeer, K. (1996). Sexual abuse history and associated multiple risk behavior in adolescent runaways. *American Journal of Orthopsychiatry, 66,* 390–400.

Rotheram-Borus, M. J., Marelich, W. D., & Srinivasan, S. (1999). HIV risk among homosexual, bisexual, and heterosexual male and female youths. *Archives of Sexual Behavior, 28,* 159–177.

Saewyc, E. M. (1999). Meanings of pregnancy and motherhood among out-of-home pregnant adolescents. *Dissertation Abstracts International-B, 60*(11), 5437. (UMI No. 9952892)

Saewyc, E. M. (2003). Influential life contexts and environments for out-of-home pregnant adolescents. *Journal of Holistic Nursing, 21,* 343–367.

Saewyc, E. M., Bauer, G. R., Skay, C. L., Bearinger, L. H., Resnick, M. D., Reis, E., & Murphy, A. (2004). Measuring sexual orientation in adolescent health surveys: Evaluation of eight school-based surveys. *Journal of Adolescent Health,*

35, 345e.1-345e.15. Retrieved October 1, 2004, from http://journals.elsevier health.com/periodicals/JAH

Saewyc, E. M., Bearinger, L., Blum, R., & Resnick, M. (1999). Sexual intercourse, abuse and pregnancy among adolescent women: Does sexual orientation make a difference? *Family Planning Perspectives, 31,* 127–131.

Saewyc, E. M., Magee, L., & Pettingell, S. (2004). Teenage pregnancy and associated risk behaviors among sexually abused adolescents. *Perspectives in Sexual and Reproductive Health, 36,* 98–105.

Saewyc, E. M., Pettingell, S. L., & Magee, L. L. (2002, June). *Pregnancy among sexually abused adolescents: Models of risk and protective factors.* Paper presented at the 13th International Congress on Women's Health Issues, Seoul, Korea.

Saewyc, E. M., Pettingell, S. L., & Magee, L. L. (2003). The prevalence of sexual abuse among adolescents in school. *Journal of School Nursing, 19,* 266–272.

Saewyc, E. M., Pettingell, S. L., & Skay, C. L. (2004). Teen pregnancy among sexual minority youth in population-based surveys of the 1990s: Countertrends in a population at risk [Abstract]. *Journal of Adolescent Health, 34,* 125–126.

Saewyc, E. M., Skay, C., Bearinger, L., Blum, R., & Resnick, M. (1998a). Demographics of sexual orientation among American Indian adolescents. *American Journal of Orthopsychiatry, 68,* 590–600.

Saewyc, E. M., Skay, C., Bearinger, L., Blum, R., & Resnick, M. (1998b). [Gender responses on the National American Indian Adolescent Health Survey]. Unpublished raw data.

Saewyc, E. M., Skay, C., Bearinger, L., Blum, R., & Resnick, M. (1998c). Sexual orientation, sexual behaviors, and pregnancy among American Indian adolescents. *Journal of Adolescent Health, 23,* 238–247.

Saewyc, E. M., Skay, C. L., & Pettingell, S. L. (2004). Hazards of stigma: The sexual and physical abuse of gay, lesbian, and bisexual adolescents in the U.S. and Canada [Abstract]. *Journal of Adolescent Health, 34,* 115–116.

Simari, C. G., & Baskin, D. (1982). Incestuous experiences within homosexual populations: A preliminary study. *Archives of Sexual Behavior, 11,* 329–343.

Stevens, S. C., & Reichert, S. (1994). Sexual abuse, adolescent pregnancy, and child abuse: A developmental approach to an intergenerational cycle. *Archives of Pediatrics and Adolescent Medicine, 148,* 23–27.

Troiden, R. R. (1988). Homosexual identity development. *Journal of Adolescent Health Care, 9,* 105–113.

Ward, M. (1995). Early childbearing: What is the problem and who owns it? In F. D. Ginsburg & R. Rapp (Eds.), *Conceiving the new world order: The global politics of reproduction* (pp. 140–158). Berkeley: University of California Press.

Widom, C., & Kuhns, J. (1996). Childhood victimization and subsequent risk for promiscuity, prostitution, and teenage pregnancy: A prospective study. *American Journal of Public Health, 86,* 1607–1611.

Zabin, L. S., Astone, N. M., & Emerson, M. R. (1993). Do adolescents want babies? The relationship between attitudes and behavior. *Journal of Research on Adolescence, 3,* 67–86.

6

RELIGION AND HEALTH AMONG LESBIAN, GAY, AND BISEXUAL YOUTHS: AN EMPIRICAL INVESTIGATION AND THEORETICAL EXPLANATION

MARGARET ROSARIO, ANN MARIE YALI, JOYCE HUNTER, AND MARYA VIORST GWADZ

In the United States, Gallup polls consistently find that approximately 96% of the population believe in God, 90% say religion is "very important or fairly important" in their lives, 75% pray regularly, approximately 40% attend religious worship weekly, and 60% attend monthly (Gallup, 1995, 1996). Religion is often viewed as a source for coping with life's existential questions such as "What is the meaning of life?" "How do I deal with death, suffering, and injustice?" and "What do I do about my failings and shortcomings?" (Batson, Schoenrade, & Ventis, 1993; Baumeister, 1991;

This work was supported by center Grant P50-MH43520 from the National Institute of Mental Health. Margaret Rosario, principal investigator, HIV Risk and Coming Out Among Gay and Lesbian Adolescents; Anke A. Ehrhardt, principal investigator, HIV Center for Clinical and Behavioral Studies. We extend our appreciation to Brenda Cole, Tracey Revenson, and Eric Schrimshaw for their comments on an earlier version of this chapter.

Pargament, 1997). In addition, religion has salutary effects on physical and psychological health (e.g., Koenig, 1997; Levin & Schiller, 1987; Worthington, Kurusu, McCullough, & Sandage, 1996); indeed, those who are religiously involved live longer than those who report little or no religious involvement (Hummer, Rogers, Nam, & Ellison, 1999; McCullough, Hoyt, Larson, Koenig, & Thoreson, 2000). However, religion's impact on health may not generalize to all segments of the population. For lesbian, gay, and bisexual (LGB) individuals, the effects of religion on mental and physical health are largely unknown. Given the condemnation of homosexuality by a majority of religious groups, one might predict that religion would have a negative effect on the physical and psychological health of this group. In this chapter, we provide an empirical investigation and theoretical explanation of the associations of religion with the health and protective factors of LGB youths.[1]

EVIDENCE OF RELIGION'S IMPACT ON HEALTH AND PROTECTIVE FACTORS

Most of the research on religion and health behaviors has been conducted with adult populations. However, there is some evidence that religion has similar benefits for adolescents (Weaver et al., 2000). Religious values and involvement tend to be associated with less alcohol and drug use among adolescents (McBride, Mutch, & Chitwood, 1996; Wallace & Forman, 1998) and with abstinence from premarital sex (Woodroof, 1985). In a large midwestern sample of young people, 12 to 18 years of age, religiosity was associated with less suicide ideation, greater self-esteem, less alcohol use, less binge drinking, less marijuana and cigarette smoking, and fewer sexual encounters (Donahue & Benson, 1995).

Gender differences and differences among ethnic groups have been found with regard to religion, but those differences do not moderate health-related behaviors. Across several studies of younger adolescents and college students who were asked to rate how important religion is to them, girls rated religion as more important than did boys, and minority groups (Blacks and Latinos) rated religion as more important than did Whites (Hyde, 1990; Silber & Riley, 1985). With respect to health-related behaviors, Zaleski

---

[1] In this chapter, we use the term *religion* broadly. According to Pargament (1997) and *Webster's Concise Dictionary* (Landau, 1997), religion has multiple defining facets, such as affiliation or identity, practices, religiosity, spirituality, and institutions of dogma. We concentrate primarily, although not exclusively, on religion as identity and religiosity. The aim of the chapter is not to engage in a discussion of the facets and their relative associations with health and protective factors. The aim is more modest: to understand and investigate the connections between (any aspect of) religion and the health and protective factors of LGB youths.

and Schiaffino (2000) found that higher rates of religiosity were related to being more likely to be sexually abstinent, regardless of gender, among freshmen attending a Roman Catholic university in New York. However, among the sexually active youths in this study, those who were more religious tended to use condoms inconsistently, regardless of gender.

The overwhelming majority of studies on religion and health do not report the sexual orientation of their participants and, thus, it is assumed that the samples are predominantly heterosexual. In addition, the failure to study the influence of religion in the lives of LGB individuals is not surprising. The predominant religions tend to view homosexuality as unnatural and sinful (Gillis, 1998), and researchers may have failed to include religion in their studies because they assumed that most LGB individuals had severed their childhood religious connections because of the negative views about their lifestyle.

The small but growing literature on spirituality and religion among LGB individuals is beginning to shed light on the role and importance of religion for these individuals. For example, one might predict that such individuals would not self-identify as being religious on the basis of the historical negative treatment of gay men and lesbians by religious people and religious institutions. Indeed, in an early study, Bell and Weinberg (1978) found that the majority of 976 LGB adults reported that they were not at all or not too religious, although a large minority said they were moderately to very religious (22% of White men, 35% of Black men, 19% of White women and 38% of Black women). It is interesting to note that the rate of church attendance was higher among men than women.

Few empirical studies of LGB individuals focus on the relations between religion and health and protective factors. In one study, religion predicted improved immune functioning and emotional health in gay men with HIV (Woods, Antoni, Ironson, & Kling, 1999). Religious behavior (e.g., reading religious material, having spiritual discussions, attending religious services) was associated with a higher CD4+ T cell count, accounting for 15% of the variance in immune status, independent of disease-progression factors.[2] Moreover, religious coping (e.g., putting trust in God, seeking God's help, finding comfort in religion) was associated with less depression, accounting for 10% of the variance. Similarly, an early study of gay men attending the Gay Metropolitan Church reported significantly higher levels of self-confidence than nonattendees who were recruited from gay bars and friendship networks (Clingman & Fowler, 1976). However, other studies have

---

[2] Immune function is measured in several ways. For HIV infection, a common marker of immune functioning is CD4+ T cell count. The assault of HIV on the immune system is assessed by decreased CD4+ count.

found greater guilt and alienation and lower self-esteem among gay men with a religious affiliation (Greenberg, 1973).

We have found only one study that examined religious factors among LGB youths. Of the participants, ages 14 to 23 years, close to 80% reported that they were not at all religious and seldom attended religious services, but nearly 85% reported a religious affiliation (Savin-Williams, 1990). Religiosity was not related significantly, for either the male or the female youths, to self-esteem or degree of self-disclosure of sexual identity to others. Unfortunately, no health behaviors were assessed.

Given the scant empirical literature and the age of this literature, we were interested in examining the associations of religion with the health and protective factors of LGB youths, expecting positive relations between religion and these factors. We also examined the relations between religion and gay-related stress, hypothesizing that religion would be associated with experiencing gay-related stress, specifically gay-related stress from kin. Further, our analyses were conducted by gender.

THE EMPIRICAL INVESTIGATION

Participants

We interviewed 164 self-identified LGB youths, ages 14 to 21 years, during October 1993 through 1994. Eight were excluded for methodological reasons or because they did not meet study protocol criteria. Detailed information about the sample and study procedures is available elsewhere (Rosario et al., 1996).

Of the final sample of 80 males and 76 females, 66% identified as gay or lesbian, 31% as bisexual, and 3% as other (e.g., "free spirit"). The mean age of the sample was 18.3 years ($SD = 1.65$). The ethnic background of the youths was diverse: 37% Latino, 35% Black, 22% White, and 7% other. Of the participants, 34% (51/151) were of lower socioeconomic status, which meant that at least one parent was reported to have received entitlement benefits (i.e., welfare, food stamps, or Medicaid). The participants were recruited in Manhattan from two college-based organizations for LGB youths (15%) and from three gay-focused community-based organizations providing social and recreational services to such youths (85%).

Measures

Religion

We developed the Religion Inventory (Rosario & Gwadz, 1993b) to assess lifetime and current religious identification and commitment. We asked the participants to specify both the religion in which they were raised and their current religious identity, using the following response scale: 1 (*evangelical religion*; e.g., *Jehovah's Witness, Pentecostal*); 2 (*other Protestant*; *specify*); 3 (*Roman Catholic*); 4 (*Jewish*); 5 (*Islam or Muslim*); 6 (*Agnostic*); 7 (*other*; *specify*); and 8 (*none*). We assessed religiosity by asking the youths, "How religious do you consider yourself to be?" using a five-point Likert response scale from 1 (*not at all*) to 5 (*a whole lot*).

Sexual Behaviors and Their Potential Risks

We used the Sexual Risk Behavior Assessment Schedule—Youth (Meyer-Bahlburg, Ehrhardt, Exner, & Gruen, 1994) to assess the youths' sexual risk behaviors over their lifetime and recently (i.e., during the last 3 months). The reader is referred elsewhere for detailed discussion of the variables reported herein (Rosario, Meyer-Bahlburg, Hunter, & Gwadz, 1999). Here, we primarily define or clarify terms. A "sexual encounter" involves a sexual meeting in which the youth engages in one or more sexual practices with the partner(s). "Ever having a risky partner" refers to at least one same-sex or other-sex partner who had injected drugs, had a sexually transmitted disease (STD), or had HIV or AIDS. Youths were asked if they ever exchanged sex for goods (i.e., money, drugs, or lodgings). Numbers of recent unprotected anal or oral sexual episodes with the same sex were computed for male youths, as were unprotected oral and vaginal–digital episodes with the same sex for female youths. Positively skewed data (i.e., numbers of lifetime and recent partners and encounters and numbers of unprotected sexual episodes) were transformed logarithmically to normalize the distributions in preparation for parametric statistical analyses.

The Health Inventory for Adolescents (Rosario, Hunter, & Gwadz, 1993) was developed to assess ever having an STD (i.e., gonorrhea, syphilis, genital herpes, venereal warts, chancroid, chlamydia, and any other STD).

Substance Use

Rosario and Gwadz (1993a) developed the Alcohol and Drugs Schedule to assess, for this chapter, lifetime and recent (i.e., during the last 3 months) use of cigarettes, alcohol, and illicit drugs (i.e., marijuana, inhalants, cocaine, hallucinogens, heroin, barbiturates, sedatives, tranquilizers, amphetamines, stimulants, analgesics, estrogens, and steroids) for nonmedical or recreational purposes. An indication of using illicit drugs for each time period was based on whether the youths reported using any of these drugs.

Psychological Distress

The Brief Symptom Inventory (Derogatis, 1993) was used to assess anxiety (e.g., "suddenly scared for no reason") and depression (e.g., "feeling hopeless about the future") during the past week, using a five-point response scale from 0 (*not at all*) to 4 (*extremely*) distressing. The mean of each scale was computed and a high score indicated elevated emotional distress (Cronbach's α = .80 for anxiety and .82 for depression).

Conduct problems were assessed by means of the conduct problems identified in the *Diagnostic and Statistical Manual of Mental Disorders* (3rd ed., rev.; American Psychiatric Association, 1987). A scale of 13 items was constructed to measure the prevalence (i.e., *yes* or *no*) of each conduct problem during the past 6 months (e.g., "started a physical fight with others"). Our index was a count of the indicated conduct problems.

Protective Factors

The Rosenberg (1965) Self-Esteem Scale was used, with its 10 items (e.g., "I feel I have a number of good qualities") and 4-point Likert response scale from 1 (*strongly agree*) to 4 (*strongly disagree*). The mean of the response scores was computed to assess self-esteem, with a high score indicating high self-esteem (Cronbach's α = .86). An adapted version of Procidano and Heller's (1983) measure of social support from friends and family was used (e.g., "I rely on my [friends/family] for emotional support."), deleting items that might be redundant with mental health. The two resulting 12-item measures assessed emotional and informational support, using a response scale of 1 (*yes*) and 0 (*no*). The indicator of social support from friends (Cronbach's α = .80) comprised a count of the items focusing on friends. The indicator of social support from family (Cronbach's α = .90) comprised a count of the items focusing on family.

Gay-Related Stress

A 12-item checklist was developed to assess stressful life events associated with being LGB (Rosario, Schrimshaw, Hunter, & Gwadz, 2002). It assessed whether arguments and difficulties with others (e.g., family, teachers, friends, police), as well as physical assault, had occurred during the past 3 months. We dichotomized the number of events to assess whether any gay-related stressful event was or was not (1 = *was*; 0 = *was not*) experienced, given the number of events was skewed.

Social Desirability

The tendency to provide socially favorable responses was measured with the Marlowe-Crowne Social Desirability Scale (Crowne & Marlowe, 1964). Our factor analysis of the self-administered scale resulted in a single factor, with 12 items loading ($\geq$ .40) on the factor. A count of the 12 items endorsed by the youths indicated social desirability (Cronbach's α = .74).

FINDINGS

Table 6.1 contains information about the youths' religious identity and religiosity. Fifty percent of the male and female participants were raised as Roman Catholic and 23% as Protestant; these findings are comparable to 1990 survey data of New York City residents (43% and 32%, respectively; Kosmin & Lachman, 1993). The religions in which the youths were raised and the religions with which they currently identified were related, $\chi^2(9, N = 155) = 81.1, p < .001$. However, an observable change in religious identity occurred over time, with a decrease in the number of youths who currently identified with a religion and a corresponding increase in the number with no current religious affiliation (see Table 6.2).

The male and female youths indicated that they were "a bit" religious (i.e., $M = 2.3, SD = 1.23$ on a 5-point response scale). We expected that the degree of religiosity would vary with current religious affiliation such that youths who currently identified with a religion would be more religious than those who did not. An association was found, $F(3, 151) = 15.8, p < .001$. Follow-up tests supported our hypothesis, with significant differences in religiosity between each of the three religious affiliations as compared with the group with no current religious affiliation (Ms ranged from 2.7–3.0 for the religious denominations vs. a mean of 1.7 for no religious affiliation).

The religious variables were related significantly ($p < .05$) to a number of sociodemographic factors and social desirability. Male youths were more religious than their female peers ($r = -.20$). Older youths as compared with their younger peers were less likely to have a current religious affiliation ($r = -.17$), especially a Roman Catholic affiliation ($r = -.19$). Youths who provided more as compared with fewer socially desirable responses were marginally more likely to have a current religious affiliation ($r = .14, p < .10$) and to report being more religious ($r = .13, p < .10$). Religious affiliation was associated with ethnicity, both with the religion in which the youths were raised, $\chi^2(9, N = 155) = 51.76, p < .001$, and with their current religious affiliation, $\chi^2(9, N = 155) = 29.22, p < .005$. The majority of Latino and White youths were raised Roman Catholic (77% and 50%, respectively), whereas Black youths were raised Protestant (48%) and, to a lesser extent, Roman Catholic (28%). With respect to current affiliation, nearly half of Latino, White, and Black youths did not identify with a religion (50%, 47%, and 48%, respectively). Therefore, it was unsurprising that no significant association was found between ethnicity and religiosity.

Given the significant findings that emerged linking religion and our sociodemographic and social desirability factors, we imposed controls for gender, age, social desirability, and ethnicity when investigating the unique relations between religion and its correlates. Although the religion variables were not associated with socioeconomic status or self-identification as

TABLE 6.1
Religious Information About Male and Female Youths

| | Male youths (n = 80) | | | | | | Female youths (n = 75) | | | | | |
| | Raised as | | Currently is | | Religiosity | | Raised as | | Currently is | | Religiosity | |
Affiliation	%	n	%	n	M	SD	%	n	%	n	M	SD
Catholic	53	42	26	21	3.1	1.0	47	35	19	14	2.8	0.7
Protestant	24	19	18	14	3.4	1.2	23	17	11	8	2.4	1.3
Other	13	10	11	9	2.7	1.5	13	10	16	12	2.7	1.3
None	11	9	45	36	1.9	1.1	17	13	55	41	1.6	1.0
Overall					2.6	1.3					2.1	1.2

Note. Percentages may not sum to 100 because of rounding. Religiosity ranges from not at all (1) to a whole lot (5).

TABLE 6.2
Change in Religious Identity Among Male and Female Youths

Raised as	Number of youths currently identifying as				
	Catholic	Protestant	Other	None	Total
Catholic	31	5	7	34	77
Protestant	1	17	2	16	36
Other	2	0	9	9	20
None	1	0	3	18	22
Total	35	22	21	77	155

Note. Other religions in which the youths were raised included Jewish (7), East Asian religions (e.g., Buddhism; 3), Greek Orthodox (1), Islam (1), and combinations of two religions such as Roman Catholic and Baptist or Lutheran and Jewish (8). Other religions with which the youths currently identified were Jewish (4), East Asian religions (4), Greek or Eastern Orthodox (2), Islamic (2), and Agnosticism (9).

lesbian, gay, or bisexual, these two variables were included as controls because they have been shown to be related to some of the risk and protective factors of this youth sample (e.g., Rosario et al., 1999; Rosario, Hunter, & Gwadz, 1997).

Simple Associations Between Religion and Risk and Protective Factors

Table 6.3 contains the simple bivariate correlations between any current religious affiliation and religiosity and the risk and protective factors. A glance at Table 6.3 indicates that many more relations were significant for the male youths than for the female youths.

Male Youths

Religion and sexual risk behaviors were related among male youths. Those who currently identified with any religion, as compared with those who had no current religious identity, reported fewer lifetime same-sex encounters. They also were less likely to report ever having a risky partner. With respect to recent sexual activity, male youths who currently identified with any religion indicated having fewer same-sex partners and sexual encounters, as well as fewer unprotected episodes of anal sex with their male partners. It is interesting to note that youths with a religious identity reported more lifetime other-sex partners.

Similar patterns of significant findings were found between religiosity and the sexual risk behaviors, including a positive relation between religiosity and ever impregnating a female partner. In addition, youths who were more religious were significantly less likely to have recently used any illicit drugs. They also were marginally less depressed and less anxious than youths who

TABLE 6.3
Pearson Correlation Coefficients for Current Religious Identity and Religiosity

Variable	Male youths (n = 80)		Female youths (n = 75)	
	Any religion[a]	Religiosity[b]	Any religion[a]	Religiosity[b]
Lifetime sexual behaviors				
No. of same-sex partners	-.22†	-.26*	.06	-.02
No. of same-sex encounters	-.30**	-.35**	-.06	.01
No. of other-sex partners	.22*	.07	-.06	.05
No. of other-sex encounters	.21†	-.01	-.16	-.06
Ever a risky male or female partner	-.30**	-.31**	-.08	-.06
Ever a risky male partner	-.36**	-.33**	-.02	.06
Ever exchanged sex for goods	-.15	-.26*	.00	-.05
Ever a sexually transmitted disease	-.25*	-.10	-.10	.04
Ever pregnant or impregnated someone[c]	.04	.23*	-.20†	-.12
Recent sexual behaviors (last 3 months)				
No. of same-sex partners	-.28*	-.30**	.11	-.10
No. of same-sex encounters	-.30**	-.34**	.14	.02
Unprotected anal sex (no. of times)	-.41**	-.32†	—	.05
Unprotected oral sex (no. of times)	-.21	-.32*	.07	.20
Unprotected vaginal–digital sex (no. of times)	—	—	.22	
Lifetime substance use				
Ever cigarettes	-.02	.04	.02	.02
Ever alcohol	-.04	-.21†	-.08	-.02
Ever any illicit drugs	.06	-.20†	-.01	.11
Recent substance use (last 3 months)				
Ever cigarettes	.03	.05	.02	.02
Ever alcohol	-.02	-.21†	.00	.11
Ever any illicit drugs	-.03	-.23*	.03	.03

	1	2	3	4
Psychological distress				
Anxiety	−.13	−.21†	−.04	.07
Depression	−.21†	−.23†	−.15	−.02
Conduct problems	−.18	−.11	.07	−.02
Protective factors				
Self-esteem	.07	.28*	.10	.05
Social support by friend	.26*	.14	−.01	.03
Social support by family	.06	−.01	−.02	.11
Stress (last 3 months)				
Any gay-related stress	−.03	.03	.22†	.13
From family	.02	.10	.24*	.18
From another source	.02	.01	.12	.00

aAny religion contrasts youths who currently identify with a religion (1) with youths who have no current religious identity (0). bReligiosity ranges from *not at all* religious (1) to *a whole lot* (5). cTen of the male youths had impregnated a female partner at least once; similarly, 10 female youths reported being pregnant at least once.
†p < .10. *p ≤ .05. **p ≤ .01.

were not as religious. Those who were more religious reported increased self-esteem.

Female Youths

Current religious identity and religiosity were essentially unrelated to the risk and protective factors. The one significant exception indicated that youths with a religious identity reported experiencing gay-related stress, particularly from family members.

Multivariate Associations Between Religion and Risk and Protective Factors

Hierarchical multiple and logistic regressions were conducted to examine the relations between religion and risk and protective factors after controlling for potential confounders (identified earlier). The religion variables were entered after the confounders. Specifically, for each risk and protective factor, three regression equations were conducted by gender: (a) current religious identity as compared with none, (b) Catholic identity as compared with none and non-Catholic religious identity as compared with none, and (c) religiosity. Multiple regression was used when the risk or protective outcome was a continuous variable, and logistic regression was used when the outcome was a dichotomy. Reported results are measures of effect size: betas (β) for multiple regression and odds ratios (OR) that estimate the change in odds of membership in the target group for one unit of increase in the prediction variable (Grimm & Yarnold, 1995). Given this is one of the only empirical investigations of religion and health among LGB youths, if not the only one, no controls were imposed for Type I error.

Male Youths

Youths with a current religious identity, as compared with youths with no current religious identity, engaged in fewer risky behaviors, evidenced less emotional distress, and indicated more social support (see Table 6.4). For example, youths with a current religious identity were less likely to have ever had a risky male sexual partner or an STD. They reported fewer numbers of recent same-sex partners, sexual encounters, and unprotected episodes of anal sex. They also indicated more social support from friends. On another note, male youths with a current religious identity reported more lifetime numbers of female sexual partners and encounters.

Analyses comparing different current religious identities with no current religious identity added more information to our understanding of the youths' risk and protective factors. Catholic youths reported fewer risky behaviors and more protective behaviors, including fewer episodes of unpro-

TABLE 6.4

Hierarchical Multiple and Logistic Regression of Current Religious Identity and Religiosity Among Male Youths

Variable	Any religion versus none[a]		Catholic identity versus none[b]		Non-Catholic identity versus none[c]		Religiosity[d]	
	β	OR	β	OR	β	OR	β	OR
Lifetime sexual behaviors								
No. of same-sex partners	−.15		−.18		−.09		−.16	
No. of same-sex encounters	−.23*		−.24*		−.18		−.28**	
No. of other-sex partners	.23*		.05		.33**		.01	
No. of other-sex encounters	.25*		.07		.35**		−.03	
Ever a risky male or female partner		.29*		.16*		.42		.56*
Ever a risky male partner		.17**		.17*		.18*		.46*
Ever exchanged sex for goods		.43		.15		.90		.45*
Ever a sexually transmitted disease		.03*		.00		.07		.81
Ever impregnated someone		3.88		2.77		5.02		3.02†
Recent sexual behaviors (last 3 months)								
No. of same-sex partners	−.24*		−.21†		−.22†		−.24*	
No. of same-sex encounters	−.27*		−.29*		−.20		−.30**	
Unprotected anal sex (no. of times)	−.49**		−.42*		−.49**		−.40*	
Unprotected oral sex (no. of times)	−.23		−.33†		−.13		−.33*	
Lifetime substance use								
Ever cigarettes		1.05		.72		1.50		1.08
Ever alcohol		.92		1.05		.82		.73
Ever any illicit drugs		2.06		2.12		2.01		.76

(continued)

TABLE 6.4   (Continued)

Variable	Any religion versus none[a]		Catholic identity versus none[b]		Non-Catholic identity versus none[c]		Religiosity[d]	
	β	OR	β	OR	β	OR	β	OR
Recent substance use (last 3 months)								
Ever cigarettes		1.02		1.04		.99		1.02
Ever alcohol		.95		.82		1.09		.69†
Ever any illicit drugs		1.04		1.02		1.06		.64†
Psychological distress								
Anxiety	-.14		-.17		-.08		-.21†	
Depression	-.18		-.26*		-.08		-.23*	
Conduct problems	-.15		-.22†		-.06		-.07	
Protective factors								
Self-esteem	.00		.07		-.05		.26*	
Social support by friend	.28*		.27*		.24†		.16	
Social support by family	.05		.10		-.01		.00	
Stress (last 3 months)								
Any gay-related stress		.75		.67		.83		.96
From family		.99		.80		1.20		1.06
From another source		.95		.82		1.10		.92

Note. Statistical controls were imposed for age, socioeconomic status, ethnicity, social desirability, and sexual self-identification as lesbian, gay, or bisexual. [a]Any religion contrasts youths who currently identify with a religion (1) with youths who have no current religious identity (0). [b]Catholics (1) are contrasted with youths with no religious identity (0). [c]Non-Catholics are contrasted with youths with no religious identity (0). [d]Religiosity ranges from *not at all* religious (1) to a *whole lot* (5). OR = odds ratio of logistic regression.
†p ≤ .10. *p ≤ .05. **p ≤ .01.

tected anal sex. They also indicated decreased depression and marginally fewer conduct problems. Non-Catholic youths generated fewer significant findings than Catholic youths. However, non-Catholic youths reported more lifetime female sexual partners and encounters than youths with no religious identity. The findings for the non-Catholic youths, as well as the findings for any religious identity versus none, were replicated when the youths who currently identified as Agnostic were excluded from the analyses. The exclusion was based on the possibility that Agnosticism might indicate either a unique religious perspective or atheism. Given the latter possibility, any relation involving Agnostics might be artificially inflated.

Female Youths

Youths with any current religious identity were three times (OR = 3.37, p < .05) more likely to experience gay-related stress associated with kin (no table). Subsequent analyses indicated that it was non-Catholic youths, as compared with youths with no current religious identity, who were three times (OR = 3.54, p < .10) more likely to experience gay-related stress associated with kin. There was also a marginal relation between religiosity and gay-related stress from kin (OR = 1.64, p < .10). The findings for the non-Catholic youths were replicated when those who currently identified as Agnostic were excluded from the analyses.

CONCLUSION

Summary of Findings

The youths' religious history indicated that the vast majority was raised with a religious background. However, many youths had abandoned their childhood religions and had not currently substituted another religion for the abandoned childhood religion. Moreover, few attempts were made to reach out to alternative religious congregations in the gay community of New York (e.g., Dignity, the Metropolitan Church); only 6 (4%) male and female youths had done so.

The potential benefits of religion for health and protective factors were apparent for the gay and bisexual male youths. Those with any current religious identity, as compared with those with no current religious identity, reported fewer sexual risk behaviors, including decreased frequency of unprotected anal sex with male partners. In particular, Roman Catholic youths, as compared with youths with no religious identity, evidenced these and additional benefits, including decreased symptoms of depression. Non-Catholic youths also demonstrated some of these benefits. The fewer significant findings for the non-Catholic group may have been a function of the group's diversity, which included, for example, Protestants, Jews, and Buddhists. The findings just discussed with respect to comparisons between any religious identity versus none or between a Catholic identity versus none were supported by findings involving degree of religiosity. In addition, youths who were more religious reported increased self-esteem.

For the lesbian and bisexual females in this study, there were essentially no relations between the religion variables (i.e., identity indicators and religiosity) and the health and protective factors. For example, of the 28 possible associations involving current religious identity, only 1 (3%) was significant at the .05 probability level. We address why religion may have been unrelated to these factors among our lesbian and bisexual female youths at the end of the next section.

Explanation of Findings: Theory of Religion and Health

Among the general population, into which LGB individuals are born and in which they are raised, the beneficial influences of religion on health and protective factors can be attributed to a combination of religious and social psychological processes. Many of the world religions advocate behaviors that reduce risk and promote health (e.g., abstinence from sex before marriage, admonishments against gluttony that reduce the likelihood that the individual will be overweight or addicted to alcohol and, by extension, any other drugs). The advocated behaviors are repeated by the clergy, inscribed in sacred texts, communicated among the lay population, and passed down through the generations. They are normative prescriptions.

The religious population is linked by shared values, beliefs, and attitudes that transcend time and inform its language and normative behaviors. Social identity and social categorization processes (Tajfel, 1981; Turner, Hogg, Oakes, Reicher, & Wetherell, 1987) unfold early in the lives of this population's members as the corpus of information, of a sense of community, and of selfhood devolves on each succeeding generation. The particular cognitive and behavioral practices reinforced by the religious group (i.e., the social reference group) become internalized with respect to how one views and defines the self (cf. self-perception theory; Bem, 1972). Thus, engaging in health and protective behaviors and avoiding risk and health-threatening behaviors as prescribed by the religion become part of the experience of self.

Social influence processes are brought to bear by the religious population on its individual members, ensuring fidelity to and continuation of shared cognitive and behavioral practices. The holy texts and stories, as well as religious rituals, serve to forge a social bond among the population. Thus, religion provides individuals with a sense of belonging and social support. It fulfills a basic need for affiliation, especially for individuals who are actively involved in group worship and meetings. In addition, the social influence of a religious group may take the form of conformity to group norms and obedience to the religious authority (Batson et al., 1993). There may be grave consequences for violating group norms or disobeying rules (e.g., banishment from the group, such as excommunication). Thus, the religious group may foster maintenance of positive health behaviors and avoidance of risky behaviors in its members by means of social influence.

For LGB individuals raised in a religious family or community, conflict or psychological tension may result from the condemnation of homosexuality professed by many religions and the self-awareness that one is an object of religious censure (Mahaffy, 1996; Thumma, 1991). This conflict or cognitive dissonance (Festinger, 1957) stems from the juxtaposition of the individual's religious identity and his or her unfolding LGB identity. Thus, one might hypothesize that religion would have negative, even toxic, consequences for the health and protective behaviors of LGB individuals, if this conflict were not resolved. That is, unless the individual suppresses or represses behavioral expression of the self, the LGB individual knows that he or she is persona non grata to many religions. It is unlikely that an individual can withstand such a blow to self-esteem and selfhood without paying a heavy toll with respect to mental and physical health and related adaptational indicators.

Cognitive dissonance must be resolved to reduce the psychological tension it creates (Festinger, 1957). As others have suggested (Rodriguez & Ouellette, 2000; Thumma, 1991), some LGB individuals may attempt to reject their same-sex identity by means of defense mechanisms (e.g., suppression, repression), self-directed interventions (e.g., avoidance of gay and lesbian individuals, immersion in heterosexual activity), or therapeutic endeavors (e.g., reparative therapy). However, the likelihood that homosexuality may have biological roots (Bailey et al., 1999; Hamer, Hu, Magnuson, Hu, & Pattatucci, 1993; LeVay, 1991; Whitam, Diamond, & Martin, 1993; Williams et al., 2000) raises serious doubts about the long-term success of such strategies, and concerns about the potential negative effects of such strategies on health.

These and other individuals may attempt to resolve the conflict by compartmentalizing their religious and gay identities into two nonintersecting sets or by integrating the two identities. Compartmentalization may be difficult to maintain for any length of time because it fails to resolve the cognitive dissonance. Therefore, compartmentalization is likely to be a transitional phase that either evolves into rejection of religion or attempts to integrate the religious and LGB identities. Rejection of religion may be an attempt to protect the self and, by implication, one's health. If the rejection is coupled with a search for another or alternative spiritual or religious connection, health and protective behaviors are expected to be maintained as the integration takes place. However, rejection of religion without an equivalent substitute in place may result in poor health and decreased protective factors for two reasons. First, internally based stress increases because an important identity is abandoned, and a reconfiguration of the self is required. Until a satisfactory reconfiguration occurs, psychological distress may be elevated, self-esteem may be decreased, and physical health may be influenced negatively. Second, rejection of religion may extend to encompass its teachings, including those that pertain to promoting health-enhancing behaviors and controlling impulsive drives (e.g., libido). In other words, rejection of religion may result in increasing risky behaviors (e.g., substance use, sexual activity) that have negative implications for health.

Individuals also may resolve the cognitive dissonance by seeking to integrate the two identities. They might screen out all aspects of religion that touch on homosexuality, refusing to accept the negative evaluations of homosexuality in scripture or religious doctrine. Individuals integrating their religious and gay identities might forge a meta-identity in which their religion's emphasis on a moral and righteous life infuses their intimate relationships and commitments with others of the same sex. They may retain their childhood religious identification or search for a religious group that is more welcoming of their LGB identity. Regardless, these are the individuals who are expected to demonstrate the strongest beneficial influence of religion on health and protective factors. Indeed, several authors report that LGB individuals seek to integrate their same-sex identity with their religious beliefs (e.g., Lynch, 1996; Rodriguez & Ouellette, 2000; Weinberg & Williams, 1974). Although some LGB individuals belong to mainstream churches, others have joined gay churches (e.g., Metropolitan Community Church) or gay-positive religious groups (e.g., Dignity), or they have created their own ceremonies and rituals to fill their spiritual needs (Perlstein, 1996). Haldeman (1996) suggested that spirituality may be as intrinsic to identity for some LGB individuals as is sexual orientation.

Managing the cognitive dissonance associated with the religious and LGB identities takes time and involves a complex process of investigation and experimentation by the individual. A solution might not be reached until the individual experiments with responses to the cognitive dissonance. Ultimately, a stable solution is reached, resulting, for most individuals, in rejection of religion or integration of religious and LGB identities. As we have indicated, the interplay or interaction between religious and LGB identities is expected to influence mental and physical health, as well as protective behaviors.

Indeed, our data are consistent with this theoretical perspective. The gay and bisexual male youths who identified with a religion or who were religious reported more health and protective behaviors than peers who did not identify with a religion or who were less religious, suggesting that some of the youths may have integrated their religious and gay or bisexual identities. By comparison, the lesbian and bisexual female youths, for whom few significant relations were found, may still not have decided whether to reject or integrate their religious and lesbian or bisexual identities, given the following. The male and female youths in this study began their psychosexual development as lesbian, gay, or bisexual at the same age, an average of 11.4 years, but the female youths were delayed during the process, requiring an extra year before they were first aware that they really were lesbian or bisexual, at age 15.1 years on average (for details, see Rosario et al., 1996). This delay may have affected related processes in other developmental areas, including the youths' evaluation and resolution of their religious identity in light of their lesbian and bisexual identity. Clearly, longitudinal data would be required to examine the validity of this conjecture.

Directions for Future Research

The data presented here indicate the need to take a new look at religion and to acknowledge its potential beneficial influences in the lives of LGB individuals. The limitations of our study can serve as a springboard for future research endeavors. First, this study was exploratory, a first attempt to determine if associations existed between religion and the health and protective factors of LGB youths. The findings support this relation and encourage one to identify and confirm the mechanisms by which religion might confer benefits on health and protective factors. Researchers should carefully examine possible avenues for reducing cognitive dissonance aroused by the juxtaposition of religious and LGB identities, determining whether religious and LGB identities are compartmentalized or integrated, or whether one identity or the other is rejected. We have argued that individuals who integrate their religious and LGB identities are most likely to experience health benefits. In addition, researchers may wish to consider alternative theories to explain the connection between religion and health and protective factors, such as self-discrepancy theory (Higgins, 1987) and the notion of possible selves (Markus & Nurius, 1986).

Although our data are cross-sectional, future investigations will need longitudinal and prospective data to assess changes in the youths' connections to religion and to ascertain the direction of associations. In addition, future studies should have larger samples than were available to us. Among youth samples, researchers may wish to consider assessing the influence of the family's religiosity on the youths' relation between religiosity and health-related behaviors. Moreover, researchers may want to consider whether the Marlowe-Crowne scale thoroughly assesses social desirability, particularly as more religious individuals may be prone to providing socially favorable responses in order to impress others with their righteousness or minimize their anxiety over their risky behaviors. Researchers also should have more diverse samples than we had in order to assess the generalizability of findings beyond our urban sample of youths recruited from gay-focused organizations. Finally, studies of LGB adults are needed to investigate the issues we have raised in this chapter, including generalizability of findings to different periods of development.

Implications for Service Providers

Individuals who work with LGB youths must realize that these youths are undergoing processes of identity development with respect to their sexual orientation and their religion, and that each identity process has implications for the youths' health and protective behaviors, as we have demonstrated here and elsewhere (Rosario, Hunter, Maguen, Gwadz, & Smith, 2001). Sensitivity toward and nonjudgmental responses to the youths' comments and queries about religion seem essential. Having and sharing information with youths about religious groups in the community that might welcome the youths seem helpful. Attempts to identify and engage nonjudgmental clergy who are willing to minister to and work with the youths also seem necessary. In addition, a greater expenditure of time and effort might be warranted with those youths who reject their religious backgrounds because, according to our findings, these youths appear to be most at risk for poor health and decreased protective behaviors. Primary prevention efforts also should attempt to identify and focus on youths who might be having problems integrating their religious and LGB identities because these youths might be most likely to reject their religious background.

REFERENCES

American Psychiatric Association. (1987). *Diagnostic and statistical manual of mental disorders* (3rd ed., rev.). Washington, DC: Author.

Bailey, J. M., Pillard, R. C., Dawood, K., Miller, M. B., Farrer, L. A., Trivedi, S., & Murphy, R. L. (1999). A family history study of male sexual orientation using three independent samples. *Behavior Genetics, 29,* 79–86.

Batson, C. D., Schoenrade, P., & Ventis, W. L. (1993). *Religion and the individual: A social-psychological perspective.* New York: Oxford University Press.

Baumeister, R. F. (1991). *Meanings of life.* New York: Guilford Press.

Bell, A. P., & Weinberg, M. S. (1978). *Homosexualities: A study of diversity among men and women.* New York: Simon & Schuster.

Bem, D. J. (1972). Self-perception: An alternative interpretation of cognitive dissonance phenomena. *Psychological Review, 74,* 183–200.

Clingman, J., & Fowler, M. G. (1976). Gender roles and human sexuality. *Journal of Personality Assessment, 40,* 276–284.

Crowne, D. P., & Marlowe, D. (1964). *The approval motive: Studies in evaluative dependence.* Westport, CT: Greenwood Press.

Derogatis, L. R. (1993). *BSI, Brief Symptom Inventory: Administration, scoring, and procedures manual.* Minneapolis, MN: National Computer Systems.

Donahue, M. J., & Benson, P. L. (1995). Religion and the well-being of adolescents. *Journal of Social Issues, 51,* 145–160.

Festinger, L. (1957). *A theory of cognitive dissonance.* Stanford, CA: Stanford University Press.

Gallup, G. H., Jr. (1995). *The Gallup poll: Public opinion 1995.* Wilmington, DE: Scholarly Resources.

Gallup, G. H., Jr. (1996). *Religion in America, 1996.* Princeton, NJ: Gallup Organization.

Gillis, J. R. (1998). Cultural heterosexism and the family. In C. J. Patterson & A. R. D'Augelli (Eds.), *Lesbian, gay, and bisexual identities in families: Psychological perspectives* (pp. 249–269). New York: Oxford University Press.

Greenberg, J. S. (1973). A study of the self-esteem and alienation of male homosexuals. *Journal of Psychology, 83,* 137–143.

Grimm, L. G., & Yarnold, P. R. (1995). *Reading and understanding multivariate statistics.* Washington, DC: American Psychological Association.

Haldeman, D. C. (1996). Spirituality and religion in the lives of lesbians and gay men. In R. P. Cabaj & T. S. Stein (Eds.), *Textbook of homosexuality and mental health* (pp. 881–896). Washington, DC: American Psychiatric Press.

Hamer, D. H., Hu, S., Magnuson, V., Hu, N., & Pattatucci, A. M. L. (1993, July 16). A linkage between DNA markers on the X chromosome and male sexual orientation. *Science, 261,* 321–327.

Higgins, E. T. (1987). Self-discrepancy: A theory relating self and affect. *Psychological Review, 94,* 319–340.

Hummer, R. A., Rogers, R. G., Nam, C. B., & Ellison, C. G. (1999). Religious involvement and U.S. adult mortality. *Demography, 36,* 273–285.

Hyde, K. E. (1990). *Religion in childhood and adolescence: A comprehensive review of the research.* Birmingham, AL: Religious Education Press.

Koenig, H. G. (1997). *Is religion good for your health? The effects of religion on physical and mental health.* New York: Haworth Press.

Kosmin, B. A., & Lachman, S. P. (1993). *One nation under God: Religion in contemporary American society.* New York: Harmony Books.

Landau, S. I. (Ed.). (1997). *The new international Webster's concise dictionary of the English language.* Naples, FL: Trident Press International.

LeVay, S. A. (1991, August 30). A difference in hypothalamic structure between heterosexual and homosexual men. *Science, 253,* 1034–1037.

Levin, J. S., & Schiller, P. L. (1987). Is there a religious factor in health? *Journal of Religion and Health, 26,* 9–36.

Lynch, B. (1996). Religious and spirituality conflicts. In D. Davies & C. Neal (Eds.), *Pink therapy: A guide for counselors and therapists working with lesbian, gay, and bisexual clients* (pp. 199–207). Buckingham, England: Open University Press.

Mahaffy, K. A. (1996). Cognitive dissonance and its resolution: A study of lesbian Christians. *Journal for the Scientific Study of Religion, 35,* 392–402.

Markus, H., & Nurius, P. S. (1986). Possible selves. *American Psychologist, 41,* 954–969.

McBride, D. C., Mutch, P. B., & Chitwood, D. D. (1996). Religious beliefs and the initiation and prevention of drug use among youth. In C. B. McCoy, L. R. Metsch, & J. A. Inciardi (Eds.), *Intervening with drug-involved youth* (pp. 110–130). Thousand Oaks, CA: Sage.

McCullough, M. E., Hoyt, W. T., Larson, D. B., Koenig, H. G., & Thoreson, C. (2000). Religious involvement and mortality: A meta-analytic review. *Health Psychology, 19,* 211–222.

Meyer-Bahlburg, H. F. L., Ehrhardt, A. A., Exner, T. A., & Gruen, R. S. (1994). *Sexual Risk Behavior Assessment Schedule—Youth.* Unpublished instrument, Columbia University, New York.

Pargament, K. I. (1997). *The psychology of religion and coping: Theory, research, and practice.* New York: Guilford Press.

Perlstein, M. (1996). Integrating a gay, lesbian, or bisexual person's religious and spiritual needs and choices into psychotherapy. In C. J. Alexander (Ed.), *Gay and lesbian mental health: A source book for practitioners* (pp. 173–188). New York: Harrington Park Press.

Procidano, M. E., & Heller, K. (1983). Measures of perceived social support from friends and from family: Three validation studies. *American Journal of Community Psychology, 11,* 1–24.

Rodriguez, E. M., & Ouellette, S. C. (2000). Gay and lesbian Christians: Homosexual and religious identity integration in the members and participants of a gay-positive church. *Journal for the Scientific Study of Religion, 39,* 333–347.

Rosario, M., & Gwadz, M. (1993a). *Alcohol and Drugs Schedule.* Unpublished instrument, City University of New York.

Rosario, M., & Gwadz, M. (1993b). *Religion Inventory.* Unpublished instrument, City University of New York.

Rosario, M., Hunter, J., & Gwadz, M. (1993). *The Health Inventory for Adolescents.* Unpublished instrument, City University of New York.

Rosario, M., Hunter, J., &, Gwadz, M. (1997). Exploration of substance use among lesbian, gay, and bisexual youth: Prevalence and correlates. *Journal of Adolescent Research, 12,* 454–476.

Rosario, M., Hunter, J., Maguen, S., Gwadz, M., & Smith, R. (2001). The coming-out process and its adaptational and health-related associations among gay, lesbian, and bisexual youths: Stipulation and exploration of a model. *American Journal of Community Psychology, 29,* 133–160 .

Rosario, M., Meyer-Bahlburg, H. F. L., Hunter, J., Exner, T. M., Gwadz, M., & Keller, A. M. (1996). The psychosexual development of urban lesbian, gay, and bisexual youths. *Journal of Sex Research, 33,* 113–126.

Rosario, M., Meyer-Bahlburg, H. F. L., Hunter, J., & Gwadz, M. (1999). Sexual risk behaviors of gay, lesbian, and bisexual youths in New York City: Prevalence and correlates. *AIDS Education and Prevention, 11,* 476–496.

Rosario, M., Schrimshaw, E. W., Hunter, J. & Gwadz, M. (2002). Gay-related stress and emotional distress among gay, lesbian, and bisexual youths: A longitudinal examination. *Journal of Consulting and Clinical Psychology, 70,* 967–975.

Rosenberg, M. (1965). *Society and adolescent self-image.* Princeton, NJ: Princeton University Press.

Savin-Williams, R. C. (1990). *Gay and lesbian youth: Expressions of identity.* New York: Hemisphere Publication Services.

Silber, M. J., & Riley, M. (1985). Spiritual and religious concerns of the hospitalized adolescent. *Adolescence, 20,* 217–224.

Tajfel, H. (1981). *Human groups and social categories: Studies in social psychology.* London: Cambridge University Press.

Thumma, S. (1991). Negotiating a religious identity: The case of the gay evangelical. *Sociological Analysis, 52,* 333–347.

Turner, J. C., Hogg, M. A., Oakes, P. J., Reicher, S. D., & Wetherell, M. S. (1987). *Rediscovering the social group: A self-categorization theory.* Oxford, England: Basil Blackwell.

Wallace, J. M., & Forman, T. A. (1998). Religion's role in promoting health and reducing risk among American youth. *Health, Education and Behavior, 25,* 721–741.

Weaver, M. J., Salford, J., Morgan, M. J., Lookdown, A. I., Larson, D. B., & Garbarino, J. (2000). Research on religious variables in five major adolescent research journals: 1992 to 1996. *Journal of Nervous and Mental Disorders, 188,* 36–44.

Weinberg, T. S., & Williams, C. J. (1974). *Male homosexuals: Their problems and adaptations.* New York: Penguin.

Whitam, F. L., Diamond, M., & Martin, J. (1993). Homosexual orientation in twins: A report on 61 pairs and three triplet sets. *Archives of Sexual Behavior, 22,* 187–206.

Williams, T. A., Pepitone, M. E., Christensen, S. E., Cooke, B. M., Huberman, A. D., Breedlove, N. J., et al. (2000, March 30). Finger-length ratios and sexual orientation. *Nature, 404,* 455–456.

Woodroof, J. T. (1985). Premarital sex and religious adolescents. *Journal for the Scientific Study of Religion, 24,* 343–366.

Woods, T. E., Antoni, M. H., Ironson, G. H., & Kling, D. W. (1999). Religiosity is associated with affective and immune status in symptomatic HIV-infected gay men. *Journal of Psychosomatic Research, 46,* 165–176.

Worthington, E. L., Jr., Kurusu, T. A., McCullough, M. E., & Sandage, S. J. (1996). Empirical research on religion and psychotherapeutic processes and outcome: A 10-year review and research prospectus. *Psychological Bulletin, 119*, 448–487.

Zaleski, E. H., & Schiaffino, K. M. (2000). Religiosity and sexual risk-taking behavior during the transition to college. *Journal of Adolescence, 23*, 223–227.

II
ADULTS

7

ESTIMATING PREVALENCE OF MENTAL AND SUBSTANCE-USING DISORDERS AMONG LESBIANS AND GAY MEN FROM EXISTING NATIONAL HEALTH DATA

SUSAN D. COCHRAN AND VICKIE M. MAYS

Over the past half century, perspectives on the relationship between homosexuality and mental health disorders have undergone at least three major transformations (Cochran, 2001). These transformations have both influenced and been influenced by the normative research methodologies used by scholars in the field. For example, if one goes back to the early 1970s, social and medical scientists presumed, like most of America, that homosexuality was psychopathology (Stein, 1993). Thus, it was reasonable, and not especially biasing, to look for lesbians and gay men in psychiatric settings. It is not surprising that these researchers found high levels of psychiatric difficulties in their lesbian and gay male participants. It took

This work was supported by the National Institute of Allergy and Infectious Disease (AI 38216), the National Institute of Mental Health (MH 61774), the National Institute of Drug Abuse (DA 15539), and the National Center for Minority Health and Health Disparities (MD 000508).

143

pioneering work by Evelyn Hooker, a psychologist from the University of California, Los Angeles (UCLA), in the late 1950s (Hooker, 1993), and others who recruited nonpsychiatric samples to demonstrate empirically that homosexuality was not ipso facto psychopathology.

In a second wave of social science research beginning with some enthusiasm in the 1970s (Bell & Weinberg, 1978; Nurius, 1983; Saghir, Robins, Walbran, & Gentry, 1970; Siegelman, 1972; Thompson, McCandless, & Strickland, 1971), social scientists now presumed that lesbians and gay men were not necessarily sick. However, they still needed to recruit participants from a small, hidden population. At the time, lesbians and gay men lacked widely visible social institutions or presence in the American consciousness, so social scientists looked for sites in which lesbians and gay men were thought most likely to congregate, such as gay bars, bath houses, and occasional feminist and gay political or social meetings. The research repeatedly found no elevation in rates of general psychiatric morbidity, for the most part, among gay men and lesbians when compared with heterosexual men and women. But as might be expected, these scientists also found that lesbians and gay men drank alcohol and used drugs more than other women and men (Fiefield, 1975; Lohrenz, Connely, Coyne, & Spare, 1978) and, parenthetically, were predominantly feminists or gay activists (Peplau, Cochran, Rook, & Padesky, 1978). Often these studies included no comparison groups of heterosexuals, making it difficult to interpret the observed prevalences of disorders. The characteristics of these samples reflected the characteristics of the populations from which they were drawn. Confounding of outcome variables with selection strategies continued to be an important methodological weakness of this early work.

In a third wave of research evolving over the past 15 years, scientists began to revisit the question of possible excess psychiatric morbidity among lesbians and gay men, influenced by the HIV epidemic and by increasing interest in the social sciences, in general, in the possible harmful effects of social inequality due to social status, including ethnicity, race, gender, and social class (Fife & Wright, 2000; Kessler, Mickelson, & Williams, 1999; Markowitz, 1998; Mays & Cochran, 1995, 1998, 2001; Mays, Cochran, & Roeder, 2004; Meyer, 1995; Otis & Skinner, 1996; Wright, Gronfein, & Owens, 2000). Many in the field of lesbian and gay psychology (Haldeman, 1991; Herek, Gillis, Cogan, & Glunt, 1997; Rothblum, 1990) noted that lesbians and gay men face particular social stressors over the course of their lives, especially in adolescence and young adulthood, including harassment and maltreatment (Bradford, Ryan, & Rothblum, 1994; Corliss, Cochran, & Mays, 2002), discrimination (Cochran & Mays, 1994; Mays, Cochran, & Rhue, 1993), and victimization (D'Augelli, Hershberger, & Pilkington, 1998; Herek & Berrill, 1992). Psychosocial models of stress-induced distress predict that these experiences, if common and severe enough, should lead to higher rates of distress and some stress-sensitive mental disorders (Dohrenwend, 2000; Kendler et al., 1995; Lin & Ensel, 1989; Mazure, 1995; Meyer, 1995).

The methodology of this third wave of research was shaped by a growing sophistication in research on gay life, generated in part by the influx of funding attached to HIV-related studies, which enabled researchers interested in gay topics to pursue them in a much more rigorous and comprehensive manner. This work for the first time put scientific articles addressing gay life somewhat routinely into top medical and behavioral science journals. To do this, researchers (Bradford et al., 1994; Cochran, Bybee, Gage, & Mays, 1996; Cochran et al., 2001; Mays & Cochran, 1988; McKirnan & Peterson, 1989; Otis & Skinner, 1996; Skinner, 1994; Skinner & Otis, 1996; Sorensen & Roberts, 1997) had to overcome the methodological limitations of earlier studies, such as small sample sizes and restricted sampling frames of dubious generalizability. This was accomplished by several changes in common research methodologies then used. These changes included using multiple recruitment strategies to reduce sampling bias, increasing the numbers of respondents in studies to enhance power, and seeking out reference estimates for the prevalences of psychiatric morbidity that were observed. Scientists became increasingly sophisticated in the use of snowball strategies, membership lists, and street recruitment to develop more diverse samples consistent with the diversity of the lesbian and gay male population. Surveys were conducted at women's music festivals, the marches on Washington, and the gay pride festivals. Also sample sizes ballooned from rather small numbers to fairly large ones including several thousand participants or more (Cochran et al., 2001; Gage, 1994; McKirnan & Peterson, 1989), though comparably sampled groups of heterosexuals remained rare. Finally, researchers began to attempt comparisons to population-based estimates of mental health morbidity. For example, in our own research (Cochran & Mays, 1994) in a study published in the early 1990s, we compared depressive distress measured in large samples of African American lesbians and gay men with published population-based estimates for African American women and men, finding much higher rates of depression in the lesbian and gay male samples. In a second study (Cochran et al., 1996), we contrasted prevalence of crack and cocaine use among nearly 8,000 lesbians from two independently conducted surveys with estimates for U.S. women generated separately from national health data. We found much higher rates of crack or cocaine use among lesbians than would be expected among women in general.

This strategy of comparing estimates from convenience-based samples with population-based estimates has many obvious limitations. As an example, Bell and Weinberg (1978), in a classic study of gay men and lesbians from the late 1970s, the results of which are still widely cited today, recruited heterosexual women by population-based household sampling, but the sampling frame for lesbians was developed by using public advertising (18%), bar attendance (30%), mailing lists (9%), and personal social networks (42%). It is not surprising that this methodology found that lesbians as compared with heterosexual women were more likely to report such behaviors as being arrested. But one wonders if arrest rates among heterosexual women would have differed much from those of lesbians if 30% of these women, too, had been recruited from local bars that at the time put women at risk for arrest.

Sampling bias and the absence of heterosexual control groups stand as two of the major difficulties today in interpreting the body of empirical evidence that has accumulated suggesting that lesbians and gay men experience greater than expected rates of depression, alcohol and drug use, and psychiatric help-seeking (Alcohol, Drug Abuse, and Mental Health Administration [ADAMHA], 1989; Atkinson et al., 1988; Bux, 1996; Cochran, 2001; Cochran et al., 1996; Cochran & Mays, 1994; Cochran & Mays, 2000a; D'Augelli & Hershberger, 1993; D'Augelli et al., 1998; Faulkner & Cranston, 1998; Hershberger & D'Augelli, 1995; Hershberger, Pilkington, & D'Augelli, 1997; Hunter, 1990; McKirnan & Peterson, 1989; Remafedi, Farrow, & Deisher, 1993; Remafedi, French, Story, Resnick, & Blum, 1998).

Population-based psychiatric surveys that measure sexual orientation could go far in clarifying the nature of possible excess risk, but these have been extremely rare until quite recently. Two early studies, one using commercial lists to draw a random neighborhood sample (Bloomfield, 1993) and the other using neighborhood household sampling (Stall & Wiley, 1988), examined alcohol use patterns in gay men and lesbians recruited from high-density gay neighborhoods in San Francisco. Both found no strong evidence of excess risk of alcoholism in lesbians or gay men as compared with heterosexual women and men recruited in the same surveys. More recently, several studies (Faulkner & Cranston, 1998; Garofalo, Wolf, Wissow, Woods, & Goodman, 1999; Remafedi et al., 1998) have looked at the possibility of excess risk of suicide attempts among high school students in samples drawn by general population-based methods. These studies found that gay men, and perhaps lesbians, are, in fact, at higher risk than heterosexually classified individuals. In addition, there are two large, university-based women's health cohort studies under way, the Nurses' Health Study (Case, 1997) and the Women's Health Initiative (Valanis et al., 2000), that have measured sexual orientation, but neither represents population-based sampling.

USING NATIONAL POPULATION-BASED DATA SETS

Since the late 1990s our research team at UCLA has increasingly turned to existing national health data sets to study issues related to psychiatric morbidity among lesbians and gay men (Cochran, 2001). The advantages to this pioneering technique are many. These data sets, often routinely collected by federal agencies to track the health of all Americans, offer a level of methodologic sophistication in sampling, survey development, quality control, and data collection procedures that is generally unavailable to most researchers. Second, they offer a population-based approach to estimating psychiatric burden in the lesbian and gay male population. This avoids common sources of sampling bias that plague volunteer-based surveys of individuals when respondents are recruited using sampling frames dependent on participation in the visible lesbian and gay male community. Convenience-based samples tend to draw heavily from specific demographic groups (e.g., young, White, male, highly educated), confounding the observed prevalences with other known correlates of mental health outcomes (Cochran, Keenan, Schober, & Mays, 2000). Third, both heterosexuals and lesbians and gay men, often from similar demographic settings, are recruited in these studies, offering opportunity to compare rates of morbidity across individuals. However, very few of these data sets actually include direct measures of sexual orientation or sexual behavior assessments that can be used as a proxy for sexual orientation.

National Health and Nutrition Examination Survey III

In one of our early efforts (Cochran & Mays, 2000a), we capitalized on information that lay untouched in the Third National Health and Nutrition Examination Survey (NHANES III; Centers for Disease Control, 1996). The NHANES III is based on a complex, multistage sample of the civilian noninstitutionalized U.S. population. In the course of data collection from these participants in the years 1988 to 1994, those respondents who were between the ages of 15 and 39 years ($N = 8,786$) were interviewed for presence of lifetime affective disorders and related symptoms, including suicidal behaviors. In addition, only men who were age 17 to 59 years ($N = 5,731$) were asked the gender of their lifetime sexual partners. From these two questions we were able to select a final total sample of 3,503 men on whom we had information about both their sexual and psychiatric histories. These men were all between the ages of 17 and 39 years of age. Approximately 3% reported a history of sex with men. For the most part, these men did not differ demographically from other men who reported exclusively female sex partners. The one exception was a lower family income.

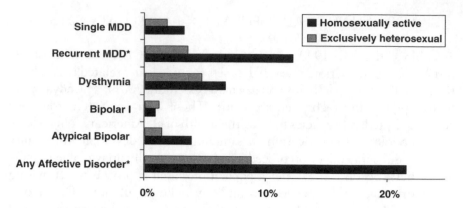

Figure 7.1. Lifetime prevalence of affective disorders among sexually active men, age 17–19, in the Third National Health and Nutrition Examination Survey. Data from Cochran and Mays (2000a). MDD = Major Depressive Disorder.
*p < .05.

When we examined prevalence of affective disorders in this same sample, comparisons of sexually active men revealed that those who reported any male sex partners during their lifetime were significantly more likely than exclusively heterosexually experienced men to meet diagnostic criteria for lifetime prevalence of recurrent depression (see Figure 7.1). These depressions also started early in life. Homosexually experienced men were 5 years younger (*M* age = 14.8 years, *SE* = 1.7) than exclusively heterosexually experienced men (*M* age = 20.3 years, *SE* = 1.7) when they first experienced depressive symptoms $t(3501)$ = 2.48, p < .05. In all, approximately 15% (confidence interval: 2.6%–28.0%) of men reporting any male sex partners met criteria in the *Diagnostic and Statistical Manual of Mental Disorders* (3rd ed., rev., *DSM–III–R*; American Psychiatric Association, 1987). Overall they were also more likely to meet criteria for at least one of the affective disorders measured in the study (e.g., major depression, dysthymia, bipolar I disorder, or atypical bipolar disorder).

The other major finding from this study pertained to histories of suicidal symptoms. Like others (Faulkner & Cranston, 1998; Fergusson, Horwood, & Beautrais, 1999; Herrell et al., 1999; Remafedi et al., 1998), we found greater prevalence of prior suicide attempts among homosexually experienced men (see Figure 7.2). But this risk appeared concentrated in younger age groups. All but one of the homosexually experienced men interviewed who reported a prior suicide attempt were under age 30 at the time of the interview, $\chi^2(1, N = 3,503)$ = 9.21, p < .01. In contrast, among heterosexually experienced men, age at the time of interview was unrelated to positive reports of suicide attempts.

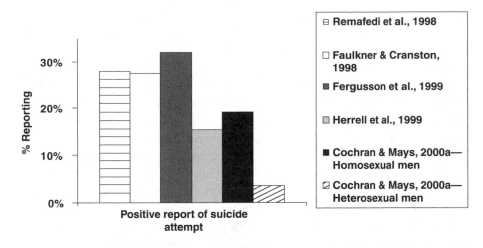

Figure 7.2. Lifetime prevalence of suicide attempts among homosexually active males (vs. exclusively heterosexual males in the Third National Health and Nutrition Examination Survey).

From this study, we drew three major conclusions. First, despite whatever increased risk we observed, most homosexually experienced men did not evidence positive lifetime histories of affective disorders. Second, men with homosexual histories may be at somewhat increased risk for recurrent major depressions. Because of the difficulties associated with the small numbers of possibly gay men in NHANES III and the ways in which controlling demographic confounding seemed to attenuate differences to close to chance levels, we were a bit tentative in this second conclusion. The third finding of importance was, again, the documenting of greater risk for prior suicide attempts among probable gay men. We observed that these men were five times as likely to report having attempted suicide than those classified as heterosexual. Nevertheless, the prevalence we observed was somewhat lower than that found in three surveys involving youths (Faulkner & Cranston, 1998; Fergusson et al., 1999; Remafedi et al., 1998) but similar to another survey involving adult men (Herrell et al., 1999). In the NHANES III, reports of prior suicide attempts among homosexually experienced men were clustered among those under 30 years of age. This supports other work (ADAMHA, 1989; D'Augelli & Hershberger, 1993; D'Augelli et al., 1998; Faulkner & Cranston, 1998; Hershberger & D'Augelli, 1995; Hershberger et al., 1997; Hunter, 1990; Remafedi et al., 1993, 1998) that emphasizes the risk of suicide attempts among gay youths. At the same time, our findings, as well as those of Herrell et al. (1999), suggest that this elevated risk might not continue through later adulthood.

National Household Survey on Drug Abuse

In a second study (Cochran & Mays, 2000b), we used data from the 1996 National Household Survey on Drug Abuse (NHSDA) produced by the Substance Abuse and Mental Health Services Administration (SAMHSA; 1996b). Like the NHANES III, the NHSDA is a national household probability sample of the noninstitutionalized civilian U.S. population. In that year, serendipitously, the interview indirectly measured homosexuality in adults by asking a single question concerning the genders of sex partners in the year prior to interview. Also, the survey collected information on both alcohol and drug use and the presence of six psychiatric syndromes (SAMHSA, 1996a). Four were measured because of a general interest by SAMHSA in studying comorbidity between drug and alcohol use and psychiatric disorders. The other two were alcohol and drug dependency syndromes. Diagnoses were made on the basis of what is coming to be called syndromal diagnosis, that is, there is no attempt to establish that the participants meet all diagnostic criteria by some gold standard such as *DSM–III–R*. Instead, a positive diagnosis represents probable caseness for the disorder in question. It is best to think of it as a positive screening decision (Epstein & Gfroerer, 1995). Syndromal, as opposed to diagnostic, methods are typically used in survey research to limit respondent burden.

In all, the 1996 NHSDA interviewed over 12,000 (N = 12,387) adults. Of these, 79% of women and 78% of men reported only opposite-gender sex partners. But 1% of women and 2% of men indicated that they had had sex with at least one same-gender sex partner in the past year. These individuals were classified as probable lesbians or gay men.[1] An additional 20% of women and men reported no sex partners and were dropped from the study.

As in the NHANES III, there were few demographic differences between those of differing sexual orientation. Probable lesbians were somewhat younger than the women we classified as heterosexual. And probable gay men were significantly more educated than probable heterosexual men. Otherwise, there were no statistically significant differences in demographic backgrounds. The typical demographic skewing frequently observed in

---

[1]The association between lesbian or gay male sexual orientation as an identity and homosexual sexual behavior is not invariant. In a population-based sample of Americans, we estimated (Cochran et al., 2000), using data from Laumann et al.'s (1994) survey of Americans and sexuality, that perhaps half of individuals who report same-gender sexual behavior in adulthood will identify as lesbian, gay, or bisexual if asked, but fewer than 2% of heterosexuals will report adult same-gender sexual contact. Thus, sexual behavior as a proxy accurately classifies heterosexuals, but many with same-gender sexual contact are in fact misclassifed heterosexuals. Bailey (1999) noted that this may result in overestimation of psychiatric risk among sexual minorities because heterosexuals with psychiatric disorders may be more likely to have positive histories of homosexual sexual behavior than heterosexuals without such histories.

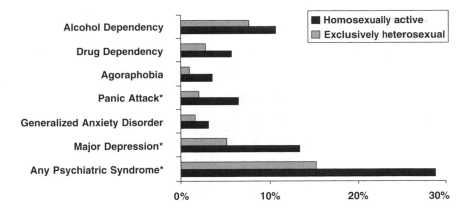

Figure 7.3. One-year prevalence of psychiatric syndromes among sexually active men in the 1996 National Household Survey on Drug Abuse. Data from Cochran and Mays (2000b).
*p < .05.

convenience-based surveys of lesbians and gay men to profiles that are overwhelmingly younger, more male, more educated, and more White than the U.S. population was relatively absent in both of the two national data sets.

The 1996 NHSDA, as noted previously, measured six psychiatric syndromes. Because men and women vary substantially in the prevalence of these disorders, we examined differences separately by gender. Among men, probable gay men were significantly more likely than probable heterosexual men to meet syndromal criteria for 1-year prevalence of major depression and panic attack (see Figure 7.3). But they did not differ from other men in their prevalence of generalized anxiety disorder, agoraphobia, drug dependency, or alcohol dependency. These findings related to depression are consistent with our earlier study using the NHANES III and provide further support for concerns that gay men may in fact experience somewhat greater risk for major depression than heterosexual men. In addition, to our knowledge, there has been only one prior study of the prevalence of anxiety disorders among gay men, and in that study all of the participants were ill with HIV disease (Atkinson et al., 1988). To what extent the excess risk for panic attacks in probable gay men that we observed in our study is or is not related to coping with the HIV epidemic is simply unknown.

When analyses were conducted examining possible differences between probable lesbians and probable heterosexual women, we observed a different pattern of excess risk (see Figure 7.4). Although probable lesbians were no more likely to meet criteria for depression or the anxiety syndromes assessed, they were significantly more likely to evidence drug and alcohol dependency syndromes. Questions about excess morbidity for drug and

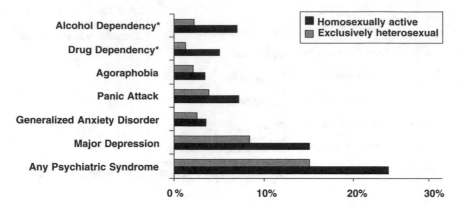

Figure 7.4. One-year prevalence of psychiatric syndromes among sexually active women in the 1996 National Household Survey on Drug Abuse. Data from Cochran and Mays (2000b).
*p < .05.

alcohol use in the lesbian and gay community are a long-standing concern of researchers (Burgard, Cochran, & Mays, 2005; Bux, 1996; Cochran, Ackerman, Mays, & Ross, 2004; Cochran et al., 1996; Cochran, Keenan, Schober, & Mays, 2000; Cochran & Mays, 1999; Cochran, Sullivan, & Mays, 2003; McKirnan & Peterson, 1989; Paul, Stall, & Bloomfield, 1991). Our findings concerning drug and alcohol dependency were consistent, in part, with prevailing views that social factors and discrimination greatly encourage dysfunctional alcohol and drug consumption in the gay community, at least for women (Bux, 1996; Hughes & Wilsnack, 1994; McKirnan & Peterson, 1989; Paul et al., 1991). But there is another viable possibility. Perhaps the greater prevalence is simply a consequence of the greater prevalence of functional alcohol and drug use in the community. How is this possible? Continuity models of risk factors for morbidity assume that risk accrued to individuals is dependent to some extent on the extent to which behaviors that create the risk are prevalent in the population (Cochran et al., 2000; Rose, 1989). So those populations with higher mean intake of alcohol will experience greater prevalence of alcohol-related morbidity simply because more individuals are placed at risk for developing disorders. If one takes two hypothetical populations with nearly the same distribution but in one most people do not drink and in the other most people drink some, then even if the right-handed tail (of higher alcohol consumption) has the same shape, in the population in which most people drink some there will be greater density in the heavy drinking category. From this perspective, it may be that lesbians are at greater risk for drug- or alcohol-related disorders simply because, on the whole, they are more likely than other women to consume drugs and alcohol routinely and in moderation (Cochran et al., 2000).

There is certainly support for this perspective in the 1996 NHSDA (Cochran et al., 2000). For example, probable lesbians were more likely than other sexually active women to indicate that they had consumed alcohol (no matter what the time frame of interest in the question asked) and did so more frequently and in larger amounts. These women also began drinking at a younger age than women who had only male sex partners.

Finally, we also estimated in this study that both men and women who reported same-gender sex partners were significantly more likely than others to indicate that they had received mental health or substance use services in the year prior to interview. This suggests lesbians and gay men may be overrepresented among those seeking and receiving psychological treatment. This should concern us because other studies have demonstrated that lesbians and gay men face particular difficulties in receiving adequate and appropriate mental health care (Cochran, 2001; Garnets, Hancock, Cochran, Goodchilds, & Peplau, 1991; Mays, Beckman, Oranchak, & Harper, 1994).

From this survey we drew four major conclusions. As with the earlier study, we found further evidence that probably around three fourths of lesbians and gay men did not meet criteria for recent psychiatric disorders. The fact that both the NHANES III and the 1996 NHSDA are population-based samples drawn without reference to either sexual orientation or levels of psychopathology supports the view that homosexuality is not usually accompanied by psychiatric disturbance. Despite this, we again found some increased risk for some psychiatric disorders, though differentially for men and women. For men, the risk appears to lie in major depressions and perhaps panic attacks. For women, the greater risk is from alcohol and drug dependency. We could not examine prevalence of suicidal symptoms because the NHSDA does not directly measure these.

National Comorbidity Survey

In an effort to further explore these ideas, we collaborated with researchers from the National Comorbidity Survey in a third study (Gilman et al., 2001) using data from this national household survey of more than 8,000 respondents representative of the U.S. population, age 15 to 54 years. Ronald Kessler at Harvard University is the principal investigator for this study, partially funded by both the National Institute on Drug Abuse and the National Institute of Mental Health. From reports of the genders of sexual partners in the subset of the sample who were questioned ($n = 5,877$) about their sexual histories, we divided the sample into those who reported

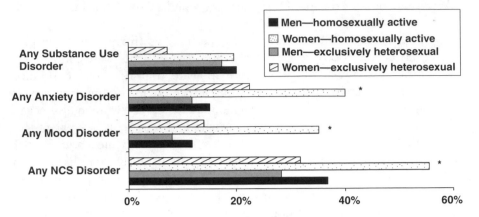

Figure 7.5. One-year prevalence of psychiatric syndromes among sexually active women and men in the National Comorbidity Survey (NCS). Data from Gilman et al. (2001).

*p < .05., comparisons within gender.

only opposite-gender sexual partners in the 5-year period prior to interview (97% of sexually active individuals) and those (3% of sexually active men and 2% of women) who reported at least one same-gender sexual partner, to compare prevalence of lifetime and 1-year psychiatric disorders using *DSM–III–R* criteria. Like the other two studies, there were few demographic differences between those individuals we classified as probably heterosexual or lesbian, gay, or bisexual. As with the previous two studies, there was some elevation of risk for 1-year prevalence of anxiety, mood, and substance use disorders among homosexually active persons, but it achieved statistical significance only among women and only for depression, posttraumatic stress disorder, and simple phobia (see Figure 7.5). No statistically significant differences were observed between homosexually and exclusively heterosexually active men, though in part that appeared due to the limited power we had. Further analyses showed that the elevated 1-year risk we found for women was largely due to higher lifetime prevalences rather than to earlier ages of onset or greater persistence of disorders.

This third study again demonstrated the existence of excess risk for psychiatric morbidity among a small subset of individuals reporting same-gender sexual behavior. But it is important to underscore that all three of these studies did not measure sexual orientation directly. As has been noted (Bailey, 1999), there may be substantial bias introjected by use of a sexual behavior proxy for sexual orientation because, for example, heterosexuals experimenting with same-gender sexual behavior will be included in the homosexually classified sample and, because of the rarity of homosexuality in the population, these misclassified heterosexuals may even outnumber the correctly classified lesbians and gay men (Cochran, 2001).

National Survey of Midlife Development in the United States

To overcome this limitation, we recently completed another study (Cochran et al., 2003) examining risk for psychiatric disorders using data from the National Survey of Midlife Development in the United States, a nationally representative survey of adults age 25 to 74 years (Brim et al., 1996) funded by the MacArthur Foundation. This household telephone and questionnaire-based survey assessed 1-year prevalence of depressive, anxiety, and substance dependency disorders and mental health treatment utilization among 2,917 respondents self-identified as homosexual, bisexual, or heterosexual. As with the previous studies, demographic differences among individuals of different sexual orientation were few, providing further evidence that convenience-based sampling has probably injected predictable volunteer-biasing effects (Rothman & Greenland, 1998) into many studies that have been reported over the years. Results from these four population-based studies, as well as work done elsewhere (Alm, Badgett, & Whittington, 2000) hint that the demographic distribution of lesbians and gay men may be fairly similar to that of other Americans in racial and ethnic background, for example. In gender-specific analyses, we found evidence of higher rates of depression and panic attacks in gay and bisexual men as compared with heterosexual men (see Figure 7.6). In contrast, we observed only higher rates of generalized anxiety disorder in lesbian and bisexual women as compared with heterosexual women. Respondents were also asked to rate their mental health at two ages: currently and at age 16 years. Among men, gay and bisexual men rated both their current and their retrospective mental health as significantly worse than did heterosexual men. Among women, this sexual-orientation-related difference was observed only for ratings of mental health at age 16. At the time of being surveyed, lesbian and bisexual women did not report higher rates of psychological distress than did heterosexual women. An important observation in this study was greater prevalence of psychiatric comorbidity in both lesbian or bisexual women and gay or bisexual men as compared with their same-gender counterparts. In addition, rates of mental health treatment utilization were higher among lesbian, gay, and bisexual (LGB) individuals when compared with heterosexual women and men.

Taken as a whole, results of these studies support concerns that some lesbians and gay men experience somewhat higher rates of stress-sensitive psychiatric disorders than other Americans and may be more likely to use

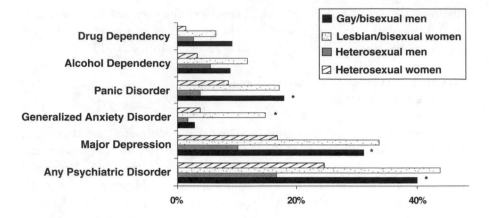

Figure 7.6. One-year prevalence of psychiatric syndromes among sexually active women and men in the National Survey of Midlife Development in the United States. Data from Cochran et al. (2003).
*p < .05., comparisons within gender.

mental health services in the United States. At the same time, the excess risk does not mean that lesbians and gay men universally experience mental health problems. In each of these studies somewhere between half and three quarters of sexual minority respondents did not meet criteria for any measured disorder. Given the very small numbers of possibly LGB individuals surveyed in each of these studies and our limited understanding of the potential effects of nonresponse and response bias in the results we observed (Cochran, 2001; Cochran et al., 2000), the results should be viewed as still tentative at this time.

FUTURE DIRECTIONS

Clearly there are many, many questions remaining. For example, we do not know or understand the causes of these observed differences. And these four studies are only initial, and imprecise, estimates of the broad range of differences in the burden of mental health disorders that might exist. Future work, including ongoing studies from our research group, can profitably explore linkages between social factors, such as discrimination, and mental health outcomes in LGB populations. Further, given the small numbers of individuals identified as lesbian, gay, or bisexual in each of these studies, specification of how other demographic factors such as age, race, or ethnicity interact with sexual orientation is currently beyond the reach of this methodology, though future work may remedy this limitation.

In conclusion, national health surveys offer a rarely tapped means of estimating mental health risks and morbidity among lesbians and gay men and may represent an important methodologic improvement in the next wave of research on mental health issues in this population. As the Women's Health Initiative (Valanis et al., 2000) and the Nurses' Health Study (P. Case testimony, cited in Solarz, 1999), have discovered, asking women directly about their sexual orientation does not affect rates of participation or responses. In addition, the NHANES 2000 is currently experimenting with a sexual orientation question, which, if all goes well, means that within a decade there will be a rich data set available to ask and answer the many questions related to lesbian and gay health that remain unexplored.

Other federally collected health data sets, such as the annual National Survey on Drug Use and Health (NSDUH, formerly the National Household Survey on Drug Abuse) and the annual National Health Interview Survey, could provide additional leadership in establishing the nature and extent of mental health risk among lesbians and gay men if questions related to sexual orientation or same-gender sexual behavior were included or, in the case of the NSDUH, reinserted. Although some may wish to view the asking of sexual orientation questions in health surveys as a political play, we as researchers are very clear that it is not. To meet the federal mandate of disease surveillance for all in the U.S. population, federal agencies need to collect information on respondents' sexual orientation in those surveys where we have suspicions that sexual orientation is associated with differential rates of morbidity or mortality. This information, in some instances, may be as important as our need to collect data on other demographic characteristics such as gender, age, and ethnic or racial background. The importance of including sexual orientation concerns became evident in the recent construction of health promotion and disease prevention targets for *Healthy People 2010* (Mays & Cochran, 1999). Targets for preventive health efforts are decided on the basis of information obtained from national data, typically derived from data sets under the sponsorship of the National Center for Health Statistics and other federal agencies. When providers and policymakers concerned about lesbian and gay men's health began requesting that disease prevention targets be more inclusive of this population's health concerns beyond sexually transmitted disease control in gay men, the lack of existing data worked to prevent the inclusion of other disease targets in the official report. Some references to sexual orientation were eventually added to *Healthy People 2010* after extensive advocacy by organizations and individuals concerned about lesbian and gay health (Gay and Lesbian Medical Association, 2001).

But at the same time, one should not underestimate the hidden nature of lesbian and gay life, its nuances and values, or the extent of prejudice against this population, expressed, in part, in negative stereotypes

(Herek, 2000; LaMar & Kite, 1998; Mays & Cochran, 2001). Although it is extremely simple to include assessment of sexual orientation in a survey, that alone does not make the research team competent to conduct this work. Knowing how to make sense of the data in a manner that results in better health outcomes for the population is just as important as being able to collect it. For example, is the higher risk of alcohol dependency among lesbians seen in the 1996 NHSDA due to stress or really due simply to higher rates of functional drinking? The former interpretation is consistent with stereotypes, and some who are not knowledgeable about the lives of these women may think no further about the problem. But the latter, and far less pejorative, interpretation about this population is also consistent with the data. Both of these hypotheses have radically different implications for prevention of dysfunctional alcohol use. Over the last decade and a half, we have seen repeatedly in HIV-related research the ways in which researchers who were unfamiliar with the gay community have had difficulties making useful interpretations about relationships between behavior and outcomes.

We hope that the federal government, as well as individual researchers, will not repeat many of the techniques used in efforts elsewhere to access and gather data from this population. These approaches, particularly in ethnic minority populations, have generated community conflict and wasted precious resources (Mays & Cochran, 1990, 1995; Mays, Cochran, & Zamudio, 2004). They include forced collaborations and partnerships, often limited funding, a devaluing of the community's own knowledge about itself, and underestimating the value and skills of researchers who are already a part of the community under study. Individuals involved in research, policy, and health care planning continue to struggle with how to include as equal partners those not a part of their formal structure. The public health response to the HIV epidemic was several years into its efforts before it developed the community health planning process we have today that includes the input of community-based organizations.

Finally, it is critical that as we develop an agenda on mental health issues among lesbians and gay men, we not include simply a call for research on pathology. Given the long history of stereotyping gay men and lesbians as mentally defective, it is also important that we explore those things that keep people safe and highly functional despite negative views of homosexuality. What is it that allows this small group of Americans to develop healthy, happy, and fulfilling lives in the context of pervasive and unrelenting discrimination? There is much that we can learn from this population about how people cope well with social inequality. In the long run, this will benefit not only lesbians and gay men but also the broader society through identifying mechanisms for the achievement and maintenance of psychological well-being in the face of social stress.

REFERENCES

Alcohol, Drug Abuse, and Mental Health Administration. (1989). *Report of the secretary's task force on youth suicide: Vol. 3. Prevention and interventions in youth suicide* (DHHS Publication No. 89-1621). Rockville, MD: Author.

Alm, J., Badgett, M. V. L., & Whittington, L. A. (2000). Wedding bell blues: The income tax consequences of legalizing same-sex marriage. *National Tax Journal, 53,* 201–214.

American Psychiatric Association. (1987). *Diagnostic and Statistical Manual of Mental Disorders* (3rd ed., rev.). Washington, DC: Author.

Atkinson, J. H., Jr., Grant, I., Kennedy, C. J., Richman, D. D., Spector, S. A., & McCutchan, J. A. (1988). Prevalence of psychiatric disorders among men infected with human immunodeficiency virus: A controlled study. *Archives of General Psychiatry, 45,* 859–864.

Bailey, J. M. (1999). Homosexuality and mental illness. *Archives of General Psychiatry, 56,* 883–884.

Bell, A., & Weinberg, M. S. (1978). *Homosexualities: A study of diversity among men and women.* New York: Simon & Schuster.

Bloomfield, K. (1993). A comparison of alcohol consumption between lesbians and heterosexual women in an urban population. *Drug and Alcohol Dependence, 33,* 257–269.

Bradford, J., Ryan, C., & Rothblum, E. D. (1994). National Lesbian Health Care Survey: Implications for mental health care. *Journal of Consulting and Clinical Psychology, 62,* 228–242.

Brim, O. G., Baltes, P. B., Bumpass, L. L., Cleary, P. D., Featherman, D. L., Hazzard, W. R., et al. (1996). *National Survey of Midlife Development in the United States (MIDUS), 1995–1996* [Data file]. Available from the Harvard Medical School Web site: http://midmac.med.harvard.edu/research.html

Burgard, S. A., Cochran, S. D., & Mays, V. M. (2005). Alcohol and tobacco use patterns among heterosexually and homosexually sexually experienced California women. *Drug and Alcohol Dependency, 77,* 61–70.

Bux, D. A., Jr. (1996). The epidemiology of problem drinking in gay men and lesbians: A critical review. *Clinical Psychology Review, 16,* 277–298.

Case, P. (1997, September). *Disclosure of sexual orientation in the Nurses' Health Study II.* Paper presented at the Institute of Medicine meetings on lesbian health research, Washington, DC.

Centers for Disease Control and Prevention. (1996). *Third National Health and Nutrition Examination Survey, 1988–1994* [Data files; Documentation No. 76200]. Hyattsville, MD: U.S. Department of Health and Human Services.

Cochran, S. D. (2001). Emerging issues in research on lesbians' and gay men's mental health: Does sexual orientation really matter? *American Psychologist, 56,* 931–947.

Cochran, S. D., Ackerman, D., Mays, V. M., & Ross, M. W. (2004). Prevalence of non-medical drug use and dependency among homosexually active men and women in the U.S. population. *Addictions, 99,* 989–998.

Cochran, S. D., Bybee, D., Gage, S., & Mays, V. M. (1996). Prevalence of self-reported sexual behaviors, sexually transmitted diseases, and problems with drugs and alcohol in three large surveys of lesbian and bisexual women. *Women's Health: Research on Gender Behavior and Policy, 2,* 11–34.

Cochran, S. D., Keenan, C., Schober, C., & Mays, V. M. (2000). Estimates of alcohol use and clinical treatment needs among homosexually active men and women in the U.S. population. *Journal of Consulting and Clinical Psychology, 68,* 1062–1071.

Cochran, S. D., & Mays, V. M. (1994). Depressive distress among homosexually active African American men and women. *American Journal of Psychiatry, 151,* 524–529.

Cochran, S. D., & Mays, V. M. (1999). Are lesbians more at risk for psychiatric disorders? Evidence from the 1996 National Household survey of Drug Abuse. In *Proceedings of the National Center for Health Statistics Conference on National Health Statistics* (CD-ROM; DHHS Publication No. PHS 99-1016). Washington, DC: U.S. Department of Health and Human Services.

Cochran, S. D., & Mays, V. M. (2000a). Lifetime prevalence of suicidal symptoms and affective disorders among men reporting same-sex sexual partners: Results from the NHANES III. *American Journal of Public Health, 90,* 573–578.

Cochran, S. D., & Mays, V. M. (2000b). Relation between psychiatric syndromes and behaviorally defined sexual orientation in a sample of the U.S. population. *American Journal of Epidemiology, 151,* 516–523.

Cochran, S. D., Mays, V. M., Bowen, D., Gage, S., Bybee, D., Roberts, S. J., et al. (2001). Cancer-related risk indicators and preventive screening behaviors among lesbian and bisexual women. *American Journal of Public Health, 91,* 591–597.

Cochran, S. D., Sullivan, J. G., & Mays, V. M. (2003). Prevalence of psychiatric disorders, psychological distress, and treatment utilization among lesbian, gay, and bisexual individuals in a sample of the U.S. population. *Journal of Consulting and Clinical Psychology, 71,* 53–61.

Corliss, H. L., Cochran, S. D., & Mays, V. M. (2002). Reports of parental maltreatment during childhood in a United States population-based survey of homosexual, bisexual and heterosexual adults. *Child Abuse and Neglect, 26,* 1165–1178.

D'Augelli, A. R., & Hershberger, S. L. (1993). Lesbian, gay, and bisexual youth in community settings: Personal challenges and mental health problems. *American Journal of Community Psychology, 21,* 421–448.

D'Augelli, A. R., Hershberger, S. L., & Pilkington, N. W. (1998). Lesbian, gay, and bisexual youth and their families: Disclosure of sexual orientation and its consequences. *American Journal of Orthopsychiatry, 68,* 361–371.

Dohrenwend, B. P. (2000). The role of adversity and stress in psychopathology: Some evidence and its implications for theory and research. *Health and Social Behavior, 41,* 1–19.

Epstein, J., & Gfroerer, J. C. (1995, August). *Estimating substance abuse treatment need from a national household survey.* Paper presented at the 37th International Congress on Alcohol and Drug Dependence, San Diego, CA.

Faulkner, A. H., & Cranston, K. (1998). Correlates of same-sex sexual behavior in a random sample of Massachusetts high school students. *American Journal of Public Health, 88,* 262–266.

Fergusson, D. M., Horwood, L. J., & Beautrais, A. L. (1999). Is sexual orientation related to mental health problems and suicidality in young people? *Archives of General Psychiatry, 56,* 876–880.

Fifield, L. (1975). *On my way to nowhere: Alienated, isolated, drunk.* Los Angeles: Gay Community Services Center.

Fife, B. L., & Wright, E. R. (2000). The dimensionality of stigma: A comparison of its impact on the self of persons with HIV/AIDS and cancer. *Journal of Health and Social Behavior, 41,* 50–67.

Gage, S. (1994, June). *Preliminary findings: The national lesbian and bi women's health survey.* Paper presented at the National Lesbian and Gay Health Conference, New York.

Garnets, L., Hancock, K. A., Cochran, S. D., Goodchilds, J., & Peplau, L. A. (1991). Issues in psychotherapy with lesbians and gay men: A survey of psychologists. *American Psychologist, 46,* 964–972.

Garofalo, R., Wolf, R. C., Wissow, L. S., Woods, E. R., & Goodman, E. (1999). Sexual orientation and risk of suicide attempts among a representative sample of youth. *Archives of Pediatrics and Adolescent Medicine, 153,* 487–493.

Gay and Lesbian Medical Association. (2001). *Healthy People 2010: Companion document for lesbian, gay, bisexual, and transgender (LGBT) health.* Retrieved May, 13, 2003, from http://www.glma.org/policy/hp2010

Gilman, S. E., Cochran, S. D., Mays, V. M., Hughes, M., Ostrow, D., & Kessler, R. C. (2001). Prevalences of DSM-III-R disorders among individuals reporting same-gender sexual partners in the National Comorbidity Survey. *American Journal of Public Health, 91,* 933–939.

Haldeman, D. C. (1991). Sexual orientation conversion therapy for gay men and lesbians: A scientific examination. In J. C. Gonsiorek & J. D. Weinrich (Eds.), *Homosexuality: Research implications for public policy* (pp. 149–160). Thousand Oaks, CA: Sage.

Herek, G. M. (2000). The psychology of sexual prejudice. *Current Directions in Psychological Science, 9,* 19–22.

Herek, G. M., & Berrill, K. T. (1992). Documenting the victimization of lesbians and gay men: Methodological issues. In G. M. Herek & K. T. Berrill (Eds.), *Hate crimes: Confronting violence against lesbians and gay men* (pp. 270–286). Newbury Park, CA: Sage.

Herek, G. M., Gillis, J. R., Cogan, J. C., & Glunt, E. K. (1997). Hate crime victimization among lesbian, gay, and bisexual adults. *Journal of Interpersonal Violence*, *12*, 195–212.

Herrell, R., Goldberg, J., True, W. R., Ramakrishnan, V., Lyons, M., Eisen, S., & Tsuang, M. T. (1999). Sexual orientation and suicidality: A co-twin control study in adult men. *Archives of General Psychiatry*, *56*, 867–874.

Hershberger, S. L., & D'Augelli, A. R. (1995). The impact of victimization on the mental health and suicidality of lesbian, gay, and bisexual youths. *Developmental Psychology*, *31*, 65–74.

Hershberger, S. L., Pilkington, N. W., & D'Augelli, A. R. (1997). Predictors of suicide attempts among gay, lesbian, and bisexual youth. *Journal of Adolescent Research*, *12*, 477–497.

Hooker, E. (1993). Reflections of a 40-year exploration: A scientific view on homosexuality. *American Psychologist*, *48*, 450–453.

Hughes, T. L., & Wilsnack, S. C. (1994). Research on lesbians and alcohol: Gaps and implications. *Alcohol Health & Research World*, *18*, 202–205.

Hunter, J. (1990). Violence against lesbian and gay male youths. *Journal of Interpersonal Violence*, *5*, 295–300.

Kendler, K. S., Kessler, R. C., Walters, E. E., MacLean, C., Neale, M. C., Heath, A. C., & Eaves, L. J. (1995). Stressful life events, genetic liability, and onset of an episode of major depression in women. *American Journal of Psychiatry*, *152*, 833–842.

Kessler, R. C., Mickelson, K. D., & Williams, D. R. (1999). The prevalence, distribution, and mental health correlates of perceived discrimination in the United States. *Journal of Health and Social Behavior*, *40*, 208–230.

LaMar, L., & Kite, M. (1998). Sex differences in attitudes toward gay men and lesbians: A multidimensional perspective. *Journal of Sex Research*, *35*, 189–196.

Laumann, E. O., Gagnon, J. H., Michael, R. T., & Michaels, S. (1994). *The social organization of sexuality: Sexual practices in the United States*. Chicago: University of Chicago Press.

Lin, N., & Ensel, W. M. (1989). Life stress and health: Stressors and resources. *American Sociological Review*, *54*, 382–399.

Lohrenz, L., Connely, J., Coyne, L., & Spare, L. (1978). Alcohol problems in several midwest homosexual populations. *Journal of Studies on Alcohol*, *39*, 1959–1963.

Markowitz, F. E. (1998). The effects of stigma on the psychological well-being and life satisfaction of persons with mental illness. *Journal of Health and Social Behavior*, *39*, 335–347.

Mays, V. M., Beckman, L. J., Oranchak, E., & Harper, B. (1994). Perceived social support for help-seeking behaviors of Black heterosexual and homosexually active women alcoholics. *Psychology of Addictive Behaviors*, *8*, 235–242.

Mays, V. M., & Cochran, S. D. (1988). The Black women's relationship project: A national survey of Black lesbians. In M. Shernoff & W. A. Scott (Eds.),

The sourcebook of lesbian/gay health care (2nd ed., pp. 54–62). Washington, DC: National Gay and Lesbian Health Foundation.

Mays, V. M., & Cochran, S. D. (1990). Methodological issues in the assessment and predictions of AIDS risk-related sexual behaviors among Black Americans. In B. Voeller, J. Reinisch, & M. Gottlieb (Eds.), *AIDS and sex: An integrated biomedical and biobehavioral approach* (pp. 97–120). New York: Oxford University Press.

Mays, V. M., & Cochran, S. D. (1995). HIV/AIDS in the African American community: Changing concerns, changing behaviors. In M. Stein & A. Baum (Eds.), *Chronic diseases* (pp. 259–272). New York: Erlbaum.

Mays, V. M., & Cochran, S. D. (1998). Racial discrimination and health outcomes in African Americans. *Proceedings of the 27th Public Health Conference on Records and Statistics and the National Committee on Vital and Health Statistics 47th Annual Symposium* [CD-ROM], Washington, DC.

Mays, V. M., & Cochran, S. D. (1999, July). *Gay men and Healthy People 2010.* Paper presented at the Gay Men's Health Summit, Boulder, CO.

Mays, V. M., & Cochran, S. D. (2001). Mental health correlates of perceived discrimination among lesbian, gay and bisexual adults in the United States. *American Journal of Public Health, 91,* 1869–1876.

Mays, V. M., Cochran, S. D., & Rhue, S. (1993). The impact of perceived discrimination on the intimate relationships of black lesbians. *Journal of Homosexuality, 25,* 1–14.

Mays, V. M., Cochran, S. D., & Roeder, M. R. (2004). Depressive distress and prevalence of common problems among homosexually active African American women in the United States. *Journal of Psychology and Human Sexuality, 15,* 27–46.

Mays, V. M., Cochran, S. D., & Zamudio, A. (2004). HIV prevention research: Are we meeting the needs of African American men who have sex with men? *Journal of Black Psychology, 30,* 78–105.

Mazure, C. M. (Ed.). (1995). *Does stress cause psychiatric illness?* Washington, DC: American Psychiatric Press.

McKirnan, D. J., & Peterson, P. L. (1989). Alcohol and drug use among homosexual men and women: Epidemiology and population characteristics. *Addictive Behavior, 14,* 545–553.

Meyer, I. H. (1995). Minority stress and mental health in gay men. *Journal of Health and Social Behavior, 36,* 38–56.

Nurius, P. S. (1983). Mental health implications of sexual orientation. *Journal of Sex Research, 19,* 119–136.

Otis, M. D., & Skinner, W. F. (1996). The prevalence of victimization and its effect on mental well-being among lesbian and gay people. *Journal of Homosexuality, 30,* 93–121.

Paul, J. P., Stall, R., & Bloomfield, K. A. (1991). Gay and alcoholic: Epidemiologic and clinical issues. *Alcohol Health and Research, 5,* 151–160.

Peplau, L. A., Cochran, S., Rook, K., & Padesky, C. (1978). Loving women: Attachment and autonomy in lesbian relationships. *Journal of Social Issues, 34*, 7–27.

Remafedi, G., Farrow, J. A., & Deisher, R. W. (1993). Risk factors for attempted suicide in gay and bisexual youth. In L. D. Garnets & D. C. Kimmel (Eds.), *Psychological perspectives on lesbian and gay male experiences* (pp. 486–499). New York: Columbia University Press.

Remafedi, G., French, S., Story, M., Resnick, M. D., & Blum, R. (1998). The relationship between suicide risk and sexual orientation: Results of a population-based study. *American Journal of Public Health, 88*, 57–60.

Rose, G. (1989). The mental health of populations. In P. Williams, G. Wilkinson, & K. Rawnsley (Eds.), *The scope of epidemiological psychiatry* (pp. 77–85). New York: Routledge.

Rothblum, E. D. (1990). Depression among lesbians: An invisible and unresearched phenomenon. *Journal of Gay and Lesbian Psychotherapy, 1*, 67–87.

Rothman, K., & Greenland, S. (1998). *Modern epidemiology* (2nd ed.). Philadelphia: Lippincott-Raven Publishers.

Saghir, M. T., Robins, E., Walbran, B., & Gentry, K. A. (1970). Homosexuality: IV. Psychiatric disorders and disability in the female homosexual. *American Journal of Psychiatry, 127*, 147–154.

Siegelman, M. (1972). Adjustment of homosexual and heterosexual women. *British Journal of Psychiatry, 120*, 477–481.

Skinner, W. F. (1994). The prevalence and demographic predictors of illicit and licit drug use among lesbians and gay men. *American Journal of Public Health, 84*, 1307–1310.

Skinner, W. F., & Otis, M. D. (1996). Drug and alcohol use among lesbian and gay people in a southern U.S. sample: Epidemiological, comparative, and methodological findings from the Trilogy Project. *Journal of Homosexuality, 30*, 59–92.

Solarz, A. (Ed.). (1999). *Lesbian health: Current assessment and directions for the future*. Washington, DC: National Academy Press.

Sorensen, L., & Roberts, S. J. (1997). Lesbian uses of and satisfaction with mental health services: Results from the Boston Lesbian Health Project. *Journal of Homosexuality, 33*, 35–49.

Stall, R., & Wiley, J. (1988). A comparison of alcohol and drug use patterns of homosexual and heterosexual men: The San Francisco Men's Health Study. *Drug and Alcohol Dependence, 22*(1–2), 63–73.

Stein, T. S. (1993). Overview of new developments in understanding homosexuality. In J. M. Oldham, M. B. Riba, & A. Tasman (Eds.), *Review of psychiatry* (Vol. 12, pp. 9–40). Washington, DC: American Psychiatric Press.

Substance Abuse and Mental Health Services Administration. (1996a). *Mental health estimates from the 1994 National Household Survey on Drug Abuse* (DHHS Publication No. SMA 96–3103, Advance Report No., 15). Rockville, MD: Author.

Substance Abuse and Mental Health Services Administration. (1996b). *National Household Survey on Drug Abuse* [Data file]. Available from the Inter-University Consortium for Political and Social Research Web site: http://www.icpsr. umich.edu

Thompson, N. L., McCandless, B. R., & Strickland, B. R. (1971). Personal adjustment of male and female homosexuals and heterosexuals. *Journal of Abnormal Psychology, 78*, 237–240.

Valanis, B. G., Bowen, D. J., Bassford, T., Whitlock, E., Charney, P., & Carter, R. A. (2000). Sexual orientation and health. *Archives of Family Medicine, 9*, 843–853.

Wright, E. R., Gronfein, W. P., & Owens, T. J. (2000). Deinstitutionalization, social rejection, and the self-esteem of former mental patients. *Journal of Health and Social Behavior, 41*, 68–90.

8

INVESTIGATING LESBIANS' MENTAL HEALTH AND ALCOHOL USE: WHAT IS AN APPROPRIATE COMPARISON GROUP?

TONDA L. HUGHES, SHARON C. WILSNACK, AND TIMOTHY P. JOHNSON

Research on the mental health of lesbians (and gay men) has a long history that includes at least three phases (Cochran & Mays, 1999). In the earliest phase, homosexuality was viewed as synonymous with psychopathology. Because many early studies used samples of lesbians from psychiatric settings, research findings tended to support the assumption that lesbians had higher rates of mental health problems than heterosexual women. In the 1970s, particularly following the removal of homosexuality as a diagnostic

This research was funded by the University of Illinois (UIC) Campus Research Board and the UIC College of Nursing Internal Research Support Program. Development of this chapter was supported by a research grant (K01 AA00266, Tonda Hughes, principal investigator) from the National Institute on Alcohol Abuse and Alcoholism (NIAAA) and the Office of Research on Women's Health, National Institutes of Health (NIH). The National Study of Health and Life Experiences of Women, the source of the heterosexual comparison sample and the interview questionnaire, was supported by Research Grants R01 and R37 AA04610 from NIAAA/NIH (Sharon Wilsnack, principal investigator).

category from the *Diagnostic and Statistical Manual of Mental Disorders* (2nd ed.; American Psychiatric Association, 1973), studies were increasingly conducted using nonclinical samples. However, researchers had to rely on organizations' mailing lists, or use social settings where lesbians could be found in large numbers, for recruitment of study samples. Therefore, research findings continued to reflect the characteristics of the populations from which the samples were drawn. For example, most studies of lesbians' use of alcohol conducted during this phase collected all or some portion of their samples in gay bars (e.g., Fifield, Latham, & Phillips, 1977; Morales & Graves, 1983; Saghir & Robins, 1973). It is not surprising that lesbians in these studies reported high rates of alcohol abuse or alcoholism.

Very few studies in the first two phases of research on lesbians' mental health included comparison groups of heterosexual women. Because health data are often used to document the need for new or improved programs or policies, and because such data are most compelling if they can demonstrate risk relative to some known standard, the ability to compare indicators of lesbians' health with those of women in the general population is important. During the past 10 to 20 years researchers investigating lesbians' mental health have made greater efforts to include comparison groups, or to at least provide comparison data. Although these attempts clearly represent improvement over earlier phases of research in which studies seldom included a basis of comparison, little attention has been paid to the appropriateness of the comparisons used. Because lesbian health research has relied on nonrandom, convenience sampling, women in these studies are often more homogeneous (a majority are generally White, middle class, and well educated) than are women in general population studies. Therefore, comparisons between data from lesbians and from women in general population surveys can be problematic.

Over the past 10 years we and our colleagues have worked to address some of the methodological limitations in research on lesbians (Hughes, Haas, & Avery, 1997; Hughes, Haas, Razzano, Cassidy, & Matthews, 2000; Hughes, Johnson, & Wilsnack, 2001; Hughes & Wilsnack, 1994, 1997; Matthews & Hughes, 2001; Matthews, Hughes, Johnson, Razzano, & Cassidy, 2002; Nawyn, Richman, Rospenda, & Hughes, 2000; Parks, Hughes, & Matthews, 2004).

In 1993–1994 we conducted a study on lesbian health that used a novel strategy for obtaining a heterosexual comparison group (Hughes et al., 1997). Lesbians were recruited from Chicago and surrounding suburbs using multiple sources to ensure as diverse a sample as possible. Each lesbian who completed the self-administered survey questionnaire was asked to give a color-coded, duplicate copy to a woman presumed to be heterosexual and whose work role closely matched the lesbian's own. Demographic characteristics of the heterosexual women (n = 134) recruited using this method were remarkably similar to the lesbian (n = 284) sample. Further, differences in most of the mental health and alcohol problem indicators were smaller than those reported in earlier lesbian health studies. Replications of the Chicago study were subsequently conducted in Minneapolis–St. Paul and New York City (Hughes et al., 2000; Hughes, Matthews, Razzano, & Aranda, 2003; Matthews et al., 2002) and in Columbus, Ohio (Bernhard & Applegate, 1999).

In this chapter we report select findings from a study of lesbians' mental health and alcohol use to illustrate the strengths and limitations of two types of comparison groups of heterosexual women in research with lesbians. Although data from lesbians in this study were collected in Chicago, the issues we highlight have broad application to research on lesbians' mental health. The first comparison group was obtained using a method similar to the one in our earlier studies in which lesbian participants were asked to assist with the recruitment of the heterosexual comparison group; the second is an urban, age-matched subsample from a national study of women in the general population. Because data in both studies were collected using the same study instrument and interview protocol, this design permits multiple comparisons: Chicago lesbians with Chicago heterosexual women, Chicago lesbians with national heterosexual women, and Chicago heterosexual women with heterosexual women in the national study.

We compare the demographic characteristics of the three samples and present data on several variables of particular importance to lesbians' mental health. Identifying similarities and differences in demographic and health variables in the three samples, and in the relationships between the demographic and health variables, provides not only substantive findings of interest but also important information about the strengths and limitations of these two methods of selecting comparison groups for use in lesbian health research.

DATA SOURCES AND STUDY METHODS

Data are from the Chicago Health and Life Experiences of Women (CHLEW) pilot study[1] and the National Study of Health and Life Experiences of Women (NSHLEW). The CHLEW was conducted in 1997 to test the inclusiveness for lesbians of the instrument and methods used in the NSHLEW (see Hughes, 2003; Hughes et al., 2001). In the CHLEW women

---

[1] Chapter 9 of this volume also reports data from the CHLEW.

who self-identified as lesbian, were English speaking, and were 18 years old or older were recruited using a broad range of ascertainment sources (lesbian and gay bars were excluded). For example, advertisements were placed in local newspapers, and flyers were posted in churches and bookstores and distributed to formal organizations and through formal and informal social events and social networks. Our recruitment efforts specifically targeted racial and ethnic minority and other hard-to-reach women (e.g., older lesbians and those with lower incomes). Interested women were asked to call the project office to schedule an interview at a time and location convenient to them. During the initial telephone contact, each lesbian participant was asked to help us recruit a heterosexual woman who was of the same race and who had a job or (in the case of students or retirees) a role similar to the lesbian's own. These recruitment strategies resulted in 63 lesbians and a comparison group of 57 heterosexual women.

The second comparison group included 128 age-matched, urban-dwelling heterosexual women from the 1991 NSHLEW survey. The NSHLEW is an ongoing longitudinal study of drinking behavior and drinking-related problems in women. The National Opinion Research Center (NORC) conducted the sampling and fieldwork for each of the NSHLEW surveys in 1981, 1986, 1991, 1996, and 2001 (see, e.g., R. W. Wilsnack, Wilsnack, & Klassen, 1984; R. W. Wilsnack, Wilsnack, Kristjanson, & Harris, 1998; S. C. Wilsnack, Klassen, Shur, & Wilsnack, 1991).

The 1981 NSHLEW interviewed a probability sample of U.S. women age 21 and older who resided in noninstitutional settings. The sample was stratified by screening interviews to include all women who reported that they consumed four or more drinks per week (approximately 20% of U.S. women in 1981) and one fourth of the women who reported that they drank less than this or abstained from alcohol. In sampled households, 94% of the adult women completed screening interviews; of the women identified as eligible for the study, 86% completed survey interviews. The final 1981 sample included 498 "moderate-to-heavy drinking" women (four or more drinks per week) and 413 lighter drinking and abstaining women.

In 1991, NORC located 92% of the original 1981 sample, and reinterviewed 696 (92%) of the 757 living respondents who were not too seriously ill to be interviewed. Analyses of attrition from the 1981 sample found that women lost to follow-up were older, as expected from mortality rates. Interviews were also completed with a new cohort of 403 women ages 21 to 30 (91% completion rate), stratified as in 1981 to oversample moderate to heavy drinkers. Statistical weighting compensated for the stratified sampling and for variations in response rates and allowed the two subsamples to be combined to represent the noninstitutionalized U.S. female population age 21 and older in 1991. With a few exceptions, distributions of age, ethnicity, and age-specific marital status in the 1991 weighted sample did not differ from the 1991 U.S. adult female population as described in the 1992 *Statistical Abstract of the United States*.

To provide the closest match with the lesbian sample in Chicago we selected from the 1991 NSHLEW data only urban-dwelling heterosexual women who were 21 to 69 years old.[2] Lesbians in the CHLEW ranged in age from 19 to 69 years old (only four lesbians were younger than 21 years).

The Health and Life Experiences of Women Questionnaire

The CHLEW study used a slightly adapted version of the interview questionnaire from the NSHLEW. The Health and Life Experiences of Women Questionnaire (HLEW) has been developed over the past 20 years and used to collect data from more than 2,000 women (see R. W. Wilsnack et al., 1984; S. C. Wilsnack et al., 1991). The HLEW was designed to gather data on drinking behavior and drinking-related problems, physical and mental health, and a variety of life experiences. The nearly 400 questions permit assessment of the individual and combined effects of a large number of variables identified in previous theory or research as being associated with women's drinking (e.g., social roles, relationship characteristics, depression and anxiety, physical and sexual abuse). Questions, indexes, and scales used in the initial (1981) HLEW were selected, whenever possible, from instruments that had been well validated in previous research. The HLEW has been extensively pretested prior to each wave of data collection and refined over time to retain the variables with the greatest predictive value. Sexual orientation questions focusing on sexual identity, behavior, and attraction were developed in two focus groups with lesbians in Chicago. The CHLEW questionnaire, with the new sexual orientation questions and some changes in wording to make other questions more inclusive of lesbians' experiences, was pretested in 1996 with 15 lesbians (Skrocki, 1996). The sexual orientation questions are now included in the NSHLEW, making possible future comparisons of lesbian and heterosexual women in this national study.

Sexual Orientation

Although the CHLEW included multiple measures of sexual orientation for our purposes here, women in the Chicago sample were considered

---

[2] We chose to use 1991 data because the 2001 NSHLEW survey had not been completed at the time this chapter was written and because the 1996 survey included only a subset of the total sample. Because many of the strongest predictors of women's drinking in the 1981, 1986, and 1991 surveys were aspects of their relationships with spouses or intimate partners, the 1996 survey interviewed only women who were between 26 to 54—the age group most likely to be drinkers and to have partners—together with their marital or cohabiting partners.

lesbian if they answered "mostly" or "only" homosexual, lesbian, or gay to the question asking "How do you define your sexual identity?" and heterosexual if they answered "mostly" or "only" heterosexual. Because resources limited the number of interviews in the CHLEW we chose to exclude women who identified as bisexual in the telephone screening for the study. Because the 1991 NSHLEW did not include a specific question about sexual identity, we used two questions about lifetime sexual behavior (male partners only, female partners only, or both) and sexual attraction or pleasure ("Would you say that sex with another woman might be enjoyable for you?") to exclude women from the heterosexual comparison group who might be lesbian or bisexual. Only women who reported that their sexual partners have been only men, and who answered "no" to the question asking whether sex with another woman might be enjoyable, were included in the NSHLEW comparison sample.

Depression

Lifetime experience of depression was measured by questions and diagnostic criteria from the National Institute of Mental Health Diagnostic Interview Schedule (Robins, Helzer, Croughan, & Ratcliff, 1981). Participants were asked about the following symptoms: decreased appetite; unexplained weight loss or weight gain; problems with sleeping (too much or too little); fatigue; talking or moving more slowly than usual; restlessness or pacing; reduced interest in sex; feelings of worthlessness, sinfulness, or guilt; and thoughts of death. If three or more of these symptoms had lasted for at least 2 weeks and were accompanied by feeling sad, blue, or depressed or by loss of interest or pleasure in things usually cared about, the participant was given a positive score for lifetime depression. The analyses reported here dichotomized lifetime depressive episodes into *none* (0) versus *one or more* (1).

Suicidal Ideation and Suicide Attempts

Participants were asked, "Have you ever felt so low that you wanted to die?" and "Have you ever attempted suicide?" Responses to both questions were dichotomous (*yes* or *no*). These questions were from the Diagnostic Interview Schedule (DIS; Robins et al., 1981). Although the DIS question about thoughts of wanting to die is technically a measure of "death ideation" rather than "suicide ideation" we included this question (rather than a separate question that asked "Have you ever felt so low you thought of committing suicide?") because we felt it was less subject to social desirability bias against admitting thoughts of wanting to kill oneself.

Drinking Measures

The CHLEW and HLEW included multiple measures of drinking behavior and drinking-related problems including 30-day drinking, 12-month, and lifetime quantity and frequency of drinking as well as past year and lifetime experiences of alcohol-related problems.

Drinking Levels

Participants were asked beverage-specific questions about frequency of drinking wine, beer, and liquor during the past 30 days, and number of drinks of each beverage consumed on a typical day when they drank that beverage. Drinking frequency, quantity, average drink sizes, and ethanol content for all beverages were combined to calculate average daily consumption. This measure was used to classify participants' levels of drinking as lifetime abstainers, 12-month abstainers (no alcohol consumed in the previous 12 months), temporary or 30-day abstainers, light drinkers (less than 0.22 oz of ethanol per day), moderate drinkers (0.22–0.99 oz of ethanol per day), and heavy drinkers (1 oz or more of ethanol per day).[3] More detail about the drinking measures is provided in R. W. Wilsnack et al. (1984).

Drinking-Related Problems

We used two measures of drinking-related problems. Eight questions asked about adverse drinking consequences: Six from previous drinking surveys (e.g., Cahalan, 1970; Clark & Midanik, 1982) asked about (a) driving while drunk or high from alcohol; (b) starting arguments or fights with partner or (c) with persons outside the family when drinking; (d) drinking-related harm to work or job chances; and (e) complaints about participant's drinking by her partner or (f) by relatives or close friends. Two newer questions asked about (g) drinking-related accidents in the home and (h) interference by drinking with housework or chores.

Symptoms of potential alcohol dependence were drawn from national drinking surveys (e.g., Cahalan, 1970; Clark, 1979; Polich & Orvis, 1979) and were selected in part on the basis of their prevalence in pretests of the NSHLEW. Questions asked about (a) memory lapses while drinking (blackouts); (b) rapid drinking; (c) inability to stop drinking before becoming intoxicated; (d) inability to stop or reduce alcohol consumption over time; and (e) morning drinking. Both measures assessed both lifetime and past-12-month experiences.

---

[3] A standard drink of beer (12-oz can), wine (4- to 5-oz glass), or liquor (1 oz) contains approximately one half-ounce of ethanol.

Other Problem Drinking Indicators

Both the CHLEW and the NSHLEW included questions that asked each participant whether she had ever wondered if she was developing a drinking problem ("Have you ever wondered at any time if you were developing a drinking problem?"). An additional question asked about lifetime and current alcohol treatment ("Have you ever gone to anyone—a treatment agency, Alcoholics Anonymous, anyone at all—for help with a drinking problem of your own?").

DATA COLLECTION AND ANALYSIS

Both the Chicago and the national studies collected data in face-to-face interviews. Interviews generally lasted 90 minutes, but were longer or shorter depending on how many of the questions applied to individual participants. Women were interviewed individually in a private setting by a trained female interviewer. Confidential self-administered handouts were used to collect data on sensitive topics such as those related to sexual experiences. In Chicago, lesbians were given $20 for their interview and $10 for assisting with a successful contact and interview of a heterosexual counterpart. Heterosexual women interviewed in Chicago also received $20. Women in the NSHLEW were not given a monetary stipend in 1991.

Descriptive statistics were used to summarize bivariate relationships. A series of two-variable multinomial logistic regression models (Agresti, 1990) were used to compare the three samples. This analytic approach has the advantage of providing pairwise comparisons of all three samples within a single model. It thus permits direct assessments of similarities and differences in the prevalence of key participant characteristics, experiences, or behaviors across the three samples. Significant differences for each pair of sample comparisons are summarized in Tables 8.1 and 8.2. To compensate for the number of statistical tests conducted, we set the significance level at .01, rather than the less stringent level of .05.

Description of the Samples

Demographic characteristics of the three groups of women are summarized in Table 8.1. The lesbian sample is much more diverse than those included in most previous research on lesbian health. Recruitment methods used in the Chicago study (having lesbian participants assist in the recruitment of heterosexual work-role counterparts who were of the same race) resulted in samples of lesbian and heterosexual women who were demographically very similar.

TABLE 8.1
Demographic Characteristics of Samples

Demographic	Chicago				U.S. heterosexual women (n = 128)	
	Heterosexual women (n = 57)		Lesbians (n = 63)			
	n	%	n	%	n	%
Age (years)[a]						
18–29	14	25	18	29	38	30
30–39	14	25	21	33	39	31
40–49	10	18	7	11	22	17
50–59	12	21	12	19	17	13
60 or older	7	12	5	8	12	9
Race/Ethnicity[b, c]						
African American (non-Hispanic)	16	28	13	21	32	25
White (non-Hispanic)	21	37	22	35	84	66
Hispanic	11	19	20	31	10	8
Other[d]	9	16	8	13	2	2
Education[b, c]						
HS or less	8	14	10	16	49	37
Some college or a BA or BS	30	53	37	59	64	50
Advanced degree	19	33	16	25	14	11
Employment						
Full time	36	63	35	56	68	53
Part time	9	16	11	18	21	16
Unemployed	12	21	17	27	39	31
Annual household income						
<$10,000	9	16	14	22	19	16
$10,000–49,999	35	61	33	52	72	60
$50,000 or greater	13	23	16	25	30	25
Married or in committed relationship	33	58	36	57	71	55
Legally married[b, c, e]	11	19	2	3	60	47
Cohabiting[c]	12	21	20	32	11	9
Committed relationship, not living together[b, c]	10	18	13	22	—	—
Children living at home[b, f]	15	27	7	12	64	50

[a]Mean age of Chicago heterosexual women = 42; mean age of Chicago lesbians and U.S. heterosexual women = 39. [b]Chicago heterosexuals and U.S. heterosexuals differ at $p \leq .001$. [c]Chicago lesbians and U.S. heterosexuals differ at $p \leq .001$. [d]Includes bi- and multi-race/ethnic identity. [e]Chicago heterosexuals and Chicago lesbians differ at $p \leq .01$. [f]Chicago heterosexuals and U.S. heterosexuals differ at $p \leq .01$.

The average age of the Chicago lesbian sample was 39—the same as heterosexual women in the national sample; mean age of the Chicago heterosexual women was 42. Although age differences were not statistically significant, the national sample differed substantially from the Chicago samples in racial and ethnic composition and education. Two thirds of the national sample was non-Hispanic White, compared with only about one third of the Chicago samples. Relatively few participants (8%) in the national sample were Hispanic (compared with 19% of heterosexual women and 31% of lesbians in the CHLEW). In addition, samples in the two studies reported quite different levels of education. The heterosexual women in the national study were more than twice as likely as the lesbians and heterosexual women in Chicago to report having a high school education or less.

Equal proportions (55%–58%) of each of the three groups reported that they were either married or in a committed relationship. However, significantly more heterosexual women from the national study than women in either Chicago sample were married; conversely, more women in the Chicago samples reported that they were living with a partner in a committed (cohabiting) relationship. To be more inclusive of lesbians' experiences, the Chicago study question about relationship status included the response category "in a committed relationship, but not living together." This response category (not included in the national study) was endorsed by similar proportions of lesbians (22%) and heterosexual women (18%) in the Chicago study. Lesbians were less likely than either of the heterosexual samples to report having children living at home; heterosexual women in the Chicago study were less likely than those in the national study to report having children living at home.

Mental Health and Alcohol Variables

Table 8.2 summarizes the findings related to the mental health and problem drinking indicators. Whereas lesbian and heterosexual women in the Chicago study did not differ significantly on the depression and suicide measures, both Chicago samples were more likely than the national sample to report past depression, suicidal ideation, and suicide attempts.

Similarly, there were no significant differences in overall levels of drinking among the three groups. These findings, however, must be interpreted in light of the fact that 18% of the lesbians in the Chicago study were in recovery for alcohol-related problems (Hughes et al., 2001) and thus did not answer questions about past 12-month alcohol consumption or alcohol-related problems. Only 2% of the heterosexual women in the Chicago study were in recovery. The numbers and percentages of lesbian and heterosexual women in the Chicago study who described themselves as in recovery correspond exactly to the figures for lifetime treatment for alcohol-related problems. Although the 1991 national survey did not include a specific question about recovery, the percentage of heterosexual women in the national study who reported lifetime treatment for alcohol-related problems (4%) is likely a close approximation of the percentage of women who were in recovery in that sample.

TABLE 8.2
Mental Health and Alcohol Variables

Variable	Chicago Heterosexual women (n = 57)		Chicago Lesbians (n = 63)		U.S. heterosexual women (n = 128)	
	n	%	n	%	n	%
Lifetime depressive episodes (1 or more)[a, b]	30	53	42	67	41	32
Suicidal ideation (ever)[a, b]	35	61	41	65	25	20
Suicide attempts (ever)[b, c]	12	21	19	30	7	6
Drinking levels						
Lifetime abstainer	7	13	0	—	18	14
12-month abstainer	2	4	15	25	16	13
Temporary abstainer[d]	8	15	8	13	12	9
Light drinker	26	47	25	41	40	32
Moderate drinker	11	20	10	16	30	24
Heavy drinker	1	2	3	5	11	9
Drinking-related problems (12-month drinkers only)[e]						
Alcohol dependence symptoms (0–5): Any symptoms past 12 months	7	15	13	28	23	25
Adverse drinking consequences (0–8): Any consequences past 12 months	7	15	17	37	34	37
Ever wondered if had drinking problem[f, g]	8	14	29	46	31	24
Alcohol treatment (lifetime)	1	2	11	18	6	4

[a]Chicago heterosexuals and U.S. heterosexuals differ at $p \leq .001$. [b]Chicago lesbians and U.S. heterosexuals differ at $p \leq .001$. [c]Chicago heterosexuals and U.S. heterosexuals differ at $p \leq .01$. [d]Had consumed alcohol in the past 12 months but not in the past 30 days. [e]For Chicago heterosexual women and Chicago lesbians, $n = 46$; for U.S. heterosexual women, $n = 93$. [f]Chicago heterosexuals and Chicago lesbians differ at $p \leq .001$. [g]Chicago lesbians and U.S. heterosexuals differ at $p \leq .01$.

There were also no significant differences in the proportions of lesbian and heterosexual women who reported one or more alcohol dependence symptoms or adverse drinking consequences in the past 12 months. However, almost one half (46%) of lesbians in this study, compared with only 14% of heterosexual women in the Chicago study and 24% of those in the national study, reported that they had wondered at some time in the past if they might be developing a drinking problem.

Previous research on women's drinking suggests that drinking outcomes such as level of drinking, binge drinking, and drinking-related problems have different predictors (e.g., R. W. Wilsnack et al., 1998) and thus may vary according to the demographic characteristics of study samples. To further explore potential differences between lesbian and heterosexual women, we conducted a series of regression analyses comparing the two heterosexual samples (combined) with the lesbians in the Chicago study. In these analyses (results not shown), interactions between sexual orientation and age, race, education, and income were examined to determine the degree to which sexual orientation may moderate the effects of demographic characteristics on alcohol-related problems. We found a significant interaction effect between level of education and sexual orientation in predicting the number of adverse drinking consequences and alcohol dependence symptoms reported. Specifically, although lesbian and heterosexual women who reported having some college education or a bachelor's degree and those with graduate or professional education reported very similar numbers of alcohol problems, lesbians with no more than a high school education reported significantly more alcohol-related problems than did heterosexual women of the same educational level; both groups of more educated women reported fewer problems than did less educated lesbians. It is interesting to note that the interaction effect between income and sexual orientation was not significant. This finding may be explained, at least in part, by a discrepancy between lesbians' levels of education and income reported by some researchers (e.g., Bradford, Ryan, & Rothblum, 1994).

DISCUSSION OF FINDINGS

Results from these analyses support earlier findings suggesting that lesbians are at heightened risk for alcohol abuse and suicidal ideation. Results also suggest that findings may differ substantially depending on the particular sample of lesbians included in a study and—when compared with heterosexual women—how similar the demographic characteristics of the comparison group are to those of the lesbian sample. Studies of lesbian health have typically included convenience samples that are predominately urban, White, and well educated. In addition, lesbians who participate in research are generally younger—usually between 25 and 40 years old—than are samples in most general population studies. Each of these characteristics likely influences findings related to health behaviors and problems. For example, in studies of women in the general population, being a current drinker is associated with higher levels of education, younger age, being White versus African American or Hispanic, and residence in an urban area (NIAAA, 2000). Differences in the demographic composition of samples may help explain why studies of lesbians' drinking that have used national probability samples for comparison (Bergmark, 1999; McKirnan & Peterson, 1989; Skinner & Otis, 1996) have found substantially higher rates of drinking among lesbians. Studies using comparison groups of heterosexual women that are more closely matched (e.g., Bloomfield, 1993; Hughes et al., 1997), as in the present study, have found fewer differences.

The Chicago samples of lesbian and heterosexual women in this study were very similar in their responses to the questions on depression and suicide (ideation and attempts). Conversely, both groups differed from the heterosexual women in the national study on each of these measures. The major differences in the drinking measures were in participants' reports that they had ever wondered if they were developing a drinking problem and in reports of treatment for alcohol-related problems; lesbians were more likely to report each of these than were heterosexual women in either the Chicago or the national samples. Although differences in these indicators of drinking-related problems may be explained, at least in part, by the context of lesbian subculture (e.g., normative use of psychotherapy, which may contribute to greater sensitivity about or willingness to acknowledge and report drinking problems), the magnitude of differences supports earlier assumptions of heightened risk.

IMPLICATIONS FOR FUTURE RESEARCH

The similarities between the mental health and drinking variables reported by the lesbian and heterosexual women in the Chicago study, and the differences between the Chicago samples and the heterosexual women in the national study, highlight the strengths and limitations of each of the types of comparison groups used in this study. On the one hand, the method we used in Chicago provides a comparison that controls for many demographic and life-experience factors—other than sexual orientation—that might have influenced the drinking and mental health variables in the study, so differences between the two groups can more confidently be attributed to sexual orientation. On the other hand, the heterosexual comparison group from the national study is more representative of the general population of women. Comparing lesbians with this group helps to reveal "clusters" of characteristics (e.g., demographic, personality, lifestyle) that may be associated with a lesbian sexual orientation (but not unique to that orientation, as indicated by the lack of differences in these characteristics between the lesbian sample from the Chicago study and the more closely matched Chicago control participants) and that may distinguish lesbians from the more heterogeneous heterosexual female population. By including both comparison groups, it may be possible to detect whether lesbian sexual orientation has only additive effects with these clusters of associated characteristics or whether it interacts with the clusters to produce even greater effects on health outcomes. However, unless studies of lesbians are designed to replicate population-based studies (as the CHLEW was), such multiple comparisons may not be feasible.

Researchers are beginning to explore other innovative methods of obtaining comparison groups for studies of lesbian health. In a recent study of lesbians' mental health, Rothblum and Factor (2001) used the sisters of lesbians as a control group. Consistent with previous research findings lesbians in this study reported higher levels of education than did their heterosexual sisters. Rothblum and Factor suggested that higher levels of education are associated with lesbians' lower likelihood of being married and having children. Each of these factors (higher levels of education, unmarried status, not having children) likely exert an important influence on lifestyle behaviors and mental health. For example, lesbians in Rothblum and Factor's study were found to have higher self-esteem than their heterosexual sisters.

Consistent findings of higher education among lesbians emphasize the limitations of simple comparisons with heterosexual women and highlight the importance of paying attention to (and when appropriate, controlling for) demographic variables—such as education—that may influence study results, even when comparison groups are carefully selected.

Notwithstanding consistent findings of higher education among lesbians, a fundamental theme emerging from the literature on lesbians' health is the tremendous variability within the lesbian population. This heterogeneity poses formidable theoretical and methodological challenges to researchers. Although the criticism leveled at lesbian health research for its inclusion of mostly White, middle-class women is not without merit, an argument can also be made that more research is needed that focuses on homogeneous subgroups within the lesbian population. In this study, lesbians with lower education reported more adverse drinking consequences and alcohol dependence symptoms than did lesbians with higher levels of education. Similarly, in another recent study, we found that racial and ethnic minority lesbians and lesbians with lower levels of education appear to be at very high risk for smoking (Hughes, Johnson, & Matthews, 2004). Because of the relatively small sample size in the current study, there were too few women to conduct in-depth comparisons of the subgroups. Until large-scale national studies that permit comparisons among subgroups of lesbians are more feasible, smaller descriptive studies of particular subgroups can provide important information about risk and protective factors specific to these groups. Methodological challenges can make research with lesbians more demanding and expensive than studies of women in the general population. Researchers should be encouraged to assume these challenges and funding agencies should be prepared to recognize the methodological requirements and support this research.

Despite recent efforts such as recommendations made by the Institute of Medicine's Committee on Lesbian Health Research (Solarz, 1999) and the Healthy People 2010 companion document (Gay and Lesbian Medical Association, 2001), research on lesbians' mental health lags far behind research conducted with women in the majority population. The insights gained through the development and testing of complex models for explaining and predicting alcohol abuse or other mental health problems among lesbians will inform understanding of the health of all women in the United States.

STRENGTHS AND LIMITATIONS

In contrast to previous studies of lesbians' mental health, our lesbian sample is very diverse in terms of race and ethnicity, age, education, and income. This internal diversity helps to minimize the potential for systematic bias that may influence study findings. Nevertheless, the sample most likely represents primarily women who are "out" or comfortable with their sexual orientation. At best, generalizability is limited to women who are "out" enough to identify as lesbian in a confidential interview.

Our inclusion of two heterosexual comparison groups is also a strength. However, the comparison groups we used are not without limitations. Among the most notable are differences in data collection time frames and definitions of sexual orientation in the CHLEW and NSHLEW. First, although there have not been marked shifts in prevalence of alcohol or mental health disorders over the past 10 years, the 5- to 6-year difference in the time periods in which data were collected in the NSHLEW and the CHLEW may have had subtle influences on women's alcohol use or mental health and resulted in larger (or smaller) differences between these two samples. Second, because the 1991 NSHLEW did not include a question about sexual identity, we used questions about sexual behavior and sexual attraction to "define" the sexual orientation of women in the national sample. Although sexual identity is highly correlated with behavior and attraction (Hughes et al., 1997; Laumann, Gagnon, Michael, & Michaels, 1994), a substantial proportion of women who have sex with other women do not identify as lesbian. Some evidence suggests that women who engage in same-sex behavior but do not identify as lesbian may be more likely than self-identified lesbians to engage in risky behaviors, such as substance abuse (Cochran & Mays, 2000; McCabe, Hughes, & Boyd, 2004; Scheer et al., 2003). Thus, different dimensions of sexual orientation may be associated with different levels of drinking or with mental health status. Because new questions about sexual orientation (including a question about sexual identity) are now in the NSHLEW, future comparisons of lesbians and heterosexual women will be based on more consistent definitions of sexual orientation.

It is time that we enter a new phase of lesbian health research. This phase should be one in which researchers of all studies—both large-scale and small—carefully define sexual orientation, include heterosexual comparison groups that are most appropriate to the research questions, use the most rigorous methods possible, and are thoughtful when interpreting findings.

REFERENCES

Agresti, A. (1990). *Categorical data analysis*. New York: Wiley.

American Psychiatric Association. (1973). *Diagnostic and statistical manual of mental disorders* (2nd ed.). Washington, DC: Author.

Bergmark, K. H. (1999). Drinking in the Swedish gay and lesbian community. *Drug and Alcohol Dependence, 56,* 133–143.

Bernhard, L. A., & Applegate, J. M. (1999). Comparison of stress and stress management strategies between lesbian and heterosexual women. *Health Care for Women International, 20,* 335–347.

Bloomfield, K. A. (1993). A comparison of alcohol consumption between lesbians and heterosexual women in an urban population. *Drug and Alcohol Dependence, 33,* 257–269.

Bradford, J., Ryan, C., & Rothblum, E. D. (1994). National Lesbian Health Care Survey: Implications for mental health care. *Journal of Consulting and Clinical Psychology, 62,* 228–242.

Cahalan, D. (1970). *Problem drinkers: A national study*. San Francisco: Jossey-Bass.

Clark, W. B. (1979). *Use of alcoholic beverages* [NIAAA Contract ADM-281-77-0021]. Berkeley: University of California, Social Research Group.

Clark, W. B., & Midanik, L. (1982). Alcohol use and alcohol problems among U.S. adults: Results of the 1979 national survey. In National Institute on Alcohol Abuse and Alcoholism, *Alcohol and health: Alcohol consumption and related problems* (pp. 3–52; Monograph No. 1, DHHS Pub. No. ADM 82–1190). Washington, DC: U.S. Government Printing Office.

Cochran, S. D., & Mays, V. M. (1999, August). *Are lesbians more at risk for psychiatric disorders? Evidence from the 1996 National Household Survey on Drug Abuse*. Paper presented at the National Conference on Health Statistics. Washington, DC: Department of Health and Human Services.

Cochran, S. D., & Mays, V. M. (2000). Relation between psychiatric syndromes and behaviorally defined sexual orientation in a sample of the US population. *American Journal of Epidemiology, 151*(5), 1–8.

Fifield, L. H., Latham, J. D., & Phillips, C. (1977). *Alcoholism in the gay community: The price of alienation, isolation, and oppression*. Unpublished monograph, Gay Community Services Center, Los Angeles.

Gay and Lesbian Medical Association. (2001). *Healthy People 2010: Companion document for lesbian, gay, bisexual, and transgender (LGBT) health.* Retrieved May 1, 2003, from http://www.glma.org/policy/hp2010

Hughes, T. L. (2003). Lesbians' drinking patterns: Beyond the data. *Substance Use and Misuse, 38,* 1739–1758.

Hughes, T. L., Haas, A. P., & Avery, L. (1997). Lesbians and mental health: Preliminary results from the Chicago Women's Health Survey. *Journal of the Gay and Lesbian Medical Association, 1*(3), 133–144.

Hughes, T. L., Haas, A. P., Razzano, L., Cassidy, R., & Matthews, A. (2000). Comparing lesbians' and heterosexual women's mental health: Findings from a multi-site study. *Journal of Gay and Lesbian Social Services, 11*(1), 57–76.

Hughes, T. L., Johnson, T. P., & Matthews, A. (2004). Sexual orientation and smoking: Results from a multi-site women's health study. Manuscript submitted for publication.

Hughes, T. L., Johnson, T. P., & Wilsnack, S. C. (2001). Sexual assault and alcohol abuse: A comparison of lesbian and heterosexual women. *Journal of Substance Abuse, 13,* 515–532.

Hughes, T. L., Matthews, A., Razzano, L., & Aranda, F. (2003). Psychological distress in African American lesbian and heterosexual women. *Journal of Lesbian Studies, 7*(1), 51–68

Hughes, T. L., & Wilsnack, S. C. (1994). Research on lesbians and alcohol: Gaps and implications. *Alcohol Health and Research World, 18*(3), 202–205.

Hughes, T. L., & Wilsnack, S. C. (1997). Use of alcohol among lesbians: Research and clinical implications. *American Journal of Orthopsychiatry, 66*(1), 20–36.

Laumann, E. O., Gagnon, J. H., Michael, R. T., & Michaels, S. (1994). *The social organization of sexuality: Sexual practices in the United States.* Chicago: University of Chicago Press.

Matthews, A., & Hughes, T. L. (2001). Mental health service utilization by African American women: Exploration of differences by sexual identity. *Cultural Diversity and Ethnic Minority Psychology, 7*(1), 75–87.

Matthews, A., Hughes, T. L., Johnson, T., Razzano, L., & Cassidy, R. (2002). Prediction of depressive distress in a community sample of women: The role of sexual orientation. *American Journal of Public Health, 92,* 1131–1139.

McCabe, S. E., Hughes, T. L., & Boyd, C. (2004). Alcohol and other drug use and misuse: Are bisexual women at greater risk? *Journal of Psychoactive Drugs, 36*(2), 217–225.

McKirnan, D. J., & Peterson, P. L. (1989). Alcohol and drug use among homosexual men and women: Epidemiology and population characteristics. *Addictive Behaviors, 14,* 545–553.

Morales, E. S., & Graves, M. A. (1983). *Substance abuse: Patterns and barriers to treatment of gay men and lesbians in San Francisco.* San Francisco: San Francisco Department of Public Health.

National Institute on Alcohol Abuse and Alcoholism. (2000). *Quick facts: Self-reported amounts and patterns of alcohol consumption.* Retrieved January 5, 2000, from http://silk.nih.gov/silk/niaaa1/database/qf.htm

Nawyn, S., Richman, J., Rospenda, K., & Hughes, T. L. (2000). Sexual identity and alcohol-related outcomes: Contributions of workplace harassment. *Journal of Substance Abuse, 11,* 289–304.

Parks, C., Hughes, T. L., & Matthews, A. K. (2004). Race/ethnicity and sexual orientation: Intersecting identities. *Cultural Diversity and Ethnic Minority Psychology, 10*(3), 241–254.

Polich, J. M., & Orvis, B. R. (1979). *Alcohol problems: Patterns and prevalence in the U.S. Air Force.* Santa Monica, CA: Rand Corporation.

Robins, L. N., Helzer, J. E., Croughan, J., & Ratcliff, K. S. (1981). National Institute of Mental Health Diagnostic Interview Schedule: Its history, characteristics, and validity. *Archives of General Psychiatry, 38,* 381–389.

Rothblum, E. D., & Factor, R. (2001). Lesbians and their sisters as a control group: Demographic and mental health factors. *Psychological Science, 12,* 63–69.

Saghir, M. T., & Robins, E. (1973). *Male and female homosexuality: A comprehensive investigation.* Baltimore: Williams & Wilkins.

Scheer, S., Parks, C. A., McFarland, W., Page-Shafer, K., Delgado, V., Ruiz, J. D., et al. (2003). Self-reported sexual identity, sexual behaviors and health risks: Examples from a population-based survey of young women. *Journal of Lesbian Studies, 7*(1), 69–83.

Skinner, W. F., & Otis, M. D. (1996). Drug and alcohol use among lesbian and gay people in a Southern U.S. sample: Epidemiological, comparative, and methodological findings from the trilogy project. *Journal of Homosexuality, 30*(3), 59–91.

Skrocki, F. E. (1996). *Use of focus groups to validate an existing instrument for use with lesbians.* Unpublished master's thesis, University of Illinois College of Nursing, Chicago.

Solarz, A. L. (Ed.). (1999). *Lesbian health: Current assessment and directions for the future.* Washington, DC: National Academy Press.

Wilsnack, R. W., Wilsnack, S. C., & Klassen, A. D. (1984). Women's drinking and drinking problems: Patterns from a 1981 national survey. *American Journal of Public Health, 74,* 1231–1237.

Wilsnack, R. W., Wilsnack, S. C., Kristjanson, A. F., & Harris, T. R. (1998). Ten-year prediction of women's drinking behavior in a nationally representative sample. *Women's Health: Research on Gender, Behavior and Policy, 4,* 199–230.

Wilsnack, S. C., Klassen, A. D., Shur, B. E, & Wilsnack, R. W. (1991). Predicting onset and chronicity of women's problem drinking: A five-year longitudinal analysis. *American Journal of Public Health, 81,* 305–318.

9

SEXUAL BEHAVIOR AND SEXUAL DYSFUNCTION IN A COMMUNITY SAMPLE OF LESBIAN AND HETEROSEXUAL WOMEN

ALICIA K. MATTHEWS, TONDA L. HUGHES, AND JESSICA TARTARO

Although establishing sexually intimate relationships is an important maturational milestone for healthy adults, empirically based studies of sexual functioning among lesbians are largely absent. Most studies of lesbians' sexual behaviors have been conducted in the context of couples' relationships and have focused on frequency of sexual activity. Blumstein and Schwartz (1983) compared sexual frequency and satisfaction among single heterosexual women and men, heterosexual married couples, and lesbian and gay male couples. Of the three types of couples studied, lesbian couples reported the lowest frequency of sexual activity. Lower frequency of sexual activity in lesbian couples has been reported in a number of subsequent studies (e.g., Decker, 1984; Hawton, Gath, & Day, 1994; Kaufman, Harrison, & Hyde, 1984; Nichols, 1988). Female socialization and underdeveloped sex drive in women has been posited as potential explanations of lesbians' lower frequency of sexual activity (Nichols, 1988). Further, Blumstein and Schwartz (1983) suggested that the failure of one or both members of lesbian couples to assume responsibility for initiation of sexual activity likely contributes to its lower frequency. Other authors suggest that compared with men, lesbians are less likely to pressure a reluctant partner to have sex, resulting in less frequent sexual activity (Nichols, 1987b).

Despite less frequent sexual activity, lesbians in relationships report sexual satisfaction levels equivalent to those of heterosexual and gay male couples (Blumstein & Schwartz, 1983; Herbert, 1996). High sexual satisfaction ratings in the absence of frequent genital sexual activity are thought to result from the value placed by lesbians on the emotional and nonphysical aspects of relationships (Blumstein & Schwartz, 1983; Hawton et al., 1994; Hurlbert & Apt, 1993; Leigh, 1989; Schreurs, 1993). However, Blumstein and Schwartz (1983) found that half of the lesbians in couples with low frequency of genital sexual contact were dissatisfied with the sexual aspect of their relationships. Given conflicting results and methodological and sampling limitations of existing studies, more research on sexual functioning and sexual satisfaction among lesbians is clearly needed.

What is known about sexual functioning among women in general? The National Health and Social Life Survey (Laumann, Gagnon, Michael, & Michaels, 1994) assessed sexual function in a national probability sample of women and men ages 18 to 59. Sexual problems assessed in the study were consistent with the criteria for sexual dysfunction in the *Diagnostic and Statistical Manual of Mental Disorders* (4th ed., *DSM–IV*; American Psychiatric Association, 1994). These included (a) lack of desire, (b) arousal difficulties (lubrication), (c) inability to achieve climax, (d) anxiety about sexual performance, (e) climaxing too rapidly, (f) pain during intercourse, and (g) not finding sex pleasurable. The data on prevalence of sexual dysfunction was compared by gender. Overall, 43% of women surveyed met the criteria for sexual dysfunction (on the basis of the presence of one or more of these symptoms). Variables associated with higher rates of sexual dysfunction among women included younger age, being unmarried, having lower levels of education, poorer health status, lower socioeconomic status, history of infrequent sexual activity, sexual victimization, and unsatisfying relationships (Laumann, Paik, & Rosen, 1999). History of any same-sex activity did not appear to be related to sexual dysfunction among this sample of women.

Studies focused more specifically on lesbians have reported mixed findings regarding prevalence of sexual dysfunction. Sexual desire problems including decreased desire, inhibited desire, or desire discrepancy problems have been cited as the most frequently reported problems among lesbians seeking services for sexual problems (Hall, 1988; Nichols, 1987a, 1987b, 1988). Other research suggests that primary anorgasmia (absence of orgasm following a normal sexual excitement phase) is uncommon among lesbians

(Herbert, 1996); however, secondary (absence of an orgasm only in the context of an ongoing, committed relationship) and situational anorgasmia (absence of orgasm that is limited to certain types of stimulation, situations, or partners) has been reported by sex therapists and other clinical providers (Masters & Johnson, 1979; Nichols, 1987a, 1987b, 1988).

What factors are known to be associated with healthy sexual functioning among women? The biopsychosocial model views health or illness outcomes as the consequence of the interplay between biological, psychological, and social factors (Engel, 1980; Schwartz, 1982). This model can be applied to understanding sexual functioning. As suggested by the model, sexual problems likely result from an interaction among physiological, psychological, and interpersonal factors. For example, sexual dysfunction may be caused by an illness (von Eschenback & Schrover, 1989). The cumulative impact of physiological changes associated with illness or its treatment may result in reduced sexual excitement and response, insufficient lubrication, and painful intercourse (Auchincloss, 1991). Sexual problems may also be associated with psychological factors such as anxiety, depression, anger, fear of rejection by a partner, and stress (Barlow, 1986). Interpersonal factors such as relationship intimacy, satisfaction, and distress are believed to influence sexual activity and satisfaction, especially among women (Baldwin & Baldwin, 1997; Hatfield, Sprecher, Pillemer, Greenberger, & Wexler, 1989; Morokoff & Gilliland, 1993; Regan & Berscheid, 1996). In addition, history of physical or sexual trauma has been associated with difficulty establishing trusting interpersonal and sexual relationships (Briere, 1992; Browne & Finkelhor, 1986; Laumann et al., 1999). Other authors have suggested that childhood sexual abuse may play a role in development of sexual dysfunction involving pain associated with sexual intercourse but may not be as strong a predictor of sexual interest or orgasmic functioning (S. C. Wilsnack, Vogeltanz, Klassen, & Harris, 1997).

We described and compared sexual behavior and sexual functioning in a community sample of lesbian and heterosexual women. Specifically, we examined sexual history (including age of initiation of sexual activity), current sexual behaviors (frequency of sex, feelings about sex with current or most recent partner, and perception of discrepancy in sexual desire between the respondent and her current or most recent partner), and rates of sexual dysfunction (pain, lack of interest in sex, and lack of interest in orgasms). Finally, we used a biopsychosocial framework to examine relationships between sexual functioning and biological (health status), psychological (mood disturbance, history of childhood sexual abuse), and social (relationship satisfaction) variables. We hypothesized that higher levels of sexual dysfunction would be associated with problems in each of the three domains of the theoretical model.

This study used data from the Chicago Health and Life Experiences of Women (CHLEW) pilot study. Detailed information about sample recruitment, study instrument, and data collection are included in chapter 8 of this volume.

Sexual Orientation

Sexual orientation is generally understood as a person's predisposition toward sexual attraction to persons of the same sex, the opposite sex, or both sexes (Diamond, 2000). The following question was used to assess sexual orientation: How would you describe your sexual orientation? The response categories ranged from "only homosexual, lesbian, or gay" to "only heterosexual."

Sexual History

Assessment of sexual history included the following questions:

1. Have you ever had sexual intercourse with a man?
2. During the past 12 months, how many partners have you had sexual activity with?
3. In the past 5 years, when having sex with a partner, how regularly have you come to sexual climax? (1 = *no sexual relations*; 6 = *about all the time*)
4. In your lifetime has it been possible to enjoy being sexual by yourself (masturbating)? (1 = *never happened*; 4 = *usually possible*)
5. During your lifetime, how important has sex been to you? (1 = *could have gotten along without it*; 5 = *very important*).

Questions related to early onset of sexual activity included the following:

1. What was your age when you first had sexual intercourse after puberty?
2. What was your age when you first had sexual activity with a partner, other than intercourse?
3. What was your age the first time you came to a sexual climax by masturbation?

Consistent with S. C. Wilsnack et al. (1997), precocious onset of sexual activity was based on recent findings suggesting that the modal age of first intercourse in women is between 16 and 17 years (Laumann et al., 1994). Age of first sexual activity, intercourse, and masturbation were dichotomized into age 14 and younger versus age 15 and older. Respondents in the CHLEW were not asked to specify the gender of their first sexual partners. Also, we did not access whether sexual activities were consensual or forced when determining age of initiation of sexual activity.

Current Sexual Behavior and Satisfaction

Current sexual behavior and satisfaction were assessed by asking respondents about the frequency of sexual activity with their current or most recent partner (0 = *none*; 5 = *more than 3 times weekly*); satisfaction with sexual activity with current or most recent partner (0 = *prefer it didn't happen*; 3 = *very good*); and desire discrepancy in the relationship ("My partner wants sex more often than I do" and "My partner does not want sex as often as I do"; 0 = *false*; 1 = *true*). Responses to the last two questions were combined and dichotomized to create a measure of *sexual desire discrepancy* between the respondent and her sexual partner (0 = *no discrepancy*; 1 = *any discrepancy*).

Sexual Dysfunction

Sexual dysfunction questions are based on work by Kaplan (1974, 1979) and S. C. Wilsnack et al. (1997). Questions address (a) lifetime lack of sexual interest ("I have never had any interest in sex"), (b) lifetime lack of orgasm with a partner ("I have never come to sexual climax during sexual activity with a partner"), (c) pain that prevents intercourse ("sexual relations have been so painful that I could not have intercourse"), and (d) infrequent orgasm ("having a sexual climax on 25% or fewer occasions of sex with a partner"). In addition, a fifth question ("sexual relations have sometimes been physically painful for me") was included. Responses to these questions were coded 0 (*false*) or 1 (*true*). An index of sexual dysfunction was created by summing responses. To identify moderately high levels of sexual dysfunction, this index was dichotomized into one or none versus two or more of the symptom indicators.

Biopsychosocial Factors

Consistent with a biopsychosocial model of health, variables believed to negatively influence sexual functioning were also examined. Specifically, we examined the following variables: perceived health status, childhood sexual abuse, relationship dissatisfaction, and mood disturbance. The following describes the variables and how they were measured.

Health Status

Global, single-item measures of perceived overall health have been shown to be reliable and valid (Cunny & Perri, 1991) and to predict mortality (Hays, Schoenfeld, Blazer, & Gold, 1996) and changes in functional status (Idler & Kasl, 1995). Perceived level of health over the past year was assessed with a single-item question of perceived health status. Self-rating of health ranged from *poor* (1) to *excellent* (4).

Childhood Sexual Abuse

Child Sexual Abuse (CSA) was assessed using two measures (S. C. Wilsnack et al., 1997; Wyatt, 1985). The first measure included (a) any intrafamilial sexual activity before age 18 that was unwanted by the participant or involved a family member 5 or more years older and (b) any unwanted extrafamilial sexual activity before age 18, or before age 13 that involved another person 5 or more years older (referred to in Tables 9.3 and 9.4 as *Wyatt* CSA). Responses were dichotomized, with 0 (*no CSA*) and 1 (*an affirmative response to either question*). Self-perception of CSA included the question "Do you feel you were sexually abused when you were growing up?"

Mood Disturbance

Anxiety was measured by a single question regarding the respondent's self-perception as a "nervous or anxious person" (*yes* or *no*). A second question asked respondents how much anxiety had interfered with their lives, with a scale ranging from 0 (*not at all*) to 4 (*a great deal*). Depression was measured using questions intended to approximate *DSM–IV* diagnostic criteria for depression (Robins, Helzer, Croughan, & Ratcliff, 1981). Respondents were asked about the following symptoms of depression: decreased appetite; unexplained weight loss or weight gain; sleeping problems; fatigue; talking or moving more slowly than usual; reduced interest in sex; feelings of worthlessness, sinfulness or guilt; and thoughts of death. If at least three of these symptoms co-occurred for at least a 2-week period and were accompanied by feeling sad, blue, or depressed or by loss of interest or pleasure in things usually cared about, the respondent was coded as having an episode of depression. A dichotomous variable indicating one or more episodes of lifetime history of depression was created.

Relationship Satisfaction

Among respondents who were currently in a relationship, level of relationship satisfaction was assessed by asking (a) How often do you and your partner discuss or consider separation or divorce? (b) How often do you quarrel? (c) How often do you regret this relationship? and (d) How often do you "get on each other's nerves"? Response options ranged from 0 (*never*) to 5 (*all the time*). A composite score was created by summing responses to these questions and ranged from 0 to 20 ($\alpha = .85$). Higher scores were associated with greater relationship dissatisfaction.

Coping Strategies

Stress and coping research has shown a robust relationship between coping efforts and adjustment. Problem-focused or emotion-focused approaches are generally associated with better psychological outcomes (Ball, Tannenbaum, Armistead, & Mageun, 2002) and avoidant–passive coping strategies with poorer adjustment (Domanico & Crawford, 2000). In this study, we examine the effect of two potential methods of coping with sexual problems: (a) the use of alcohol during sexual activity and (b) the use of mental health services for sexual problems.

Use of Alcohol During Sex

Respondents were asked about use of alcohol during sex with their current or most recent partner. Responses were rated from 0 (*never*) to 3 (*usually*). Three questions measuring positive expectancies about the role of alcohol during sexual activity included (a) I feel less inhibited during sex with alcohol, (b) sexual activity is more pleasurable with alcohol, and (c) I feel less reluctant to have sex with alcohol. Responses to these questions were on a 3-point scale ranging from 0 (*never true*) to 2 (*usually true*).

Mental Health Services

Sexual problems can be reduced by professional intervention (Besharat, 2001). One such method is to seek sexual counseling from a mental health professional. Use of mental health services was assessed by asking participants whether they had sought help for sexual problems in the past 5 years (0 = *no*; 1 = *yes*).

STUDY FINDINGS

Data analyses included frequency distributions and descriptive statistics. Calculation of percentages, cross-tabulations, and chi-square analyses were conducted to examine similarities and differences between lesbian and heterosexual women. Independent groups' *t* tests were conducted for continuous variables, and Pearson's product–moment correlation coefficients (Pearson's *r*) were used to identify simple bivariate associations between study variables. All significant differences reported had probabilities of $p \leq .05$.

Sample Demographics

Data from 63 lesbian and 57 heterosexual respondents were included in these analyses (see chap. 8, this volume, for full description of sample). The average age of participants was 40 years. Overall, 36% of the women were Caucasian, 24% African American, 25% Hispanic or Latina, and 15% of another racial or ethnic heritage. The majority of women in the study were married or in a committed relationship (88%), had more than a high school education (85%), and were employed (75%). The median household income was $30,000 to $39,000. Overall, respondents perceived themselves to be in good health. No significant differences were found between the lesbian and heterosexual groups on key demographic variables.

Sexual History and Behaviors

As shown in Table 9.1, most women in the sample reported a history of sexual intercourse. The age of first sexual intercourse did not differ between lesbians ($M = 19$, $SD = 10.9$) and heterosexual women ($M = 21$, $SD = 10.6$). Higher, but not statistically different, proportions of lesbians reported sexual activity prior to age 14, including masturbation, sexual intercourse, and noncoital sexual activity. Differences were observed in how typical it was for lesbian and heterosexual women to masturbate, $\chi^2(4, N = 117) = 16.8$, $p \leq .001$. Heterosexual women (32%) were more likely than lesbians (5%) to report that they had never masturbated. Similar proportions of lesbian and heterosexual women had no sexual partners in the past 12 months (12% vs. 19%, ns); however, lesbians were more likely to have more than one sexual partner in that time period (35% vs. 11%), $\chi^2(1, N = 107) = 8.5$, $p < .01$. Lesbians (92%) and heterosexual women (84%) differed little in feeling positive about sex with past sexual partners (ns) and in frequently reaching sexual climax during sexual activity (72% vs. 60%, ns). Although not statistically significant, lesbians were more likely than heterosexual women to endorse a high level of importance of sex during their lifetime (56% vs. 41%, ns).

Respondents were asked to describe the gender of their sexual partners since they were 18 years old. Sixteen percent of lesbians reported that their partners had been mostly men, and 19% reported that they had about the same number of male and female sexual partners; only one of the heterosexual women reported any same-sex sexual partners since age 18, $\chi^2(5, N = 116) = 112.2$, $p < .001$. When asked about sexual partners in the past 5 years, the majority of lesbians (81%) reported "mostly" or "only" female sexual partners.

Just over half of the lesbian sample (52%) reported being attracted only to women (40% mostly to women); 75% of heterosexual women re-

TABLE 9.1
Sexual Experience

Sexual experience	Heterosexual (n = 57)		Lesbian (n = 63)		
	n	%	n	%	p
Ever had sexual intercourse	53	93	53	84	.12
Masturbation to climax under age 14	9	27	26	44	.11
Noncoital sexual activity under age 14	10	19	20	33	.09
First intercourse under age 14	5	10	10	21	.12
Never masturbated	18	32	3	5	.01
Regularly achieve orgasm during sex	31	60	41	72	.21
More than one sex partner in past 12 months	5	11	21	35	.01
Sexual activity at least once weekly	36	64	38	60	.27
Since age 18 sexual partners mostly/only men	52	96	10	16	.01
Since age 18 sexual partners mostly/only women	0	0	40	65	.01
Since age 18 sexual partners both men/women	1	2	12	19	.01
Have typically felt pretty/very good about sex	46	84	56	92	.10
Sex has been important during their lifetime	23	41	34	56	.20
Childhood sexual abuse	27	47	42	68	.05
Self-perception of sexual abuse	11	19	23	37	.03

Note. The sample size for each analysis may vary because of missing data or lack of sexual activity during the specified time frame.

ported being attracted only to men (16% mostly to men). Similar and lower proportions of lesbians (8%) and heterosexual women (9%) reported being equally attracted to both men and women.

Childhood Sexual Abuse

For women who provided sufficient information (three lesbian and eight heterosexual women did not provide sufficient information to determine whether they met study criteria for CSA), significantly more lesbian (70%) than heterosexual women (55%) met the study definition of CSA, $\chi^2(2, N = 119) = 5.96, p < .05$. In addition, lesbians (37%) were more likely than heterosexual women (19%) to report that they perceived themselves to have been sexually abused when they were growing up, $\chi^2(1, N = 120) = 4.6, p < .05$.

TABLE 9.2
Sexual Problems

Sexual problem	Heterosexual (n = 57)		Lesbian (n = 63)		p
	n	%	n	%	
Any sexual dysfunction	23	50	16	30	.12
Lifetime lack of sexual interest	0	0	2	3	.17
Lifetime lack of orgasm with partner	2	4	4	7	.51
Low frequency of orgasm with partner (25% or less)	10	22	11	20	.83
Pain associated with sexual activity	16	34	8	14	.02
Pain that prevents intercourse	10	21	3	5	.02
Sexual dysfunction index[a]	1	22	4	8	.05
Partner desires sex more often	30	60	19	33	.01
Respondent desires sex more often	8	17	25	44	.01
Desire discrepancy in the relationship	33	70	37	69	.98
Sought treatment for sexual problems	1	5	7	16	.19

Note. The sample size for each analysis may vary because of missing data or lack of sexual activity during the specified time frame.
[a]Sums lifetime lack of sexual interest, lifetime lack of orgasm with partner, pain associated with sexual relations, pain that prevents intercourse, and low frequency of orgasm with a partner.

Current Sexual Activity

Level of current sexual activity was similar for lesbian and heterosexual women. Sixty percent of lesbian and 64% of heterosexual women reported having sex at least once per week. The majority of lesbian (87%) and heterosexual women (92%) reported high levels of positive feelings about sex with their current partner. Although similar proportions of lesbian (69%) and heterosexual women (70%) reported any discrepancy in the level of sexual desire between themselves and their sexual partners, direction of the discrepancy varied by sexual orientation. Only 33% of lesbians compared with 60% of heterosexual women reported that their partner wanted sex more often than they did, $\chi^2(1, N = 107) = 7.63, p \leq .01$. In contrast, 44% of lesbians compared with 17% of heterosexual women reported wanting sex more often than their partners, $\chi^2(1, N = 105) = 8.94, p \leq .01$.

Sexual Dysfunction

Overall, 41% of the sample reported at least one symptom of sexual dysfunction. As shown in Table 9.2, lack of interest in sexual activity was low in both groups; only 3% of lesbians and none of the heterosexual women reported no interest in sexual activity. About one third (34%) of heterosexual women compared with 14% of lesbians reported pain associated with sexual activity, $\chi^2(1, N = 104) = 5.8$, $p \leq .05$. Further, heterosexual women were also more likely than lesbians (21% vs. 5%) to report that pain prevented sexual intercourse, $\chi^2(1, N =103) = 5.8$, $p \leq .05$. Anorgasmia and low frequency of orgasm (less than 25% of sexual encounters) were reported equally by both groups. Fewer lesbian (8%) than heterosexual (22%) women met criteria for moderately high levels of sexual dysfunction (2 or more indicators), $\chi^2(1, N = 99) = 4.0$, $p < .05$. Of women reporting use of therapy in the previous 5 years, higher but not statistically significant proportions of lesbian (16%) than heterosexual women (5%) sought mental health services specifically for sexual problems, $\chi^2(1, N = 67) = 1.7$, ns.

Alcohol Use

All lesbian and 87% of heterosexual respondents reported ever drinking alcohol, $\chi^2(1, N = 120) = 8.2$, $p < 001$. Among lifetime drinkers, lesbians were more likely to report that alcohol helped them to feel less sexually inhibited (30% vs. 26%), $\chi^2(3, N = 113) = 8.05$, $p < .05$. Higher (but not statistically significant) proportions of lesbians reported that alcohol made sex more pleasurable (13% vs. 6%) and helped them feel less reluctant to have sex (19% vs. 10%). Among current drinkers, 27% of heterosexual women and 15% of lesbians reported use of alcohol during sexual activity (ns).

Relationship Satisfaction

Group means on the composite measure of relationship satisfaction were similar for lesbians ($M = 5.3$) and heterosexual women ($M = 6.6$). Although differences were not statistically significant, more heterosexual women than lesbians reported considering divorce or separation (15% vs. 6%); frequent quarreling (24% vs. 15%); feeling regret about forming the relationship (6% vs. 3%); and "getting on each other's nerves" (24% vs. 12%).

Mood Disturbance

Reports of lifetime anxiety were high for both lesbians (87%) and heterosexual women (90%). However, lesbians (64%) were more likely than heterosexual women (47%) to report that anxiety or nervousness had interfered with everyday life or activities, $\chi^2(4, N = 120) = 12.6$, $p < .01$. Almost two thirds (67%) of lesbian and 53% of heterosexual women met the study criteria for lifetime history of depression, $\chi^2(1, N = 120) = 2.45$, $p = .08$.

Associations Between Study Variables

Findings from bivariate correlation analyses suggest partial support for the hypothesized relationship between sexual dysfunction and study predictor variables. For the entire sample combined, higher levels of sexual dysfunction were associated with heterosexuality ($r = .20$, $p < .05$), poor health status ($r = -.23$, $p < .05$), depression ($r = .26$, $p < .01$), and drinking alcohol before sexual activity ($r = .25$, $p < .05$), but not with lifetime anxiety ($r = -.04$, $p > .05$), history of CSA ($r = .05$, $p > .05$), or relationship satisfaction ($r = .01$, $p > .05$). Sexual dysfunction was also not associated with participation in therapy for sexual problems ($r = .17$, $p > .05$).

Additional analyses were conducted to examine similarities and differences in the relationships between study variables for lesbian and heterosexual women. As shown in Table 9.3, among lesbians, sexual dysfunction was not correlated with health status, mood, or relationship satisfaction. Instead, higher scores on our indicator of sexual dysfunction were associated with both positive and negative coping strategies including obtaining mental health services for a sexual problem ($r = .37$, $p < .05$) and drinking with current sexual partner ($r = .48$, $p < .01$). As shown in Table 9.4, both biological and psychological factors were associated with sexual dysfunction among heterosexual women including self-reported poor health ($r = -32$, $p < .05$) and depression ($r = .40$, $p < .01$).

DISCUSSION OF FINDINGS

The purpose of this study was to describe and compare sexual behavior and sexual functioning in a community sample of lesbian and heterosexual women. A biopsychological model of sexual functioning was used to examine correlates of sexual behaviors, satisfaction, and dysfunction. We discuss the main study findings here, as well as study limitations and future directions for research.

Sexual Satisfaction and Activity

Lesbian and heterosexual women were equally likely to report positive feelings about sexual activity with their partners. In contrast to previous research suggesting lower frequency of sexual activity in lesbian couples than in heterosexual or gay male couples (e.g., Blumstein & Schwartz, 1983), lesbian and heterosexual women in the study did not differ on frequency of sexual activity. Though differences were not statistically significant, heterosexual women were more likely to report the absence of sexual activity in their current or most recent relationships.

TABLE 9.3
Correlation Matrix: Lesbian Women

Variable	1	2	3	4	5	6	7	8	9	10	11	12
1. Early nonintercourse sexual activity	—											
2. Early sexual intercourse	.579**	—										
3. Sexual dysfunction	.231	.137	—									
4. Discrepancy in sexual desire	-.108	-.248	-.017	—								
5. Health status	-.040	-.145	-.140	-.209	—							
6. Depression	-.082	.105	.188	.085	-.153	—						
7. Anxiety	-.142	.056	-.100	.054	-.183	.135	—					
8. Wyatt CSA	.083	-.158	-.005	.036	.021	.067	.114	—				
9. Self-rated sexual abuse	.249*	.446**	.097	-.168	.066	.056	.096	.720	—			
10. Relationship satisfaction	-.242	-.328	-.107	.316*	-.090	-.271	.154	-.061	-.286	—		
11. Drink during sex with partner	-.088	-.292*	.480**	.139	-.003	.087	.056	-.126	-.091	-.177	—	
12. Therapy for sexual problems	-.025	.477**	.374*	-.247	-.240	.101	.152	-.025	.036	-.113	.365*	—

Note. Wyatt CSA = child sexual abuse as evaluated by the measure in Wyatt (1985).
*p < .05. **p < .01.

TABLE 9.4
Correlation Matrix: Heterosexual Women

Variable	1	2	3	4	5	6	7	8	9	10	11	12
1. Early nonintercourse sexual activity	—											
2. Early initiation of intercourse	-.058	—										
3. Sexual dysfunction	-.139	-.075	—									
4. Discrepancy in sexual desire	-.269	.097	.077	—								
5. Health status	-.213	.011	-.324*	-.183	—							
6. Depression	-.027	.135	.399**	.293*	-.241*	—						
7. Anxiety	.156	.049	-.024	.077	.141	-.241	—					
8. Wyatt CSA	.166	.132	.228	-.052	-.169	.263*	.120	—				
9. Self-rated sexual abuse	.260**	-.058	.106	.111	-.177	.286	.168	.481**	—			
10. Relationship satisfaction	.046	.021	.029	.164	-.194	.283	-.023	.022	-.216	—		
11. Drink during sex with partner	.132	-.015	.066	.190	-.129	.161	.189	.162	.303*	-.137	—	
12. Therapy for sexual problems	-.108	-.096	-.141	.141	-.358	-.356	-.690	-.239	-.165	-.164	.030	—

Note. Wyatt CSA = child sexual abuse as evaluated by the measure in Wyatt (1985).
*p < .05. **p < .01.

Despite similar frequency of sexual activity, an interesting pattern was observed regarding desire for sexual activity. Whereas reports of desire discrepancies between themselves and their sexual partners did not differ, heterosexual women were more likely than lesbians to report that their partners wanted sex more often than they. However, lesbians were more likely to report wanting sex more often than their partners. Further, discrepancies in sexual desire were associated with higher rates of relationship dissatisfaction among lesbians and may be an important issue for mental health providers working with lesbian couples.

Sexual Dysfunction

Overall rates of sexual dysfunction approximated those reported in previous studies of sexual functioning in women (Read, King, & Watson, 1997; Laumann et al., 1999). Forty percent of the women in our study reported at least one symptom of sexual dysfunction. Pain associated with sexual activity (34%) was the most frequently reported symptom among heterosexual women and low frequency of orgasm (20%) the most frequently reported symptom reported by lesbians. Fewer (8%) lesbians than heterosexual women (22%) met criteria for moderately high levels of sexual dysfunction (two or more indicators).

A biopsychosocial model was used in our study to explore factors associated with sexual dysfunction. For the combined sample, sexual dysfunction was associated with poor health status and history of depression. After examining study variables separately by sexual orientation, the same associations between sexual dysfunction and health and mood were observed among heterosexual women. However, none of the biopsychosocial variables were associated with sexual dysfunction among lesbians. Several factors may account for this finding. The relatively small sample size of the study combined with the low base rates of sexual dysfunction in lesbians may have reduced our ability to detect relationships between the study variables. Further, the sexual dysfunction measure used in this study is likely more relevant to the experiences of heterosexual women (i.e., pain associated with intercourse) and may not be a valid measure of sexual dysfunction for lesbians. For example, although the Health and Life Experiences of Women (HLEW) instrument included questions about the importance of sex during respondents' lifetimes, general feelings about sexual activity with current or most recent partners, and similarities or discrepancies in respondents and their partners' desire for frequency of sexual activity, we were unable to fully assess level of sexual desire. Thus, more research with larger samples of lesbians that includes measurement of a wider range of sexual function is needed.

Previous studies have described a relationship between sexual dysfunction and alcohol use among women in the general population (e.g., Beckman

& Ackerman, 1995; Klassen & Wilsnack, 1986) and in clinical samples of female alcoholics (S. C. Wilsnack, Klassen, Shur, & Wilsnack, 1991). In the current study, higher levels of sexual dysfunction among lesbians were associated with the use of alcohol during sex. Although alcohol use can lead to problems with sexual functioning, some women may use alcohol as a compensatory strategy for increasing sexual enjoyment or reducing anxiety or distress, or to avoid unwanted negative thoughts or images associated with past traumatic sexual experiences. Given the high rates of CSA and depression reported by lesbians in this study, as well as high rates of alcohol problems reported in previous analyses of data from this study (Hughes, Johnson, & Wilsnack, 2001), mental health providers treating lesbians with sexual problems should evaluate whether alcohol is being used as a method of coping. Likewise, women treated for alcohol-related problems should also be assessed for sexual functioning.

Despite higher rates of sexual dysfunction in heterosexual women, lesbians were three times as likely to report seeking mental health services for sexual problems. Although this finding may be confounded by substantially higher rates of overall mental health service use by lesbians—nearly 80% in some studies (Bradford & Ryan, 1987; Hughes, Haas, & Avery, 1997)— it may also reflect a healthy coping strategy more readily used by lesbian than heterosexual women. Additional research is needed to determine the potential moderating effect of therapy or counseling on sexual problems among lesbians.

Nonnormative Sexual Behavior

Consistent with earlier studies, lesbians were more likely than heterosexual women to report activities that are normally suppressed among women (Kinsey, Pomeroy, Martin, & Gebhard, 1953; Laumann et al., 1994; Loulan, 1987, 1988). For example, lesbians were more likely to report masturbating, engaging in sexual activity at an earlier age, and having a greater number of sexual partners in the past 12 months. Previous studies suggest that these behaviors are associated with a history of sexual abuse (Finkelhor & Browne, 1986; Greene, 1993; Laumann et al., 1994; Oliver & Hyde, 1993; S. C. Wilsnack et al., 1997). In the current study, a substantial proportion of lesbians and heterosexual women reported histories of CSA. However, only self-perception of CSA was associated with early sexual intercourse. The lack of association between CSA and the other sexual experience variables may be due in part to the smaller sample size in this study compared with the national studies. Alternatively, these findings may reflect lesbians' openness to a broader range of sexual expression (e.g., masturbation). Future studies would be strengthened by explicitly assessing attitudes regarding sexual behavior and experiences.

Strengths and Limitations

This study addressed a greatly underresearched area of lesbian health. In addition, unlike the majority of previous studies of lesbians, this study included a diverse sample of lesbians and a demographically matched heterosexual comparison group. Moreover, this study used an existing survey instrument and previously validated measures of sexual function from the National Study of Health and Life Experiences of Women (R. W. Wilsnack, Wilsnack, & Klassen, 1984; S. C. Wilsnack et al., 1991).

Despite these important strengths, several limitations must be noted. First, the sample was recruited using nonrandom, convenience methods. Second, the measure of sexual dysfunction used in this study emphasizes sexual intercourse and thus may underestimate actual sexual dysfunction or satisfaction among lesbians in the study. Further, the sexual dysfunction measure did not permit assessment of level of sexual desire. This omission is important given findings of low sexual desire in clinical reports on lesbians' sexual functioning. Finally, we were unable to assess the temporal order of the dependent and independent variables. Because women's identification as lesbian, bisexual, or heterosexual and women's actual sexual behavior may vary over time (e.g., Peplau & Garnets, 2000), longitudinal studies are needed to more accurately identify variables that predict healthy sexual functioning in lesbians and to make stronger inferences regarding cause and effect. These limitations suggest that caution be used in the interpretation and generalization of the findings.

Future Directions

Overall, findings suggest that lesbians may enjoy higher levels of sexual satisfaction and lower levels of sexual problems than suggested by earlier studies. Results suggest that for heterosexual women, sexual problems are influenced by both health-related and psychosocial factors. Variables included in our model of sexual dysfunction had less clear relevance for lesbians. Future research is needed that includes assessments of sexual problems and identifies variables relevant to lesbians' experiences. Such information can inform the development of measures sensitive to the sexual experiences and relationship dynamics of lesbians as well as clinical interventions with lesbians who have problems related to sexual functioning.

REFERENCES

American Psychiatric Association. (1994). *Diagnostic and statistical manual of mental disorders* (4th ed.). Washington, DC: Author.

Auchincloss, S. (1991). Sexual dysfunction after cancer treatment. *Journal of Psychosocial Oncology, 9,* 23–42.

Baldwin, J. D., & Baldwin, J. I. (1997). Gender differences in sexual interest. *Archives of Sexual Behavior, 26,* 181–210.

Ball, J., Tannenbaum, L., Armistead, L., & Mageun, S. (2002). Coping and HIV infection in African-American women. *Women and Health, 35,* 17–36.

Barlow, D. H. (1986). Causes of sexual dysfunction: The role of anxiety and cognitive interference. *Journal of Consulting and Clinical Psychology, 54,* 140–148.

Beckman, L. J., & Ackerman, K. T. (1995). Women, alcohol, and sexuality. *Recent Developments in Alcoholism, 12,* 267–285.

Besharat, M. A. (2001). Management strategies of sexual dysfunctions. *Journal of Contemporary Psychotherapy, 31,* 161–180.

Blumstein, P., & Schwartz, P. (1983). *American couples: Money, work, and sex.* New York: Morrow.

Bradford, J. B., & Ryan, C. (1987). *National lesbian health care survey: Mental health implications for lesbians* (Report No. PB88-201496/AS). Bethesda, MD: National Institute of Mental Health.

Briere, J. (1992). *Child abuse trauma: Theory and treatment of the lasting effects.* Newbury Park, CA: Sage.

Browne, A., & Finkelhor, D. (1986). Initial and long-term effects: A review of the research. In D. Finkelhor (Ed.), *A source book on child sexual abuse* (pp. 143–179). Newbury Park, CA: Sage.

Cunny, K. A., & Perri, M. (1991). Single-item vs. multiple-item measures of health-related quality of life. *Psychological Reports, 69,* 127–130.

Decker, B. (1984). Counseling gay and lesbian couples. *Journal of Social Work and Human Sexuality, 2,* 39–52.

Diamond, L. M. (2000). Sexual identity, attractions, and behavior among young sexual minority women over a 2-year period. *Developmental Psychology, 36,* 241–250.

Domanico, R., & Crawford, I. (2000). Psychological distress among HIV-impacted African American and Latino males. *Journal of Prevention and Intervention in the Community, 19,* 55–78.

Engel, G. L. (1980). The clinical application of the biopsychosocial model. *American Journal of Psychiatry, 137,* 535–544.

Finkelhor, D., & Browne, A. (1986). The traumatic impact of child sexual abuse: A conceptualization. In S. Chess & A. Thomas (Eds.), *Annual progress in child psychiatry and child development* (pp. 632–648). New York: Brunner/Mazel.

Greene, A. H. (1993). Child sexual abuse: Immediate and long-term effects and interventions. *Journal of the American Academy of Child & Adolescent Psychiatry, 32,* 890–902.

Hall, M. (1988). Sex therapy with lesbian couples: A four stage approach. In E. Coleman (Ed.), *Integrated identity for gay men and lesbians: Psychotherapeutic approaches for emotional well-being* (pp. 137–156). New York: Harrington Park Press.

Hatfield, E., Sprecher, S., Pillemer, J. T., Greenberger, D., & Wexler, P. (1989). Gender differences in what is desired in the sexual relationship. *Journal of Psychology and Human Sexuality, 1,* 39–52.

Hawton, K., Gath, D., & Day, A. (1994). Sexual function in a community sample of middle-aged women with partners: Effects of age, marital, socioeconomic, psychiatric, gynecological, and menopausal factors. *Archives of Sexual Behavior, 23,* 375–395.

Hays, J. C., Schoenfeld, D., Blazer, G. G., & Gold, D. T. (1996). Global self-ratings of health and mortality: Hazard in the North Carolina Piedmont. *Journal of Clinical Epidemiology, 49,* 969–979.

Herbert, S. (1996). Lesbian sexuality. In R. Cabaj & T. Stein (Eds.), *Textbook of homosexuality and mental health* (pp. 723–742). Washington, DC: American Psychiatric Press.

Hughes, T. L., Haas, A. P., & Avery, L. (1997). Lesbian and mental health: Preliminary results from the Chicago women's health survey. *Journal of the Gay and Lesbian Medical Association, 1,* 133–144.

Hughes, T. L., Johnson, T., & Wilsnack, S. C. (2001). Sexual assault and alcohol abuse: A comparison of lesbian and heterosexual women. *Journal of Substance Abuse, 13,* 515–532.

Hurlbert, D., & Apt, C. (1993). Female sexuality: A comparative study between women in homosexual and heterosexual relationships. *Journal of Sex and Marital Therapy, 19,* 315–327.

Idler, E. L., & Kasl, S. V. (1995). Self-ratings of health: Do they also predict changes in functional ability? *Journal of Gerontology and Social Science, 50,* s344–s353.

Kaplan, H. S. (1974). *The new sex therapy: Active treatment of sexual dysfunctions.* New York: Brunner-Mazel.

Kaplan, H. S. (1979). *Disorders of sexual desire and other new concepts and techniques in sex therapy.* New York: Simon & Schuster.

Kaufman, P., Harrison, E., & Hyde, M. (1984). Distancing for intimacy in lesbian relationships. *American Journal of Psychiatry, 141,* 530–533.

Kinsey, A. C., Pomeroy, W. B., Martin, C. E., & Gebhard, P. H. (1953). *Sexual behavior in the human female.* Oxford, England: Saunders.

Klassen, A. D., & Wilsnack, S. C. (1986). Sexual experience and drinking among women in a U.S. national survey. *Archives of Sexual Behavior, 15,* 363–392.

Laumann, E. O., Gagnon, J. H., Michael, R. T., & Michaels, S. (1994). *The social organization of sexuality: Sexual practices in the United States.* Chicago: University of Chicago Press.

Laumann, E. O., Paik, A., & Rosen, R. C., (1999). Sexual dysfunction in the United States: Prevalence and predictors. *Journal of the American Medical Association, 281,* 537–544.

Leigh, B. (1989). Reasons for having and avoiding sex: Gender, sexual orientation, and relationship to sexual behavior. *Journal of Sex Research, 26,* 199–209.

Loulan, J. (1987). *Lesbian passion.* Minneapolis, MN: Spinsters Ink.

Loulan, J. (1988). Research on the sex practices of 1566 lesbians and their clinical applications. *Women and Therapy, 7,* 221–234.

Masters, W. H., & Johnson, V. E. (1979). *Homosexuality in perspective.* Boston: Little, Brown.

Morokoff, P. J., & Gillilland, R. (1993). Stress, sexual functioning, and marital satisfaction. *Journal of Sex Research, 30,* 43–53.

Nichols, M. (1987a). Doing sex therapy with lesbians: Bending a heterosexual paradigm to fit a gay life-style. In Boston Lesbian Psychologies Collective (Eds.), *Lesbian psychologies: Explorations and challenges* (pp. 242–260). Chicago: University of Illinois Free Press.

Nichols, M. (1987b). Lesbian sexuality: Issues and developing theory. In Boston Lesbian Psychologies Collective (Eds.), *Lesbian psychologies: Explorations and challenges* (pp. 97–125). Chicago: University of Illinois Free Press.

Nichols, M. (1988). Low sexual desire in lesbian couples. In S. R. Leiblum & R. C. Rosen (Eds.), *Sexual desire disorders* (pp. 387–412). New York: Guilford Press.

Oliver, M. B., & Hyde, J. S. (1993). Gender differences in sexuality: A meta-analysis. *Psychological Bulletin, 114,* 29–51.

Peplau, L. A., & Garnets, L. D. (2000). A new paradigm for understanding women's sexuality and sexual orientation. *Journal of Social Issues, 56,* 329–350.

Read, S., King, M., & Watson, J. (1997). Sexual dysfunction in primary medical care: Prevalence, characteristics and detection by the general practitioner. *Journal of Public Health Medicine, 19,* 387–391.

Regan, P. C., & Berscheid, E. (1996). Beliefs about the state, goals, and objects of sexual desire. *Journal of Sex and Marital Therapy, 22,* 110–120.

Robins, L. N., Helzer, J. E., Croughan, J., & Ratcliff, K. S. (1981). National Institute of Mental Health Diagnostic Interview Schedule: Its history, characteristics, and validity. *Archives of General Psychiatry, 38,* 381–389.

Schreurs, K. (1993). Sexuality in lesbian couples: The importance of gender. *Annual Review of Sex Research, 4,* 49–66.

Schwartz, G. E. (1982). Testing the biopsychosocial model: The ultimate challenge facing behavioral medicine? *Journal of Consulting and Clinical Psychology, 50,* 1040–1053.

von Eschenback, A. C., & Schrover, L. R. (1989). The role of sexual rehabilitation in the treatment of patients with cancer. *Cancer, 54,* 2662–2667.

Wilsnack, R. W., Wilsnack, S. C., & Klassen, A. D. (1984). Women's drinking and drinking problems: Patterns from a 1981 national survey. *American Journal of Public Health, 74,* 1231–1237.

Wilsnack, S. C., Klassen, A. D., Shur, B. E., & Wilsnack, R. W. (1991). Predicting onset and chronicity of women's problem drinking: A five-year longitudinal analysis. *American Journal of Public Health, 81,* 305–318.

Wilsnack, S. C., Vogeltanz, N. D., Klassen, A. D., & Harris, T. R. (1997). Childhood sexual abuse and women's substance abuse: National survey findings. *Journal of Alcohol Studies, 58,* 264–271.

Wyatt, G. E. (1985). The sexual abuse of Afro-American and White-American women in children. *Child Abuse and Neglect, 9,* 507–519.

10

HOMOPHOBIA, POVERTY, AND RACISM: TRIPLE OPPRESSION AND MENTAL HEALTH OUTCOMES IN LATINO GAY MEN

RAFAEL M. DÍAZ, EDWARD BEIN, AND GEORGE AYALA

The social and sexual lives of many Latino gay men have been impacted by three socially oppressive forces—homophobia, poverty, and racism—that, acting in an unfortunate synchrony, tend to produce devastating experiences of social alienation and personal shame. Although many men have responded to the oppression with creative acts of personal agency, ranging from committed social activism to acts of personal heroism, others have been deeply troubled and debilitated by financial hardship, family rejection, and discriminatory practices that prevent their fair participation in professional life and in the gay community.

Because a relationship between social discrimination and poor health outcomes has been well documented (Krieger, 1999; Williams, Neighbors, & Jackson, 2003), it is expected that the experience of triple oppression

The research presented in this chapter was supported by Grant R01-HD32776 from the National Institute of Child Health and Human Development.

will predict a wide range of health-related problems for Latino gay men in the United States. However, little is known about the physical or mental health of Latino gay men; the few empirical studies that exist have been conducted in the context of HIV prevention research (see review in Díaz, 1998). Most of what we know in important areas of health in this population, such as a history of childhood sexual abuse or substance abuse, has been examined and reported only as predictors of sexual risk behavior (Carballo-Diéguez & Dolezal, 1995; Díaz, Morales, Bein, Dilán, & Rodríguez, 1999). In the present chapter, we address this gap by examining experiences of social discrimination as predictors of symptoms of psychological distress.

The specific purpose of this chapter is twofold: First, we describe qualitatively and quantitatively the experiences of triple oppression in the lives of Latino gay men who live in the United States; second, we examine and assess the impact of such oppression on mental health, as manifested in symptoms of anxiety, depression, and suicidal ideation. This chapter is based on data collected in a study of Latino gay and bisexual men in three U.S. cities. Data collected in the study allowed us to determine the prevalence of social discrimination and of psychological symptoms in the population of Latino gay and bisexual men and also test a multivariate model on the relationship between the two sets of variables. We first turn to a description of the study.

NUESTRAS VOCES/OUR VOICES: THE NATIONAL STUDY OF LATINO GAY MEN

Funded by the National Institute of Child Health and Human Development (NICHD/NIH), the 4-year study was designed to document the role of sociocultural factors in predicting three important health-related outcomes: sexual practices that involve the risk of HIV transmission, substance use and abuse, and symptoms of psychological distress. Although virtually no data exist on substance use patterns or mental health status of Latino gay and bisexual men in the United States (a notable exception is Dolezal, Carballo-Diéguez, Nieves-Rosa, & Díaz, 2000), there is ample evidence that this population is highly overrepresented in both prevalence and incidence of HIV infection (Valleroy et al., 2000). Our study thus attempted to assess prevalence of other health and mental health outcomes, in addition to HIV risk. More important, our study is the first one to measure both qualitatively and quantitatively actual experiences of social discrimination on account of race, class, and sexual orientation, in an attempt to document and test their impact on the health and well-being of Latino gay and bisexual men in the United States. The study was conducted from 1996 to 2000 in Miami, Los Angeles, and New York; the three cities were chosen not only because of their obvious regional diversity but also because of their Latino populations, which represent the three largest Latino ethnic subgroups in the United States, namely, Cubans in Miami, Puerto Ricans in New York, and Mexicans in Los Angeles.

Men were included in the study if they reported a Latino self-identification (e.g., Latino, Hispanic, any Latin American nationality, or any other recognized Latino ethnic descriptor, such as "Raza" or "Chicano") and a nonheterosexual sexual identity. We thus excluded heterosexually identified men from the study. It is important to note that we studied not simply men who have sex with men, but rather men whose same-sex attractions, desires, and behavior impact their sexual identity. We were also interested in studying men who are closely connected to and participate in the Latino community and therefore recruited men from social venues identified as both gay and Latino, such as Latino-identified gay bars or Latino nights in mainstream gay bars.

By studying Latino self-identified gay and bisexual men, we were addressing a population seldom represented in the literature. Because research instruments are seldom available in Spanish, studies of gay men tend to include mostly English-speaking, highly acculturated, U.S.-born Latinos. Similarly, because attempts are seldom made to include sexual minorities, studies of Latino populations tend to leave out self-identified gay and bisexual men. The study was named "*Nuestras Voces*/Our Voices" because both our theorizing and our assessment tools were based on the subjective experiences and personal meanings (the *voices*) of men in the target population.

The study was conducted bilingually, with all study measurement tools and materials—advertisement, recruitment materials, screeners, focus group questions, and survey items—available in both English and Spanish and administered according to participant-stated language preference.

The study was conducted in three distinct but interrelated phases: Phase 1 involved a qualitative study—conducted between November 1996 and March 1997—in which we interviewed approximately 300 Latino gay men in the context of 24 focus groups in the three cities. Phase 2 involved a measurement development study. During this phase, the transcribed focus group discussions were used to create items for the quantitative survey, with the concern that survey items should reflect as closely as possible the lived subjective experiences of men who experience multiple sources of discrimination. Between 1997 and 1998, 18 months were devoted to an analysis of the qualitative data and the construction and pilot testing of the questionnaire with 150 participants to ensure its sensitivity, appropriateness, and psychometric quality. In Phase 3, a probability sample of 912 Latino gay men was drawn from men entering social venues (bars, clubs, and weeknight events identified as Latino and gay) in the cities of New York (n = 309), Miami (n = 302), and Los Angeles (n = 301). A detailed description of the probability sampling, recruitment procedures, and participation rates and a demographic description of the population estimated from the probability sample can be found in Díaz, Ayala, Bein, Henne, and Marin (2001) as well as in Díaz and Ayala (2001). Recruited men who agreed to participate were interviewed face to face individually by carefully trained interviewers. The rich database is currently under analysis; we present in this chapter only findings related to social discrimination and mental health variables.

The study was designed to address the following gap in the existing literature on health disparities: The relation between social inequality and disease has been mostly inferred from differences in health outcomes between groups that are differentially disadvantaged, discriminated against, and oppressed, such as the observed health disparities among African American, Latino, and White populations in the United States. Rarely have studies measured and examined specific factors of discrimination as they impact the health, behavior, and risk of individuals within the most affected groups. Such analysis within specific groups affected by social discrimination is essential to understand both their specific lived experiences and the specific mechanisms by which oppression impacts the most affected individuals within those groups. In our study, we measured individual differences in experiences of social discrimination and then tested their predictive utility in explaining negative health outcomes in the population.

NUESTRAS VOCES: THE FOCUS GROUP STUDY

Between December 1996 and March 1997, a total of 397 men were recruited in 24 Latino-identified gay bars in the cities of New York, Los Angeles, and Miami. Guided by a brief screening questionnaire, administered at the bar, men were invited to participate in the study only if they identified as Latino or Hispanic and as other than heterosexual. As required by the study design, approximately half the men recruited were under the age of 30 ("younger men") and the other half were 30 or above ("older men"); also, because half the focus groups were conducted in Spanish, half of the sample had to indicate both dominance and preference in the Spanish language, as assessed by the screening instrument.

Our recruitment strategies were aimed at obtaining a sample of self-identified Latino gay and bisexual men who vary in age, acculturation, and geographical location. By recruiting study participants in the context of Latino-identified gay bars, we aimed to include men who for reasons of language, race, and class tend to feel uncomfortable and do not participate in venues and activities associated with the mainstream (mostly White and middle-class) gay community. Men were assigned to 24 different focus groups, with 2 groups within each of the 12 cells created by the 3 (Miami/New York/Los Angeles) × 2 (older/younger) × 2 (Spanish/English) design.

Interview Procedures

Men recruited at the bars were invited to participate in a 2-hour focus group discussion for Latino gay and bisexual men about issues related to HIV. On the basis of answers to screening questions, men were assigned and scheduled to participate in the appropriate age (younger vs. older) and language (English vs. Spanish) groups. Focus group interviews, ranging from 4 to 15 participants, took place in marketing research facilities that were easily accessible to men in each city. The focus group interviews were audiotaped and later transcribed for qualitative analysis. Focus group questions centered on experiences of discrimination on account of being Latino and gay, issues of gay life as a man of color in the respective cities, sexuality, social and family networks, general well-being, the impact of AIDS, and reasons for unprotected sex for Latinos in their respective cities. Immediately following the focus group discussion, participants were asked to fill out a four-page, self-administered questionnaire, including demographic items, which took about 15 minutes to complete. After which the short survey, men were thanked and given $50 each, in compensation for their participation.

Study Participants

Of the 397 men recruited for the study, 293 men participated in the focus group interviews, for a participation rate of 74%. The majority of the sample (86%) identified as gay or homosexual. An assessment of acculturation level, based on language use and length of residence in the United States, shows that the sample falls mostly on the lower end of the acculturation scale. The majority (75%) of the sample are immigrants, with 39% having been in the United States 10 years or less, and 83% reporting substantial use of the Spanish language with peers. Thus, as originally intended by recruitment in Latino-identified gay bars, we were successful in obtaining a sample of men who self-identify as gay or homosexual and who remain close to the Latino community and culture. Unlike the highly acculturated gay Latinos that are typically recruited in mainstream gay venues, this sample can give us the perspective of gay men who also experience the social and economic hardships of ethnic minority groups in the United States. Even though this is a relatively young (84% between 20–40 years of age) and highly educated group of men (69% reported some college or more), only 54% of the sample was employed full time at the time of the study, with a reported unemployment rate of 27%.

RESULTS: THE EXPERIENCE OF TRIPLE OPPRESSION

The qualitative data yielded a wealth of information regarding men's experiences of homophobia, racism, and financial hardship, documented in the following paragraphs and quotes. Men told us about experiencing both verbal and physical abuse, police harassment, and decreased economic opportunities on account of their being gay or effeminate. They told us about powerful messages—both explicit and covert—in their communities, telling them that their homosexuality made them "not normal" nor truly men; that they would grow up alone without children or families; and that ultimately their homosexuality is dirty, sinful, and shameful to their families and loved ones.

In the words of one participant,

> I was a devout Catholic, hated gay people, and was married twice, and actually put two women through a lot because I couldn't accept myself. I came out when I was 30 and it was very difficult for me to deal with being gay. I tried to commit suicide . . . and when I had the strength to say, "Well, this is who I am," my family didn't speak to me for over 15 years.

Another participant added the following:

> You also grow up being told that being gay, you're going to be punished for it. It's something dirty. And I guess being told that from when you're little, it's somewhere in the back of your head, that I'm going to be punished no matter what.

Men told us about having to opt for exile and migration to live as a gay man away from their loved ones, whom they perceived that they would hurt if they opted to live openly their homosexual desires. And many others told us about having to live double lives and pretend to be straight to sustain social connections and employment opportunities.

Similarly, men reported multiple instances of discrimination, verbal and physical violence, police harassment, and decreased sexual and social opportunities on account of their being Latino, immigrant, or having a darker skin color. A great deal of racism was experienced in the context of gay community and gay venues, where men reported not feeling at ease, not welcomed, and some even "escorted out" on account of their different looks, color, and accent.

Some men felt sexually objectified by White boyfriends and lovers, who stereotypically paid more attention to their skin color or Spanish accents than to who they truly are, giving the men a feeling of invisibility and of being used just for fantasy material rather than attempting a more authentic and equitable relationship.

With some White gay men it's like they see you as, again, a piece of meat. Something they could go to bed with, you know, they had their Latino boy or whatever and I've been in situations where I start talking and they're like, "Oh, you can think too?" Latinos also treat each other like that. We sometimes incorporate or believe those stereotypes about each other and we play into it.

Some have encountered overt racist rejection in the context of sexual and romantic relations. One of our New York participants stated the following:

My first lover was White, and his White friends were on his case about why is he living with a Puerto Rican lover. . . . The fact is that they can fuck with Puerto Ricans, but not have one as a lover. They had a big problem with that because you know, I'm just Puerto Rican, why is he with me?

Above all, men felt that the gay community and the gay venues that represent it are highly stratified along race and class dimensions.

Well, my experience in growing up in a gay world . . . it's kind of almost like if you are not Caucasian, you do not even deserve to be gay, in the sense of . . . you know, like what are you doing here in these kinds of clubs? These are gay Caucasian kinds of clubs, and unless you go to a specific Hispanic club, I personally feel that you're not treated equally, not only as an individual, but because you are different, you know, race. You can also be homosexual, which I would think would be enough of a unity, [but] just because you are gay like someone else does not unify you to any kind of organization or group. It's not enough. I feel . . . it's almost like a hindrance being Puerto Rican, . . . to be accepted in the gay community.

This race and class stratification extends to intragroup segregation of immigrant and U.S.-born Latinos:

I came to realize a long time ago that Los Angeles is very stratifying, and I realized that because of the way the clubs would segregate. I just realized that White guys would go one place and the Black guys would go somewhere else, and the Mexican guys would go somewhere else. And within the Mexican or within the Latino community itself, they would even stratify even more. The Chicanos would go to a certain club, to me it's mainly Circus and Arena. The Mexicanos who just got here, straight off the boat, would go to places like La Barcito. So I began to realize that here was a huge stratification of people.

Many men reported experiencing poverty both while growing up and in the present. Men talked about difficulties in meeting their day-to-day living expenses and often struggled with inconsistent employment and sources of income. Many reported having neither health insurance nor access to decent health care. Others reported not having their own place to live, having to rely on friends or relatives for temporary housing.

For many, anger surfaced when remembering the poor conditions of their families of origin, in the face of obvious social inequality:

> In my home it was pretty much hand-to-mouth, and later on I began to realize that a lot of what we considered luxuries was commonplace with these other folks, and they didn't live but maybe two blocks down the street from me. It made me probably just a little sad, I guess. I don't think anger came into it yet, because I didn't have an analysis of the economic situation.

Others had to face the harsh reality of extreme poverty in the inner city, with a deep sense of lack of control and unsettled resignation. Here's a voice from the South Bronx, one of the poorest and most devastated areas in the country, in the context of an implicit connection between the poverty of the neighborhood and the inevitability of HIV infection:

> Me for instance, I have this impending doom. You know what I'm saying? Like the world is going to come to an end, we're going to die . . . and a lot of my friends as well, being poor, living in the South Bronx, they say "fuck it," it's going to be like this . . . I accept it like that, that's the way life is.

In summary, the focus group transcripts made obvious that the lives of Latino gay men—their family, social, and sexual lives—have unfolded within a grid of oppressive social forces that deeply impact their sense of self, their relationships, and their social and professional opportunities.

NUESTRAS VOCES: THE QUANTITATIVE SURVEY

Our research team converted the focus group narratives into a survey instrument that would reliably measure men's experiences of oppression in their lives, from childhood to adulthood. Whereas the qualitative focus group data informed us with richness and depth about men's experiences of discrimination and oppression, only the quantitative data could give us the true dimensions of the problem, namely, how many men did actually have those experiences? The quantitative data could then be used to ask the major question addressed in this chapter: Are those experiences truly related to or predictive of mental health outcomes?

A Quantitative Measure of Oppression

Our ambitious goal was, as much as possible, to take every item in our survey questionnaire verbatim from the voices of the men, as transcribed from the focus groups. We set this goal in full awareness that our research findings, to be maximally useful to service delivery and policy making, must reflect the actual experiences and struggles of those we intend to serve. We came close to our goal, creating reliable scales that measured experiences of homophobia (sample questions: "As you were growing up, how often did you feel that your homosexuality hurt and embarrassed your family?" "As an adult, how often have you had to pretend that you are straight to be accepted?"); experiences of racism ("How often have you been turned down for a job because of your race or ethnicity?" "In sexual relationships, how often do you find that men pay more attention to your race or ethnicity than to who you are as a person?"); and experiences of poverty or financial hardship ("In the last 12 months, how often did you run out of money for your basic necessities?" "In the last 12 months, how often have you had to borrow money from a friend or a relative to get by financially?").

Sampling, Recruitment, and Interviewing Procedures

Between October 1998 and March 1999, the probability sample noted earlier under Phase 3 was drawn from men entering social venues in New York, Miami, and Los Angeles. We were able to approach a total of 5,097 men in the three cities. Of those, 3,086 (61%) agreed to be screened at the venue at time of recruitment. Of those whom we screened at the venues, 1,546 (50%) met qualifying criteria for inclusion in the study. Of those who qualified, 1,324 (86%) gave contact information to be interviewed.

Appointments for individual interviews were made either at time of recruitment or through the contact information. Interviews were conducted individually, with participants responding verbally to an interviewer in a face-to-face format. Interviews were administered in either English or Spanish according to the participant's stated language preference. Interviews occurred in various accessible locations (typically interviewing rooms of marketing research companies) in the three different cities. Interviewing stopped when we reached (actually, slightly exceeded) our goal. A discussion of results by different cities is beyond the scope of the present chapter; thus, all data and analyses are reported for the combined three-city sample. It should be noted, however, that all statistical analyses were conducted controlling for the effects of city, age, and degree of acculturation as measured by reported language use with friends.

Analysis of the weighted data yielded the following demographic profile for the population of men studied. Within the population of nonheterosexual men who attend Latino gay venues in the cities of Miami, New York, and Los Angeles, 54% (50.9–56.5 [95% confidence interval]) self-identify as gay, 30% (27.5–32.1) as homosexual, 15% (13.8–16.8) as bisexual, and 1% (0–1.3) as "other," using labels such as "queer," "pansexual," "maricon," or "joto" (the latter two labels are, respectively, Spanish and Mexican equivalents of the word *faggot*). Many Spanish-speaking men identified themselves with the label "gay" as directly incorporated into the Spanish language or used the Spanish word *homosexual*, spelled the same as in English but pronounced differently in the Spanish language. The overwhelming majority (72.2%; 67.3–77.1) are immigrants, with about half of all immigrants (52.6%; 46.7–58.5) having been in the United States for 10 years or less. Over one third of the participants use "only" or "mostly" Spanish to interact with friends. As expected from a population of bar patrons, the population is relatively young; the estimated mean age is 31.2 (30.0–32.4) with 86.8% (83.1–90.5) between the ages of 20 and 40. Even though this is a highly educated population, with 64.2% (58.8–69.5) having some college education or more, the rate of unemployment is surprisingly high (27.3%; 21.0–33.6). On the basis of self-report, a conservative measure of HIV status, 21.8% (13.8–29.8) are HIV positive, 67.3% (60.3–74.3) are HIV negative, and 10.9% (7.9–13.9) do not know their HIV serostatus.

MEASURES

Our quantitative assessment was based on measures of these four factors: symptoms of psychological distress; experiences of homophobia, racism, and poverty; social isolation and low self-esteem; and resiliency.

Symptoms of Psychological Distress

Symptoms of psychological distress were assessed through a five-item scale, responded to with a 4-point frequency Likert scale (0 = *never*; 1 = *once or twice*; 2 = *a few times*; 3 = *many times*). Items in this scale measured symptoms of anxiety, depression, and suicidality for the last 6 months (e.g., "In the last six months, how often have you felt sad or depressed?" and "In the last six months, how often have you thought of taking your own life?"). A reliability analysis of the scale showed strong internal consistency (Cronbach's α = .75), and high scores indicated higher psychological distress.

Experiences of Homophobia, Racism, and Poverty

Eleven items measured experiences of homophobia both as children and as adults. Within the Homophobia scale, four questions about experiences of verbal harassment and physical assaults were asked in relation to both perceived sexual orientation and gender nonconformity (e.g., "As you were growing up, how often were you hit or beaten up for being homosexual or effeminate?"). Ten items measured experiences of racism as children and as adults, and three items measured recent (in the last 12 months) experiences of poverty or financial hardship. All items on the three different scales were responded to by the 4-point frequency Likert scale, with responses ranging from *never* to *many times,* as previously described. The three scales showed the following high levels of internal consistency: Homophobia (α = .75), Racism (α = .82), and Poverty (α = .71).

Social Isolation and Low Self-Esteem

To test our hypothesis that the impact of social discrimination on mental health outcomes is mediated by a sense of social isolation and low self-esteem, we developed measures for these two constructs. The measure of low self-esteem contained eight items that assessed satisfaction with one's life and personality and perceived levels of self-care and self-respect, as well as a general sense of self-determination and purpose in life (e.g., "Do you like most aspects of your personality?" and "Do you feel you have a sense of direction and purpose in your life?"). The Self-Esteem scale (α = .77) was responded to with a 4-point agreement Likert scale (0 = *definitely yes;* 1 = *somewhat yes;* 2 = *somewhat no;* 3 = *definitely no*). The scale was scored so that higher scores reflect poorer self-esteem. The measure of social isolation (α = .78) contained seven items such as "How often do you feel you lack companionship?" and "How often do you feel there is no one you can turn to?". For this scale four items were responded to with the 4-point frequency Likert scale (from *never* to *many times*) previously described; the other three items were responded to with the 4-point agreement Likert scale (from *definitely yes* to *definitely no*), also previously described. The scale was scored so that higher scores reflect higher levels of social isolation.

Resiliency

The Resiliency scale included in the survey was based not only on the transcripts of the focus groups but also on conversations we had with community leaders and service providers about the factors they view as sources of strength in the community that can be protective against health risks, such as substance abuse and HIV. These factors can be divided into five domains: "outness" to family and peers (e.g., "Have you told your mother or female guardian that you're homosexual/bisexual?"); family acceptance (e.g., "Is there at least someone in your immediate family that you can talk openly with about your homosexuality/bisexuality?"); life satisfaction (e.g., "Are you satisfied with your sex life?"); community involvement with referent social group (e.g., "Are you involved with Latino gay organizations?"); and the presence of a gay role model while growing up (e.g., "Growing up, were there older gay friends or relatives whom you looked up to or who served as role models for you?"). The five different factors, however, did not factor out independently in the statistical analysis. Rather, all 14 items clustered along one internally consistent scale, labeled Resiliency. The Resiliency scale (α = .71) contained the 14 items that were responded to with the 4-point agreement scale, ranging from *definitely yes* to *definitely no*. High scores indicate greater resiliency.

QUANTITATIVE RESULTS

Our population prevalence estimates show that the overwhelming majority of Latino gay men have experienced homophobia personally and quite intensely. For example, 64% were verbally insulted as children for being gay or effeminate; 70% felt that their homosexuality hurt and embarrassed their family; 64% had to pretend to be straight to be accepted; 71% heard as a child that gays would grow old alone; 29% had to move away from their family on account of their homosexuality; and 20% have experienced police harassment on account of their homosexuality. In addition, about one third have experienced racism in the form of verbal harassment as children (31%) and by being treated rudely as adults on account of their race or ethnicity (35%). One out of four men (26%) have experienced discomfort in mostly White gay spaces because of their ethnicity, and more than one out of five (22%) have experienced racially related police harassment. The majority (62%) have experienced racism in the form of sexual objectification from other gay men. In terms of financial hardship, within a 1-year period, more than half of the sample ran out of money for basic necessities (61%) and had to borrow money to get by (54%). Close to half of the men (45%) had to look for work in the past year.

Symptoms of Psychological Distress

The most frequently reported symptoms were depressed mood and sleep difficulties. For the last 6 months, an estimated 80% of Latino gay men experienced feelings of sadness and depression at least once or twice during the time period, with 22% experiencing a depressed mood at a relatively high frequency (*many times*). Sleep problems were experienced by 61% at least once or twice during the previous 6 months, with 20% experiencing sleep problems many times. Feelings of anxiety (i.e., experiences of fear or panic with no apparent reason) and a general feeling of being sick or not well were experienced by about half of Latino gay men at least once or twice during a 6-month period. The most serious symptom of psychological distress—thoughts of taking one's own life—was experienced by 17% at least once or twice during a 6-month period, with 6% having suicidal ideation a few times or more.

The Relationship Between Social Discrimination and Suicidal Ideation

We examined the relations between experiences of social discrimination and the single most severe symptom of psychological distress in the scale, namely, suicidal ideation in the last 6 months. For this analysis, both types of variables—experiences of social discrimination and suicidal ideation—were dichotomized as occurring at least once versus never; the univariate associations between the two types of variables were then tested using chi-square analysis. Those who reported any suicidal ideation in the last 6 months were assigned to a suicidal ideation group; prevalence of experiences of oppression in the suicidal group was compared with the prevalence of oppression for those who did not report suicidal ideation. The relationship between experiences of oppression and suicidal ideation was then tested by comparing the different percentages of men within each suicidal ideation group who reported the experience of discrimination. For example, 81% of men who had suicidal ideation in the last 6 months reported being made fun of as a child for being gay or effeminate, whereas only 61% of those who did not have suicidal ideation reported the same type of discriminatory mocking in childhood. This difference is statistically significant ($p < .001$). Overall, the data showed very strong relationships between life experiences of homophobia and racism, recent experiences of financial hardship, and suicidal ideation within the last 6 months. For all items that measured oppression, those who reported suicidal ideation also reported more frequent experiences of oppression. Specifically, of the 24 chi-square analyses conducted, 18 (75%) were statistically significant; of the remaining six tests, three had marginally significant probabilities between .06 and .10. In all cases, the suicidal ideation group reported higher rates of experienced oppression (see Díaz et al., 2001, for a more detailed report of these findings).

The Relationship Between Oppression and Mental Health

After a careful study of our qualitative data, we hypothesized that increased experiences of social oppression would predict symptoms of psychological distress both directly and indirectly through a sense of social isolation and low self-esteem. In other words, we hypothesized that the impact of social oppression on health is mediated to a large extent by its effects on both social isolation and low self-esteem, which in turn impact psychological well-being. In addition, we examined the role of reported sources of resiliency and strength—such as family acceptance, supportive social networks, and participation in social activism—in alleviating social isolation and low self-esteem. It should be clear, however, that the different aspects of resiliency did not emerge as independent factors in factor analysis, but rather as a single internally consistent 14-item scale, as described in the previous section titled Measures.

Our theoretical model states that social oppression (operationalized as experiences of homophobia, poverty, and racism) impacts mental health (operationalized as symptoms of psychological distress) by affecting two crucial psychosocial factors: social isolation and low self-esteem. We further hypothesized that the impact of social discrimination would be counteracted by the independent effects of resiliency factors that diminish social isolation and increase self-esteem. To test our multivariate model, and given the fact that all constructs in our model—predictors as well as outcome variables— were measured as continuous variables using reliable scales, we used multiple linear regression techniques. We first tested the predictive strength of the full model in a hierarchical regression, with psychosocial variables entered as a first step, social oppression variables entered as a second step, and the resiliency variable entered as a third step. In addition, we tested the mediation model, with procedures suggested by Baron and Kenny (1986).

Social isolation and low self-esteem predicted 26% of the variance of psychological symptoms, with experiences of social oppression predicting an additional 11% of the variance, and resiliency an additional 1%. The full model is statistically significant, $F(6, 77) = 88.27, p < .000001$, predicting a substantive 38% of the variance in symptoms of psychological distress. All the variables in the final model, except for racism and resiliency, were statistically significant.

To test the mediation model of psychological symptoms, in which social isolation and low self-esteem were hypothesized to mediate the effects of social oppression and resiliency, we followed the approach suggested by Baron and Kenny (1986). They suggested procedures for determining mediation through three different regression equations, showing first that the independent variable must affect the mediator in the first equation; second, the independent variable must be shown to affect the dependent variable in the second equation; and third, the mediator must affect the dependent variable in the third equation when independent variables are also included in the equation. The authors suggested further that "if these conditions all hold in the predicted direction, then the effect of the independent variable on the dependent variable must be less in the third equation than in the second. Perfect mediation holds if the independent variable has no effect when the mediation is controlled" (p. 1177).

In our analysis, the independent variable was constituted by experiences of oppression and the Resiliency scale, the mediator was constituted by social isolation and low self-esteem, and the dependent variable was constituted by psychological symptoms of distress. We thus performed three multiple regressions examining whether (a) social oppression and resiliency predict social isolation and low self-esteem; (b) social oppression and resiliency predict psychological symptoms; and (c) social isolation and low self-esteem predict psychological symptoms, even when social oppression and resiliency are included in the equation. These three steps correspond to Baron and Kenny's (1986) test of a mediation model.

The multiple linear regression analysis showed the following:

1. Experiences of homophobia, racism, financial hardship, and resiliency are strong predictors of social isolation, $R^2 = .27$, $F(4, 79) = 40.57$, $p <. 0001$, and of low self-esteem, $R^2 = .17$, $F(4, 79) = 33.34$, $p <. 0001$, with all four predictors contributing independently and, as expected, resiliency negatively associated to the outcome variable in the two different equations.
2. Experiences of homophobia, racism, financial stress, and resiliency significantly predict symptoms of psychological distress, $R^2 = .27$, $F(4, 79) = 38.29$, $p <.0001$.
3. When both independent and mediator variables were entered in the equation, social isolation and low self-esteem remained strong and significant predictors of psychological symptoms, whereas the effects of social oppression and resiliency diminished.

These analyses confirmed the hypothesized mediational model, in which social alienation and low self-esteem mediate the effects of social oppression and resiliency on symptoms of psychological distress. However, because in the final equation two measures of oppression (homophobia and poverty) still predicted symptoms of psychological distress, our model cannot be considered a "perfect" mediation. In other words, experiences of oppression appear to affect mental health outcomes both directly and indirectly, through their mediated impact on social isolation and low self-esteem.

CONCLUSION

Our study shows that social oppression directly and negatively affects levels of perceived social support and self-esteem, whereas resiliency factors enhance them. Men who have been physically and verbally mistreated on account of their being gay, gender nonconformity, or ethnicity are more likely to feel socially disconnected and feel worse about who they are and the lives they live. Psychological symptoms of distress, in turn, are more prevalent among those who both are socially isolated and have a low sense of self-esteem. Our findings thus support a theoretical model in which the hypothesized impact of social oppression on mental health outcomes is mediated by its impact on social isolation and low self-esteem. However, our findings also reveal that social oppression, in particular experiences of homophobia and financial hardship, also has direct or nonmediated effects on mental health outcomes; the mechanisms or pathways by which these direct effects occur are not yet clear and must be the subject of future research.

The fact that resiliency factors alleviate social isolation and low self-esteem underscores the need to focus on the strengths of those individuals who, in spite of severe oppression, manage to avoid the expected negative health outcomes. Our study reveals that a cluster of factors, ranging from family acceptance to antidiscrimination activism, serves important protective functions for members of oppressed groups. It is important to note that in our study, resiliency factors—family acceptance, satisfaction with social and sexual networks, presence of gay role models—are in fact factors of social support, that is, supportive characteristics in the individuals' social environment and developmental history, rather than simply intrapersonal factors such as cognitive ability, behavioral skills, or educational success. This finding underscores the importance and prevention potential of interventions that focus on social contexts and social support systems. Our findings, for example, would support interventions that support Latino families in their understanding and acceptance of their gay children as a way to improve the mental health outcomes in Latino gay men.

In summary, the data from the present study suggest that a very large proportion of Latino gay men who live in U.S. urban centers show a relatively high frequency of symptoms of psychological distress that compromise their mental health and general well-being. Their psychological symptoms, however, cannot be merely understood as a product of individual pathology. The negative mental health outcomes observed in this study are deeply connected to a lifelong history and current experiences of social discrimination due to sexual orientation and racial or ethnic inequalities, as well as to high levels of financial hardship resulting from severe unemployment and poverty. Our analysis suggests that the three measured oppressive factors—experiences of poverty, racism, and homophobia—all contribute independently and negatively to the mental health of those who are most affected. The fact that such relationships were found by examining individual variations within a socially vulnerable group provides strong evidence of the close relationship that exists between social oppression and health. Our findings echo Paul Farmer's (1999) statement that "disease emergence is a socially produced phenomenon" (p. 5).

It is important to note that our findings must be considered in light of three important limitations. First of all, we did not use standardized measures of mental health outcomes (e.g., depression and anxiety), and thus it is not possible to establish the clinical significance of the negative mental health outcomes reported, other than the face validity of self-reported symptoms of psychological distress. Second, throughout the chapter we use the term *impact* somewhat liberally when referring to the relation between oppression and mental health. Our claim is based mostly on the fact that, for the most part, experiences of oppression temporally preceded the health outcomes measured in the study. However, because we only used a cross-sectional design, any references to causality must be treated with caution. Finally, because we recruited from social venues identified as both Latino and gay, our findings cannot be properly generalized to those Latino gay men in urban centers who do not attend such venues.

REFERENCES

Baron, R. M., & Kenny, D. A. (1986) The moderator–mediator variable distinction in social psychological research: Conceptual, strategic, and statistical considerations. *Journal of Personality and Social Psychology, 51,* 1173–1182.

Carballo-Diéguez, A., & Dolezal, C. (1995). Association between history of childhood sexual abuse and adult HIV-risk sexual behavior in Puerto Rican men who have sex with men. *Child Abuse & Neglect, 19,* 595 605.

Díaz, R. M. (1998). *Latino gay men and HIV: Culture, sexuality, and risk behavior.* New York: Routledge.

Díaz, R. M., & Ayala, G. (2001). *Social discrimination and health: The case of Latino gay men and HIV risk.* New York: Policy Institute of the National Gay and Lesbian Task Force.

Díaz, R. M., Ayala, G., Bein, E., Henne, J., & Marin, B. V. (2001). The impact of homophobia, poverty, and racism on the mental health of gay and bisexual men: Findings from three U.S. cities. *American Journal of Public Health, 91,* 927–932.

Díaz, R. M., Morales, E., Bein, E., Dilán, E., & Rodríguez, R. (1999). Predictors of sexual risk in Latino gay/bisexual men: The role of demographic, developmental, social cognitive and behavioral variables. *Hispanic Journal of Behavioral Sciences, 21,* 481–501.

Dolezal, C., Carballo-Diéguez, A., Nieves-Rosa, L., & Díaz, F. (2000). Substance use and sexual risk behavior: Understanding their association among four ethnic groups of Latino men who have sex with men. *Journal of Substance Abuse, 11,* 323–336.

Farmer, P. (1999). *Infections and inequalities: The modern plagues.* Berkeley: University of California Press.

Krieger, N. (1999). Embodying inequality: A review of concepts, measures, and methods for studying health consequences of discrimination. *International Journal of Health Services, 29,* 295–352.

Valleroy, L. A., MacKellar, D. A., Karon, J. M., Rosen, D. H., Macfarland, W., Shehan, D. A., et al. (2000). HIV prevalence and associated risks in young men who have sex with men. *Journal of the American Medical Association, 284,* 198–204.

Williams, D. R., Neighbors, H. W., & Jackson, J. S. (2003). Racial/ethnic discrimination and health: Findings from community studies. *American Journal of Public Health, 93,* 200–208.

11

LESBIANS AND GAY MEN AT WORK: CONSEQUENCES OF BEING OUT

THEO G. M. SANDFORT, HENNY BOS, AND RAYMOND VET

In this chapter we explore what it means to be lesbian or gay in work situations. Building on existing research we present findings from a study, carried out in the Netherlands, about the consequences of discriminatory experiences and openness about one's homosexuality for job satisfaction, health, and sick leave. We pay special attention to the role of *burnout*.

Given the private character of sexuality one might assume that sexual orientation and work are completely unrelated. For lesbians and gay men this is, however, not the case. Being lesbian or gay has an impact that goes far beyond people's private lives (Troiden, 1989). Lesbians and gay men live in an environment that is implicitly assumed to be heterosexual by most people who participate in it, and in which homosexuality is stigmatized. This has several consequences for them (Herek, 1996). Having a homosexual orientation negatively affects the way people are perceived and interacted with in general, with potential negative consequences for their well-being. We assume this also to be the case in work environments.

This study was carried out with support from the Dutch labor union Abvakabo FNV. Completion of the manuscript was supported by a grant from the National Institute of Mental Health (P30 MH43520, Anke A. Ehrhardt, principal investigator).

The experiences of lesbians and gay men at work have been the subject of various studies. These studies, predominantly carried out in the United States, were summarized by Croteau (1996; see also Diamant, 1993; Ellis, 1996). Croteau showed that because of the variety of research designs, general conclusions from these studies can only be drawn with caution. Most of these studies looked at the prevalence of discrimination. Given that the samples studied were not representative and the information reported could not be verified, "true" estimates of discrimination are not possible. These studies, however, suggest that discrimination in the workplace is pervasive. Negative actions toward workers due to their homosexual orientation are reported by 25% to 66% of the participants in these studies. According to Croteau, these studies also show that fear or anticipation of discrimination is pervasive. This fear is often reported to be an important consideration in how workers manage their sexual identities at work. Regarding the latter, studies show a wide variation in concealment or openness in the workplace.

That one's sexual orientation indeed matters at work has been shown in a study among almost 5,000 members of a Dutch labor union working for local governments and in health care (Sandfort & Bos, 1998). In this study lesbians and gay men were compared with heterosexual people on a broad range of aspects of their work experience, such as the importance of work in one's life, feedback on their job performance, social support, burnout, and job satisfaction.

What is special about this study is that a probability sample has been used, rather than a convenience sample. As a consequence, a diverse group of lesbians and gay men participated in the study, not just those who were comfortable with their sexual orientation and open about it, and more inclined to volunteer as participants in a study (cf. Lonborg & Phillips, 1996). Furthermore, the various aspects of work experience were assessed without reference to one's sexual orientation, making the comparison between gay or lesbian and heterosexual employees more objective. Sexual orientation was assessed with one question at the end of the questionnaire. Of course this limits the possibility of differentiating within the group of lesbians and gay men. Nothing was known about their behavior and identity and, probably more relevant, the way they dealt with their homosexuality at work. Regardless of this limitation, the findings of this study showed that the way in which lesbian and gay employees experienced their work differed consistently from that of heterosexual persons. Whenever there were differences, these differences were to the disadvantage of lesbian and gay employees. Compared with heterosexual employees, lesbian and gay employees experienced their relationships with colleagues and their boss as less positive, and they experienced less social support from their colleagues. The feeling that colleagues accepted one's lifestyle was lower among gay or lesbian employees than among their heterosexual peers. Lesbians and gay men experienced more symptoms of burnout than their heterosexual counterparts. Finally, as a consequence of these differences, the incidence of sick leave was higher among gay and lesbian employees than among heterosexual employees. Work experiences also differed, depending on gender and on work setting. Men were generally better off than women, regardless of sexual orientation. In addition, the health care setting seemed to be a more supportive working environment than local government. It is unclear to what extent findings from this study can be generalized to other, less service-oriented work settings and to countries with a different social climate regarding homosexuality. The findings, however, strongly indicate that sexual orientation matters at work and make one wonder how these differences in work experience actually come about.

It is likely that lesbian and gay employees' work experience is also dependent on how they deal with their sexual orientation at work. Several, mostly qualitative studies have identified a variety of strategies. In a study on lesbian and gay teachers, Griffin (1991), for instance, identified four strategies: passing, covering, and being implicitly or explicitly out. *Passing* refers to making other people, who are assumed not to be informed about one's homosexual orientation, believe that one is heterosexual, for instance by making up intimate partners of the other sex. People who apply a *covering* strategy also assume that other people do not know about their sexual orientation, but instead of lying about it, they censor information about themselves. For instance, by not sharing specific information they try to prevent coworkers from finding out about their homosexuality. People who are *implicitly out* will not avoid the truth about their sexual orientation, but they will not explicitly refer to themselves as gay men or lesbians. These people are likely to be open to friends and parents, but less so to coworkers. Lesbians and gay men who are *explicitly out* at work are open with colleagues about their sexual orientation. They have adopted a lesbian or gay identity, present themselves as such, and want to be seen as lesbians or gay men. People who are explicitly out are supposed to have a better integration between personal and professional aspects of the self.

Hall (1989) identified an overlapping set of strategies among a small group of lesbians working in large organizations. In addition, Hall based her typology on how women dealt with homophobic remarks. Overlapping with the strategy of passing is what Hall called *deception*. She observed that this strategy might cause inner conflicts and force people to find ways to avoid seeing themselves as dishonest. Other strategies that Hall observed were *denial* and *dissociation*. The first strategy was used to characterize women who considered themselves not to be in the closet at work even though they had never informed coworkers about their sexual orientation. The strategy of dissociation refers to people who said that they felt comfortable about homophobic remarks by thinking that it was not they who were being discussed contemptuously. Finally, Hall identified the strategy of *distraction*: By presenting oneself as a feminist or a liberal and cultivating that image, one distracts the attention of people from the more discrediting (homosexual) aspect of one's identity.

At this moment, no comprehensive, conceptually defined and empirically based typology of strategies is available. In general, these strategies can be put on a continuum, indicating the extent to which people are open about their homosexuality.

Being open about one's homosexuality is usually considered to be a basic stage in the process of sexual identity formation and indicative of acceptance of one's own sexuality. Franke and Leary (1991), however, demonstrated that willingness to come out to others is largely a matter of the degree to which one is concerned about other people's reactions and how negative such reactions are perceived to be. There are obvious advantages to not disclosing one's sexual orientation: It is an effective means of protecting oneself against so-called innocent jokes, ridicule, rejection, or harassment. Avoidance of potential discrimination seems to be a legitimate reason not to disclose at the workplace. There is some evidence that more open workers experience greater frequency of discrimination (Badgett, 1996). Not disclosing might, however, also involve various costs. Hiding one's orientation requires a continuing vigilance regarding the personal information one shares with other people. It requires keeping a perfect split between two worlds and maintaining two separate selves. Not disclosing might induce feelings of being dishonest and disconnect or alienate one from colleagues. As a consequence, one might not get support from others when it is needed. Because not disclosing might also affect one's job satisfaction and productivity, it could also have negative consequences for the organization in which one works.

Conversely, being open about one's homosexuality might have positive benefits. Herek (1996) distinguished three broad categories of reasons why people might reveal their sexual orientation: improving interpersonal relationships, enhancing one's mental and physical health, and changing society's attitudes. These categories match the various considerations for self-disclosure mentioned by respondents in a study by Wells and Kline (1987). For this study 20 lesbians and gay men were interviewed with an open-ended questionnaire assessing how, when, where, why, and to whom they disclosed their sexual orientation. Reasons for self-disclosure mentioned by the respondents were honesty; increasing the likelihood of developing close relationships; the need to be one's self; the need to be affirmed by supportive others; helping heterosexual people to understand gayness and lesbianism; and contributing to liberalizing attitudes toward homosexuality. Reasons mentioned only by women were reducing sexual pressure from others and finding sexual partners.

Few studies have actually addressed the consequences of being open at work. One notable exception is Day and Schoenrade's study (1997) about the relationships between communication about sexual orientation and work attitudes. Controlling for various potentially confounding variables, they found that workers who are more open are more committed to the organization where they work, experience less conflict between work and home, and have higher job satisfaction.

It is of course not always up to lesbians and gay men themselves to decide whether or not they want to be open about their homosexuality. Even though homosexuality, unlike race and gender, is traditionally considered to be a stigmatized characteristic that people can conceal, this is not necessarily the case. One's presented identity may not coincide with one's observed identity (cf. Troiden, 1989). One might present oneself as nonhomosexual and have the illusion that people are not able to perceive one's homosexuality; colleagues might think differently, however. Various clues might suggest that someone is gay or lesbian. One's homosexuality can also become public knowledge without one's consent by what is called *outing*, disclosure by third parties.

Consequences of being open about one's homosexuality will depend on the context, on the interpersonal as well as the societal level. In a country with a rather tolerant climate toward homosexuality, such as the Netherlands (Van den Akker, Halman, & De Moor, 1994; Widmer, Treas, & Newcomb, 1998), it might be easier to be open about one's homosexuality as the risk of negative reactions is smaller. As Dutch research about sexual orientation and mental health suggests, the consequences of a more tolerant climate should not be overrated (Sandfort, de Graaf, Bijl, & Schnabel, 2001).

On the basis of previous research, we would like to take the subject of homosexuality and work one step further by introducing the concept of burnout (Schaufeli & Van Dierendonck, 1993). Burnout, a syndrome of emotional exhaustion, depersonalization, and reduced sense of personal competence, is usually assumed to be a consequence of an unbearable workload. We hypothesized that symptoms of burnout could also result from not being open about one's homosexual orientation. Not disclosing one's sexual orientation might induce negative evaluations of oneself or a lack of personal energy and create a detached response to coworkers. However, actual disclosing, albeit not in each and every situation and not necessarily unconditionally, might prevent symptoms of burnout by fostering psychological and physical well-being, validation of one's experiences, and the development of personal relationships (Kowalski, 1999).

Burnout might also result from negative experiences that lesbians and gay men have at the workplace in interactions with colleagues. Such negative experiences may result from discrimination, harassment, or seemingly less intrusive behaviors such as bullying or mobbing (Einarsen, Raknes, & Matthiesen, 1994). Einarsen et al. defined mobbing as behavior that "over a period of time" causes a person to feel "subjected to negative acts that one can not defend oneself against" (p. 383). The most negative and most frequently observed forms of mobbing were social isolation and exclusion, devaluation of one's work and efforts, and exposure to teasing, insulting remarks, and ridicule.

In addition to informal discrimination, lesbians and gay men might also encounter formal discrimination at work, in the form of career obstacles, or obstructions in the development of one's career, because of one's homosexual orientation. We expected this formal discrimination also to induce feelings of burnout by negatively affecting one's feelings of competence and successful achievement.

We expected not being open about one's homosexuality at work, informal homonegative experiences, and career obstacles all to be positively associated with burnout. To the extent that these associations were found, we also wanted to explore whether these three phenomena independently contributed to feelings of burnout. Furthermore, we examined these relationships with three specified kinds of burnout: emotional exhaustion, depersonalization, and sense of reduced personal competence (Schaufeli & Van Dierendonck, 1993). Emotional exhaustion refers to a sense of being totally "empty" or "exhausted" in relation to one's work. It gets expressed in such feelings as being tired when getting up with a working day ahead or the notion that a full day's work is too heavy a load. Depersonalization refers to a cold, indifferent, cynical, and impersonal attitude to one's work and to colleagues. Reduced personal competence reflects feelings of being less capable of doing one's work well than previously was the case.

Other studies have shown that burnout induces lower job satisfaction, a decline in health status, and, related to that, more days away from work because of sickness (Van Veldhoven & Meijman, 1994). Would burnout in lesbians and gay men have the same consequences, and, if so, which specific forms of burnout would be operative? If this was the case, burnout might mediate the consequences of homonegative experiences with colleagues, career obstacles, and concealment of one's homosexuality for job satisfaction, health, and sick leave. We explored whether this indeed was the case. Although we did not expect this, it could of course also be that these three factors might contribute to job satisfaction, health, and sick leave, independently of burnout.

Figure 11.1 illustrates the relationships described here and was used to guide the analysis of the data and the interpretation of our findings.

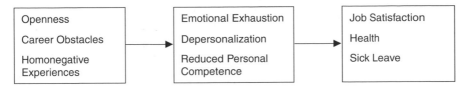

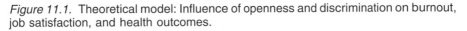

Figure 11.1. Theoretical model: Influence of openness and discrimination on burnout, job satisfaction, and health outcomes.

THE STUDY

In 1998, we recruited respondents for this study among members of a lesbian and gay interest group in one of the major Dutch labor unions. This union is predominantly for workers in service-oriented fields, such as health care, social work, governmental administration, and education. The members of this interest group received a written questionnaire through the mail, with a prepaid postage return envelope. Of the 368 questionnaires that had been sent out, 174 were returned (47%). Failure to respond was due partly to the fact that about 15% of the entries on the mailing list were for organizations rather than individuals. For practical reasons these addresses could not be removed from the mailing list.

Of the 174 persons who participated in the study, 40% were female. The respondents' age ranged from 27 to 58 years, and as Table 11.1 shows, the mean age was 41 years. Compared with the general population, the average level of education was high. Most respondents lived in urban areas. Over 75% of the respondents were involved in steady relationships, women significantly more often than men (87% vs. 69%). Across all respondents, 20% had one or more children; more women than men had children (29% vs. 13%).

Almost all variables were measured with scales, most of which had been used in other studies or were derived from scales successfully used by others. A scale especially developed for this study measured the extent to which people were open at work. This Being Open at Work scale contained nine statements, which referred to various strategies for managing one's sexual orientation at work such as passing, covering, and being implicitly and explicitly out (Griffin, 1991). Examples of statements included are "If people at work think that I am straight then I'll leave it like that," "I only inform colleagues whom I can trust about my homosexuality," and "It is perfectly clear at my work that I am lesbian/gay." Participants were asked to indicate their agreement with the statements on a 5-point scale (1 = *completely agree*; 5 = *completely disagree*). Some scores were reversed in such a way that higher scores on all items indicated more openness about one's homosexuality at work. The alpha for this scale was .76.

TABLE 11.1
Characteristics of Study Participants

Characteristic	Gay men (n = 105)	Lesbian women (n = 69)	Total (N = 174)
Age (years)			
M	41.78	40.50	41.28
SD	6.96	7.63	7.23
Education (%)			
Primary, basic vocational	5.8	2.9	4.6
Lower secondary	15.4	11.6	13.9
Higher secondary	10.6	7.2	9.2
Higher professional, university	68.3	78.3	72.3
Involved in steady relationship (%)	69.2	87.0	76.3[a]
Openness[b]			
M	4.23	4.46	4.32
SD	0.64	0.51	0.60[c]
Career obstacles[d]			
M	1.09	1.11	1.10
SD	0.23	0.29	0.25
Homonegative experiences[d]			
M	1.22	1.16	1.19
SD	0.30	0.33	0.32
Emotional exhaustion[b]			
M	2.92	2.80	2.87
SD	1.06	0.92	1.01
Depersonalization[b]			
M	2.71	2.80	2.75
SD	1.08	0.96	1.03
Reduced personal competence[b]			
M	2.98	2.92	2.95
SD	0.84	0.78	0.81
Job satisfaction[b]			
M	3.68	3.66	3.67
SD	0.95	0.91	0.93
Health[b]			
M	3.82	3.83	3.82
SD	0.59	0.55	0.57
Sick leave (days in preceding year)			
M	9.91	13.10	11.22
SD	15.28	19.03	16.94

[a]$\chi^2(1, N = 172) = 7.207, p < .05.$ [b]$1 = low, 5 = high.$ [c]$t(1) = 6.141, p < .05.$ [d]$1 = none, 5 = many.$

The occurrence of homonegative experiences at work was assessed with a 9-item scale based on the Leidse Mobbing Schaal (Hubert, 1996) and the Leymann Inventory of Psychological Terrorization (Leymann, 1990). Because the length of the original scales was not appropriate for a mail-in questionnaire, we reduced the number of items. We decided to select items from these scales that specifically referred to ridiculing, marginalizing, or exclusion. Examples of the selected items are "Colleagues made you look ridiculous," "Colleagues mocked your private life," and "Colleagues called you names." Participants were asked to indicate on a 3-point scale (1 = *never*; 3 = *two times or more often*) how frequently the various forms of mobbing had happened to them in the past 6 months in relation to their homosexual orientation. The alpha for this scale was .83.

To determine the occurrence of formal discrimination we assessed whether people had experienced any obstructions in the development of their career in their current job (career obstacles). The scale is based on the Dutch questionnaire Beleving en Beoordeling van de Arbeid (Experience and Assessment of Labor; Van Veldhoven & Meijman, 1994), which assesses the occurrence of experiences such as being removed from a task, being denied a promotion, and not being allowed to attend a specific course. Items were reworded in such a way that these occasions had to be related to one's homosexuality. The scale consisted of five items. People were asked to indicate whether (*yes* or *no*) they had experienced the included obstructions. The alpha for this scale was .91.

The three dimensions of burnout were assessed with a short form of the Dutch version of the Maslach Burnout Inventory (Schaufeli & Van Dierendonck, 1993). Items on this scale refer to various symptoms of burnout. For this study the original scale was shortened to reduce the time needed to fill it out. We selected items with the highest item–total correlations as indicated by Schaufeli and Van Dierendonck (1991) in their report on the construction of the scale. Emotional exhaustion, depersonalization, and reduced competence were measured with five, four, and seven items respectively. Participants had to indicate on a 7-point scale how often the various symptoms occurred (1 = *never*; 7 = *always*). Examples of items are "I feel mentally exhausted by my work" (Emotional Exhaustion), "I have noticed that I have become too distant from my work" (Depersonalization), and "I doubt the usefulness of my work" (Reduced Personal Competence). The alphas for the three subscales in this study were .87, .71, and .81, respectively.

As potential consequences of burnout we assessed job satisfaction, health, and sick leave. Job satisfaction was assessed by asking respondents to indicate on a 5-point scale (1 = *very unsatisfied*; 5 = *very satisfied*) how they experienced their work overall. General health status was evaluated with a 4-item scale assessing how people felt in general about their health (1 = *badly*; 5 = *excellent*), how often they were troubled by various physical problems such as stomach ache, heart palpitations, dizziness, and headaches, and how frequently they used sleeping pills or related narcotics. The alpha for this scale was .60. Sick leave was assessed with one question asking how many days people had missed work in the past year because of illness.

In addition to these variables we collected sociodemographic information and asked questions about various aspects of each participant's function and position. One of these questions was whether the participant's work included contacts with people other than colleagues. Examples of other characteristics of the job that we assessed were whether the job was temporary or steady, whether it was a full- or a part-time position, and how long the participant had been working for the current employer.

We used the path model in Figure 11.1 to guide our analyses of the data. We first looked at whether openness, homonegative experiences, and career obstacles were related to the three specified forms of burnout: emotional exhaustion, depersonalization, and reduced personal competence. Next, we used regression analysis to see which of the factors that were bivariately related to burnout contributed to the explanation of burnout independently. In a second series of analyses, we applied the same procedure to assess the relationships of the three forms of burnout to job satisfaction, health, and sick leave.

Subsequently, we explored the role of burnout as a mediator between openness, homonegative experiences, and career obstacles, on the one hand, and job satisfaction, health, and sick leave, on the other hand. We did this only in the following cases (cf. Baron & Kenny, 1986): The outcome variable (job satisfaction, health, or sick leave) had to be independently related to at least one form of burnout; the respective form(s) of burnout had to be independently related to one or more independent variables (openness, homonegative experiences, or career obstacles); and the respective outcome variable had to be independently related to one or more independent variables (openness, homonegative experiences, or career obstacles). We assessed the role of burnout as a mediator with hierarchical regression analyses. Burnout was considered to be a mediator, if controlling for burnout would eliminate or reduce the effect of the independent variables.

All analyses were carried out for the total group as well as for the gay men and the lesbians separately. The pattern of outcomes for men and women differed substantially. Therefore, we present most of the findings separately for men and women. Results for the total group are only reported if the analyses showed the same results for men and women.

Openness, Homonegative Experiences, and Career Obstacles

The mean level of openness in this sample was relatively high (Table 11.1). Lesbians were more open with colleagues about their homosexual orientation than were gay men. Being open was not related to age or to whether people lived in urban or rural areas. Gay men with a higher level of education were more open about their homosexuality ($r = .25$, $p < .05$). Lesbians and gay men were less open if they were not involved in a steady relationship ($r = .29$, $p < .01$). Being open was not related to characteristics of the job, such as whether the job was temporary or steady, whether it was a full- or a part-time position, and how long one had been working for the current employer. Gay men who had job-related contacts with people outside of the organization were more open at work about their homosexuality compared with gay men without such contacts ($r = .32$, $p < .001$). For lesbians, there was no such relationship.

Men and women did not differ with respect to the level of homonegative experiences they had had in interactions with colleagues. The most frequently reported experience was that colleagues gossiped about the respondents; this experience was reported by 42% of the gay men and 34% of the lesbians. Twenty-one percent of the gay men and 13% of the lesbians said that suggestions they made at work were rejected. It was somewhat less frequently reported that colleagues mocked the respondents' private lives (14% of the men and 13% of the women) and made the respondents look ridiculous (19% of the men and 13% of the women). Other types of homonegative experiences were reported by smaller proportions of respondents.

Having had homonegative experiences at work was not related to age, relationship status, whether people lived in urban or rural areas, or characteristics of the job. The only distinction in any of these areas was that gay men who had job-related contacts with people outside of the organization had fewer homonegative experiences than gay men without such contacts ($r = -.42$, $p < .001$). Lesbian women with a permanent appointment reported fewer homonegative experiences in their current position than lesbian women with temporary appointments ($r = -.36$, $p < .01$).

Men and women had experienced obstacles in their career development in relation to their homosexual orientation to more or less the same degree (Table 11.1). The most frequently reported obstacle was that respondents felt that their careers were thwarted, a response reported by 13% of the gay men and 14% of the lesbians. Being removed from a specific task was reported by 7% of the gay men and 6% of the lesbians. Fewer men and women reported the other two obstacles: being denied promotion and not being allowed to get special training.

Career obstacles were more often reported by gay men with a lower level of education ($r = -.22$, $p < .05$). Reported career obstacles were not related to characteristics of the job, except for permanent versus temporary employment of gay men. Gay men with a permanent appointment reported fewer career obstacles in their current position than did gay men with temporary appointments ($r = -.30$, $p < .01$).

One might expect that being open at work about one's homosexuality increases the risk of being exposed to negative experiences. However, we did not find such a relationship. Openness at work was not related to having experienced career obstacles or homonegative experiences (Table 11.2). However, both lesbian and gay respondents who reported having experienced career obstacles in relation to their homosexuality were also more likely to

TABLE 11.2
Intercorrelations Between Homosexuality-Related Factors, Burnout, and Outcome Measures

Variable	1	2	3	4	5	6	7	8	9
1. Openness about homosexuality	—	.09	.01	.03	-.03	-.13	-.04	-.01	.19
2. Career obstacles	-.07	—	.38***	-.04	.25*	.05	-.29*	.04	.06
3. Homonegative experiences	-.18	.21*	—	.16	.14	.01	-.24*	-.06	.17
4. Emotional exhaustion	-.28**	.18	.42***	—	.39***	.38***	-.43***	-.50***	.24*
5. Depersonalization	-.23*	.06	.31***	.59***	—	.47***	-.68***	-.09	.15
6. Reduced personal competence	-.28**	.14	.11	.42***	.50***	—	-.42***	-.21	.20
7. Job satisfaction	.33***	-.12	-.22*	-.47***	-.60***	-.52***	—	.04	-.09
8. Health	.05	.01	-.15	-.47***	-.12	-.13	.14	—	-.34**
9. Sick leave	.01	.17	.19	.38***	.24**	.10	-.09	-.38***	—

Note. Results for lesbian women are above the diagonal; results for gay men are below the diagonal.
*$p < .05$. **$p < .01$. ***$p < .001$.

have had homonegative experiences in interactions with colleagues (for the total group: $r = .29$, $p < .001$).

Burnout, Job Satisfaction, Health, and Sick Leave

Men and women did not differ on the three dimensions of burnout (Table 11.1). The three dimensions were strongly interrelated ($.38 < r < .59$, $p < .001$ for all three; Table 11.2). Men and women also did not differ in their job satisfaction, their health status, and the number of days they had missed work because they were sick. Job satisfaction was unrelated to health status and sick leave. As might be expected, health and sick leave were negatively related (for the total group, $r = .36$, $p < .001$). People who overall were less healthy had missed work more days.

Burnout as a Consequence of Openness, Career Obstacles, and Homonegative Experiences

We subsequently wanted to test whether not being open at work, homonegative experiences in interactions with colleagues, and obstacles in one's career development seen as related to one's homosexual orientation were related to burnout, and to which form of burnout specifically. In those cases in which more than one factor was related to a specific form of burnout, a regression analysis (forward) was performed to assess whether the contribution of each factor in the explanation of burnout was independent.

For gay men, openness about one's homosexuality and homonegative experiences were both related to burnout (Table 11.2). Gay men who were less open about their homosexuality at work experienced more symptoms of emotional exhaustion (feeling completely empty and exhausted at work), depersonalization (feeling negative or distant toward one's work), and reduced personal competence (feeling less able to do one's work than in the past). Having had homonegative experiences at work was positively related to both emotional exhaustion and depersonalization by participants who reported more homonegative experiences, indicating higher levels of emotional exhaustion and depersonalization. The number of career obstacles gay men had experienced as a consequence of their homosexuality was not related to any dimension of burnout. The regression analyses showed that for gay men, emotional exhaustion was predicted by both the level of openness about one's homosexuality and the occurrence of homonegative experiences at work ($R^2 = .22$, $p < .001$). Depersonalization was independently predicted only by homonegative experiences and not by openness ($R^2 = .10$, $p < .001$).

Fewer significant effects were found for the lesbians. Openness about one's homosexuality and having had homonegative experiences were not related to any of the three forms of burnout. Lesbians only had a higher level of depersonalization when they had experienced more career obstacles due to their homosexuality (Table 11.2).

Job Satisfaction, Health, and Sick Leave as a Consequence of Burnout

The relationships of the three forms of burnout to job satisfaction, health, and sick leave were similar in lesbians and gay men (Table 11.2). Job satisfaction was negatively related to emotional exhaustion, depersonalization, and reduced personal competence for both groups. Women and men with higher levels of these three forms of burnout reported lower levels of job satisfaction. Gay men with higher levels of emotional exhaustion reported more sick leave; the same pattern was found among women. Emotional exhaustion was related to diminished health in both men and women. Depersonalization and reduced personal competence were not related to health, either in men or in women, and reduced personal competence was not related to sick leave.

We performed regression analyses to see which forms of burnout independently contributed to job satisfaction and sick leave. For gay men, job satisfaction was independently related to depersonalization and reduced personal competence, and not to emotional exhaustion ($R^2 = .42, p < .001$). Participants who felt more distant and negative about work and had a stronger sense of not being able to do one's work reported less job satisfaction. For lesbians, only depersonalization, and neither of the other two forms of burnout, independently predicted job satisfaction ($R^2 = .46, p < .001$). Women who felt negative and distant about their work were overall less satisfied with their work.

Is Burnout a Mediator?

We expected that burnout would mediate potential relationships between openness, homonegative experiences, and career obstacles, on the one hand, and openness, career obstacles, and homonegative experiences, on the other hand. Before assessing this, we first explored which of the three independent variables—openness, homonegative experiences, and career obstacles—were independently related to the outcome variables.

For gay men, being open and having had homonegative experiences were both associated with job satisfaction. Men who were more open about their homosexuality at work reported being more satisfied with their job. Men who reported more homonegative experiences at work reported less job satisfaction. Only openness was independently and positively related to job satisfaction ($R^2 = .11, p < .001$).

For lesbians, homonegative experiences and career obstacles were both negatively related to job satisfaction, indicating that women, who experienced more homonegative experiences and more career obstacles that they

TABLE 11.3
Hierarchical Regression Analysis for Openness,
Homonegative Experiences, Career Obstacles, and
Burnout as Predictors of Job Satisfaction

Step	Gay men	Lesbian women
Step 1		
Openness about homosexuality	−.33***	—
Career obstacles	—	−.29*
R^2	.11***	.09*
Step 2		
Openness about homosexuality	.16*	—
Career obstacles	—	−.14
Depersonalization	−.43***	−.64***
Reduced personal competence	−.26***	—
R^2	.44***	.48***
ΔR^2	.34***	.39***

Note. Data are standardized multiple regression coefficients (β).
*$p < .05$. ***$p < .001$.

attributed to their homosexuality, reported less overall satisfaction with their job. Only career obstacles were independently related to job satisfaction ($R^2 = .09$, $p < .05$).

None of the independent factors was related to health or sick leave, either in gay men or in lesbians. Consequently, we explored only the role of burnout as a mediator for job satisfaction in gay men and lesbians. In gay men specifically, depersonalization and reduced personal competence could mediate the relationship between openness about homosexuality and job satisfaction. In lesbians, depersonalization could mediate the relationship between career obstacles and job satisfaction.

Table 11.3 shows the outcomes of the hierarchical regression analyses. For gay men, the significant effect of openness on job satisfaction was reduced when controlling for depersonalization and reduced personal competence (from $\beta = .33$, $p < .001$, to $\beta = .16$, $p < .05$, $\Delta R^2 = .34$, $p < .001$). This suggests that in gay men burnout indeed mediates the relationship between being open about one's homosexual orientation and job satisfaction. For lesbians, the significant effect of career obstacles on job satisfaction was eliminated when controlling for depersonalization (from $\beta = -.29$, $p < .05$, to $\beta = -.14$, *ns*, $\Delta R^2 = .39$, $p < .001$), suggesting that burnout does indeed mediate the relationship between career obstacles and job satisfaction.

DISCUSSION

The lesbians and gay men in this study were all rather open at work about their homosexuality. Relatively few of them had experienced obstacles in their career development in relation to their homosexuality. The level of discrimination that was experienced by these lesbians and gay men seems not to have been as pervasive as that usually found in American studies (Croteau, 1996). Being open about one's homosexuality also does not necessarily promote homonegative experiences, contrary to what has been suggested previously (Badgett, 1996). It is quite possible, though, that in specific cases, dependent on the context or the ways one manifests homosexuality, openness could indeed lead to more homonegative experiences. What we did find is that people who had experienced more career obstacles in relation to their homosexuality were also more likely to have had homonegative experiences in interactions with their colleagues.

This study supports the importance of the concept of burnout to understand gay men's work experiences in particular. Gay men, who were less open about their homosexuality at work and reported more homonegative experiences in their interactions with colleagues, had higher levels of burnout. Lesbians who reported career obstacles felt more cold, indifferent, cynical, and impersonal in relation to colleagues and their work. Among the lesbians and gay men studied, burnout was also related to the outcome variables, in particular to job satisfaction. Higher levels of burnout seemed to result in lower levels of job satisfaction. The outcomes of the study also suggest that burnout, or specifically emotional exhaustion, is related to diminished health and more frequent sick leave.

Burnout seemed to play a role as mediator for job satisfaction. The findings for gay men suggest that not being open about one's homosexuality induces burnout, which subsequently decreases the satisfaction men experience in their job. For lesbians burnout mediated the relationship between career obstacles and job satisfaction. The findings suggest that lesbians who experience more career obstacles in relation to their sexual orientation experience more burnout, which subsequently reduces the overall satisfaction with their job.

Some of the relationships we expected to find were not supported by the findings. There is, for example, no support for the idea that not being open about one's homosexuality, homonegative experiences, or career obstacles makes people less healthy and results in more sick leave, directly or indirectly. It is quite possible that health status and sick leave are more determined than job satisfaction by factors that are external to the work situation.

The observed differences between lesbians and gay men are remarkable. It could well be that in work environments—usually dominated by heterosexual men—the work experience of lesbians is more affected by the fact that they are female. Their sexual orientation might be less salient. This links to findings in the probability sample (Sandfort & Bos, 1998). When asked for the reasons they were harassed or mobbed, 13% of the gay men and 4% of the lesbians mentioned their sexual orientation. Gender as a perceived reason for being mobbed was mentioned by none of the gay men and by 5% of the lesbians.

This study has a few limitations. First, using a convenience sample, more particularly members of an interest group within a labor union, likely resulted in the selection of people who are more open and more at ease with their sexual orientation (Sandfort, 1997), reducing variance in the data and resulting in less power to establish significant relationships (Croteau, 1996). Comparing this sample with a non–self-selected group of lesbians and gay men who were part of a probability sample of all members of the same union illustrates this selectivity (Sandfort & Bos, 1998). Lesbians and gay men in the probability sample had lower levels of education, lived relatively more often in rural than in urban areas, were or had been (heterosexually) married more often, and more often had children. Job satisfaction was lower in the probability sample whereas occurrence of sick leave was higher (Bos & Sandfort, 1999). Other limitations are the reliance on self-report, meaning that participants' perceptions and attributions do not necessarily accurately reflect what actually happened. Some of the scales were used for the first time and have not yet been validated.

The generalizability of the findings is limited because of the use of a convenience sample of people in predominantly service-oriented professions and the relatively tolerant Dutch climate toward homosexuality. Furthermore, regardless of one's sexual orientation, it is our impression that compared with people in the United States, Dutch people are more open at work about private aspects of their lives and share more personal information. It is also possible that in the Netherlands there is a strong social norm regarding openness about one's homosexuality. The combined effect of these factors might affect the relationship of being open with factors influencing openness and consequences of being open in other work environments.

PRACTICAL IMPLICATIONS AND DIRECTIONS FOR FUTURE RESEARCH

The findings from this study have various practical implications. They suggest that formal and informal discrimination based on one's sexual orientation does occur in work situations. It is in the interest of both employers and employees to create working environments in which lesbians and gay men can come out safely and in which neither formal nor informal discrimination occurs. Lesbians and gay men should also be supported in finding ways to develop more positive feelings about their own homosexuality and in constructively disclosing their sexual orientation at work.

It is obvious that more research in the field of sexual orientation and work is needed to better understand and address the situations lesbians and gay men face in their work environments. Future research might also further our understanding of the consequences of self-expression in interpersonal relationships at work and the ways in which stigma affects interactions with coworkers.

As in almost all research among lesbians and gay men, the issue of sampling needs more attention in future studies. Our findings suggest that selective samples affect the outcomes of the study. Even though opportunities to study more representative samples might be limited, attempts should be made to recruit lesbians and gay men who are less open about their homosexuality.

Future research should also explore the role of the context in which lesbians and gay men work. It is quite likely that experiences of lesbians and gay men are dependent on the environment in which they work. One relevant dimension could be whether people are working in traditionally more masculine or more feminine professions.

Qualitative research will be particularly useful for understanding coming out in work situations as a process, the trajectories that people follow in revealing their homosexual orientation and considerations involved, including those related to career development. Incidents of homonegative experiences might be better understood through qualitative research, including the perspectives of lesbians and gay men themselves as well as those of their coworkers.

Our finding that openness about one's homosexuality at work was related to having a steady relationship warrants further investigation, independent of the work setting. It is quite possible that being in a relationship increases one's respectability, which makes it easier to come out. A negative consequence of the growing recognition of same-sex relationships could then be that life for single lesbians and gay men becomes more difficult.

Finally, our findings suggest the importance of distinguishing between lesbians and gay men in future studies. Even though lesbians and gay men have common political aims, their actual situations are not identical. Comparative research on men and women, lesbian, gay, and heterosexual, will help us to understand these differences.

REFERENCES

Badgett, M. V. L. (1996). Employment and sexual orientation: Disclosure and discrimination in the workplace. In A. L. Ellis & E. D. B. Riggle (Eds.), *Sexual identity on the job: Issues and services* (pp. 29–52). New York: Haworth Press.

Baron, R. M., & Kenny, D. A. (1986). The moderator–mediator variable distinction in social psychological research: Conceptual, strategic, and statistical considerations. *Journal of Personality and Social Psychology, 51*, 1173–1182.

Bos, H., & Sandfort, T. G. M. (1999). *Homoseksuele mannen en vrouwen over hun werksituatie: "De prijs die ik betaal"*[Homosexual men and women on work conditions: "The price that I pay"]. Zoetermeer, the Netherlands: Abvakabo FNV.

Croteau, J. M. (1996). Research on the work experiences of lesbian, gay, and bisexual people: An integrative review of methodology and findings. *Journal of Vocational Behavior, 48*(2), 195–209.

Day, N. E., & Schoenrade, P. (1997). Staying in the closet versus coming out: Relationships between communication about sexual orientation and work attitudes. *Personnel Psychology, 50*(1), 147–163.

Diamant, L. (Ed.). (1993). *Homosexual issues in the workplace.* Philadelphia: Taylor & Francis.

Einarsen, S., Raknes, B. I., & Matthiesen, S. B. (1994). Bullying and harassment at work and their relationships to work environment quality: An exploratory study. *European Work and Organizational Psychologist, 4,* 381–401.

Ellis, A. L. (1996). Sexual identity issues in the workplace: Past and present. In A. L. Ellis & E. D. B. Riggle (Eds.), *Sexual identity on the job: Issues and services* (pp. 1–16). New York: Haworth Press.

Franke, R., & Leary, M. R. (1991). Disclosure of sexual orientation by lesbians and gay men: A comparison of private and public processes. *Journal of Social and Clinical Psychology, 10,* 262–269.

Griffin, P. (1991). From hiding out to coming out: Empowering lesbian and gay educators. *Journal of Homosexuality, 22*(3–4), 167–196.

Hall, M. (1989). Private experiences in the public domain: Lesbians in organizations. In J. Hearn, D. L. Sheppard, P. Tancred-Sheriff, & G. Burrell (Eds.), *The sexuality of organizations* (pp. 125–138). London: Sage.

Herek, G. M. (1996). Why tell if you're not asked? Self-disclosure, intergroup contact, and heterosexuals' attitudes toward lesbians and gay men. In G. M. Herek, J. B. Jobe, & R. M. Carney (Eds.), *Out in force: Sexual orientation and the military* (pp. 197–225). Chicago: University of Chicago Press.

Hubert, A. B. (1996). *Mobbing, pestgedrag op de werkplak: Een exploratief onderzoek* [Mobbing, teasing at work: An exploratory study]. Leiden, the Netherlands: Rijksuniversiteit.

Kowalski, R. M. (1999). Speaking the unspeakable: Self-disclosure and mental health. In R. M. Kowalski & M. R. Leary (Eds.), *The social psychology of emotional and behavioral problems* (pp. 225–247). Washington, DC: American Psychological Association.

Leymann, H. (1990). Mobbing and psychological terror at workplaces. *Violence and Victims, 5,* 119–126.

Lonborg, S. D., & Phillips, J. M. (1996). Investigating the career development of gay, lesbian, and bisexual people: Methodological considerations and recommendations. *Journal of Vocational Behavior, 48*(2), 176–194.

Sandfort, T. G. M. (1997). Sampling male homosexuality. In J. Bancroft (Ed.), *Researching sexual behavior: Methodological issues* (pp. 261–275). Bloomington: Indiana University Press.

Sandfort, T. G. M., & Bos, H. (1998). *Sexual preference and work: This is what makes the difference*. Zoetermeer, the Netherlands: Abvakabo FNV.

Sandfort, T. G. M., de Graaf, R., Bijl, R. V., & Schnabel, P. (2001). Same-sex sexual behavior and psychiatric disorders: Findings from the Netherlands Mental Health Survey and Incidence Study (NEMESIS). *Archives of General Psychiatry, 58*, 85–91.

Schaufeli, W. B., & Van Dierendonck, D. (1991). *Burnout, a concept measured: The Dutch version of the Maslach Burnout Inventory (MBL-NL)*. Nijmegen, the Netherlands: Catholic University.

Schaufeli, W. B., & Van Dierendonck, D. (1993). The construct validity of two burnout measures. *Journal of Organizational Behavior, 14*, 631–647.

Troiden, R. R. (1989). The formation of homosexual identities. *Journal of Homosexuality, 17*(1–2), 43–73.

Van den Akker, P., Halman, L., & De Moor, R. (1994). Primary relations in Western societies. In P. Ester, L. Halman, & R. De Moor (Eds.), *The individualizing society: Value change in Europe and North America* (pp. 97–127). Tilburg, the Netherlands: Tilburg University Press.

Van Veldhoven, M., & Meijman, T. F. (1994). *Het meten van psychosociale arbeidsbelasting met een vragenlijst: De Vragenlijst Beleving en Beoordeling van de Arbeid (VBBA)* [Measuring psychosocial workload with a questionnaire: The Questionnaire Experience and Assessment of Labor (QEAL)]. Amsterdam, the Netherlands: Nederlands Instituut voor Arbeidsomstandigheden.

Wells, J. W., & Kline, W. B. (1987). Self-disclosure of homosexual orientation. *Journal of Social Psychology, 127*, 191–197.

Widmer, E. D., Treas, J., & Newcomb, R. (1998). Attitudes toward nonmarital sex in 24 countries. *Journal of Sex Research, 35*, 349–358.

12

SOCIAL THREAT, PERSONAL IDENTITY, AND PHYSICAL HEALTH IN CLOSETED GAY MEN

STEVE W. COLE

To protect themselves from societal prejudice, many gay men and lesbians conceal their sexual orientation from at least some social audiences (Goffman, 1963; Herek, 1996, 2000; Weinberg & Williams, 1974). *Closeting* is generally believed to be stressful, but little empirical research has directly examined the implications of concealing a homosexual identity for psychological or physical well-being (for a notable exception, see Weinberg & Williams, 1974). This lacuna is somewhat surprising given that gay men in particular already are at elevated risk for health threats ranging from assault and suicide to hepatitis and HIV-1 infection (Herek, 1989; Ungvarski & Grossman, 1999). In the mid-1990s, my colleagues and I conducted several studies that revealed a heightened risk of physical illness in gay men who

Thanks to Gregory Herek, Margaret Kemeny, and George Solomon for their thoughtful discussions. The research reviewed here was supported by the University of California Universitywide AIDS Research Program, the National Institute of Allergy and Infectious Disease, the UCLA AIDS Institute, and the Norman Cousins Center for Psychoneuroimmunology. This work is dedicated to the memory of George Freeman Solomon, who gave life to the field of psychoneuroimmunology and inspired a generation of its researchers with his intellect, curiosity, courage, and integrity.

concealed their sexual orientation (Cole, Kemeny, & Taylor, 1997; Cole, Kemeny, Taylor, & Visscher, 1996; Cole, Kemeny, Taylor, Visscher, & Fahey, 1996). Relative to gay men who were "out of the closet," those who concealed their homosexuality showed an increased risk of several disease outcomes ranging from upper respiratory infections to accelerated HIV-1 disease progression. This chapter analyzes the psychological, social, and biological processes involved in those results and considers their implications for psychological theory, physical health, and the social advancement of gay men and lesbians.

Minding George Engel's (1977) maxim that all disease is biopsychosocial in origin, our analyses were guided by a conceptual model of homosexual identity management that emphasizes the impact of external social forces on internal psychological processes that mediate both social identity display behaviors and physiologic stress responses (Figure 12.1). In this model, negative social attitudes toward homosexuality ("sexual prejudice," Herek, 2000) represent a fundamental ecological threat that forces gay men and lesbians to negotiate conflicting cultural demands for authentic self-presentation and the expression of a heterosexual identity. These pressures impact a variety of internal goals and motives such as the desire to express oneself freely, to maintain congruity between public and private selves, to affirm homosexuality, and to receive positive evaluation from others. Because no self-presentational course simultaneously satisfies all these motives, gay men and lesbians must decide whether to express or conceal their homosexuality on the basis of a rational "cost–benefit analysis" of the alternatives. Costs of publicly expressing a homosexual identity might include social rejection or physical harm, and the benefits may include maintenance of congruent personal and social identities or public affirmation of homosexuality's legitimacy. Also weighing in are the costs and benefits of concealment, including protection from social rejection, constraints on self-expression, and the social risk of being "discreditable" (Goffman, 1956). In these calculations, it is the *perceived* consequences of a given course of action that represent the most proximal determinants of personal decisions and subsequent social behavior (Goffman, 1956; Ross & Nisbett, 1991). Under standard expectancy-value theories, perceived costs and benefits represent the projected likelihood of a given outcome weighted by its anticipated impact (e.g., the probability of a social rejection multiplied by the subjective pain anticipated). Individuals with different subjective values or expectations may come to differing conclusions about the desirability of publicly expressing a homosexual identity in the same social ecology.

Subjective values and expectations also influence the experienced stress of being "in" versus "out" of the closet. Neither course is stress free, and the same subjective estimations that influence behavioral social identity decisions also serve as the fundamental catalysts for physiologic stress re-

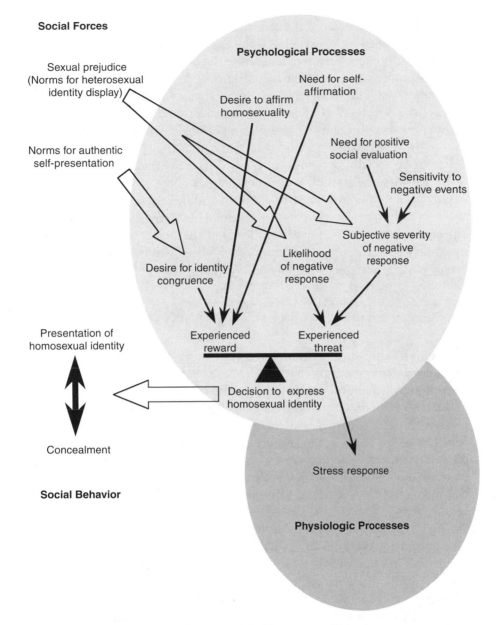

Social Forces

Sexual prejudice
(Norms for heterosexual
identity display)

Psychological Processes

Need for self-
affirmation

Desire to affirm
homosexuality

Need for positive
social evaluation

Norms for authentic
self-presentation

Sensitivity to
negative events

Desire for identity
congruence

Likelihood
of negative
response

Subjective severity
of negative
response

Presentation of
homosexual identity

Experienced
reward

Experienced
threat

Decision to express
homosexual identity

Concealment

Stress response

Social Behavior

Physiologic Processes

Figure 12.1. The experienced threat model of homosexual identity management.

sponses (Sapolsky, 1998). Each individual is likely to choose a self-presentational strategy that minimizes experiences of stress and threat, but which strategy achieves that goal may well vary depending on people's differing sensitivities to the threat of social rejection versus embarrassment at being discovered to have deceived others, or of physical assault versus the burdens of restricted self-expression, and so forth. We term the set of processes outlined in Figure 12.1 as the experienced threat model of homosexual identity management to emphasize the role of subjective psychological factors in influencing both self-presentational decision making and ensuing stress responses. This model does not imply that sexual prejudice is "all in the mind of the perceiver." Rather, it seeks to understand individual responses to sexual prejudice through the lens of the personal goals, values, and motives that are threatened by prejudice. To the extent that people differ in their desire to be socially accepted, to publicly present their personal identity, or to advance the naturalization of homosexuality, sexual prejudice may impact them differently and thus provoke different behavioral responses and varying perceptions of personal threat. This analytic approach has been especially valuable in efforts to understand the health effects of closeting in comparatively tolerant environments where the true degree of social threat may be variable or ambiguous.

HEALTH RISK AND CONCEALMENT

Our research on the health effects of closeting began in an effort to test the long-standing psychosomatic hypothesis that psychological inhibition is physiologically harmful. As far back as the second century A.D., the Greek physician Galen noted that people who were socially and emotionally inexpressive suffered an increased incidence of infectious diseases and cancer (Siegel, 1968). More recent theorists have proposed that an inexpressive phenotype reflects the experience and subsequent inhibition of social and emotional impulses (Gross, 1989; Pennebaker, 1993; Weinberger, Schwartz, & Davidson, 1979), which is hypothesized to enhance sympathetic nervous system activity (Gross & Levenson, 1993; Pennebaker & Chew, 1985; Wegner, Shortt, Blake, & Page, 1990) and, thus, detract from physical health (Pennebaker, 1988). Epidemiologic studies have documented a heightened incidence and severity of several diseases among inexpressive individuals (Gross, 1989; Pennebaker, 1993; Solomon & Moos, 1964; Sommers-Flanagan & Greenberg, 1989), and experimental studies suggest that expressing thoughts and feelings may lead to measurable improvements in physical health (Pennebaker, 1988, 1997). However, these studies have not decisively supported "conflict" theories of psychological inhibition because it is unclear whether lack of expression reflects the generation and subsequent inhibition of psychological events or the failure to experience such events in the first place. Given this background, concealed homosexual identity represented a good model of psychological inhibition because both the occurrence of subjectively significant psychological events and their subsequent expression versus concealment could be directly measured. Closeting, by definition, inhibits gay men and lesbians from openly expressing thoughts and feelings related to personal aspirations, romantic and physical attraction, social events, interpersonal relationships, and a wide variety of other subjectively significant topics.

In our initial study, we examined the relationship between closeting and HIV-1 disease progression in 80 self-identified gay men participating in the Natural History of AIDS Psychosocial Study (NHAPS) as part of the Los Angeles component of the Multicenter AIDS Cohort Study (MACS; Cole, Kemeny, Taylor, Visscher, & Fahey, 1996). Early in its course, the NHAPS assessed closeting using an established ordinal scale that asked participants whether they were *completely out of the closet, out of the closet most of the time, half in and half out, in the closet most of the time,* or *completely in the closet* relative to other gay men (Weinberg & Williams, 1974). Focusing on all cohort members who were HIV positive but physically and immunologically healthy at study entry, we tracked several indicators of disease progression over the ensuing 10 years, including CD4+ T cell levels, the incidence of AIDS-defining clinical conditions, and HIV-specific mortality. Figure 12.2 summarizes the results.

Relative to gay men who were *mostly* or *completely* out of the closet, those who indicated being *half or more* in the closet suffered a 40% acceleration in times to a critically low CD4+ T cell level, a 38% acceleration in times to diagnosis with an AIDS-defining illness, and a 21% acceleration in times to death due to HIV-related pathology. Across all measures examined, closeting was associated with a 2- to 4-year acceleration in the median 10-year HIV-1 disease trajectory. These differences occurred despite the fact that closeted participants entered the study with the same good physical health as the remainder of the sample and despite the fact that analyses controlled for a variety of potential confounders including CD4+ T cell levels at study entry, age, ethnicity, income, education, recreational drug use, antiretroviral treatment, health care utilization, high-risk sexual activity, and estimated time since infection. Survival analyses showed a strong "dose–response" relationship, with times to a critically low CD4+ T cell level, AIDS diagnosis, and HIV-specific mortality decreasing by 7% to 14% with each scale point increase between *completely out of the closet* and *completely in the closet.*

In an effort to define the breadth of health risk associated with concealment, we subsequently surveyed the 5-year incidence of physician-diagnosed infectious diseases and cancer in 220 HIV-1 seronegative MACS–NHAPS participants (Cole, Kemeny, Taylor, & Visscher, 1996). The incidence of both outcomes increased dose-dependently with the degree of concealment (Figure 12.3), and the health risks associated with closeting could not be explained by differences in behavior or demographic characteristics. Closeting thus appeared to represent a generalized physical health risk factor.

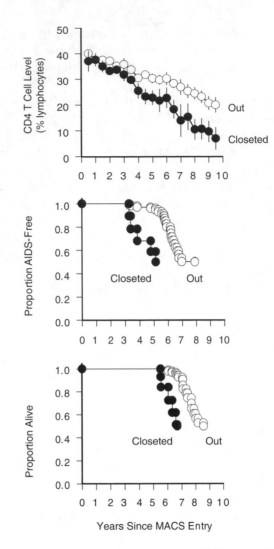

Figure 12.2. CD4+ T cell trajectories and times to AIDS (1987 CDC case definition) and HIV-specific mortality for gay men who are "in" (solid symbol) versus "out" of the closet (open symbol). From "Accelerated Course of Human Immunodeficiency Virus Infection in Gay Men Who Conceal Their Homosexual Identity," by S. W. Cole, M. E. Kemeny, S. E. Taylor, B. R. Visscher, and J. L. Fahey, *Psychosomatic Medicine, 58*, p. 224. Copyright 1996 by Lippincott Williams & Wilkins. Adapted with permission. MACS = Multicenter AIDS Cohort Study.

Psychological Mediators

The epidemiologic data outlined in the previous section support hypotheses linking psychological inhibition to physical illness, but the specific mechanisms involved remain unclear because of those studies' correla-

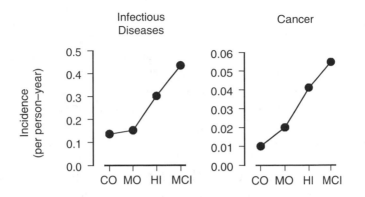

Infectious
Diseases

Cancer

Figure 12.3. Incidence of infectious and neoplastic diseases as a function of degree of concealment of homosexual identity. Adapted from "Elevated Physical Health Risk Among Gay Men Who Conceal Their Homosexual Identity," by S. W. Cole, M. E. Kemeny, S. E. Taylor, and B. R. Visscher, 1996, *Health Psychology, 15*, pp. 243–251. Copyright 1996 by the American Psychological Association. CO = completely "out," MO = mostly "out," HI = half "in" and half "out," MCI = mostly or completely "in."

tional structure. One group of psychological inhibition theories emphasizes the causal influence of inhibition on physiologic processes (Gross & Levenson, 1993; Pennebaker, 1988; Wegner et al., 1990), whereas another group treats inhibited behavior as a dimension of stable individual difference that stems from stable, underlying biological differences (reviewed by Pennebaker, 1993). The latter approach is exemplified by Kagan's (1994) concept of "inhibited temperament," in which socially withdrawn behavior is proposed to stem from variations in threat sensitivity mediated by genetically based differences in central nervous system (CNS) activity. In addition to its academic implications, the cause-and-effect question also has significant implications for social policy and the mitigation of health effects (Lanou, 2001). If psychological inhibition represents a causal determinant of physical health, then coming out of the closet should enhance physical health. If psychological inhibition instead reflects underlying differences in temperament, then coming out of the closet may not have any effect. Coming out might even be harmful if concealment functions as a "social defense mechanism" to shield constitutionally sensitive individuals from the stress of social rejection (Cloninger, 1986; Kramer, 1992). These theoretical and practical concerns motivated us to search for psychological mechanisms mediating links between closeting and physical illness.

Analyses of the MACS–NHAPS data showed that closeted individuals did not differ from those who were "out" on standard measures of depression, anxiety, generalized negative and positive affectivity, or an array of other mood facets (Cole, Kemeny, Taylor, & Visscher, 1996; Cole, Kemeny,

Taylor, Visscher, & Fahey, 1996). Closeted individuals also showed comparable levels of social support, including objective indicators of network size and subjective measures of loneliness, isolation, and dissatisfaction with available relationships. These similarities are not surprising given that closeted participants in our samples concealed their sexual orientation from only some social audiences—primarily at work or school, or in other public settings—and typically reported satisfactory numbers of gay male friends. Given the lack of association between closeting and the most prominent psychosocial health risk factors, we sought to identify other psychological dimensions that might distinguish closeted individuals from those who were "out." Among more than 40 psychological, social, and behavioral variables surveyed, closeted individuals differed only in (a) showing a greater concern for others' impressions of them, on the Marlowe-Crowne Social Desirability Scale (MCSD); (b) more frequent display of a repressive coping style—primarily as a function of the previous result, because the MCSD represents a major component of the operational definition of repressive coping style (Weinberger et al., 1979); (c) reporting greater discomfort in social settings in which their homosexuality might be salient to strangers or the general public, on the Social Situations Scale (SSS; McDonald, 1984); and (d) reporting lower levels of emotional expressiveness, particularly for negative affect, on the Emotional Expressiveness Questionnaire (EEQ; King & Emmons, 1990). This array of differences shows a striking correspondence to Galen's original description of melancholic individuals as well as a variety of empirically derived personality syndromes falling under the general rubric of "social inhibition," such as Kagan's inhibited temperament, Weinberger and colleagues' repressive coping style, Solomon's immunodysregulatory personality, and the "Type C" cancer-prone personality (Gross, 1989; Kagan, 1994; Rogentine et al., 1979; Solomon & Moos, 1964; Weinberger et al., 1979). Associations between closeting and socially inhibited characteristics emerged in analyses of both the HIV-1 seropositive and the seronegative MACS–NHAPS cohorts and in the subsequent West L.A. Autonomic Study sample described later in this chapter.

Relationships between closeting and social inhibition are telling in the context of the experienced threat model because most "inhibited personality" theories propose that individual differences in threat sensitivity motivate socially inhibited behavior. In the context of homosexual identity management, temperamental characteristics may set an internal threshold for the experience of personal threat from sexual prejudice and thereby unleash physiologic stress responses and self-protective concealment in direct proportion to the degree of individual sensitivity. This temperament-based perspective is not incompatible with ecological influences on closeting and may actually help explain certain environmentally linked dynamics. For example, variations in the prevalence of closeting across different social environments would be expected if differing levels of sexual prejudice exceed the tolerance of varying fractions of the gay male population. One implication of this perspective suggests that personality-selective migration patterns might result if dispositionally sensitive individuals disproportionately leave intolerant social environments for more accepting locales. This hypothesis has not yet been examined, but it illustrates the heuristic value of temperament theory in explaining sociological dynamics.

Consistent with the temperament account, associations between closeting and illness risk were rendered nonsignificant in mediational analyses that controlled for socially inhibited personality characteristics (a standardized composite of the EEQ, MCSD, and SSS). In contrast, socially inhibited characteristics remained a significant predictor of disease risk in analyses that controlled for variations in closeting (Cole et al., 1997). Thus, concealment's link to physical illness appears to stem more from the characteristics of those who choose to be "in" versus "out" of the closet than from closeting per se. Weinberg and Williams (1974) drew a similar conclusion from their analysis of associations between concealment and somatic symptomatology. However, the heuristic nature of both analyses needs to be emphasized. Strong causal conclusions can never be drawn from correlational data, and a variety of technical factors can influence the relative success of "competing" predictors in mediational analyses (Miller, 1986; Rogosa, 1980). However, the most parsimonious interpretation of the observed data suggests that closeting may serve as a sociobehavioral marker for underlying differences in personality or temperament.

Correlations between closeting and temperament raise the question of whether concealment serves as a purely incidental marker of social inhibition, or whether it might represent an active strategy used by sensitive individuals to protect themselves from the high subjective costs of negative social reactions. To test this hypothesis, we undertook a more complex analysis of the HIV-1 disease progression data by distinguishing generalized effects of closeting that pertained to all individuals from person-specific protective effects that varied in proportion to the degree of social inhibition (Cole et al., 1997). These studies were carried out in the context of regression-based survival analyses that used a factorial structure to separate fixed effects of personality on disease progression (a social inhibition main effect), fixed effects of closeting on disease progression (a closeting main effect), and effects of closeting that varied as a function of personality (Social Inhibition × Closeting interaction). Two major results are summarized in Figure 12.4.

First, there appears to be a generalized *cost of closeting*. Above and beyond any effect of personality, closeting was associated with an average 10% acceleration in times to critically low CD4+ T cell levels, AIDS

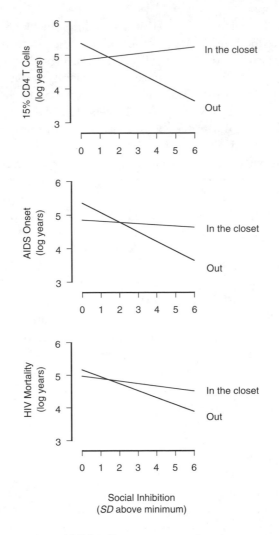

Figure 12.4. Regression of HIV-1 disease progression times on social inhibition for gay men who are "in" versus "out" of the closet. Adapted from "Social Identity and Physical Health: Accelerated HIV Progression in Rejection-Sensitive Gay Men," by S. W. Cole, M. E. Kemeny, and S. E. Taylor, 1997, *Journal of Personality and Social Psychology, 72*, pp. 320–336. Copyright 1997 by the American Psychological Association.

diagnosis, and HIV-specific mortality (a significant closeting main effect). The second result involved relationships between personality and HIV-1 disease progression. Social inhibition was associated with accelerated disease progression among only those individuals who were out of the closet (a significant Social Inhibition × Closet interaction). Among closeted participants, increasing levels of social inhibition were not associated with any significant acceleration in HIV-1 disease progression. Graphically, this is represented by the steeper slope of regression lines relating social inhibition to disease progression times for individuals who were out of the closet versus closeted. These results are consistent with the idea that closeting exerts a protective effect by reversing an individual-specific disease vulnerability linked to social inhibition. Such findings imply that both causal perspectives on psychological inhibition may apply in the context of homosexual identity management. As predicted by conflict theories of social inhibition, closeting incurs a generalized cost—a downward shift in the regression line intercept. However, closeting also appears to shield temperamentally sensitive individuals from the increasing health risks associated with high levels of social inhibition (flattening the downward slope). The net effect of these two dynamics depends on the individual's degree of social inhibition, with protective effects exceeding the cost of closeting only at high levels of social inhibition—values to the right of the regression lines' intersection in Figure 12.4.

Strategic parametrization of the statistical models allowed us to estimate the magnitude of the generalized cost of closeting as well as its *sparing effect*. Again referring to Figure 12.4, the cost of closeting was estimated by the vertical shift in regression line intercepts—the effect of closeting for individuals with minimal levels of social inhibition who should derive minimal protective benefits. This effect was significantly greater than 0 for each disease endpoint. Superimposed on this generalized cost of closeting is a sparing effect represented by the vertical distance from the "out" regression line to the "closeted" regression line—the net health benefit accrued by closeting. This "benefit" is clearly negative over low ranges of social inhibition, where the cost of closeting outweighs its protective effects. However, for all three disease progression endpoints, the protective effects of closeting began to exceed the generalized cost of closeting near the 80th percentile of the social inhibition distribution (the abscissa value corresponding to the crossover points in the regression lines of Figure 12.4). The empirical likelihood of being in the closet also climbed substantially in the same vicinity, with most individuals above the 85th percentile being *half or more* in the closet. The close correspondence between the empirical prevalence of closeting and the relative dominance of its health-protective effect suggests that people accurately anticipate the impact of various identity management strategies on their level of psychological and physiologic stress. Specific individuals are unlikely to use the kind of population-based cost–benefit analyses illustrated here, but psychological and somatic stress reactions may provide sufficient feedback to optimize subjective comfort over the course of an individual's social experience.

Biological Mediators

To determine how these social and psychological dynamics impact physical well-being, we have focused a substantial portion of our research on relationships between psychological inhibition and physiologic function. Previous studies have shown elevated levels of autonomic nervous system (ANS) activity in socially inhibited individuals, particularly under ambiguous or threatening conditions (Block, 1957; Buck, Miller, & Caul, 1974; Field, 1982; Jones, 1935, 1950, 1960; Kagan, Reznick, & Snidman, 1988). This led us to recruit a new cohort of 56 HIV-1 seropositive gay men to assess relationships among personality characteristics, closeting, ANS activity, and HIV-1 disease progression. Participants were recruited by flyers in the West Los Angeles and West Hollywood metropolitan areas and through news media accounts of the initial findings with the MACS–NHAPS cohort. Screening interviews ensured that participants had no history of AIDS-defining conditions (including low CD4+ T cell levels), no indications of HIV-induced CNS or ANS disturbance, and no medical conditions or medication histories that might influence nervous system activity, immune system function, or social behavior (including depression or anxiety). On two occasions 7 to 14 days apart, each participant completed an array of psychosocial measures and underwent a series of procedures assessing individual differences in ANS activity (Cole et al., 2001). Indicators of ANS activity included skin conductance, heart rate, blood pressure, finger pulse amplitude, and pulse transit time (duration between heart beat and the arrival of a blood pulse in the fingertip). Each indicator was monitored under resting baseline conditions and in response to a series of physical stimuli (e.g., standing up from a sitting position, paced deep breathing), psychological stimuli (e.g., auditory attention tones, a computer-administered visual discrimination task), and social stimuli (e.g., unexpected introduction of a novel individual, experimenter-pressured mental arithmetic, a lie-telling procedure). Stable individual differences in ANS activity were quantified by averaging standardized measures of change on each physiologic indicator over all tasks on each assessment occasion. Participants were subsequently followed over 12 to 16 months to monitor the stability of individual psychosocial characteristics and the progression of HIV-1 infection.

Data from the West L.A. Autonomic Study are still being analyzed, but a number of significant findings have already emerged. Psychometric measures of social inhibition developed in independent studies have been found to correlate with closeting, supporting the hypothesis that concealment is linked to individual differences in personality. Consistent with the experienced threat model, decisions to conceal or express a homosexual social identity have been found to vary as a function of subjective expecta-

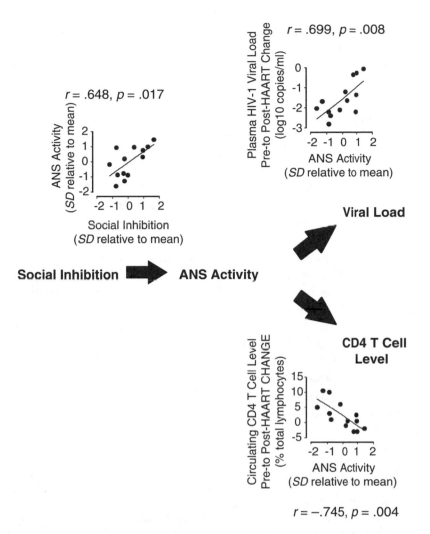

Figure 12.5. Relationships between baseline social inhibition, autonomic nervous system activity, and change in indicators of HIV-1 pathogenesis (plasma HIV-1 viral load and CD4+ T cell level) before and after highly active antiretroviral therapy.

tions about (a) others' likely response to homosexuality and (b) the impact of prejudiced social reactions on subjective well-being. Like members of other populations, gay men who showed socially inhibited personality characteristics also showed elevated ANS activity under basal conditions and in response to physical and psychosocial stimuli (Figure 12.5).

From a physical health standpoint, the most provocative result from the West L.A. Autonomic Study involves enhanced HIV-1 pathogenesis in people with constitutively high levels of ANS activity. For example, among those who began combination antiretroviral therapy during the 1-year follow-up, high ANS activity prior to treatment was associated with significantly poorer suppression of plasma viral load and poorer CD4+ T cell recovery during therapy (Cole et al., 2001; Figure 12.5). ANS-linked differences in viral and immunologic response emerged despite statistical control for pretreatment viral load and CD4+ T cell level, treatment duration and adherence, previous antiretroviral therapy, recreational drug use, and demographic characteristics. Current antiretroviral drugs do not fully eradicate HIV-1 from the body (Chun et al., 2000; Davey et al., 1999; Sharkey et al., 2000), and residual viral replication creates opportunities for the emergence of drug-resistant viral strains and subsequent treatment failure. The physiologic processes that sustain residual viral replication remain poorly understood, but the results outlined above suggest that ANS activity may play a significant role. Thus, psychological processes that impact ANS activity may still be quite relevant to the health of HIV-positive individuals even in this era of highly active antiretroviral therapy.

High ANS activity levels were also associated with elevated HIV-1 viral load in the absence of antiretroviral therapy. The spontaneous rate of viral replication in an infected individual—the viral load set point—is believed to constitute the primary physiologic determinant of differential HIV-1 disease progression rates. Thus, stress-linked differences in ANS activity may be responsible for the differential HIV-1 progression rates observed in the MACS–NHAPS studies. In addition, social inhibition emerged as a strong predictor of viral and immunologic outcomes in the West L.A. Autonomic Study. Socially inhibited individuals also showed significantly elevated levels of ANS activity, and statistical mediation analyses suggest that such differences could account for 70% to 90% of the differential disease progression associated with social inhibition. Although the correlational nature of these results needs to be considered, these findings are consistent with the idea that temperament plays a key role in the relationship between social threat and individual physiologic stress responses.

Relationships between ANS activity and HIV-1 disease progression led us to examine the effects of neural activity on viral replication—the basic biological parameter driving HIV-1 pathogenesis (Mellors et al., 1996). Viral replication takes place mainly in T lymphocytes (Zack et al., 1990), and neuroanatomic studies have identified ANS neurons in the lymph nodes, spleen, thymus, and other lymphoid organs that serve as the primary sites of HIV-1 replication (Bellinger, Lorton, Lubahn, & Felten, 2001). To determine how these neurons might impact viral replication, we examined the effects of the ANS neurotransmitter norepinephrine (NE) on HIV-1 replication in laboratory-infected human lymphocytes. As shown in Figure 12.6, NE concentrations similar to those observed in lymphoid organs can accelerate HIV-1 replication rates up to 10-fold (Cole, Korin, Fahey, & Zack, 1998).

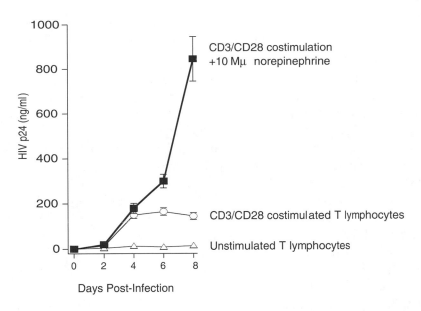

Figure 12.6. HIV-1 replication in cultured peripheral blood T lymphocytes left unstimulated (open triangles), stimulated to proliferate (open circles), or stimulated to proliferate in the presence of a 1 micromolar concentration of norepinephrine (solid squares).

In subsequent studies, we identified the specific receptor responsible for NE's effects as the lymphocyte β_2 adrenoreceptor. We also identified the biochemical signaling pathway that transmits its effects—the Protein Kinase A (i.e., PKA) signaling cascade. NE supports HIV-1 replication by (a) rendering healthy lymphocytes more vulnerable to infection and (b) increasing the capacity of already-infected lymphocytes to produce new HIV-1 viral particles (virions; Cole, Jamieson, & Zack, 1999; Cole, Korin, et al., 1998). In its first role, NE relocalizes the proteins CCR5 and CXCR4 from the inside of lymphocytes to the outside surface of the cell, where they serve as velcrolike receptors allowing HIV-1 virions to adhere to and infect a previously healthy lymphocyte (Cole et al., 1999, 2001). In its later role, NE suppresses cellular expression of the genes that encode immune system signaling molecules such as IFN-γ and IL-10, both of which suppress HIV-1 replication (Cole, Korin, et al., 1998). Additional studies suggest that NE may also enhance cellular expression of HIV-1 genes (Cole et al., 2001; Rabbi, Saifuddin, Gu, Kagnoff, & Roebuck, 1998). Thus, ANS activity can drive HIV-1 replication through multiple biological pathways that converge on the same net effect—accelerated spread of the virus and ensuing destruction of the immune system.

IMPLICATIONS AND DIRECTIONS
FOR FUTURE RESEARCH

The data outlined above present a complex but coherent portrait of the mechanisms by which social prejudice can impact physical health. One aspect of the complexity is summarized in the experienced threat model of Figure 12.1. Variations in subjective values and expectations modulate gay people's responses to contradictory cultural demands for heterosexual identity and authentic self-presentation. Regardless of which demand they appease, the same values and expectations also trigger internal physiologic responses to the personal and social threats that result. Figures 12.5 and 12.6 detail some of the biological processes that may be involved. Both correlational clinical studies and in vitro experiments show that the physiologic stress responses create a vulnerability to disease by altering cellular and molecular processes involved in viral replication. However, the interaction analyses depicted in Figure 12.4 also suggest that individual social behavior can influence the actualization of that vulnerability. If temperamental differences were unilaterally responsible for health differences, both closeted gay men and those who were out would show similar accelerations in HIV-1 disease progression with increasing levels of social inhibition. Instead, closeting appears to abrogate much of the temperament-related increase in risk, suggesting that self-presentational behavior may significantly modify the biological processes that underlie disease pathogenesis.

Behavioral effects on health have long been known, but the present results are remarkable in terms of their mechanism of action. Health-relevant behaviors such as smoking, diet, and exercise typically "gate" an individual's exposure to a physical pathogen (e.g., a disease-causing agent such as cigarette smoke or cholesterol). In our studies, the pathogen is already well established and closeting appears to exert its effects mainly by altering disease-supporting physiologic activity. These effects are fundamentally indirect and depend largely on an individual's capacity to negate a personal sense of threat by controlling external social reactions to the self. The net utility of this strategy depends on the subjective significance of that social threat. As shown in Figure 12.4, uninhibited individuals who care little about their social environment's regard for them show no benefit from closeting and actually suffer instead. However, socially inhibited individuals are highly concerned with social regard and seem to accrue significant benefits by concealing their homosexual identity. To the extent that such maneuvers block socially triggered stress responses, closeting may be construed as a social defense mechanism through which individuals regulate their own internal physiologic processes by altering the social identity they present to others. Regulation of gene expression or receptor density by selective self-disclosure would seem to strain credulity, but once we grant the power of external social events to affect internal psychology and begin to appreciate the physical and functional connections between the nervous system and the immune system, it is not a great leap to propose that personal behaviors that control the social responses of others can also have a reciprocal impact on the individual's own internal biology. Symbolic interactionists have long emphasized the power of strategic self-presentation in controlling the response of society to the individual (Cooley, 1902/1983; Goffman, 1956; Mead, 1934). The present data expand the impact of such dynamics beyond the social, political, and economic motivations traditionally analyzed to include other fundamental motives such as a desire for personal security, freedom from threat, and physical health. From this perspective, closeting can be construed as one strategy by which gay and lesbian individuals may mitigate the burdens imposed on them by sexual prejudice.

These data suggest that closeting may have protective effects under certain circumstances, but such findings should not be taken as a generalized argument in favor of concealment. Closeting may incur psychological risks that are not reflected in the physical health outcomes studied here (Herek, 1996). In addition, there may be significant social costs to concealment that are not reflected in individual well-being. Widespread public presentation of a homosexual social identity is believed to have played a central role in the social and political emancipation of gay men and lesbians (Herek, 1996). To the extent that personal decisions to remain in the closet detract from that process, some cost is borne by the entire community of homosexual people. Moreover, the present data show that closeting is generally not beneficial. As shown in Figure 12.4, the costs of closeting generally outweigh its benefits unless an individual is particularly sensitive to social rejection (above the 80th percentile of social inhibition). Whatever benefits accrue from closeting pertain to an especially vulnerable set of individuals. As discussed later in this chapter, those vulnerabilities may be better addressed through other means.

Health costs of concealing a homosexual identity have the potential to impact a variety of political controversies including the military's "don't ask, don't tell" policy (Lanou, 2001) and the politically charged practice of "outing." However, the complex interactions among social prejudice, personal characteristics, and self-presentational behavior greatly complicate the translation of research findings into "sound-bite" recommendations for social policy or personal behavior. Perhaps the only general conclusion that can be drawn regards the decisive role of individual values, perceptions, strengths, and vulnerabilities in governing the individual's adaptation to a potentially hostile environment. Once it becomes clear that individuals respond differently to social threats, it is easier to appreciate the moral importance of self-determination in matters of social identity (Stramel, 1997). Any universal policy on homosexual identity presentation may be detrimental to some, regardless of whether it enforces concealment (don't ask, don't tell) or prevents it (outing). It seems no more reasonable to demand that all individuals adhere to the same personal values, psychological sensitivities, or social presentations than it does to demand that they all practice heterosexuality.

A critical limitation of these studies involves the social context in which they were conducted. These results are based on a temporally and spatially distinct cohort of gay men in a comparatively tolerant social environment. In other settings, different cost–benefit equilibria are likely to prevail and other psychological characteristics may emerge as primary correlates of closeting. A truly psychological understanding of homosexual identity management will require more sophisticated longitudinal and cross-contextual analyses, as well as comparative studies of concealment dynamics among lesbian and bisexual individuals. Studies that directly examine the consequences of coming out of the closet for psychological and physical well-being will provide critical information about the causal impact of identity management. In parallel, studies that survey the effects of closeting in multiple social environments would provide a powerful framework for analyzing interactions between individual values and social threat.

Identification of psychological and biological mechanisms linking concealment to physical illness suggests a variety of interventions that could potentially support the well-being of gay men and lesbians as they confront sexual prejudice. Even in the absence of the most fundamentally just solution—the evolution of more humane social attitudes—the present analyses suggest that it might be possible to dissociate internal stress responses from prejudiced social reactions without incurring the costs of concealment. To the extent that socially inhibited individuals overestimate the objective likelihood of negative social responses to homosexuality, or are hypersensitive to such events, cognitive–behavioral revision of relevant belief systems may help reduce the subjective need for concealment. Approximately 80% of the participants in the West L.A. Autonomic and MACS–NHAPS studies found it feasible to live mostly or completely out of the closet, and those who were not comfortable doing so showed a profile of characteristics that suggests they might be exceptionally sensitive to social rejection. Psychosocial interventions that reduce sensitivity to prejudice-based rejection may help such individuals lead more secure and satisfying lives. Some evidence suggests that individual differences in neurobiology may create a predisposition toward social sensitivity (Cole, Knutson, Wolkowitz, & Reus, 1998; Kagan, 1994; Kramer, 1992), implying that CNS-directed interventions could conceivably help support individual autonomy. For example, it may be possible to dampen limbic system threat responses with selective serotonin reuptake inhibitors (SSRIs; Cole, Knutson, et al., 1998; Kagan, 1994; Kramer, 1992). Regardless of the particular mode of intervention, relationships between social inhibition and physical health suggest that internal psychological responses to the social environment may represent opportune targets for improving the health of the individual in society.

Interventions that support the expression of homosexual social identity are feasible only to the extent that the individual actually inhabits an objectively tolerant environment. If closeting is a necessity, the present findings suggest that it may still be possible to address concealment-related stress at the threshold of its physiologic impact. Identification of ANS activity as a potential regulator of HIV-1 pathogenesis provides a target for interventions aimed at decoupling those processes. Safe and effective pharmacological agents are already available to inhibit NE's interaction with β_2 adrenoreceptors. Clinical trials have just begun to evaluate the impact of beta blockers on HIV-1 disease, and it is not yet clear whether there will be any significant benefits. However, the general principle of attacking psychosocial health risk factors at their biological threshold could represent a valuable alternative if behavior change is not feasible. Neuropharmacological interventions also offer new opportunities to control the threat experiences underlying social inhibition. Such approaches will be critical in moving beyond the correlational research designs presented here to more clearly define the causal impact of neural activity on social behavior and physical health.

Merely considering SSRIs and beta blockers as potential adjuvants for human social existence highlights the ethical absurdity of personal adaptation to cultural prejudice. It is clearly ridiculous that people should have to drug themselves to live comfortably in society. However, to the extent that such a strategy actually preserves personal health and well-being, it seems good to at least have the option. Kramer (1992) provides a serious analysis of the tension between pharmacological self-adjustment and personal integrity in the face of a rejecting environment. From a moral perspective, the fundamental flaw in all of these approaches lies in the fact that the burden of responding to social prejudice falls on its victim. The only truly just solution to the psychological conflicts created by sexual prejudice lies in shifting the onus of adaptation back on the society that instigates those conflicts. In a culture that embraces human nature rather than trying to dictate it, gay men and lesbians would not have to trade the peace of personal security for the peace of social authenticity. In that sense, the chief contribution of the present research lies in physically quantifying the personal toll exacted by social prejudice. The cumulative burden of distorting one's existence to avoid sexual prejudice may literally cost years of life.

REFERENCES

Bellinger, D. L., Lorton, D., Lubahn, C., & Felten, D. L. (2001). Innervation of lymphoid organs. In R. Ader, D. L. Felten, & N. Cohen (Eds.), *Psychoneuroimmunology* (3rd ed., pp. 55–111). San Diego, CA: Academic Press.

Block, J. (1957). A study of affective responsiveness in a lie-detection situation. *Journal of Abnormal and Social Psychology, 55*, 11–15.

Buck, R., Miller, R. E., & Caul, W. F. (1974). Sex, personality, and physiological variables in the communication of affect via facial expression. *Journal of Personality and Social Psychology, 27*, 587–596.

Chun, T. W., Davey, R. T. J., Ostrowski, M., Shawn Justement, J., Engel, D., Mullins, J. I., & Fauci, A. S. (2000). Relationship between pre-existing viral reservoirs and the re-emergence of plasma viremia after discontinuation of highly active antiretroviral therapy. *Nature Medicine, 6*, 757–761.

Cloninger, C. R. (1986). A unified biosocial theory of personality and its role in the development of anxiety states. *Psychiatric Developments, 3*, 167–226.

Cole, S. W., Jamieson, B. D., & Zack, J. A. (1999). cAMP externalizes lymphocyte CXCR4: Implications for chemotaxis and HIV infection. *Journal of Immunology, 162*, 1392–1400.

Cole, S. W., Kemeny, M. E., & Taylor, S. E. (1997). Social identity and physical health: Accelerated HIV progression in rejection-sensitive gay men. *Journal of Personality and Social Psychology, 72*, 320–336.

Cole, S. W., Kemeny, M. E., Taylor, S. E., & Visscher, B. R. (1996). Elevated physical health risk among gay men who conceal their homosexual identity. *Health Psychology, 15*, 243–251.

Cole, S. W., Kemeny, M. E., Taylor, S. E., Visscher, B. R., & Fahey, J. L. (1996). Accelerated course of Human Immunodeficiency Virus infection in gay men who conceal their homosexual identity. *Psychosomatic Medicine, 58*, 219–231.

Cole, S. W., Knutson, B. D., Wolkowitz, O. L., & Reus, V. I. (1998). *Serotonergic neurotransmission modulates socially inhibited personality characteristics in normal humans.* Los Angeles: University of California.

Cole, S. W., Korin, Y. D., Fahey, J. L., & Zack, J. A. (1998). Norepinephrine accelerates HIV replication via protein kinase A-dependent effects on cytokine production. *Journal of Immunology, 161*, 610–616.

Cole, S. W., Naliboff, B. D., Kemeny, M. E., Griswold, M. P., Fahey, J. L., & Zack, J. A. (2001). Impaired response to HAART in HIV-infected individuals with high autonomic nervous system activity. *Proceedings of the National Academy of Sciences of the United States of America, 98*, 12695–12670.

Cooley, C. H. (1983). *Human nature and the social order.* New Brunswick, NJ: Transaction Books. (Original work published 1902)

Davey, R. T., Bhat, N., Yoder, C., Chun, T. W., Metcalf, J. A., Dewar, R., et al. (1999). HIV-1 and T cell dynamics after interruption of highly active antiretroviral therapy (HAART) in patients with a history of sustained viral suppression. *Proceedings of the National Academy of Sciences of the United States of America, 96,* 15109–15114.

Engel, G. L. (1977, April 8). The need for a new medical model: A challenge for biomedicine. *Science, 196,* 129–136.

Field, T. (1982). Individual differences in the expressivity of neonates and young children. In R. S. Feldman (Ed.), *Development of nonverbal behavior in children* (pp. 279–298). New York: Springer-Verlag.

Goffman, E. (1956). *The presentation of self in everyday life.* Edinburgh, Scotland: University of Edinburgh Social Science Research Centre.

Goffman, E. (1963). *Stigma: Notes on the management of spoiled identity.* Englewood Cliffs, NJ: Prentice Hall.

Gross, J. J. (1989). Emotional expression in cancer onset and progression. *Social Science and Medicine, 28,* 1239–1248.

Gross, J. J., & Levenson, R. W. (1993). Emotional suppression: Physiology, self-report, and expressive behavior. *Journal of Personality and Social Psychology, 64,* 970–986.

Herek, G. M. (1989). Hate crimes against lesbians and gay men: Issues for research and policy. *American Psychologist, 44,* 948–955.

Herek, G. M. (1996). Why tell if you're not asked? Self-disclosure, intergroup contact, and heterosexuals' attitudes towards lesbians and gay men. In G. M. Herek, J. B. Jobe, & R. M. Carney (Eds.), *Out in force: Sexual orientation and the military* (pp. 197–225). Chicago: University of Chicago Press.

Herek, G. M. (2000). The psychology of sexual prejudice. *Current Directions in Psychological Science, 9,* 19–22.

Jones, H. E. (1935). The galvanic skin response as related to overt emotional expression. *American Journal of Psychology, 47,* 241–251.

Jones, H. E. (1950). The study of patterns of emotional expression. In M. L. Reymert (Ed.), *Feelings and emotions: The Mooseheart Symposium* (pp. 161–168). New York: McGraw-Hill.

Jones, H. E. (1960). The longitudinal method in the study of personality. In I. Iscoe & H. W. Stevenson (Eds.), *Personality development in children* (pp. 3–27). Austin: University of Texas Press.

Kagan, J. (1994). *Galen's prophecy: Temperament in human nature.* New York: Basic Books.

Kagan, J., Reznick, J. S., & Snidman, N. (1988, April 8). Biological bases of childhood shyness. *Science, 240,* 167–171.

King, L. A., & Emmons, R. A. (1990). Conflict over emotional expression: Psychological and physical correlates. *Journal of Personality and Social Psychology, 58,* 864–877.

Kramer, P. D. (1992). *Listening to Prozac: A psychiatrist explores antidepressant drugs and the remaking of the self.* New York: Penguin Books.

Lanou, J. H. R. (2001) Restricted expression and immunosuppression: How "don't ask, don't tell" may harm military readiness by increasing the risk of cancer and infectious disease in homosexuals. *George Mason Law Review, 10,* 1–32.

McDonald, G. J. (1984). *Identity congruity and identity management among gay men.* Unpublished doctoral dissertation, University of Windsor, Windsor, Ontario, Canada.

Mead, G. H. (1934). *Mind, self, and society.* Chicago: University of Chicago Press.

Mellors, J. W., Rinaldo, C. R. J., Gupta, P., White, R. M., Todd, J. A., & Kingsley, L. A. (1996, May 24). Prognosis in HIV-1 infection predicted by the quantity of virus in plasma. *Science, 272,* 1167–1170.

Miller, R. G. (1986). *Beyond ANOVA: Basics of applied statistics.* New York: Wiley.

Pennebaker, J. W. (1988). Confession, inhibition, and disease. In L. Berkowitz (Ed.), *Advances in experimental social psychology* (Vol. 22, pp. 211–242). Orlando, FL: Academic Press.

Pennebaker, J. W. (1993). Overcoming inhibition: Rethinking the roles of personality, cognition, and social behavior. In H. C. Traue & J. W. Pennebaker (Eds.), *Emotion, inhibition and disease* (pp. 100–115). Kirkland, WA: Hogrefe & Huber.

Pennebaker, J. W. (1997). Writing about emotional experiences as a therapeutic process. *Psychological Science, 8*(3), 162–166.

Pennebaker, J. W., & Chew, C. H. (1985). Behavioral inhibition and electrodermal activity during deception. *Journal of Personality and Social Psychology, 49,* 1427–1433.

Rabbi, M. F., Saifuddin, M., Gu, D. S., Kagnoff, M. F., & Roebuck, K. A. (1998). The cAMP-dependent protein kinase A and protein kinase C-beta pathways synergistically interact to activate HIV-1 transcription in latently infected cells of the monocyte-macrophage lineage. *Virology, 245,* 257–269.

Rogentine, G. N., Van Kammen, D. P., Fox, B. H., Docherty, J. P., Rosenblatt, J. E., Boyd, S. C., & Bunney, W. E. (1979). Psychological factors in the prognosis of malignant melanoma: A prospective study. *Psychosomatic Medicine, 41,* 647–655.

Rogosa, D. (1980). A critique of cross-lagged correlation. *Psychological Bulletin, 88,* 245–258.

Ross, L., & Nisbett, R. (1991). *The person and the situation: Perspectives of social psychology.* New York: McGraw-Hill.

Sapolsky, R. M. (1998). *Why zebras don't get ulcers: An updated guide to stress, stress-related diseases, and coping.* New York: Freeman.

Sharkey, M. E., Teo, I., Greenough, T., Sharova, N., Luzuriaga, K., Sullivan, J. L., et al. (2000). Persistence of episomal HIV-1 infection intermediates in patients on highly active anti-retroviral therapy. *Nature Medicine, 6*(1), 76–81.

Siegel, R. E. (1968). *Galen's system of physiology and medicine.* New York: Karger.

Solomon, G. F., & Moos, R. H. (1964). Emotions, immunity, and disease. *Archives of General Psychiatry, 11,* 657–674.

Sommers-Flanagan, J., & Greenberg, R. P. (1989). Psychosocial variables and hypertension: A new look at an old controversy. *Journal of Nervous and Mental Disease, 177*, 15–24.

Stramel, J. S. (1997). *Gay virtue: The ethics of disclosure.* Unpublished doctoral dissertation, University of Southern California, Los Angeles.

Ungvarski, P. J., & Grossman, A. H. (1999). Health problems of gay and bisexual men. *Nursing Clinics of North America, 34*, 313–331.

Wegner, D. M., Shortt, J. W., Blake, A. W., & Page, M. S. (1990). The suppression of exciting thoughts. *Journal of Personality and Social Psychology, 58*, 409–418.

Weinberg, M. S., & Williams, C. J. (1974). *Male homosexuals: Their problems and adaptations.* New York: Penguin Books.

Weinberger, D. A., Schwartz, G. E., & Davidson, R. E. (1979). Low anxious, high anxious, and repressive coping styles: Psychometric patterns and physiological responses to stress. *Journal of Abnormal Psychology, 88*, 369–380.

Zack, J. A., Arrigo, S. J., Weitsman, S. R., Go, A. S., Haislip, A., & Chen, I. S. Y. (1990). HIV-1 entry into quiescent primary lymphocytes: Molecular analysis reveals a labile, latent viral structure. *Cell, 61*, 213–222.

13

EXPLORING SEXUAL BEHAVIORS AND SEXUAL ORIENTATION: AN ETHNOGRAPHIC STUDY OF AFRICAN AMERICAN FEMALE CRACK COCAINE USERS

CLAIRE E. STERK AND KIRK W. ELIFSON

Few studies among female crack cocaine users have focused on the women's sexual orientation as opposed to their sexual behaviors. Crack, which emerged on the U.S. drug markets in the 1980s, is a type of cocaine that is sold in the form of small rocks that typically sell for five dollars. Its popularity is due in part to its affordability. Crack cocaine typically is smoked, resulting in a rapid and intense high that lasts only 3 minutes or less. On achieving the high, users experience an almost immediate crash and a craving for the next high (for more information, see Inciardi, Lockwood, & Pottieger, 1993; Sterk, 1999b).

This research was funded by the National Institute on Drug Abuse (RO1DA09819 and RO1DA10642) and the Center for AIDS Research at Emory University. The views presented in this chapter are those of the authors and do not represent those of the funding agencies.

Historically, drug use by women has been associated with prescription drugs. Only since the 1960s have studies on the use of illicit drugs by women become common, a change that coincided with the second wave of the feminist movement in the Western world. Studies conducted from the 1960s and 1970s to the present have frequently included female drug users as a comparison sample for male users. This design has resulted in findings that highlight sex and gender differences, with female users often being depicted much more negatively than their male counterparts (Binion, 1982). The emancipation thesis guided some of this research, emphasizing that as women become more "liberated," they are also more likely to become involved with criminal activities, including drug use (Adler, 1975; Ettore, 1992; Rosenbaum, 1981).

Prior to the crack cocaine epidemic, few researchers acknowledged the unique circumstances of women in the drug world. Studies show African American women to be overrepresented among crack cocaine users as compared with users of other drugs (Bourgois, 1995; National Institute on Drug Abuse, 1995), which in turn is related to the targeted marketing of crack cocaine in poor inner-city communities (Sterk, 1999b). Few scholars have conducted a holistic investigation of female crack cocaine users, one in which the women are viewed as drug users within the context of their other social roles, such as those of partner, friend, relative, or mother (Kearney, Murphy, & Rosenbaum, 1994; Sterk, 1999b). More typical are investigations that focus on limited gender-specific factors such as the women's reproductive and mothering role (Chasnoff, 1988; Chavkin, 1990) or their involvement in a new form of prostitution by directly exchanging sex for crack (Ratner, 1993; Sterk-Elifson & Elifson, 1990). Consequently, and also driven by the correlation between crack use, unsafe sex, and HIV risk, much of the research emphasis has been on the heterosexual behaviors of female crack cocaine users. In this chapter we challenge the dominance of heterocentric thinking. In addition, we highlight the presence of all types of sexual orientation among female crack cocaine users.

Sexual orientation often is measured using the one-item, one-dimensional Kinsey Scale (Kinsey, Pomeroy, Martin, & Gebhard, 1953). However, the multidimensional and complex nature of sexual orientation requires measures using multiple items, such as the one proposed by Golden (1987), which consists of three orthogonal dimensions: (a) sexual identity, (b) sexual behavior, and (c) community participation. It is important to note that these dimensions may be incongruent with each other. For example, a woman may identify as lesbian without participating in the lesbian community; or a woman may have sex with other women but not describe herself as lesbian. Others also have shown sexual identity and behaviors to vary by social context, that is, where women are and with whom (Benhabib,

1992; Boles & Elifson, 1994; Dowset, 1996; Kennedy & Davis, 1993; Stein, 1999), as well as stage of the life course (see chaps. 2 and 5, this volume).

Investigations among female crack cocaine users tend to focus on their sexual behaviors, which often are associated with strategies to support the habit, the psychopharmacological effects of cocaine, or craving for the next high (Edlin et al., 1994; Ratner, 1993; Sterk, 1988). The potential impact of the sexual identity of female crack cocaine users on their sexual activities is ignored. Our overall knowledge regarding the use of alcohol and other drugs by women with varying sexual orientations is limited. Although some researchers indicate that sexual-minority women are more likely to have used or currently use drugs than heterosexual women, others contest that conclusion (Heffernan, 1996). A similar debate occurs in studies exploring differences in alcohol use among heterosexual, bisexual, and homosexual women (Skinner & Otis, 1996; see also chap. 8, this volume). In addition, much of the scholarship on sexual identities among women is concentrated on White middle-class women (Greene, 1994; Mays & Cochran, 1998; Mays, Cochran, & Rhue, 1993). Studies including racial and ethnic-minority women and women of lower socioeconomic status are limited, and results show African American women who self-identify as lesbian reporting conflicting loyalties between the lesbian and the African American communities (Greene, 1994; Greene & Boyd-Franklin, 1996; Gutierrez & Dworkin, 1992).

In this chapter, we present narratives from in-depth interviews with 62 African American crack cocaine users, all of whom report having had sex with a woman. Using Golden's (1987) model of sexual orientation, we give specific attention to the women's discussion of the links between crack cocaine use and sexual behaviors, and between sexual behaviors and sexual orientation.

THE QUALITATIVE RESEARCH PARADIGM

We used the qualitative research paradigm to develop a complex and holistic understanding from the women's perspective. When studying "hard-to-reach" populations such as female crack cocaine users, recruitment and sampling pose unique challenges. Despite the scientific merit of involving a representative sample, this was not feasible because the parameters of the study population were unknown. In addition, our understanding of the lives of the women was limited, thereby further reducing the ability to include a representative sample. Ascending sampling methodologies, such as targeted sampling (Watters & Biernacki, 1989), appeared more appropriate. To conduct our targeted sampling, we used ethnographic mapping (Sterk, 1999a).

This mapping involved a review of existing information such as data and other documentation drawn from local drug treatment centers, health care settings, law enforcement, and other social and health service agencies. In addition, the ethnographic mapping entailed observational data collection in the geographic areas from which the women were recruited. Finally, it involved a community identification process (Tashima, Crain, O'Reilly, & Sterk-Elifson, 1996). These various techniques—review of existing information, observations and mapping, data collection from experts—allowed for a targeted sampling scheme.

Open-ended in-depth interviews were the main method of inquiry (Sterk, 1995). The underlying assumption of this type of interviewing is that the study participants are viewed as experts (Campbell & Bunting, 1991). This approach is consistent with a feminist orientation in which study participants are encouraged to learn about themselves and to reflect on their lives (Henwood, 1997). The data gathered were textual in nature, and the first step in the analysis process was to organize the data in a systematic way and to identify salient themes from the perspective of the women. We began by placing "code words" in the margins of the transcribed interviews. To ensure intercoder reliability, multiple persons coded the text analyzed. We used the constant comparison method of the grounded theory approach (Glaser & Strauss, 1967; Strauss & Corbin, 1990) to engage in an iterative process of reviewing and coding the data, while developing concepts that were "grounded" in the data. This process moved us from description to conceptualization. Central to the constant comparison method was the writing of memos that described the coding, analytical decisions, and theoretical insights (Strauss & Corbin, 1990).

METHODS: WHO, HOW, AND WHAT?

The findings presented are part of our ongoing studies of female drug users in the Atlanta area. This research began in the early 1990s. Since June 1996, we have interviewed over 400 female crack cocaine users. To be eligible, women had to be 18 years or older, actively using crack cocaine, not in drug treatment or any other institutional setting, and reside in the Atlanta area. African American women were overrepresented because of the prevalence of crack cocaine use in their communities. In an effort to learn more about women who had sex with women (WSW), we focused on 62 African American women who were active crack cocaine users and who indicated that they had had sex with other women. Although we did not specify a time frame during which the women last had sex with another woman as eligibility criteria, all of the women reported having had sex with another women within 90 days prior to the interview.

The interviews were conducted at one of two centrally located research offices, at the woman's home, or in settings such as a local fast-food restaurant, a community center, or a park bench. The main criteria were that the respondent felt comfortable and the setting provided privacy. All interviewers were women and they were experienced with open-ended data collection. Three of the interviewers were African American, one was Hispanic, and two others were White. Prior to the interview, the interviewers briefed the respondents about the nature of the study, the time required, and about the informed consent procedures. None of the women who reported for an interview declined to participate, and all study participants received $15 as an incentive for the time they gave us. The in-depth interview ranged in length from 45 minutes to 2.5 hours, with an average time of 1.5 hours. The topics discussed included demographic characteristics, drug use, sexual behavior, and sexual identity.

Each woman was assigned a study number, and no names were recorded. The interviews were audiotaped and transcribed verbatim. To ensure accuracy, we compared the transcripts with the tapes. The data set also included the methodological and analytical–theoretical memos written by the interviewers after completion of the interview as well as during the transcription process. As is common in qualitative research, the data analysis began almost simultaneously with the data collection. The quotations selected in the results were chosen because they were representative in relation to each of the categories as well as for their richness. The use of the quotations also allows us to present the voices of the women.

RESULTS

All women were active crack cocaine users who had had sex with another woman. Two thirds of them smoked crack cocaine in the 2 days prior to the interview. The women's mean age was 36.6 years, and the age range was from 18 to 52. Their mean level of education was 11.7 years, with educational attainment ranging from a few years of grade school to post-college training. Almost three fourths lived below the federal poverty level, and one third reported illegal activities as their main source of income.

Almost three fourths ($n = 42$) of the women had exchanged sex for crack cocaine or had engaged in sexual performances for which they were paid with crack cocaine. Among the groups distinguished were (a) heterosexuals: women who self-identify as heterosexual, who prefer a man as their primary sex partner, and who sometimes have sex with another woman ($n = 32$); (b) hidden lesbians: women who publicly self-identify as heterosexual but who prefer a woman as their primary sex partner, and who also have sex with men ($n = 12$); (c) women who self-identify as bisexual ($n = 6$);

and (d) women who self-identify as lesbians who are out and sometimes had sex with a man (*n* = 9).

Sexual Behavior and Crack Cocaine Use

The women described how crack cocaine initially served as a sexual disinhibitor but, over time, caused them to have unprotected sex, sex with anonymous partners, and sex with multiple partners, and to sell or barter sex for crack cocaine. They described such prostitution involvement to support their crack cocaine habit often as a last resort. As their crack cocaine habit began dominating their lives and they became less successful at committing other crimes, prostitution often was the only support strategy remaining. The women indicated that they would not be prostituting themselves if it were not for their crack cocaine habit. In the following account, one woman shared her concerns of losing her "touch" as a shoplifter and feared becoming involved in prostitution:

> If you don't know what you are doing, a crack habit gets expensive, like it takes all your money and everything you have. I used to be nasty to one of the women in the neighborhood who would do about anything to get some rock. She was like a sex machine. . . . My main thing was boosting [shoplifting] but I lost my touch. I got busted three times in a row because I was trying to do my business and getting high at the same time. . . . I don't see myself as a crack whore, but I know I need to watch out or it'll happen.

Some women sought to engage in sexual performances instead of submitting to sex with a man. This could include public masturbation or sex with another woman. Although all sex in the context of crack cocaine use was exploitive, several women referred to sex with other women as less abusive than heterosexual acts. They contended that engaging in sex with another woman provided protection from sexual harassment and abuse by male users. Sex with another woman was perceived as more gentle and provided the women with a sense of control. In the words of one woman who is a hidden lesbian,

> The guys take it out on the women. The crack makes them not come and it makes them mad. There is a reason why they call a woman who blows a guy for hours a chicken head. . . . I myself only perform, like a little stage show to turn the guys on. No messing around with straight sex, just some kissing and rubbing . . . I tell people I'm into sex with a woman. They call me names for it, but that beats having to deal with the guys.

Lesbians, including those who are out and those who are hidden, felt most strongly about sex with another woman as a protective strategy to reduce trauma. Bisexual women tended not to differentiate on the basis of the sex of their partner, whereas few heterosexuals perceived sex with men as abusive, blaming any abuse that might occur on their or their partner's crack cocaine habit. A number of the lesbians who are out and the bisexual women explained that they sometimes invited gay men to get high with them, and if they were in the mood, they had sex together.

Several women had sex in a setting where crack cocaine was being used, but where no sex-for-crack exchanges occurred. They described feeling "turned on" by crack cocaine and reported that part of the ritual of getting high was having sex, but not bartering sex. The lesbians who are out reported this perspective most often. Two of the lesbians preferred to smoke crack only with other women and, with few exceptions, engaged in sex only with other women. They preferred women-only crack settings, a context that researchers have largely ignored. One of the bisexual women explained that getting high with women, in this case lesbians, changed her drug-using experience:

> I don't have to worry about who is going to rip me off, force me to give him a blow job, or make me feel like a slut. I have been there, and it is rape all the way around. I like getting high with my group [a group of herself and five lesbian crack cocaine–using friends]. I give myself the time to enjoy the high. I know this sounds crazy with crack being an upper but I get high and I feel relaxed. It adds peace to the high . . . the sex is more peaceful, too. It is sex for joy. Nobody wants to hurt the other person.

These women also pooled their money to purchase crack cocaine and got high at one group member's home, as opposed to a more public setting. They helped each other when craving began and set boundaries about how much to smoke, how to pace their use, and how to cope with the crash.

Sexual Identity and Sexual Behavior

A salient theme in the interviews was the incongruence between the descriptions of the women's sexual identity and their sexual behaviors. With the exception of one woman, none of the heterosexual women linked their sexual behaviors with other women to a bisexual or lesbian sexual orientation. One woman acknowledged that she has sex with other women and that this challenges her sexual identity:

> Sometimes I have to sit back and wonder who I am. I mean with getting high all the time and all the bullshit that goes on in the house [a house where people smoke crack together and where sex-for-crack exchanges are the norm]. . . . At first, getting rocks was no problem. People would let me smoke theirs, or I would buy my own. . . . My habit got bigger

than my wallet . . . I didn't want to have sex with the guys, and one of the girls got me into doing it with her. The guys would watch and pay us for it. I ain't no lesbian or whatever you call a dyke. I am a woman who's trying to take care of herself.

This woman also typified many other women, mainly heterosexuals and hidden lesbians, who resented any political association with being bisexual or out and lesbian. They referred to themselves as "being into women." One woman who self-identified as a lesbian said the following:

Lesbian is not about what a person is on the inside, it is about the outside. I see a lesbian as a White dyke who has what she needs . . . like, a house, a car. Lesbians are proud of the way in which they stick with each other, all the wonderful things they do for each other. Black women have been doing that forever. We're all sisters. It has nothing to do with the guys. . . . I guess I am lesbian because I have sex with other women. That's what it is about. Sex—nothing else, no politics or all that nonsense. I don't want to be confused with that type of lesbian. That's why I always say that I have sex with women. I am into women.

The hidden lesbians emphasized the public image of being heterosexual, but in their private lives many preferred a woman as their primary partner and identified themselves as lesbian. Several hidden lesbians' concerns about being viewed as homosexual prevented them from developing a long-term relationship with another woman. Typically, the hidden lesbians were privately involved with other female crack users. As one woman said, "That is the pool I can pick from." They tended to believe that lesbians who did not use crack cocaine would not be interested in them as partners. The few women who had been involved in a lesbian relationship with a nonusing partner explained that they had to hide their use and constantly feared discovery. One woman's relationship was immediately terminated by her female partner once she discovered the crack cocaine use. Another woman pledged to her lesbian partner that she would quit, but she was unable to do so, which ultimately resulted in her partner breaking off the relationship. Many hidden lesbians preferred getting high in a heterosexual setting in which homosexual activity was tolerated. When feasible, they would orchestrate the situation so that they could be with a female partner, without others knowing of their connection or their sexual orientation. Some hidden lesbians presented their relationship with another woman as a friendship, rationalizing that a close friendship between two women was more acceptable than a sexual relationship.

Unlike the heterosexuals and hidden lesbians, the bisexual women tended not to resist being labeled as such. Although bisexuals made up the smallest subgroup in our sample, two women mentioned having had same-gender sex prior to ever having used crack cocaine. They hinted at the fact that their nonmainstream sexual orientation and their drug use were both part of their desire to distinguish themselves from others. One woman noted, "Folks are shocked when I tell them I am bi and they are shocked when they find out I am a crack head. I like to shock people, so this is cool."

The remaining bisexual women described having shifted from identifying exclusively as heterosexual to identifying as bisexual after they began using crack. Some of them claimed that the sexual exploitation by men in the sex-for-crack scene led them to become more interested in sex with women. Once they had sex with a woman, they developed an appreciation of same-gender sex.

Those women who were out as lesbians preferred sex only with women. However, to support their crack cocaine habit, they reported having sex with men—preferably oral rather than vaginal sex. When feasible, they performed sex with another woman. As one of them revealed, her comfort with sex toys was an advantage:

> I'm used to sex toys. Around here they think a dildo is from another planet. I don't play it up, but when I get a chance I will use some of them toys. It turns the guys on and they'll even throw rocks my way . . . that beats having to do them.

As described earlier, lesbians who are out viewed women-only places as the ideal setting in which to get high and have sex in the context of crack cocaine use.

DISCUSSION AND FUTURE RESEARCH

African American female crack cocaine users are not as homogenous as often presented in the literature. For example, not all female crack cocaine users exchange sex for crack (Sterk, 1999b). In addition, the sexual activity that occurs in the context of crack cocaine use is much more complex than is often assumed and goes beyond bartering sex for crack. For example, the women in this study emphasized sexual performances between women as a main strategy to prevent them from having to "sell" their bodies for crack, mainly to avoid having sexual intercourse with men.

Ethnographic research provides the opportunity to gain a better understanding of the sexual orientation of female crack cocaine users. Their sexual behaviors often are driven by the need to support their habit as well as by the social norms among those with whom they use crack cocaine. The women's accounts support the need for a multidimensional measure of sexual orientation. In addition, the inclusion of qualitative findings will allow researchers to place epidemiological or survey data in context (Sterk, Dolan, & Hatch, 1999).

There are a number of possible suggestions for future research. This study is only a first step in identifying some of the key concepts; more integrated qualitative and quantitative research is needed. In addition, this qualitative investigation does not allow for any statements regarding the prevalence of WSW among female crack users. However, it does allow for initial development of a typology consisting of four groups, namely heterosexuals, hidden lesbians, bisexuals, and lesbians who are out. Following Golden's model of sexual orientation, the third dimension of community participation appears less salient to the respondents.

REFERENCES

Adler, F. (1975). *Sisters in crime*. New York: McGraw-Hill.

Benhabib, S. (1992). *Situating the self: Gender, community, and postmodernism in contemporary ethics*. Oxford, England: Polity Press.

Binion, V. (1982). Sex differences in socialization and family dynamics of female and male heroin users. *Journal of Social Issues, 38*, 43–57.

Boles, J., & Elifson, K. (1994). Sexual identity and HIV: The male prostitute. *Journal of Sex Research, 31*(1), 39–46.

Bourgois, P. (1995). *In search of respect: Selling crack in El Barrio*. New York: Cambridge University Press.

Campbell, K., & Bunting, S. (1991). Voices and paradigms: Perspectives on critical and feminist theory in nursing. *Advancement in Nursing Science, 13*, 1–5.

Chasnoff, I. (1988). Cocaine, pregnancy, and the neonate. *Women and Health, 15*, 23–25.

Chavkin, W. (1990). Drug addiction and pregnancy: Policy crossroads. *American Journal of Public Health, 80*, 483–487.

Dowset, G. (1996). *Practicing desire: Homosexual sex in the era of AIDS*. Stanford, CA: Stanford University Press.

Edlin, B. R., Erwin, K. L., Faruque, S., McCoy, C. B., Word, C., Serrano, Y., et al. (1994). Intersecting epidemics: Crack cocaine use and HIV infection among inner city young adults. *New England Journal of Medicine, 24*, 1422–1427.

Ettore, B. (1992). *Women and substance abuse*. New Brunswick, NJ: Rutgers University Press.

Glaser, B., & Strauss, A. (1967). *The discovery of grounded theory: Strategies for qualitative research*. New York: Aldine de Gruyter.

Golden, C. (1987). Diversity and variability in women's sexual identities. In Boston Lesbian Psychologies Collective (Eds.), *Lesbian psychologies: Explorations and challenges* (pp. 19–34). Urbana: University of Illinois.

Greene, B. (1994). Lesbian women of color: Triple jeopardy. In L. Comas-Diaz & B. Greene (Eds.), *Women of color: Integrating ethnic and gender identities in psychotherapy* (pp. 389–427). New York: Guilford Press.

Greene, B., & Boyd-Franklin, N. (1996). African American lesbian couples: Ethnocultural considerations in psychotherapy. *Women & Therapy, 19*, 49–60.

Gutierrez, F., & Dworkin, S. (1992). Gay, lesbian, and African American: Managing the integration of identities. *Counseling Gay Men and Lesbians*, 141–156.

Heffernan, K. (1996). Eating disorders and weight concern among lesbians. *International Journal of Eating Disorders, 19*, 127–138.

Henwood, K. (1997). Adult mother–daughter relationships: Two phases in the analysis of a qualitative project. *Feminism and Psychology, 7*, 255–263.

Inciardi, J., Lockwood, D., & Pottieger, A. (1993). *Women and crack cocaine.* New York: Macmillan.

Kearney, M., Murphy, S., & Rosenbaum, M. (1994). Mothering on crack cocaine: A grounded theory analysis. *Social Science and Medicine, 2*, 351–361.

Kennedy, E., & Davis, M. (1993). *Boots of leather, slippers of gold: The history of a lesbian community.* New York: Routledge.

Kinsey, A. C., Pomeroy, W., Martin, C. E., & Gebhard, P. H. (1953). *Sexual behavior in the human female.* Philadelphia: W. B. Saunders.

Mays, V., & Cochran, S. (1988). The Black women's relationship project: A national survey of Black lesbians. In M. Shernoff & W. Scott (Eds.), *The sourcebook on lesbian/gay health care* (2nd ed., pp. 54–62). Washington, DC: National Lesbian and Gay Health Foundation.

Mays, V., Cochran, S., & Rhue, S. (1993). The impact of perceived discrimination on the intimate relationships of Black lesbians. *Journal of Homosexuality, 25*, 1–4.

National Institute on Drug Abuse. (1995). *Prevalence of substance use among racial and ethnic subgroups in the United States, 1991–1993.* Washington, DC: Government Printing Office.

Ratner, M. (1993). *Crack pipe as a pimp: An ethnographic investigation of sex-for-crack exchanges.* New York: Lexington Books.

Rosenbaum, M. (1981). *Women on heroin.* New Brunswick, NJ: Rutgers University Press.

Skinner, W., & Otis, M. (1996). Drug and alcohol use among lesbian and gay people in a Southern U.S. sample: Epidemiological, comparative, and methodological findings from the trilogy project. *Journal of Homosexuality, 30*, 59–92.

Stein, E. (1999). *The mismeasure of desire: The science, theory, and ethics of sexual orientation.* New York: Oxford University Press.

Sterk, C. E. (1988). Cocaine and HIV seropositivity. *Lancet, 1*, 1052–1053.

Sterk, C. E. (1995). Women and drug abuse: The application of qualitative research methods. In E. Lambert & R. Ashbury (Eds.), *Qualitative methods in drug abuse and HIV research* (pp. 65–83). Washington, DC: Government Printing Office.

Sterk, C. E. (1999a). Building bridges: Community involvement in HIV and substance abuse research. *Drugs and Society, 14,* 107–121.

Sterk, C. E. (1999b). *Fast lives: Women who use crack cocaine.* Philadelphia: Temple University Press.

Sterk, C. E., Dolan, K., & Hatch, S. (1999). Epidemiological indicators and ethnographic realities of female cocaine use. *Journal of Substance Abuse and Use, 34,* 2055–2070.

Sterk-Elifson, C. E., & Elifson, K. (1990). Drug-related violence and prostitution. In M. De La Rosa, E. Lambert, & B. Gropper (Eds.), *Drugs and violence: Causes, correlates, and consequences* (pp. 208–221). Washington, DC: Government Printing Office.

Strauss, A., & Corbin, J. (1990). *Basics of qualitative research: Grounded theory process and techniques.* Newbury Park, CA: Sage.

Tashima, N., Crain, S., O'Reilly, K., & Sterk-Elifson, C. E. (1996). The community process: A discovery model. *Qualitative Health Research, 6,* 23–48.

Watters, J., & Biernacki, P. (1989). Targeted sampling: Options for the study of hidden populations. *Social Problems, 36,* 416–430.

14

LESBIAN MOTHERS AND THEIR CHILDREN: FINDINGS FROM THE CONTEMPORARY FAMILIES STUDY

MEGAN FULCHER, ERIN L. SUTFIN, RAYMOND W. CHAN, JOANNA E. SCHEIB, AND CHARLOTTE J. PATTERSON

Parenthood is often considered to be the prerogative of heterosexual adults. In fact, substantial numbers of lesbians and gay men are parents, and many American children are being reared in families headed by these parents (Patterson & Friel, 2000). Such families have become the subject of a number of controversies in legal and public policy domains in recent years (Patterson, Fulcher, & Wainright, 2002; Patterson & Redding, 1996). Social science research on lesbian mothers, gay fathers, and their children has also emerged, and a considerable research literature has accumulated (Patterson, 2000, 2004).

The most visible group of nonheterosexual parents may be lesbian mothers. Many lesbian mothers conceived and gave birth to children within the context of heterosexual relationships but assumed a lesbian identity later in life (Kirkpatrick, 1996). More recently, observers have commented

We gratefully acknowledge the Lesbian Health Fund of the Gay and Lesbian Medical Association for support of this work, and we thank Barbara Raboy for her many contributions.

on the growing numbers of women who have chosen to have children after assuming a lesbian identity, and this trend has sometimes been referred to as a *lesbian baby boom* (e.g., Patterson, 1994; Weston, 1991). Similar trends can be observed among gay fathers, but perhaps because of their prominence in child custody cases (Patterson et al., 2002), lesbian mothers have generally drawn more attention from researchers.

To determine whether being raised by lesbian parents results in different outcomes for children, as has often been assumed in the legal system, researchers have designed studies that examined the social and personality development of such children. A few studies have focused on the normative development of children born to or adopted by women who already identified as lesbians (Flaks, Ficher, Masterpasqua, & Joseph, 1995; Gartrell et al., 1996, 1999, 2000; McCandlish, 1987; Patterson, 1995a, 1995b; Patterson, Hurt, & Mason, 1998; Steckel, 1985, 1987). Overall, these studies indicated that children of lesbian mothers were developing normally.

Similarities were revealed between the children of lesbian and heterosexual parents across a wide array of assessments of cognitive and behavioral functioning (Patterson, 2004; Perrin, 2002). More recently, Gartrell and colleagues (1996, 1999, 2000) have analyzed data from a longitudinal study of 84 lesbian-headed families who conceived their children through donor insemination. They reported that at the age of 5, the children were developing normally, and that in most cases, both parents were actively involved in the child's upbringing (Gartrell et al., 2000). These findings provide valuable information about the development of children born to lesbian mothers, as well as about the adjustment of such families over time, yet many questions remain in need of study.

One important issue concerns parental division of family labor and partners' satisfaction with their division of labor. In many families headed by heterosexual couples, mothers are responsible for the bulk of household and child-care labor (Cowan & Cowan, 1992). Lesbian couples, however, are more likely to report dividing household and child-care labor equally between partners (Kurdek, 1993; Peplau, Veniegas, & Campbell, 1996). Lesbian couples also report generally high satisfaction with division of labor arrangements in their households (Flaks et al., 1995; Koepke, Hare, & Moran, 1992). If lesbian couples with children maintain equal division of labor, and if they are satisfied with these arrangements, then parents' satisfaction with these arrangements may be associated with positive outcomes for their children.

Another important issue concerns the nature and extent of children's social networks. In particular, grandparents can contribute to the healthy development of their grandchildren on many levels, both directly and indirectly (Rossi & Rossi, 1990). Until recently very little information has been available about the social networks of lesbian mothers and their children

(Allen & Demo, 1995; D'Augelli & Patterson, 1995; Laird & Green, 1996; Patterson, 1998). In the absence of research, it has sometimes been assumed that lesbians may be estranged from their families of origin. For instance, informal reports suggest that grandparents may be less likely to remain in contact with children being raised by lesbian daughters as compared with those being raised by heterosexual daughters (Patterson, 1996; Saffron, 1996). Some anecdotal reports suggest that such stereotypes are incorrect (Laird, 1993; Lewin, 1993; Weston, 1991), but empirical research has been limited.

To examine these and other related issues, Patterson designed the Bay Area Families Study (Patterson, 1994). This study involved 4- to 9-year-old children who were conceived or adopted by a lesbian mother or mothers. This study examined the mental health of mothers, the mental health of children, division of household labor among parents, parents' relationship satisfaction, and the relations among these variables (Patterson, 1994, 1995a, 2001; Patterson et al., 1998).

The results of this study revealed several important findings. On the basis of results from standardized assessments, both mothers' and children's average levels of adjustment fell within the normal range for all measures (Patterson, 1994, 2001). Lesbian couples who took part in this study reported that they divided household labor and child care in a relatively even manner (Patterson, 1995a). A third major finding was an association between division of labor and psychosocial outcomes for mothers and their children (Patterson, 1995a). When lesbian couples shared child care more evenly, mothers were more satisfied and children were more well-adjusted. This suggested that children might benefit from egalitarian divisions of labor.

Finally, contrary to popular stereotypes, Patterson and her colleagues reported that most children of lesbian mothers in their sample were in regular contact with grandparents, relatives, and other adults outside their immediate households (Patterson et al., 1998). Consistent with expectations based on earlier research, children who had more contact with grandparents also showed fewer internalizing behavior problems than did other children (Patterson et al., 1998). Taken together with those of previous studies, results from the Bay Area Families Study suggested that children of lesbian mothers show normal psychosocial development. Although these results were valuable, a number of limitations hindered a clear-cut interpretation of them. Data for the Bay Area Families Study were drawn from a convenience sample of families who lived in a single geographical area. In addition, the study did not include a comparison group of heterosexual families. Clearly, it would be desirable to study a larger, more diverse sample of children with lesbian mothers, and it would be helpful to include a well-matched comparison sample of children with heterosexual parents.

THE CONTEMPORARY FAMILIES STUDY

The Contemporary Families Study (Chan, Brooks, Raboy, & Patterson, 1998; Chan, Raboy, & Patterson, 1998; Fulcher, Chan, Raboy, & Patterson, 2002) was designed to address these and related issues. The Contemporary Families Study involved a sample of lesbian- and heterosexual-headed families who had conceived children through donor insemination using the resources of a single sperm bank. Although all the families were clients of a single sperm bank, they actually resided in many parts of the United States, so the findings are not limited to a single geographic area. This sample allowed a comparison of heterosexual- and lesbian-headed families drawn from the same population. In addition, among families headed by couples (as opposed to a single parent), regardless of sexual orientation, one parent was genetically related to the child and one was not. This allowed the separation of questions regarding sexual orientation from those regarding genetic relatedness.

In this chapter, we describe the Contemporary Families Study itself and its principal results to date. First, we describe demographic and other characteristics of the participating families. Next, we describe assessments of adjustment of both parents and children in heterosexual- as well as lesbian-parented families, indicating parental relationship status (i.e., single or coupled). In families that were headed by couples, the study also examined key facets of couple functioning (e.g., relationship satisfaction, division of labor), and we report comparisons by parental sexual orientation. The study also investigated associations of individual differences in children's adjustment with couple functioning variables. Finally, the study also explored children's contacts with grandparents and other important adults. Although we do not provide statistical details here, all findings described as statistically significant were at the $p < .05$ level. The methods and findings are summarized briefly in the following sections, but additional details and commentary are available elsewhere (Chan, Brooks, et al., 1998; Chan, Raboy, & Patterson, 1998; Fulcher et al., 2002). There were no significant sex differences in the data presented here, so our presentation does not consider this variable.

Description of Participating Families

Families participating in this study were all former clients of The Sperm Bank of California (TSBC), which is located in Berkeley, California. TSBC has been providing reproductive services to clients regardless of sexual orientation or relationship status since 1982. Clients who had conceived and given birth prior to July 1990 were considered eligible to participate in this research (thus their children were at least 5 years old at the beginning of data collection). Six families who had already participated in Patterson's

Bay Area Families Study were excluded to maintain independence of data between the two studies. Also excluded was one family headed by a woman who identified herself as bisexual.

The sample consisted of 80 families—34 headed by lesbian couples, 21 by lesbian single mothers, 16 by heterosexual couples, and 9 by heterosexual single mothers. Children averaged 7 years of age and genetically related mothers averaged 42 years of age. There were 26 girls and 54 boys. The families were primarily Caucasian and parents were generally well educated, with most holding a college degree and most employed at least part time. They were relatively affluent, with family incomes well above national averages.

We explored the possibility that demographic differences might exist among the four family types. We found that, on average, lesbian genetic mothers had completed more years of education than had heterosexual mothers, and lesbian nongenetic mothers had completed more years of education than had heterosexual fathers. As one would expect, families headed by couples reported higher annual household incomes than did families headed by single parents. Otherwise, no significant demographic differences emerged from these analyses.

Procedures

Each eligible family was initially contacted by a letter from the executive director of TSBC. The letter gave a brief explanation of the study and asked each family to consider participation. Telephone calls from TSBC staff members followed these letters to describe the study more fully and to request each family's participation. When a family agreed to participate, a brief, structured telephone interview about family background and current family status was conducted. It was during this interview that parents responded to questions about their child's contact with grandparents and other adults. Remaining materials were then mailed to participating families along with self-addressed stamped envelopes in which the participants were asked to return questionnaires to investigators. In families that consented, a parent gave the child's teacher the Teacher's Report Form (TRF; Achenbach, 1991). Teachers returned the form in a provided self-addressed stamped envelope.

Mental Health of Mothers

Parenting stress was measured using the Parenting Stress Index–Short Form (Abidin, 1995). This short form includes 63 items on 5-point rating scales, scored from *strongly agree* to *strongly disagree*. The score reflects stress directly related to the parenting role as well as stress from other life events.

Items such as "I feel trapped by my responsibilities as a parent" are included. Higher scores indicate reports of greater stress. Depressive symptoms among parents were measured with the Center for Epidemiologic Studies Depression Scale (Radloff, 1977). On this 20-item self-report measure, respondents indicate how often they felt or behaved in a certain way on a 3-point rating scale (e.g., "I had trouble keeping my mind on what I was doing"). Higher scores indicate more depressive symptoms.

Maternal self-esteem was assessed using the Rosenberg Self-Esteem Scale (Rosenberg, 1979). This scale consists of 10 statements, each with four response alternatives, indicating the respondent's degree of agreement with each statement (e.g., "I am able to do things as well as most people"). Results were tabulated to obtain total scores, following the recommendations contained in Rosenberg (1979). Higher scores indicate higher self-esteem.

Our results indicated that the parents participating in this study were well adjusted when compared with available norms. Very few parents in this sample showed symptoms of serious depression or low self-esteem. There was no difference in parental adjustment between parents who were coupled or single. Likewise, there were no significant differences in reported stress, depressive symptoms, or self-esteem in genetic mothers as a function of sexual orientation. In families headed by couples, there were also no significant differences in adjustment measures between nongenetic fathers and nongenetic mothers. In summary, parents were generally well adjusted, and there were no significant differences in adjustment as a function of parental sexual orientation.

Assessment of Couple Functioning

To get an overall indication of couple functioning, we assessed couples' division of labor and marital satisfaction. The measures of couple functioning were given only to parents who described themselves as being involved in a coupled relationship. To assess division of labor in the household, as well as satisfaction with the division, Cowan and Cowan's (1990) Who Does What? was used. This instrument was designed to measure parents' perceptions of the current and ideal distribution of labor within the family, as well as each parent's satisfaction with their arrangements.

The Who Does What? instrument is divided into three sections: division of household tasks, decision making, and child care within a family. Minor wording changes were made to make the measure suitable for lesbian mothers. Each section began by asking respondents to rate, on a scale from 1 to 9, their actual and ideal distribution of certain family tasks (1 = *my partner does it all*; 5 = *we both do this about equally*; 9 = *I do it all*). The first section included 13 household tasks (e.g., meal preparation and cleanup), the second section included 12 family decision-making tasks (e.g., making financial decisions), and the third section included 20 child-care tasks (e.g., bathing the child). Scores around 5 indicated a relatively equal division of labor, whereas high scores indicated that the respondent reported performing more of the labor. At the end of each section of this instrument, respondents were asked to indicate their overall satisfaction with that specific area of household labor. Finally, in the decision-making and child-care sections, respondents were asked to indicate global ratings of both their own and their partner's influence over family decisions and involvement in child care.

To assess relationship satisfaction, we used two instruments. The Locke–Wallace Marital Adjustment Test (LWMAT; Locke & Wallace, 1959) was used to indicate overall relationship quality, whereas the Partnership Questionnaire (Braiker & Kelley, 1979) assessed more specific aspects of couples' relationships. The LWMAT is a 15-item self-report measure that was designed to assess marital adjustment in heterosexual marriages (e.g., "Do you confide in your partner?"). To make the instrument suitable for use with lesbian couples as well as with heterosexual couples, we made minor wording changes. Possible scores range from 2 to 158, with higher scores indicating greater satisfaction.

The Partnership Questionnaire (Braiker & Kelley, 1979) is a 25-item instrument designed to assess components of a close relationship. We used two scales: the Love scale, consisting of 10 items relating to caring and emotional attachment (e.g., "To what extent do you love your partner at this stage?"), and the Conflict scale, consisting of 5 items concerning problems and arguments (e.g., "How often do you and your partner argue with one another?"). Each partner indicates level of agreement ranging from 1 (*not at all or very little*) to 9 (*very much or very often*). Higher scores on these scales indicate, respectively, more love and more conflict.

For division of labor, the results for lesbian couples indicated that overall, household tasks, family decision making, and child care were all seen as being shared relatively equally between the partners. Lesbian genetic mothers reported doing almost the same amounts of child care as their partners. Lesbian parents also divided time spent on work outside the home about equally. Lesbian nongenetic mothers reported working longer hours in paid employment than lesbian genetic mothers, but this difference did not reach statistical significance.

There was more variation in scores for heterosexual couples. Heterosexual parents reported sharing household tasks and family decision making relatively equally. However, for child care, the results indicated an unequal distribution of labor. Mothers reported doing more child care and fathers reported doing less child care. Indeed, heterosexual mothers reported doing more child care than did lesbian genetic mothers, and heterosexual fathers reported doing less child care than did lesbian nongenetic mothers.

Comparisons were also made between actual and ideal divisions of labor. In the areas of household tasks and family decision making, both lesbian and heterosexual respondents reported sharing these responsibilities relatively equally with their partner. They also reported that this matched their ideals. In the area of child care, however, differences emerged as a function of parental sexual orientation. For ideal distribution of labor, heterosexual mothers indicated that they would prefer a more equitable distribution of child-care labor than they currently experienced. Fathers reported preferring that their wives assume most of the child care; their actual score on current child-care participation was similar to their report on their ideal amount of responsibility. However, in addition to reporting the practice of equal child care, both lesbian genetic mothers and their partners reported wanting an equal division of child care. Overall, both lesbian and heterosexual mothers preferred a more equitable division of child care than did fathers. For lesbian mothers, this desire was realized in their actual child-care arrangements, but this was not the case for heterosexual mothers.

Regardless of their actual labor arrangements, most parents reported feeling satisfied with their current division of labor. There was no significant difference between heterosexual and lesbian parents in this regard. Likewise, there were no significant differences between genetic and nongenetic parents in terms of their satisfaction with the division of child-care labor. It seems that regardless of how these couples actually divided labor they were satisfied with their arrangements.

Heterosexual and lesbian couples' scores on the LWMAT (Locke & Wallace, 1959) exceeded mean scores for similar populations, indicating high relationship satisfaction. In addition, heterosexual and lesbian couples reported high levels of love and low to moderate levels of conflict on the Partnership Questionnaire (Braiker & Kelley, 1979), suggesting that parents were generally satisfied with their relationships. Overall, lesbian and heterosexual couples reported similar levels of love, conflict, and satisfaction with their relationships.

Children's Adjustment

To assess levels of children's social competence and behavior problems, we administered the Child Behavior Checklist (CBCL; Achenbach & Edelbrock, 1983) and the TRF (Achenbach, 1991). These scales were particularly useful here because of their ability to discriminate between children in the clinical versus normative range of functioning for problems involving both internalizing (e.g., inhibited, overcontrolled) and externalizing (e.g., aggressive, antisocial, or undercontrolled) behavior. The CBCL is designed to be completed by parents, and in families headed by couples,

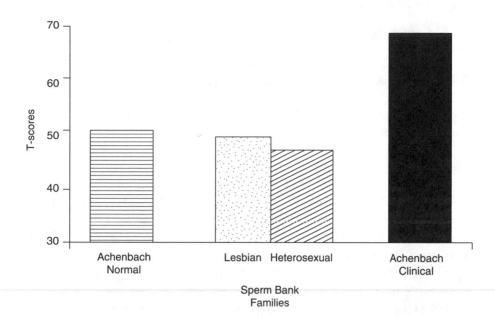

Figure 14.1. Children's total behavior problems (average of parent reports). Data from "Psychosocial Adjustment Among Children Conceived via Donor Insemination by Lesbian and Heterosexual Mothers," by R. W. Chan, B. Raboy, and C. J. Patterson, 1998, *Child Development, 69,* pp. 443–457.

each parent completed a CBCL for the target child. In addition, the CBCL scale measured social competence, whereas the TRF measured academic performance and adaptive functioning. The TRF utilized teacher reports. These scales were selected because they are widely used child assessment instruments for which national age and sex norms are available for both clinical and nonclinical populations. Moreover, sex- and age-specific raw scores can be converted to standard *t* scores that allow comparisons across age and gender groups.

Results showed that compared with a large group of normal children, children in this sample were well adjusted according to both their CBCL and TRF scores as reported by both parents and teachers. Children's average scores on the externalizing, internalizing, and total behavior problems scales fell well below clinical cutoffs (see Figure 14.1). Likewise, social competence, academic performance, and adaptive functioning scores for these children were well above clinical cutoffs. There was no significant difference in adjustment scores between children of lesbian parents and children of hetero-sexual parents. Furthermore, there was also no difference in children's adjust-ment as a function of mothers' relationship status. We found that both parents and teachers reported that children conceived through donor insemi-nation were well adjusted.

Because the family structure variables, parental sexual orientation, and relationship status were not related to children's adjustment in this sample, efforts to predict adjustment focused on other variables. Generally, we report the associations of family interactions and processes with children's adjustment across family types except when interactions are revealed between family type and children's adjustment. We turn next to results from these analyses.

Child and Parental Adjustment

Children's adjustment was significantly associated with parental adjustment. When parents reported more parenting distress and more dysfunctional parent–child interactions on the parenting stress index, children were described as showing more behavior problems. When genetic mothers reported dysfunctional interactions with their children, those children had more reported internalizing problems. Likewise, genetic mothers' reports of greater parental distress and dysfunctional interactions were associated with more reports of their children's externalizing and total behavior problems. A similar pattern emerged for nongenetic parents' reports of parental stress and dysfunctional interactions, which were also associated with children's externalizing and total behavior problems. Teachers' reports of children's behavior problems were most associated with the nongenetic parents' reports of parental distress. There was no relationship between parents' depressive symptom scores and children's behavior scores, probably because parents in this sample showed very few depressive symptoms.

There were also significant associations between children's adjustment scores and parental reports of relationship satisfaction. When couples in this sample reported higher relationship satisfaction and love, their children were less likely to show adjustment problems. For example, when genetic mothers reported higher global relationship satisfaction and higher levels of love in their couple relationship, their children showed better adjustment. Nongenetic parents' reports of relationship satisfaction and love were also associated with lower levels of children's reported behavior problems. Genetic mothers who reported higher levels of conflict with their partners also reported that their children had more behavior problems. Thus, when parents reported higher levels of relationship satisfaction and love, and lower levels of parental conflict, they also reported that their children had fewer behavior problems.

Division of Labor and Children's Adjustment

We also assessed the relationship between parents' division of labor, their satisfaction with the division of labor, and their children's adjustment.

Overall, nongenetic parents' reports of greater satisfaction with the couple's division of household labor were associated with lower externalizing behavior problems in their children, as reported by their teachers. However, some associations differed according to parental sexual orientation.

In families headed by heterosexual couples, when fathers reported greater satisfaction with the division of family decision making but lower levels of satisfaction in the division of household tasks, mothers reported lower levels of externalizing problems in their children. In lesbian-headed families, the associations among division of labor and children's adjustment were more complicated. Genetic mothers' reports of greater satisfaction with the division of household labor and family decision making were associated with lower reported levels of externalizing behavior on the part of their children. Nongenetic mothers who reported greater satisfaction with division of family decision making also reported lower levels of externalizing behavior by their children. Finally, in lesbian-headed families, when nongenetic mothers actually participated in more child-care tasks, the children were reported by genetic mothers to have fewer externalizing problems. These complicated associations between division of labor and children's adjustment were mediated by parents' satisfaction with the couple relationship. This mediation makes clearer the paths of influence, and we examine such associations next.

Relationship Satisfaction, Division of Labor, and Children's Adjustment

We were interested in whether associations between parental division of labor and children's adjustment might be mediated by parents' relationship satisfaction. The results indicated that in lesbian-headed families, nongenetic mothers' reports of their satisfaction with the division of family decision making were associated with their reports of higher relationship satisfaction and with the description of their children as having fewer externalizing behaviors. Furthermore, the results showed that this association was mediated by nongenetic mothers' satisfaction with the couple relationship. When effects of relationship satisfaction and division of family decision-making satisfaction were considered simultaneously, only parents' relationship satisfaction remained predictive. Thus, the associations between parental division of labor and children's adjustment were mediated by parents' relationship satisfaction. When parents reported higher levels of relationship satisfaction, children were described as showing fewer externalizing behaviors (see Figure 14.2). We conclude that parental satisfaction is more highly associated with child outcomes than any specific division of labor. This finding is consistent with others in the literature (based on studies that included only heterosexual families) showing that associations between

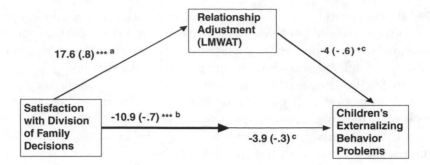

Figure 14.2. Mediation model of parental relationship satisfaction, division of labor, and children's adjustment in lesbian-parented families. Regression coefficients are given in the form $B(\beta)$. LMWAT = Locke–Wallace Marital Adjustment Test. From "Division of Labor Among Lesbian and Heterosexual Parents: Associations With Children's Adjustment," by R. W. Chan, R. C. Brooks, B. Raboy, and C. J. Patterson, 1998, *Journal of Family Psychology, 12,* 414. Copyright 1998 by the American Psychological Association. [a]Model 1: Relationship adjustment regressed on satisfaction with division of decision making, $R^2 = .66$, $F(1, 17) = 30.5$, $p < .001$. [b]Model 2: Children's externalizing behavior problems regressed on satisfaction with division of decision making, $R^2 = .56$, $F(1, 17) = 20.3$, $p < .001$. [c]Model 3: Children's externalizing behavior problems regressed on relationship adjustment and satisfaction with decision making, $R^2 = .68$, $F(2, 17) = 15.9$, $p < .001$.
$*p < .05$. $**p < .01$. $***p < .001$.

children's outcomes and parental division of labor are mediated by parents' level of marital satisfaction (e.g., Cowan & Cowan, 1992). Thus, our main finding was that parents' higher levels of satisfaction in the couple relationship were associated with lower levels of behavior problems in their children.

Children's Contacts With Grandparents and Other Adults

During the initial telephone interview, information about contact with grandparents and other adults was collected from the child's genetic mother. Mothers reported the amount of contact the target children had with grandparents. Genetic grandparents were identified by the child's genetic mother as her parents, and nongenetic grandparents were identified by the child's genetic mother as parents of the nongenetic parent. Contact was defined as a visit, a telephone call, a card, or e-mail. Contact scores ranged from 1 to 7 (1 = *no contact*; 2 = *less than once a year*; 3 = *once a year*; 4 = *every other month*; 5 = *once a month*; 6 = *once a week*; and 7 = *daily contact*). If the mother did not list nongenetic grandparents, because she was single or not in contact with a former partner, the family was not included for these comparisons. Data for children whose grandparent had died were not considered in the comparisons for that grandparent. Parents also listed up to five adults, in addition to parents and grandparents, who were seen as "important" in the child's life. The adult's gender and relationship to the child (e.g., parent's friend, relative, neighbor, child-care provider, or coach) was recorded as well. Each of these adults was also scored for contact using the scale previously described.

Most parents reported that their children were in at least monthly contact with their grandparents. There were no significant differences in amount of contact between grandparents and children of lesbian parents versus children of heterosexual parents. Among couples, this was true for both genetic grandparents and for nongenetic grandparents. However, children of both lesbian and heterosexual parents were in more frequent contact with their genetic grandparents than with their nongenetic grandparents.

The amount of contact between children and other adults also did not differ according to parental sexual orientation. Children of lesbian parents had contact with as many adult relatives as did children of heterosexual parents. Contrary to stereotypes, children of lesbian parents had contact with as many adult men as did children of heterosexual parents. Children of lesbian parents did, however, have significantly more contact with unrelated women than did children of heterosexual parents. Overall, the amount of contact with adults outside the home was similar among children of lesbian and heterosexual parents.

OVERVIEW OF RESULTS AND IMPLICATIONS

The Contemporary Families Study was designed to examine child development and family functioning among families headed by lesbian and heterosexual parents who conceived their children through donor insemination. This sample allowed us to compare parents and children in families headed by lesbian and heterosexual parents, taking into account that only one parent was genetically related to the child.

Our first major finding was that both parents' and children's average levels of adjustment fell clearly within the normative range in both family types. This finding is consistent with results from earlier studies of lesbian parents and their children (Flaks et al., 1995; Steckel, 1985, 1987). Furthermore, there were no significant differences in children's or parents' adjustment scores according to parental sexual orientation. Considering that this result is consistent with findings from other research on lesbian women in general (Gonsiorek, 1991), lesbian mothers in particular (Falk, 1989; Patterson, 1992), children of divorced lesbian and gay parents (Patterson, 1992), and children born to lesbian mothers (Flaks et al., 1995; McCandlish, 1987; Steckel, 1985, 1987), this outcome was not surprising. Particularly in light of judicial and popular prejudices against lesbian and gay families that still exist in many parts of the United States, however, the result is worthy of attention. The present data revealed not only that lesbian mothers' adjustment and self-esteem were within the normative range but also that their children's development was proceeding in normal fashion.

The second major finding was that both lesbian and heterosexual parents expressed high satisfaction and high levels of love within their couple relationships. There were no differences in satisfaction or warmth between heterosexual and lesbian couples. Although both lesbian and heterosexual parents reported relatively equal contributions to paid labor, household chores, and family decision making, differences did emerge in the division of labor involved in child care. Lesbian couples divided child care more evenly than did heterosexual couples. In families headed by heterosexual parents, mothers reported doing more child care than did their husbands. This is consistent with previous findings on child-care arrangements among heterosexual couples (Belsky & Pensky, 1988; Cowan & Cowan, 1992; Perry-Jenkins & Crouter, 1990). Parents in both family types reported satisfaction with division of child care; however children's adjustment was more strongly related to partners' satisfaction with division of labor than to their reports of actual division of labor. Therefore, in well-functioning families it may be more important for children that parents negotiate a division of labor that is satisfactory to both parents than that they adhere to an egalitarian arrangement.

Another principal finding emerging from these data was that family process variables such as parental adjustment and couple adjustment were more strongly related to children's outcomes than were family structural variables such as parental sexual orientation or relationship status. The family process variables showed the same pattern of associations in families headed by lesbian and heterosexual parents. For example, regardless of parental sexual orientation, elevated parenting stress was associated with more externalizing behavior problems among children. Parents in both family types who reported being less happy with their relationship also reported having children with more behavior problems. Patterns of family interaction were clearly related to children's outcomes, regardless of parental sexual orientation.

Finally, we found that children of lesbian and heterosexual parents who conceived through donor insemination were described by their parents as being surrounded by networks of supportive adults. Children of lesbian and heterosexual parents were described as being in equal amounts of contact with their grandparents. The lineal bridge between child and grandparent seemed to function without regard to parental sexual orientation. Our results suggested that grandparents were not less willing to invest time in grandchildren born in the context of a lesbian relationship than in those born in the context of a heterosexual one. Children were also said to have similar amounts of contact with other adults in addition to grandparents, regardless of parental sexual orientation. The only significant difference was that children with lesbian parents were in regular contact with more unrelated women than children with heterosexual parents. In short, consistent with earlier findings (Patterson et al., 1998), our results showed that children of lesbian parents in this sample were not living in isolation, nor were they lacking adult male role models.

There are several limitations of our study that must be considered when interpreting the results. First, the Contemporary Families Study was cross-sectional in design and so does not afford us the opportunity to examine children's development across time. Second, because lesbian parents were more likely than heterosexual parents to participate, our sample may be more representative of these families. Finally, the measures used here relied on self-reports or reports from parents or teachers. Future studies that are longitudinal in design and use representative samples and observational measures may be better able to clarify causal questions.

FUTURE DIRECTIONS

The results of the Contemporary Families Study have afforded some insight into families formed by lesbian and heterosexual parents who conceived through donor insemination. The study also raises many questions for further research. Questions about children's development over time would clearly benefit from longitudinal research. Questions about the role of reproductive technology could be clarified by research on lesbian and heterosexual families formed in other ways (e.g., through adoption). Questions about broader aspects of children's social worlds might also be addressed through research on other aspects of children's social development.

Lesbian-parented families may offer the opportunity for a more detailed examination of parents' role in children's gender role knowledge and stereotyping flexibility. It has been reported that heterosexual fathers' attitudes about children's sex-typed behavior are more conservative than those of mothers; fathers' attitudes and behavior have also been found to be more predictive of children's sex-typed behavior than those of mothers (Fagot & Leinbach, 1995). It would be interesting to examine the development of gender role behavior among children born to lesbian mothers who grow up without paternal influence (Stacey & Biblarz, 2001).

In an age in which children are being conceived and raised in families that are growing increasingly diverse, it is important to examine the role that family constellations play in children's development. The family structural variables studied here (e.g., number of parents and parental sexual orientation) were not associated in this sample with children's adjustment or with their frequency of contact with important adults such as grandparents. It was family process variables, such as parental relationship satisfaction, that were associated with children's adjustment. Overall, results of the Contemporary Families Study were consistent with those of other studies on lesbian mothers and their children (Gartrell et al., 2000; Patterson, 2000; Perrin, 2002; Stacey & Biblarz, 2001; Tasker & Golombok, 1995) in revealing that these families can provide supportive environments in which children can grow and develop.

REFERENCES

Abidin, R. R. (1995). *Parenting Stress Index: Professional manual* (3rd ed.). Odessa, FL: Psychological Assessment Resources.

Achenbach, T. M. (1991). *Manual for the Teacher's Report Form and 1991 profile.* Burlington: University of Vermont, Department of Psychiatry.

Achenbach, T. M., & Edelbrock, C. (1983). *Manual for the Child Behavior Checklist and Revised Child Behavior Profile.* Burlington: University of Vermont, Department of Psychiatry.

Allen, K. R., & Demo, D. H. (1995). The families of lesbians and gay men: A new frontier in family research. *Journal of Marriage and the Family, 57,* 111–127.

Belsky, J., & Pensky, E. (1988). Marital change across the transition to parenthood. *Marriage and Family Review, 12,* 133–156.

Braiker, H. B., & Kelley, H. H. (1979). Conflict in the development of close relationships. In R. L. Burgess & T. L. Huston (Eds.), *Social exchange in developing relationships* (pp. 135–168). New York: Academic Press.

Chan, R. W., Brooks, R. C., Raboy, B., & Patterson, C. J. (1998). Division of labor among lesbian and heterosexual parents: Associations with children's adjustment. *Journal of Family Psychology, 12,* 402–419.

Chan, R. W., Raboy, B., & Patterson, C. J. (1998). Psychosocial adjustment among children conceived via donor insemination by lesbian and heterosexual mothers. *Child Development, 69,* 443–457.

Cowan, C. P., & Cowan, P. A. (1990). Who does what? In J. Touliatos, B. F. Perlmutter, & M. A. Straus (Eds.), *Handbook of family measurement techniques* (pp. 447–448). Newbury Park, CA: Sage.

Cowan, C. P., & Cowan, P. A. (1992). *When partners become parents: The big life change for couples.* New York: Basic Books.

D'Augelli, A. R., & Patterson, C. J. (Eds.). (1995). *Lesbian, gay and bisexual identities over the lifespan: Psychological perspectives.* New York: Oxford University Press.

Fagot, B. I., & Leinbach, M. D. (1995). Gender knowledge in egalitarian and traditional families. *Sex Roles, 32,* 513–526.

Falk, P. J. (1989). Lesbian mothers: Psychosocial assumptions in family law. *American Psychologist, 44,* 941–947.

Flaks, D., Ficher, I., Masterpasqua, F., & Joseph, G. (1995). Lesbians choosing motherhood: A comparative study of lesbian and heterosexual parents and their children. *Developmental Psychology, 31,* 104–114.

Fulcher, M., Chan, R. W., Raboy, B., & Patterson, C. J. (2002). Contact with grandparents among children conceived via donor insemination by lesbian and heterosexual mothers. *Parenting: Science and Practice, 2,* 61–76.

Gartrell, N., Banks, A., Hamilton, J., Reed, N., Bishop, H., & Rodas, C. (1999). The national lesbian family study: 2. Interviews with mothers of toddlers. *American Journal of Orthopsychiatry, 69,* 362–369.

Gartrell, N., Banks, A., Reed, N., Hamilton, J., Rodas, C., & Deck, A. (2000). The national lesbian family study: 3. Interviews with mothers of five-year olds. *American Journal of Orthopsychiatry, 70,* 542–548.

Gartrell, N., Hamilton, J., Banks, A., Mosbacher, D., Reed, N., Sparks, C. H., & Bishop, H. (1996). The national lesbian family study: 1. Interviews with prospective mothers. *American Journal of Orthopsychiatry, 66,* 272–281.

Gonsiorek, J. (1991). The empirical basis for the demise of the illness model of homosexuality. In J. C. Gonsiorek & J. D. Weinrich (Eds.), *Homosexuality: Research implications for public policy* (pp. 115–136). Newbury Park, CA: Sage.

Kirkpatrick, M. (1996). Lesbians as parents. In R. P. Cabaj & T. S. Stein (Eds.), *Textbook of homosexuality and mental health* (pp. 353–370). Washington, DC: American Psychiatric Press.

Koepke, L., Hare, J., & Moran, P. B. (1992). Relationship quality in a sample of lesbian couples with children and child-free lesbian couples. *Family Relations, 41,* 224–229.

Kurdek, L. (1993). The allocation of household labor in homosexual and heterosexual cohabiting couples. *Journal of Social Issues, 49,* 127–139.

Laird, J. (1993). Lesbian and gay families. In F. Walsh (Ed.), *Normal family processes* (2nd ed., pp. 282–328). New York: Guilford Press.

Laird, J., & Green, R. J. (Eds.). (1996). *Lesbians and gays in couples and families: A handbook for therapists.* San Francisco: Jossey-Bass.

Lewin, E. (1993). *Lesbian mothers: Accounts of gender in American culture.* Ithaca, NY: Cornell University Press.

Locke, H., & Wallace, K. (1959). Short marital adjustment and prediction tests: Their reliability and validity. *Marriage and Family Living, 21,* 251–255.

McCandlish, B. (1987). Against all odds: Lesbian mother family dynamics. In F. W. Bozett (Ed.), *Gay and lesbian parents* (pp. 23–38). New York: Praeger Publishers.

Patterson, C. J. (1992). Children of lesbian and gay parents. *Child Development, 63,* 1025–1042.

Patterson, C. J. (1994). Children of the lesbian baby boom: Behavioral adjustment, self-concepts, and sex-role identity. In B. Greene & G. Herek (Eds.), *Contemporary perspectives on lesbian and gay psychology: Theory, research, and application* (pp. 156–175). Beverly Hills, CA: Sage.

Patterson, C. J. (1995a). Families of the lesbian baby boom: Parents' division of labor and children's adjustment. *Developmental Psychology, 31,* 115–123.

Patterson, C. J. (1995b). Lesbian mothers, gay fathers, and their children. In A. R. D'Augelli & C. J. Patterson (Eds.), *Lesbian, gay and bisexual identities over the lifespan: Psychological perspectives* (pp. 262–290). New York: Oxford University Press.

Patterson, C. J. (1996). Contributions of lesbian and gay parents and their children to the prevention of heterosexism. In E. D. Rothblum & L. A. Bond (Eds.), *Preventing heterosexism and homophobia* (pp. 184–201). Thousand Oaks, CA: Sage.

Patterson, C. J. (1998). Family lives of children with lesbian mothers. In C. J. Patterson & A. R. D'Augelli (Eds.), *Lesbian, gay and bisexual identities in families: Psychological perspectives* (pp. 154–176). New York: Oxford University Press.

Patterson, C. J. (2000). Family relationships of lesbians and gay men. *Journal of Marriage and the Family, 62,* 1052–1069.

Patterson, C. J. (2001). Families of the lesbian baby boom: Maternal mental health and child adjustment. *Journal of Gay and Lesbian Psychotherapy, 4,* 91–107.

Patterson, C. J. (2004). What difference does a civil union make? Changing public policies and the experiences of same-sex couples: Comment on Solomon, Rothblum, and Balsam. *Journal of Family Psychology, 18,* 287–289.

Patterson, C. J., & Friel, L. V. (2000). Sexual orientation and fertility. In G. Bentley & N. Mascie-Taylor (Eds.), *Infertility in the modern world: Biosocial perspectives* (pp. 238–260). Cambridge, England: Cambridge University Press.

Patterson, C. J., Fulcher, M., & Wainright, J. (2002). Children of lesbian and gay parents: Research, law, and policy. In B. L. Bottoms, M. B. Kovera, & B. D. McAuliff (Eds.), *Children, social science and the law* (pp. 176–199). New York: Cambridge University Press.

Patterson, C. J., Hurt, S., & Mason, C. D. (1998). Families of the lesbian baby boom: Children's contact with grandparents and other adults. *American Journal of Orthopsychiatry, 68,* 390–399.

Patterson, C. J., & Redding, R. E. (1996). Lesbian and gay families with children: Implications of social science research for policy. *Journal of Social Issues, 52*(3), 29–50.

Peplau, L. A., Veniegas, R. C., & Campbell, S. M. (1996). Gay and lesbian relationships. In R. C. Savin-Williams & K. M. Cohen (Eds.), *The lives of lesbians, gays, and bisexuals: Children to adults* (pp. 250–273). Fort Worth, TX: Harcourt Brace.

Perrin, C. E. (2002). Technical report: Coparent or second-parent adoption by same-sex parents. *Pediatrics, 109,* 341–344.

Perry-Jenkins, M., & Crouter, A. C. (1990). Men's provider-role attitudes: Implications for household work and marital satisfaction. *Journal of Family Issues, 11,* 136–156.

Radloff, L. S. (1977). The CES-D Scale: A self-report depression scale for research in the general population. *Applied Psychological Measurement, 1,* 385–401.

Rosenberg, M. (1979). *Conceiving the self.* New York: Basic Books.

Rossi, A. S., & Rossi, P. H. (1990). *Of human bonding: Parent–child relations across the life course.* New York: Aldine de Gruyter.

Saffron, L. (1996). *What about the children? Sons and daughters of lesbian and gay parents talk about their lives.* New York: Cassell & Co.

Stacey, J., & Biblarz, T. J. (2001). (How) Does sexual orientation of parents matter? *American Sociological Review, 65,* 159–183.

Steckel, A. (1985). *Separation–individuation in children of lesbian and heterosexual couples.* Unpublished doctoral dissertation, Wright Institute Graduate School, Berkeley, CA.

Steckel, A. (1987). Psychosocial development of children of lesbian mothers. In F. W. Bozett (Ed.), *Gay and lesbian parents* (pp. 75–85). New York: Praeger Publishers.

Tasker, F., & Golombok, S. (1995). Adults raised as children in lesbian families. *American Journal of Orthopsychiatry, 65,* 203–215.

Weston, K. (1991). *Families we choose: Lesbians, gays, kinship.* New York: Columbia University Press.

AUTHOR INDEX

Numbers in italics refer to listings in reference sections.

Cowan, P. A., 282, 286, 292, 294, *296*
Coyne, L., 144, *162*
Crain, S., 272, *280*
Cramer, D. W., 60, 69
Cranston, K., 15, 17, 18, *32*, 55, 69, 146, 148, 149, *161*
Crawford, I., 191, *202*
Croteau, J. M., 226, 240, *243*
Croughan, J., 172, *184*, 190, *204*
Crouter, A. C., 294, *298*
Crowne, D. P., 122, *137*
Cunny, K. A., 190, *202*
Cwayna, K., 106, *113*
Cyranowski, J. M., 77, *91*

Damon, W., 75, *94*
D'Augelli, A. R., 14, 18, *32*, 37, 38, 39, 40, 41, 47, 49, 50, *51*, *52*, 60, *70*, 99, 102, *113*, *114*, 144, 146, 149, *160*, *162*, 283, *296*
Davey, R. T. J., 258, *264*
Davidson, L., 55, 68, 69
Davidson, R. E., 248, *267*
Davies, G. E., 57, 69
Davis, M., 271, *279*
Dawood, K., *136*
Day, A., 185, *203*
Day, N. E., 229, *243*
DeCecco, J., 87, *91*
Deck, A., *297*
Decker, B., 185, *202*
Deisher, R. W., 37, *52*, 99, *114*, 146, *164*
Delgado, V., *184*
Demo, D. H., 283, *296*
de Graaf, R., 229, *244*
De Moore, R., 229, *244*
Derogatis, L. R., 47, *52*, 121, *137*
Dewar, R., *264*
Diament, L., 226, *243*
Diamond, L. M., 15, *31*, 40, *52*, 75, 76, 77, 78, 81, 85, 89, *91*, *94*, 102, 103, *114*, 188, *202*
Diamond, M., 133, *139*
Díaz, F., *223*
Díaz, R. M., 208, 210, 219, *223*
DiBartolo, P. M., 67, 69
Dilán, E., 208, *223*
Ding, S., 17, *33*
Dixon, J. K., 78, *91*
Docherty, J. P., *266*

Dohrenwend, B. P., 145, *161*
Dolan, K., 278, *280*
Dolezal, C., 208, *223*
Doll, L. S., 15, *32*
Domanico, R., 191, *202*
Donahue, M. J., 118, *137*
Donovan, J. E., 98, *114*
Dowset, G., 271, *278*
Dowson, G., 271, *278*
Driscoll, A. K., 15, *34*
DuRant, R. H., 15, 17, *32*, 55, 69, 101, *114*, *115*
Dworkin, S., 271, *279*

Eaves, L. J., *162*
Edelbrock, C., 288, *296*
Edlin, B. R., 271, *278*
Ehrhardt, A. A., 121, *138*
Einarsen, S., 230, *243*
Eisen, S., *162*
Elifson, K., 270, 271, *278*, *280*
Ellis, A. L., 226, *243*
Ellison, C. G., 118, *137*
Emans, S. J., 101, *115*
Emerson, M. R., 97, *116*
Emmons, R. A., 252, *265*
Engel, D., *264*
Engel, G. L., 187, *202*, 246, *265*
Ensel, W. M., 145, *162*
Epstein, J., 150, *161*
Erbaugh, J., 56, 68
Ericksen, J. A., 29, *32*
Erwin, K. L., *278*
Eshleman, S., *70*
Ettore, B., 270, *278*
Exner, T. A., 121, *138*
Exner, T. M, *115*

Factor, R., 180, *184*
Fagot, B. I., 295, *296*
Fahey, J. L., 246, 249, 250, 252, 258, *264*
Fairchild, B., 73, *91*
Falk, P. J., 293, *296*
Farmer, P., 222, *223*
Farrer, L. A., *136*
Farrow, J. A., 99, 101, 106, *114*, 146, *164*
Faruque, S., *278*
Fassinger, R., 82, 83, *93*

Weinberg, M. S., 14, *31*, 75, 76, 78, 79, 80, 84, 87, 88, 94, 119, *136*, 144, 146, *159*, 245, 249, 253, *267*
Weinberg, N. Z., 17, *35*
Weinberg, T. S., 134, *139*
Weinberger, D. A., 248, 252, *267*
Weintraub, J. K., 57, 68
Weissman, A., 56, 68
Weitsman, S. R., *267*
Wells, J. W., 83, 94, 228, *244*
Weston, K., 282, 283, 299
Wetherll, M. S., 132, *139*
Wexler, P., 187, *203*
Whisman, V., 75, 94
Whitam, F. L., 133, *139*
Whitlock, E., *165*
Whittington, L. A., 155, *159*
Widmer, E. D., 229, *244*
Widom, C., 100, 107, *116*
Wilcox, B., 29, *32*
Wiley, J., 146, *164*
Wilkinson, S., 87, 88, 92
Williams, B. I., *115*
Williams, C. J., 75, 94, 134, *139*, 245, 249, 253, *267*
Williams, D. R., 144, *162*, 207, *224*
Williams, T. A., 133, *139*
Wilsnack, R. W., 170, 171, 173, 177, *184*, 200, 201, *204*
Wilsnack, S. C., 152, *162*, 168, 170, 171, *183*, *184*, 187, 188, 189, 190, 200, 201, *203*, *204*, 205

Wissow, L. S., 19, *32*, 55, 69, 78, 92, 146, *161*
Wolf, R. C., 17, 19, *32*, 55, 69, 78, 92, *114*, 146, *161*
Wolf, T. J., 87, 93
Wolkowitz, O. L., 262, 264
Wooden, W. S., 29, *35*, 78, *94*
Woodroof, J. T., 118, *139*
Woods, E. R., 19, *32*, 55, 69, 78, 92, 146, *161*
Woods, T. E., 119, *139*
Word, C., 278
Worthington, E. L., Jr., 118, *140*
Wright, D. L., 20, *35*
Wright, E. R., 144, *161*, 165
Wyatt, G. E., 190, 197, 198, 205

Yap, L., 67, 69
Yarnold, P. R., 128, *137*
Yoder, C., 264

Zabin, L. S., 97, *116*
Zack, J. A., 258, 259, *264*, *267*
Zaleski, E. H., 118–119, *140*
Zamudio, A., 158, *163*
Zani, B., 58, *71*
Zera, D., 78, *94*
Zhao, S., 70

SUBJECT INDEX

stable interpersonal relationship and, 242

strategies, 227–228

therapeutic support, 262–263

in workplace, 227–230, 234–238, 239, 240

See also Concealed sexual orientation

Discrimination

experienced threat model of homosexual identity management, 248

gender differences, 240–241

health effects, 210, 260

within LGB community, 212–213

mental health outcomes of, 219–222

sexual orientation disclosure and risk of, 228, 235–237, 240, 246

suicidal ideation and life experiences of, 219

therapeutic responses, 263

workplace manifestations, 230

workplace prevalence, 226, 235

See also Latino gay men, health-related outcomes of discrimination against; Victimization of LGB youth

Economic functioning

experiences of Latino gay men, 213–214

in mediation of mental health-related outcomes of social oppression, 221, 222

Educational attainment, women's health and, 178, 180

Emotional functioning

affective disorder risk, 147–149

assessment, 190

burnout symptoms, 230

closeting as inhibition in, 248–249

in defining sexual orientation, 15

emotional exhaustion, 230, 238

emotional expressivity, health and, 248

patterns among women, 195

physical attraction *vs.* emotional attraction, 85–86

in sexual self-identification, 82

symptoms of psychological distress among Latino gay men, 218

Ethnographic mapping, 271–272

Expectancy-value theory, 246

Experienced threat model of homosexual identity management, 248, 252, 260

Families

discrimination experiences of Latino gay men, 212, 222

division of labor in lesbian households, 282, 283, 286–288, 290–292, 294

LGB youth and relationships with, 40, 45

grandparent relationships, 282–283

Gay bars, 29–30, 44, 98, 210, 213

Gender differences

adolescent mental health, 47

disclosure of sexual orientation, 234

psychopathology risk, 153

relationship patterns, 23

religious practice, 119, 123

same-sex romantic relationships among youths, 43

sexual orientation development, 40, 42–43, 49, 135

social relationships of LGB youth, 44

substance use among adolescents, 24–27

substance use and same-sex attraction among youth, 17–18

victimization experiences of adolescents, 46

workplace experiences, 227, 234–235, 237–239, 240–241

Grandparent relationships, 282–283

Health and Life Experiences of Women Questionnaire, 171, 199

Healthy People 2010, 157

Homelessness, 16, 99, 100–101, 106, 110

Immigrants, 213

Immune function, 257–259

Informed consent, 60

National Longitudinal Study of Adolescent Health, 14, 17–18, 29
  data collection, 19–20
  limitations of, 30
  measures, 20–22
  purpose, 19
  significance of, 30
National Study of Health and Life Experiences of Women, 169, 170, 181
National Survey of Midlife Development, 155–156
National Survey on Drug Use and Health, 150–153, 157
Norepinephrine, 258–259, 263

Panic disorders, 151, 155
Parents of LGB youth
  abusive behaviors of, 46
  ADD Health study data, 20
  sexual orientation disclosure patterns, 45
  youth mental health outcomes and, 49–50
Phobia, 154
Physical health
  biological mediators of closeting effects, 256–259
  biopsychosocial model, 246
  effects of closeting, 245–246, 249, 260–261
  psychological inhibition and, 248, 250–251, 253, 254–255
  psychological mediators of closeting effects, 251–255
Poverty, 213–214, 222
Pregnancy, in lesbian women, 281–282. See also Mothers, lesbian
Pregnancy in sexual-minority youth
  attitudes of pregnant teens toward pregnancy, 111–112
  contraceptive practices and, 103–105
  as coping response, 100–101, 111
  deviance theory, 97–98
  disclosure of sexual identity to clinician, 95–96
  explanatory models, 97–101, 110–112
  homelessness and, 106
  prevalence, 96, 109–110
  prostitution and, 106–107
  risk factors, 101

sexual abuse experience and, 99–100, 107–109, 110
sexual behavior correlates, 101–103, 110–111
stigma management theory, 98–99, 110, 111
Prostitution, 99, 100, 106–107, 110
  among female crack cocaine users, 273, 274
Protein kinase signaling, 259

Race/ethnicity
  access to social support, 66–67
  ADD Health study data, 19–20
  assessment of racism experiences, 216–217
  discrimination within LGB community, 213
  religiosity and, 123
  sampling issues in LGB research, 77
  See also Crack cocaine users, African American female; Latino gay men, health-related outcomes of discrimination against
Religion and spirituality
  among LGB individuals, 119, 120, 123–125, 131
  associated risk and protective factors, 125–132
  attitudes toward same-sex relationships, 119, 133
  benefits, 117–118
  clinical considerations, 136
  effects on health, 118–120
  integration of religious and same-sex identities, 134–135
  mechanism of health protection, 132–135
  mental health and, 118, 125–128, 131, 133
  national patterns and trends, 117
  risky behaviors and, 125, 128–131, 134
  social relations and, 132–133
  as source of cognitive dissonance, 133–134
Research
  adolescent development, 39–40
  adolescent mental health, 18–19
  adolescent substance use, 17–18

Research, *continued*
bisexual representation in, 78
children of lesbian mothers, 282
designs for discrimination outcomes studies among Latino men, 208–211, 222–223
designs for women's mental health studies, 168–176, 179–180, 181
designs for women's sexual functioning studies, 188–191, 201
evolution of mental health research, 143–146, 167–168
health surveys, 157
informed consent issues, 60
interpretation of LGB data, 157–158
lesbian-headed families, 295–296
measures of discrimination and social oppression, 214–215, 216–217
measures of sexual orientation, 15, 20–21, 103
obstacles to adolescent research, 14, 15–17, 29
pregnancy in sexual-minority youth, 110–111, 112–113
recommendations for adolescent research, 30–31, 50–51, 67–68, 135–136
sampling issues, 16–17, 50, 77, 145–146, 168, 180, 210–211, 241, 242, 271
sexual identity development, 74, 75–77, 86–90
sexual orientation identification in federally collected health data, 157
social anxiety among LGB youth, 59–66, 67–68
sociopolitical context, 29
terminology and definitions, 14
trends in youth research, 37–38
women's sexual functioning, 185
women's substance abuse, 270, 271
workplace experiences of lesbians and gays, 226, 231–234, 241–242
See also National Longitudinal Study of Adolescent Health
Resiliency
assessment, 217–218
in mediation of mental health-related outcomes of social oppression, 219–222

Romantic relationships
adolescent patterns, 22–24
assessment, 190–191, 287
causes of sexual dysfunction, 187
consistency over time among adolescents, 24
discrimination experiences of Latino gay men, 213
of female crack cocaine users, 276
gender differences among youths, 43
of lesbian mothers, 287, 290, 291–292, 294
openness about sexual orientation and, 242
as protective against alcohol abuse, 29–30
sexual desire discrepancies, 199
women's satisfaction with, 195

Selective serotonin reuptake inhibitors, 263
Self-concept, 14, 15
adolescent patterns, 28, 44, 47
age of sexual orientation awareness, 41, 49, 135
assessment, 217
biopsychosocial model of closeting effects, 246
burnout symptoms, 229–230
changes in sexual identity label after other-sex attraction, 79–80
developmental milestones of LGB youth, 41
deviance theory, 97–98
experienced threat model of homosexual identity management, 248, 252
first same-sex experience and sexual identification, 42, 43, 49
importance of sexual identity label, 82–86
maternal, 286
in mediation of mental health-related outcomes of social oppression, 219–222
mental health risks for LGB youth, 18, 66
models of sexual identity development, 73–76, 86–90
personal competence, 230, 233

Victimization experiences of Latino gay men, 212
Victimization of LGB youth
　forms of, 45
　mental health correlations, 48, 50
　milestones of sexual development and, 48
　by parents, 46
　patterns, 45–46
　by peers, 46
　risk of sexual abuse, 99
　self-esteem and, 48

Women
　alcohol use patterns, 176–179, 195
　changes in sexual attractions over time, 75–76
　designs for mental health research, 168–176, 179–180, 181
　designs for sexual functioning research, 188–191, 201
　educational attainment, 178, 180
　evolution of mental health research, 167–168
　exclusivity of sexual attractions, 78–79
　masturbation patterns, 192
　mental health patterns, 176, 195
　mental health service utilization, 200
　sexual abuse experiences, 193, 200
　sexual behavior patterns, 185–186, 192–193, 194, 196–199, 200
　sexual dysfunction patterns, 186–187, 194–195, 196, 199–200
　sexual functioning research, 185, 201
　sexual identity development, 74–75, 76–86
　sexual initiation, 188–189, 192
　sexual orientation disclosure strategies, 227–228
　sexual satisfaction patterns, 186, 192, 196, 199
　stability of sexual identity over time, 80–82
　substance abuse patterns, 145, 151–153, 158, 270
　substance abuse research, 271

suicidal ideation/behavior among, 178, 179
See also Crack cocaine users, African American female; Mothers, lesbian
Workplace experiences of lesbians and gays, 225
　career advancement, 233, 235–237, 239–240
　disclosure effects, 227–229, 235–238
　disclosure patterns, 234–235
　disclosure strategies, 227
　discrimination assessment, 232–233
　discrimination prevalence, 226, 235
　forms of discrimination, 230
　gender differences, 227, 234–235, 237–239, 240–241
　job satisfaction, 237, 238
　knowledge base, 226
　sick leave patterns, 227, 237, 238, 239
　social acceptance, 226–227
See also Burnout, workplace

Youth, LGB
　ADD Health study, 19–29, 30
　after-school social support intervention, 58
　attraction and relationship patterns, 22–24
　disclosure to parents, 45
　heterosexual sex experiences, 29, 42–43, 101–103
　mental health patterns, 28–29, 39, 47, 56–58
　mental health risks, 13–14, 18–19, 39, 55, 58
　religious beliefs and practices, 118–121, 123–125
　research challenges, 15–17, 29
　risks for, 13–14
　sexual orientation milestones, 41–43
　social anxiety among, 59, 63–67
　social relationships, 44
　substance abuse risk, 17–18
　substance use patterns, 24–28
　victimization experiences, 45–46
See also Parents of LGB youth; Pregnancy in sexual-minority youth
Youth Risk Behavior Surveys, 15, 17

ABOUT THE EDITORS

Allen M. Omoto, PhD, is a professor of psychology and the director of the Institute for Research on Social Issues at the Claremont Graduate University in Claremont, California. He is a social psychologist whose research interests include the social and psychological aspects of volunteerism; interpersonal relationships; HIV disease; and lesbian, gay, and bisexual issues. He has an ongoing program of research on volunteerism and helping relationships, including multiyear studies that have been supported by federal and private foundation grants. He also has extensive public policy experience. He helped found and administer a community-based AIDS service organization, and he worked in the U.S. Congress as the American Psychological Association's inaugural William A. Bailey AIDS Policy Congressional Fellow.

Howard S. Kurtzman, PhD, is a psychologist working for the federal government. He received a doctorate in cognitive psychology from the Massachusetts Institute of Technology and has served on the faculty at Cornell University. He has published and administered research programs in a variety of areas, including psycholinguistics, cognitive science, cognitive aspects of mental disorder, data archiving, and gender and sexual orientation. In 2002, he was a recipient of the Outstanding Achievement Award from the American Psychological Association's Committee on Lesbian, Gay, and Bisexual Concerns for his efforts to promote rigorous behavioral, social, mental health, and substance abuse research with lesbian, gay, bisexual, and transgender populations.